Spike Milligan was born in Ahmednagar in India in 1918. He received his first education in a tent in the Hyderabad Sindh desert and graduated from there, through a series of Roman Catholic schools in India and England, to the Lewisham Polytechnic. Always something of a playboy, he then plunged into the world of Show Business, seduced by his first stage appearance, at the age of eight, in the nativity play of his Poona convent school. He began his career as a band musician but has since become famous as a humorous script writer and actor in both films and broadcasting. He was one of the main figures in and behind the infamous *Goon Show*. Among the films he has appeared in are: *Suspect, Invasion, Postman's Knock* and *Milligan at Large*.

Spike Milligan's published work includes *The Little Potboiler, Silly Verse for Kids, Dustbin of Milligan, A Book of Bits, The Bed-sitting Room* (a play), *The Bald Twit Lion, A Book of Milliganimals, Puckoon, Small Dreams of a Scorpion, Transports of Delight, The Milligan Book of Records, Games, Cartoons and Commercials, Dip the Puppy, William McGonagall: The Truth at Last* (with Jack Hobbs), *The Spike Milligan Letters* and *More Spike Milligan Letters*, both edited by Norma Farnes, *Open Heart University, The Q Annual, Unspun Socks from a Chicken's Laundry, The 101 Best and Only Limericks of Spike Milligan, There's a Lot of It About, The Melting Pot, Further Transports of Delight, The Looney: An Irish Fantasy* and *The Lost Goon Shows. Milligan's War* is a selection taken from his unique and incomparable six volumes of war memoirs: *Adolf Hitler: My Part in His Downfall, Rommel: Gunner Who?, Monty: His Part in My Victory, Mussolini: His Part in My Downfall, Where Have All the Bullets Gone?* and *Goodbye Soldier*.

MILLIGAN'S
WAR

THE SELECTED WAR
MEMOIRS OF SPIKE MILLIGAN

Original editor Jack Hobbs

PENGUIN BOOKS

PENGUIN BOOKS

Published by the Penguin Group
27 Wrights Lane, London W8 5TZ, England
Viking Penguin Inc., 40 West 23rd Street, New York, New York 10010, USA
Penguin Books Australia Ltd, Ringwood, Victoria, Australia
Penguin Books Canada Ltd, 2801 John Street, Markham, Ontario, Canada L3R 1B4
Penguin Books (NZ) Ltd, 182–190 Wairau Road, Auckland 10, New Zealand

Penguin Books Ltd, Registered Offices: Harmondsworth, Middlesex, England

This selected edition first published in Great Britain by Michael Joseph 1988
Published in Penguin Books 1989
1 3 5 7 9 10 8 6 4 2

Filmset in 10/12pt Linotronic Plantin
Made and printed in Great Britain by
Richard Clay (The Chaucer Press), Ltd
Bungay, Suffolk

CONTENTS

Acknowledgements vi

ACKNOWLEDGEMENTS

Many people contributed their memories, diaries and photographs to help me write these war memoirs. In particular I should like to thank Mrs Chater Jack, widow of our CO and late Lt Colonel Chater Jack, MC DSO, for the use of the private letters, diaries and documents which she lent me; Alf Fildes for his diary; Harry Edgington for permission to publish his letters; plus the lads from the Battery who lent me the odd photo or letter – Doug Kidgell, Syd Price and Syd Carter especially. Major J. Leaman, Lt S. Pride, Lt C. Budden, BSM L. Griffin, Sgt F. Donaldson, the late Bombardier Edwards, Bombardier H. Holmwood, Bombardier S. Price, Bombardier A. Edser, Bombardier S. Kemp, Gunner 'Jam Jar' Griffin, Bombardier D. Sloggit, Lance-Bombardier R. Bennett, Gunner J. Shapiro, Gunner 'Dipper' Dye and D. Battery Reunion Committee also contributed their recollections. Thanks are due too to the Imperial War Museum and to Bart H. Vanderveen for permission to reproduce photographs.

VOLUME ONE

ADOLF HITLER:
My Part in His Downfall

HOW IT ALL STARTED

September 3rd, 1939. The last minutes of peace ticking away. Father and I were watching Mother digging our air-raid shelter. 'She's a great little woman,' said Father. 'And getting smaller all the time,' I added. Two minutes later, a man called Chamberlain who did Prime Minister impressions spoke on the wireless; he said, 'As from eleven o'clock we are at war with Germany.' (I loved the *WE*.) 'War?' said Mother. 'It must have been something we said,' said Father. The people next door panicked, burnt their post office books and took in the washing.

Almost immediately came the mournful wail of the first Air-Raid Warning. 'Is that you dear?' said Mother. 'It's a Jewish Funeral,' said Father, 'Quick! Put out the begging bowls.' It was in fact the Bata Shoe Factory lunch hooter. It caused chaos until it was changed. Uncle Willie, a pre-death mortician, who hadn't worked for years, started making small wooden mushrooms. He sent them to Air-Marshal Harris requesting they be dropped on Germany to prove that despite five days of war, British craftsmanship still flourished. They were returned with a note saying, 'Dropping wooden mushrooms during raids might cause unneces-

My father, Leo Milligan

3

sary injury.' My brother Desmond too, seized with pre-pubic patriotism, drew pictures of fantastic war machines. He showed Father: 'Son,' he said, 'these inventions will be the salvation of England.' They wasted no time: carrying the portfolio of drawings in a string bag, they hurried to Whitehall by 74 tram. After several arguments and a scuffle, they were shown into the presence of a curious nose-manipulating Colonel. He watched puzzled as Father laid out drawings of Troop-Carrying Submarines, Tank-Carrying Zeppelins and some of Troops on Rocket-Propelled Skates, all drawn on the backs of old dinner menus. 'Right,' said the Colonel, 'I'll have the brown windsor, roast beef and two veg.' Father and son were then shown the door, the windows, and finally the street. My father objected. 'You fool! By rejecting these inventions you've put two years on the war.' 'Good,' said the Colonel, 'I wasn't doing anything!' Father left. With head held high and feet held higher, he was thrown out.

I was no stranger to Military Life. Born in India on the Regimental strength, the family on both sides had been Gunners as far back as the Siege of Lucknow. Great-Grandfather, Sergeant John Henry Kettleband, had been killed in the Indian Mutiny, by his wife, his last words were, 'Oh!' His father had died in a military hospital after being operated on for appendicitis by a drunken doctor. On the tombstone was carved –

R.I.P.

In memory of
Sgt. Thomas Kettleband.
954024731.

Died of appendicitis
for his King & Country.

Now apparently it was my turn.

One day an envelope marked OHMS fell on the mat. Time for my appendicitis, I thought.

'For Christ's sake don't open it,' said Uncle, prodding it with a stick. 'Last time I did, I ended up in Mesopotamia, chased by Turks waving pots of Vaseline and shouting, "Lawrence we love you" in Ottoman.'

Father looked at his watch. 'Time for another advance,' he said and took one pace forward. Weeks went by, several more OHMS letters arrived, finally arriving at the rate of two a day stamped URGENT.

'The King must think a lot of you son, writing all these letters,' said Mother as she humped sacks of coal into the cellar. One Sunday, while Mother was repainting the house, as a treat Father opened one of the envelopes. In it was a cunningly worded invitation to partake in World War II, starting at seven and sixpence a week, all found. 'Just fancy,' said Mother as she carried Father upstairs for his bath, 'of all the people in England, they've chosen you, it's a great honour, Son.'

My mother's side. Trumpet Sergeant Kettleband, Indian Army, about 1899

Laughingly I felled her with a right cross.

It was now three months since my call-up. To celebrate I hid under the bed dressed as Florence Nightingale. Next morning I received a card asking me to attend a medical at the Yorkshire Grey, Eltham. 'Son,' said Father, 'I think after all you better go, we're running out of disguises, in any case when they see you, they're bound to send you home.' The card said I was to report at 9.30 a.m. 'Please be prompt.' I arrived prompt at 9.30 and was seen promptly at 12.15. We were told to strip. This revealed a mass of pale youths with thin, white, hairy legs. A press photographer was stopped by the recruiting Sergeant. 'For Christ's sake don't! If the public saw a photo of this lot they'd pack it in straight away.' I arrived in the presence of a grey-faced, bald doctor.

'How do you feel?' he said.

'All right,' I said.

'Do you feel fit?'

'No, I walked here.'

Grinning evilly, he wrote Grade 1 (One) in blood red ink on my card. 'No black cap?' I said. 'It's at the laundry,' he replied.

The die was cast. It was a proud day for the Milligan family as I was taken from the house. 'I'm too young to go,' I screamed as Military Policemen dragged me from my pram, clutching a dummy. At Victoria Station the RTO gave me a travel warrant, a white feather and a picture of Hitler marked 'This is your enemy.' I searched every compartment, but he wasn't on the train. At 4.30, June 2nd, 1940, on a summer's day all mare's tails and blue sky we arrived at Bexhill-on-Sea, where I got off. It wasn't easy. The train didn't stop there.

I JOIN THE REGIMENT

Lugging a suitcase tied with traditional knotted string, I made my way to Headquarters 56th Heavy Regiment Royal Artillery. Using sign language they re-directed me to D

Battery. They were stationed in a building called 'Worthingholm', an evacuated girls' school in Hastings Road. As I entered the drive, a thing of singular military ugliness took my eye. It was Battery Sergeant-Major 'Jumbo' Day. His hair was so shorn his neck seemed to go straight up the back of his hat, and his face was suffused red by years of drinking his way to promotion. 'Oi! Where yew

Very well, alone then! Gnr Milligan, 954024, defending England, June 1940

goin? It ain't a girls' school no more.' 'Isn't it? Never mind I'll join the Regiment instead,' I said.

He screwed up his eyes. 'You're not *Milligan*, are yew?'

'Actually I am.'

A beam of sadistic pleasure spread over his face.

'We've been waiting for yew!' he said, pushing me ahead of him with his stick. He drove me into what was D Battery Office. The walls once white were now thrice grey. From a peeling ceiling hung a forty watt bulb that when lit made the room darker. A Janker Wallah was giving the bare floor a stew-coloured hue by slopping a mop around, re-arranging the dirt. On the wall was a calendar with a naked tart advertising cigarettes. Below it was a newspaper cut-out of Neville Chamberlain grinning upwards. Fronting the fire-place was a trestle table covered with a merry grey blanket. A pile of OHMS letters, all addressed to me, were tucked in the corner of the blotter. In the lid of a cardboard shoe-box was a collection of rubber bands, paper-clips, sealing-wax, string and a lead weight. My pulses raced! Here was the heart of a great fighting machine. Seated behind this mighty war organ was a middle-aged, pink, puffy-faced man in his early fifties wearing a uniform in its late seventies. Parts that had frayed had been trimmed with leather; these included cuffs, elbows, pockets, gaiters and all trailing edges; for this reason he was known as 'Leather Suitcase'. His maiden name was Major Startling-Grope. 'This is Gunner Milligan sir,' said the BSM. When they'd both finished laughing, the Major spoke.

'Whair hev yew been, and whai are yew wearing civilian clothes?'

'They wouldn't let me on the train naked sir.'

'I mean, whai aren't you in uniform?'

'I'm not at war with anybody sir.'

'Silence when you speak to an officer,' said BSM.

The Major, who was fiddling with a rubber band, slid it over his finger.

'Does this mean we're engaged sir?'

'Silence!' said BSM.

'I suppose,' said Suitcase, 'you know you are three months late arriving?'

'I'll make up for it sir, I'll fight nights as well!' All these attempts at friendly humour fell on stony ground. I was marched to a bare room by a Bombardier. He pointed to a floor board.

'You're trying to tell me something,' I said.

'Your bed, right?'

'Right.'

'Right, *Bombardier!*'

'I'm a Bombardier already?'

'Oh, cheeky bastard, eh? Got the very job for yew.'

He gave me a scrubbing-brush with two bristles, showed me a three acre cook-house floor and pointed down; he was still trying to tell me something. Leering over all this was the dwarf-like Battery Cook, Bombardier Nash, who looked like Quasimodo with the hump reversed. He was doing things to sausages. Three hours' scrubbing, and the knees in my trousers went through. To make matters worse there were no uniforms in the 'Q' stores. I cut a racy figure on guard, dark blue trousers gone at the knee, powder blue double-breasted chalk-stripe jacket, lemon shirt and white tie, all set off with steel helmet, boots and gaiters. It wasn't easy.

'Halt! Who goes there?' I'd challenge. When they saw me the answer was, 'Piss Off.' I had to be taken off guard duties. In time I got a uniform. It made no difference.

'Halt, who goes there?'

'Piss Off.'

Words can't describe the wretched appearance of a soldier in a new battle-dress. Size had nothing to do with it. You wore what you got. Some soldiers never left barracks for fear of being seen. Others spent most of their time hiding behind trees. The garments were impregnated with an anti-gas agent that reeked like dead camels, and a water-proofing chemical that gave you false pregnancy and nausea. The smell of 500 newly kitted rookies could only be likened to an open Hindu sewerage works on a hot summer night by Delius. To try and 'cure' my BO I salted it and hung it outside in thunderstorms, I took it for walks, I hit it, in desperation I sprayed it with Eau de Cologne, it made little difference, except once a sailor followed me home. Overcoats were a huge, shapeless dead loss. If you wanted alterations, you took it to a garage. But the most difficult part of Army Life was the 0600 hours awakening. In films this was done by a smart bugler who, silhouetted against the dawn with the Union Jack flying, blew reveille. Not so our 'Badgey',* who stayed in bed, pushed the door open with his foot, blew reveille, then went back to sleep.

LIFE IN BEXHILL 1940–41

In Bexhill life carried on. We went on route marches which became pleasant country walks. No matter what season, the Sussex countryside was always a pleasure. But the summer of 1941 was a delight. The late lambs on spring-heel legs danced their happiness. Hot, immobile cows chewed sweet cud under the leaf-choked limbs of June oaks that were young 500 years past. The musk of bramble and blackberry hedges, with purple-black fruit offering themselves to passing hands, poppies, red, red, red, tracking the sun with open-throated petals, birds bickering aloft, bibulous to the sun. White fleecy clouds passing high, changing shapes as if uncertain of what they were. To break for a smoke, to lie in that beckoning grass and watch cabbage white butterflies dancing on the wind. Everywhere was saying bethankit. It was hop picking time. In 1941 the pickers were real cockneys who, to the consternation of the ARP Wardens, lit

* Badgey: Bugler.

bonfires at night and sang roistering songs under the stars. 'Right, fags out, fall in!' – of course, I almost forgot, the war! but people were saying it would all be over by Christmas. Good! that was in twelve weeks' time! I started to read the 'Situations Vacant' in the *Daily Telegraph*, and prematurely advertised, 'Gunner 954024, retired house-trained war hero, unexpectedly vacant. Can pull a piece of string and shout bang with confidence.'

1940 HOW WE MADE MUSIC DESPITE

I took my trumpet to war. I thought I'd earn spare cash by playing Fall In, Charge, Retreat, Lights Out, etc. I put a printed card on the Battery Notice Board, showing my scale of charges:

Fall In	1/6
Fall Out	1/–
Charge	1/9
Halt	£648
Retreat (Pianissimo)	4/–
Retreat (Fortissimo)	10/–
Lights Out	3/–
Lights Out played in private	4/–

While waiting for these commissions I'd lie on my palliasse and play tunes like, 'Body and Soul', 'Can't Get Started', 'Stardust'. It was with mixed feelings that I played something as exotic as 'You go to my Head' watching some hairy gunner cutting his toe-nails. Of course I soon contacted the Jazz addicts. I was introduced to six-foot-two dreamy-eyed Gunner Harry Edgington. A Londoner, he was an extraordinary man, with moral scruples that would have pleased Jesus. It was the start of a lifelong friendship. Harry played the piano. Self taught. He delighted me with some tunes he had composed. He couldn't read music, and favoured two keys, F sharp and C sharp! both keys the terror of the Jazz man: however, over the months I'd busk tunes with him in the NAAFI. I taught him the names of various chords and he was soon playing in keys that made life easier for me. He was game for a 'Jam' any time. And of course, start to hum any tune and Harry would be in with the harmony, and spot on. It helped life a lot to have him around. One day, with nothing but money in mind, I suggested to Harry we try and form a band. Harry grinned and looked disbelieving. 'Just the two of us?'

'We could sit far apart,' I said.

A stroke of luck. A driver, Alf Fildes, was posted to us with suspected rabies and he played the guitar! All we needed was a drummer. We advertised in Part Two Orders. 'Wanted. House Trained Drummer. Academic Training advantage, but not essential. Apply The Gunners Milligan and Edgington. No coloureds but men with names like Duke Ellington given preference.' No one came forward. We were stuck, worse still we were stuck in the Army. But! Milligan had the eye of an eagle, the ear of a dog, and the brain of a newt (we've all got to eat). One meal time, as the dining hall rang to the grinding of teeth in gritty cabbage, came the sound of a rhythmic beat; it was a humble gunner hammering on a piece of Lease Lend bacon, trying to straighten it out for the kill. This was Driver Douglas Kidgell. Would he like to be our drummer? Yes. Good. Now, where to get the drums. Gunner Nick Carter said there was a 'certain' drum kit lying fallow under the stage of Old Town Church Hall. Captain Martin, a sort of commissioned Ned Kelly, suggested we 'requisition' the 'certain' drum kit to prevent it falling into German hands. This sort of patriotism goes deep. With Germany poised to strike we couldn't waste time. We took the drums, and camouflaged them by painting on the Artillery Crest. Kidgell soon got the hang of the drums, and lo! we were a quartet!

After a month's practice, Captain Martin asked could we play for a dance. I told him we had a very limited repertoire,

Harry Edgington in a brown study

Driver Doug Kidgell, as the Khaki Pimpernel

he said 'So have I, we'll hold the dance this Saturday.' GAD! this was the big time! Saturday, The Old Town Church Hall, Bexhill! who knows, next week Broadway! In entertainment starved Bexhill, the dance was a sell-out. The old corrugated iron Hall was packed to suffocation; there were old women, kids, officers, gunners, various wives, very much a village dance affair.

After twenty minutes we had exhausted our repertoire, so we started again. I suppose playing 'Honeysuckle Rose' forty times must be some kind of record. The bar did roaring business, the barman being none other than the Reverend Clegg, Regimental Vicar. We played well on into the night. About two o'clock Captain Martin called a halt. They all stood to attention, we played 'God Save the King'. Now for the rewards. To pay us, Captain Martin led us into the Churchyard in pitch darkness. There he gave us a ten shilling note.

*The memorable first wartime dance in Bexhill Old Town
Church Hall, and the band's first engagement*

'A little something for you lads,' he said.

'Ten bob?' said Fildes painfully. 'Couldn't we raffle it?'

'Now then lads, remember there's a war on,' said Martin pocketing the rest.

That night, by a flickering candle, we all swore allegiance to Karl Marx. No matter what, next dance, unless we got paid more, we'd play the bloody awful Warsaw Concerto!

APPLICATION FOR RAF PILOT

About now, of course, the heroes of the war were the RAF pilots. It made you green with envy on leave. All the beautiful birds went out with pilots. I couldn't stand it any more. I volunteered for the Air Force. I had to be interviewed by Leather Suitcase.

'I hear you want a transfer, Milligan.'

'Yes sir, I want to join the RAF.'

'Ah yes, those are the ones that fly.'

'Yes sir, they go up whereas we just go along.'

'Have you ever flown before?'

'No sir, but I've been upstairs on a bus on my own.'

'No, what I said was, have you ever flown before. I didn't say anything about buses.'

'No sir, I have never flown before.'

'Your father has written to me about it, and I will recommend you for a transfer.'

In February 1941 I was called for an interview to Kingsway House. I waited in a room with about forty other hopefuls. After an hour I was called before a man who appeared to be wearing a pair of hairy outstretched wings under his nose.

'I see you want to join the RAF.'

'Yes, sir. I have the character and temperament that is admirably suited to that arm.'

'What would you like to be.'

'A pilot, sir.'

'Want to go out with pretty girls, eh?'

After a stringent Physical Examination they told me. 'Sorry, your eyesight isn't up to what we need for a pilot; however, we have a number of vacancies for rear gunners.'

'No sir, I don't want to be at the back, I want to drive.'

'I'm sorry lad, that's all we can offer you.'

I stood up, saluted smartly and exited. As I walked down the corridor to the street, I saw what was possibly the ugliest WAAF I had ever seen. 'Hello cheeky,' she said as I passed her. Perhaps they were right, perhaps I had got bad eyesight. I caught an evening train back to Bexhill, and arrived to be informed by Edgington that he had read in the *Melody Maker* that Harry Parry, of the BBC Radio Rhythm Club, was holding auditions to find the best unknown jazz musicians – the winners were to make a recording for broadcasting on the BBC. We wrote off to Harry Parry, c/o BBC, London. We received a reply saying could we come down on the next weekend. We approached Leather Suitcase.

'You're going to do what?'

'Do an audition for the BBC.'

'You can't join them! They're civvies!'

I explained as best I could to him, bearing in mind that contemporary opinion of jazz in those days was almost the same as that of cannabis today. However, he let me go, and the following weekend, excited out of my mind, I arrived at the BBC Studios, Maida Vale. Briefly, I was picked as the best trumpet player, and along with the winning alto, trombone and tenor players, we cut a disc. The pianist for this was the then almost unknown George Shearing, and for an hour, along with Harry Parry, we recorded six sides. It was an unforgettable day for me. I felt that I had been accepted as a jazz musician, and before I left, George Shearing said, 'I hope we meet and play again.' Man, that was praise enough.

POSTING

Posting is an evil ritual: it was with devilish glee that one unit would pass on to another a soldier who they knew to be bloody useless. However, to keep the joke going, these failures were never discharged, just posted. There must have been, at one time, thousands of these idiots, all in a state of permanent transit, spending most of their life on lorries. Lots gave lorry numbers as a forwarding address. Hundreds spent the duration on board lorries, seven were even buried on them. There is a legend that the last of these idiots was discovered as late as 1949, living on the tail-board of a burnt-out ammunition lorry in a Wadi near Alamein. When located, he was naked, save for a vest and one sock: he said he was 'waiting to be posted'.

'MONTY'

In 1941 a new power came on the scene. Montgomery! He was put in charge of Southern Command. He removed all the pink fat-faced, Huntin', Shootin' and Fishin' chota peg-swilling officers who were sittin' round waitin' to 'see off the Bosche'. To date we'd done very little Physical Training. We had done a sort of half hearted knees-up mother brown for five minutes in the morning, followed by conducted coughing, but that's all.

One morning a chill of horror ran through the serried ranks. There in Part Two Orders were the words: 'At 0600 hours the Battery will assemble for a FIVE MILE RUN!' Strong gunners fell fainting to the floor, some lay weeping on their beds. FIVE MILES? There was no such distance! FIVE MILES!?!? That wasn't a run, that was deportation! On that fateful dawn the duty Bombardier bade us rise: 'Wakey Wakey, Hands off Cocks on Socks.' The defenders of England rose wraith-like from their blankets. All silent, save those great lung-wracking coughs that follow early morning cigarettes. The cough would start in silence; first there was the great inhale, the smoke sucked deep down into the lungs, and held there while the victim started what was to be an agonised body spasm. The face would first turn sweaty lemon, the shoulders hunched, the back humped like a Brahmin bull. The legs would bend, the hand grabbed the thighs to support the coming convulsion. The cough would start somewhere down in the shins, the eyes would be screwed tight to prevent being jettisoned from the head, the mouth gripped tight to preserve the teeth. Suddenly! from afar comes a rumbling like a hundred Early Victorian Water Closets. Slowly the body would start to tremble and the bones to rattle. The first things to shake were the ankles, then up the shins travelled the shakes, and next the knees would revolve and turn jelliform; from there up the thighs to the stomach it came, now heading for the blackened lungs. This was the stage when a sound like a three ton garden roller being pulled over corrugated iron was heard approaching the heaving chest. Following this up the convulsed body was a colour pattern, from a delicate green at the ankles to layers of pinks, blue, varicose purple, and sweaty red. As the cough rose up the inflated throat, the whole six colours were pushed up into the victim's face. It had now reached the inner mouth; the last line of defence, the cheeks, were blown out the size of football bladders. The climax was nigh! The whole body was now a purple shuddering mass! After several mammoth attempts to contain the cough, the mouth would finally explode open! Loose teeth would fly out, bits of breakfast, and a terrible rasping noise filled the room. Aweeioussheiough!!! followed by a long, silent stream of spume-laden air: on and on it went until the whole body was drained of oxygen, the eyes were popping, and veins like vines standing out on the head, which was now down 'twixt knees. This atrophied pose held for seconds. Finally, with a dying attempt, fresh air was sucked back into the body, just in time to do it all over again. Bear in mind this was usually performed by some sixty men all at the same time. Whenever I see those bronzed 'Jet Set Men' whose passport to International smoking is a King Size, I can't help but recall those Bronchial Dawn Coughing Wrecks.

So to the great run. Hundreds of white shivering things were paraded outside Worthingholm. Officers out of uniform seemed stripped of all authority. Lieutenant Walker looked very like a bank clerk who couldn't. Now I, like many others, had no intention of running five miles, oh, no. We would hang behind, fade into the background, find a quiet haystack, wait for the return and rejoin them. Montgomery had thought of that. We were all put on three ton trucks and driven FIVE MILES into the country and dropped. So it started. Some, already exhausted having to climb off the lorry, were begging for the *coup de grâce*. Off we went, Leather Suitcase in front: in ten seconds he was trailing at the back. 'Rest,' he cried, collapsing in a ditch. We rested five minutes and then he called, 'Right, follow me.' Ten seconds later he collapsed again. We left him expiring by the road.

Many tried to husband their energy by running on one leg. It was too cold to walk, we had to keep moving or hoar frost got at the appendages. One by one we arrived back at the billets, behind was a five mile train of broken men. It took two hours before the last of the stragglers arrived back. As a military disaster, the run was second only to Isandhlawana. It was the end of the line for Leather Suitcase.

Our new CO was Major Chater Jack, MC, DSO. In the months that followed he ran us across two-thirds of Sussex, the whole of the South Coast, over mountains, through haystacks, along railway lines, up trees, down sewers, anywhere. If ever we had to retreat we were in tip top condition.

In the first week herds of men reported sick with sore

Major Chater Jack, MC, DSO. (This photograph shows him in 1945 when he was a lieutenant-colonel)

feet. Busty Roberts told us the cure: 'Piss in yer boots, lads, let 'em stand overnight.' By God, it worked! There were accidents; forgetful sleepers got up and plunged their feet into boots full of cold urine. What an Army! What a life! I still can't believe it happened. But of course, the Russians were advancing on all fronts, the Yanks were coming, and we had our first case of Crabs. I had no idea what the crabs (or, as Smudge Smith said, 'Sandy McNabs') were. The victim was Sergeant Cusak – he discovered he got them on the eve of a week's leave. The MO told him to apply 'Blue Unction'. Now blue unction has only one use – to destroy crabs. Knowing this, Sergeant Cusak entered Boots in Piccadilly with a prescription during the rush hour on Friday – it was crowded. He whispered to the assistant, 'Can I have some blue unction?' In a voice that could be heard up Regent Street the assistant said 'BLUE UNC-TION??' Cusak replied twice as loud, 'YES, I'VE GOT BLOODY CRABS!'

MOVING TO MILL WOOD

1941: during which the sole stratagem of the Army in England was one of continual movement. They chose the most excruciating moments. After spending months making your billet comfortable came the order 'Prepare to Move'. This time I was just about to lay my new Axminster when the order came. It was awful, I had to sell the piano. The moves were always highly secret and came in highly sealed envelopes, the contents of which usually appeared in later editions of the *Bexhill Observer*. Secrecy was impossible, enemy agents had only to follow the trail of illegitimate births. Another obsession was 'night occupation'. The swearing, the mighty oaths and clangs, told the whole area exactly what was happening. It was quite normal for a pub to empty out and give a hand pulling the gun. Most kids in Bexhill could dismantle one. Our first move was to a 'specially selected' muddy disused rubbish tip at Mill Wood, two miles from Worthingholm. The signal section under Sergeant Dawson had to start the lark of laying new lines. This was simple: you went from Point A, the OP and took the line to Point B, the Gun Position. Taking a rough bearing, we set off carrying great revolving iron drums of D5* telephone cable. We had to cross railway lines, roads, swamps, rivers, with no more than adhesive tape. We borrowed the equipment en route from houses, a ladder here, a pair of pliers there, a bit of string, a few hooks, a three course lunch, etc.

To cross roads we had to climb telegraph poles. Basically lazy, it took some half an hour of arguing and threats to get one of us to go up. It was always little Flash Gordon, he didn't want to climb the poles, but we hit him until he did.

We had a new addition to the family, a military ten line telephone exchange. This saved a great amount of cable laying; it also connected up to the GPO. It was installed in a concrete air-raid shelter at the back of Worthingholm. In 1962 I took a sentimental journey back to Bexhill. The shelter was overgrown with brambles; I pushed down the stairs and by the light of a match I saw the original telephone cables still in place on the wall where the exchange used to be. There was still a label on one. In faded lettering it said, 'Galley Hill OP' in my handwriting. The place was full of ghosts – I had to get out. One of the pleasures of Duty Signaller was listening to officers talking to their females. When we got a 'hot' conversation we plugged it straight through to all those poor lonely soldiers at their OPs and gun positions. It was good to have friends.

BURNING OF THE CLUBS (MILL WOOD)

It was during this time the Goons in the Popeye cartoon

---

* I don't know what it means either.

Me, line-laying. My tin hat had just fallen off and I was afraid of dive-bombers

appeared and tickled my sense of humour, and any soldier I thought was an idiot I called a Goon. This was taken up by those with a like sense of humour. We called ourselves the Clubbers. We built a club rack outside the marquee and, in time, we fashioned great gnarled clubs from fallen branches. They all had names – 'Nurkes Nut Nourisher', 'Instant Lumps'. The pride was a magnificent find by Gunner Devine; it was a part of a blasted oak, five feet long, almost a replica of the club of Hercules. We added to it by driving earthing irons into the head. It was solemnly christened, 'Ye Crust Modifier'. The way the Clubbers were assembled was by a trumpet call based on the Fanfare from the 'Boys from Syracuse' film. Immediately the gang would do 'Hollywood Rhubards', rush forth, grab the clubs, run into the woods hitting trees and shouting 'Death to the Goons'. This exercise was our downfall. We were caught

Shaving al fresco in Mill Wood, with the Germans only forty miles away. The cross eyes were the result of a blunt blade

one summer night by the duty officer. Drunk and naked, we were running through the woods wielding clubs and yelling 'Viva Joe Stalin'. We were ordered to destroy the weapons. We had a solemn funeral procession. They would have to burn in warriors' graves. These turned out to be the disused rubbish tip at the bottom of a gently sloping hill. Rubbish was dumped by trucks via a small gauge railway. Filling the truck with clubs, we soaked them in petrol and set them ablaze. Giving the truck a start we jumped on, Edgington in front, holding on with his arms stretched backwards, looking like a ship's figure head. The truck gathered momentum, flames built up, we were gathering speed and singing 'Round and round went the bloody great wheel', when suddenly it occurred to me there was no method of braking. As we careered towards a mountain of old tins, crying with laughter, I shouted, 'Jump for it'. We all leaped clear, save Edgington, who seemed transfixed. At the very last minute he let out a strangulated castrati scream and hurled himself sideways as the blazing truck buried itself into the mountain of tins with an ear splitting crash.

It was a fitting Viking end for the Sacred Clubs. Occasions of insanity such as this stopped us all going mad.

As the days of 1940 came to an end, Dunkirk was sliding into history. The war was spreading; there seemed very little in the way of victories, there were constant reversals in Libya and Greece. On my birthday, April 16th, 1941, London had its worst raid yet. But cheering news – May 14th was the first anniversary of – wait for it – The Home Guard!

7.2 GUNS AND THE TIGER SCHEME

Our 9.2 guns were past it. Every time they fired, bits fell off. In place of bolts and nuts were bent nails and chicken wire. Gunners on leave would rummage through their sheds for screws, pinions, etc. The end came when elastic bands, which held the gun-sight together, were no longer obtainable. The Major wrote away, asking for a new gun for Christmas. One day they arrived. Dozens of them! 7.2 gun howitzers. Huge things towed behind Giant Schamell lorries.

At once we were put into vigorous training to familiarise us with the new toys. For weeks the area rang to the clang of breech-blocks, shouted orders, grunts of the sweating ammunition numbers. The guns threw a 280 pound projectile 17,800 yards, so you weren't safe anywhere except at 18,000 yards. Momentum was mounting, we were getting new field telephones, wireless trucks, wireless sets, tommy guns, Tannoy loudspeakers that linked Command Post to the guns. The war effort was moving into top gear.

Monty sprang a giant Southern Command scheme, code name 'Tiger'. One autumn dawn the sky was a mass of grey sponges: this undoubtedly would be the day. It was. Off we went. One hour after off we went we stopped wenting. We were in the middle of a Rain Forest that appeared to be in the Mato Grosso. 'Dismount,' came the waterlogged order.

A 7.2 gun howitzer as seen from the receiving end
(The Imperial War Museum)

Soggy officers were called to the OC's car. They stood in a squelching semi-circle, holding maps. Chater Jack whipped through the map references and all that Khaki Jazz. Our officer was Tony Goldsmith. 'We've got to set up an OP at Map Reference 8975–4564★ in half an hour. Synchronise watches.' None of us had one. 'Very well,' said Goldsmith. '*I'll* synchronise watches.' Goldsmith's map reading left something to be desired, like someone to read it for him. Using his method, we had arrived at a hundred-year-old deserted chalk quarry. How can people be so heartless as to desert a hundred-year-old chalk quarry? We were two hundred feet below sea level. We got out. Goldsmith consulted his map. 'There must be something wrong,' he

★ Somewhere on the South Downs.

25

said, looking intelligent at two hundred feet below sea level. 'According to my calculations we should be on top of a hill, looking down a valley.'

Gunner Milligan said, 'But we aren't on top of a hill looking down a valley, are we sir?'

'No, we're not, Milligan. How shrewd of you to notice. This could mean promotion for you, or death. I suggest we retrace our steps to the main road. Does anybody know where it is?'

'I think I do sir,' said Driver Wenham.

We boarded the truck, and set off somewhere. 'Send a message to HQ,' said Goldsmith, still trying to maintain the illusion of efficiency. 'Say, "Truck in ditch, will be late for OP".'

I sent off the message. But received a request for Goldsmith to speak to 'Sunray' (code name for CO). What a lovely name I thought for a dripping wet CO.

Goldsmith spoke.

'Hello, Sunray, Seagull here. Over.'

Chater Jack: Tony? What the bloody hell's going on? Over.

Goldsmith: The truck's stuck, sir. Over.

Chater Jack: Well hurry up, the whole bloody battery's waiting for you.

We drove grimly on. One o'clock. 'Get the BBC news, Milligan,' said Goldsmith, 'you never know, it might be all over.' There were the opening bars of Beethoven's Fifth Symphony. 'I wonder if he gets royalties,' said Goldsmith. 'Oh yes,' I said, 'every Friday.' The news. Russians were advancing on all fronts. Then a list of current British disasters, retreats, sinkings, etc. The news concluded with a report of a two-headed calf born in Hereford.

Using all the skill of a trained Army driver, Wenham had the truck into a ditch a second time!

'Sorry sir,' said Wenham, 'I won't do it again!'

'Don't stop now man, you're just getting the hang of it,'

said Goldsmith. 'Milligan! Send another message "Truck now in second ditch."'

Back came Chater Jack.

Chater Jack: Good God, Tony, where are you man? Over.

Goldsmith: About a mile from the OP sir. Over.

Chater Jack: You're very faint. Over.

Goldsmith: It's the food sir. Over.

Chater Jack: I can't hear you. Look, we'll have to write you off. We'll get 18 Battery OP to fire us. Over.

Goldsmith: Roger sir. Over.

Chater Jack: Anything else? Over.

Goldsmith: A two-headed calf has been born at Hereford sir. Over.

Chater Jack: Two what? Over.

Goldsmith: Very good sir, anything else?

Chater Jack: No. Roger and out.

We stopped at a village of Lower Lind, where we went to the Essoldo Bioscope Cinema to see 'Black Moonlight' with Anton Walbrook, and heard that bloody awful Warsaw Concerto. Lieutenant Goldsmith paid for us all, as is fitting for a man wearing the King's uniform over his Queens' College body.

He told me a story about Jesus College, Cambridge. It was Christmas morning, the phone rang in the gate porter's lodge. 'Hello,' said the porter.

'Is that Jesus?' asked a donnish voice.

'Yes.'

The voice sang, 'Happy birthday to you.'

At six o'clock we arrived at the night rendezvous, a field of bracken resting on a lake. We got tea from a swearing cook-house crew, who took it in turns to say 'piss off' to us. We were given to understand we could have a complete night's sleep. Good. We tossed for who was to sleep in the truck. I lost. Sod. Rain. Idea! Under the truck! Laid out ground sheet, rolled myself like a casserole in three blankets. I dropped into a deep sleep. I awoke to rain falling on me. The truck had gone. Everybody had gone. There had been a surprise call to action at 0200 hours. I was alone in a fifty-acre field. I shouted into the darkness, 'Anybody there?' I was still alone in a fifty-acre field. Smell of oil – I felt my face. It was smothered. The stuff had dripped from a leaky sump. Sound of motor bike approaching. 'Help,' I said. 'Who's that?' said a voice. It was Jordy Dawson.

'It's me, Sarge! Milligan.' A torch shone.

'What in Christ has happened to you?' he said.

'I'm doing Paul Robeson impressions. You're just in time for my encore.' I started to sing: 'Ole man ribber, dat ole . . .'

'What's that on your mush?'

'Oil, Sarge! I cut an artery and struck oil. We're rich, do you hear me. We can be married.'

He started to laugh. 'You silly bugger, we've had half the bloody signal section looking for you. The scheme's over.'

'I know! Half of it's over me,' I said.

'Come on, I'll take you back.'

'Go back?' I said in a pained voice, 'but I'm happy here, here on de ole plantation, massa baws.' Seated on the pillion, he drove me back to Bexhill. Tiger had been a roaring success. The German High Command must have been ecstatic. The following is an excerpt from the Regimental war diary of the time:

When the weather was too bad for schemes out of doors, wireless and telephone exercises were held within the Regiment to increase the proficiency in communications. It was on such an occasion as this, that a message was sent reading: 'Invasion Fleet in the Channel, two miles off SEAFORD, steaming NW. Estimated strength three capital ships, sixteen destroyers, and many lesser craft.' He had omitted to prefix the message with the magic word 'PRACTICE' and by some unkind trick of fate, which has never since been accounted for, the message by-passed RHQ and was sent direct to Corps. The scheme finished, and the Regiment prepared to depart on its nightly occupations. Suddenly the peace was shattered by the frantic ringing of the telephone bell. It was a call from the War Office, who enquired, in no uncertain tones, what the thundering blazes was the meaning of our message. What steps had been taken by us: and had the Navy been informed?

By the time the matter had been sorted out, tempers were frayed and feeling was running high. It took some laughing off, but a personal visit by the CO to the War Office the following day succeeded in allaying the storm. It is an interview that few of us would have cared to undertake personally.

I think I can now safely reveal that the signal was sent by 954024, Gunner Milligan.

LARKHILL

Things had been going too smoothly to continue as they were, it really was time we had another bout of applied chaos. It came in the shape of a sudden rush to Larkhill Artillery Camp, Salisbury, hard by Stonehenge. It was January 1942, and quite the bitterest weather I could remember. We arrived after a Dawn to Sunset trip by road. Salisbury Plain was blue-white with hoar-frost. I sat in the back of a Humber Radio Car, listening to any music I could pick up from the BBC and banging my feet to keep warm. We arrived tired, but being young and tired means you could go on all night! Ha! Having parked the vehicles, we were dismissed. The signallers were shown to a long wooden hut on brick piers. We dumped our kit on the beds, with the usual fight for the lower bunk, then made for the ORs' mess and began queueing. It must have been the season for schemes, as the whole place was swarming with gunners. We were given pale sausages, not long for this world, and potatoes so watery we drank them. The camp had masses of hot showers and we spent a pleasant hour under them, singing and enjoying the luxury of hot water. There were the usual comments about the size of one's 'wedding tackle': 'Cor, wot a beauty', or 'he's bloody well hung', or 'Christ, his poor wife', etc. After a quick tea and wad in the NAAFI we went to the large cinema Nissen hut. It was The Glen Miller Orchestra in 'Sun Valley Serenade', and it was a feast of great big band sound plus at least ten good songs. Sitting in the NAAFI later, we tried to recall them; it was this way that we learnt most of the tunes for the band's repertoire. Seated at the piano, Harry tried to play some of the tunes from the film.

'Play Warsaw Concerto,' said a drunk Scottish voice.

At dawn the next day the Battery set off on the great, ice-cold, frost-hardened Salisbury Plain. Most of us had put on two sets of woollen underwear, including the dreaded 'Long Johns'. We were to practise a new speedy method of bringing a twenty-five pounder gun into action. Ahead of us would go a scouting OP; somewhere on the Plain four twenty-five pounders drawn by quads would be moving in the direction of a common map reference, all linked to the OP by wireless. Ahead the OP would establish itself at a point overlooking 'Crash Action East', or whichever compass point applied; the information was received by the gun wireless, whose operator would shout out to the gun officer the order received. The gun officer, standing up in his truck would shout to the gun crew, 'Halt, Action East'. The quad would brake sharply, the gun crew in a frenzy unlimber the gun, and face it east; while they were doing this the OP would rapidly send down the Rough Range of the Target. As soon as the gun crew had done this, they fired. In our case, from the first order to the firing of the first round was twenty-five seconds. This was the fastest time for the day.

The next ten days saw us going through rigorous training. The weather was bitterly cold. I saw Sid Price smoke a cigarette down to the stub, and burn the woollen mitten on his hand without feeling a thing. On the last day, B Subsection were firing smoke shells, when one got jammed in the breech. Sergeant Jordy Rowlands was in the process of removing the charge when it exploded in his hand. When the smoke cleared Rowlands was looking at the stump of his wrist with his right hand ten yards away on the ground. There was a stunned silence and then he said, 'Well, I'll be fooked.' Apart from initial shock he was OK, but for him the war was finished on Salisbury Plain. The severed hand was buried where it fell by Busty Roberts. As he dug a small hole Driver Watts said, 'You going to shake hands before you bury it?' Busty's reply was never recorded.

That night there was an Officers' and All-Ranks' dance in the Drill Hall. We all worked hard to extricate all the best-looking ATS girls from the magnetic pull of the officers and sergeants. Alas, we failed, so we reverted to the time honoured sanctuary of the working man – Drink. We finally reached the stage of inebriation when we were willing to do the last dance with any good-looking Lance Bombardier. Next day, Saturday, the last day at Camp, we were allowed into Salisbury. I went to see the Cathedral. I'll never forget the feeling of awe when I walked in. A boys' choir was singing something that sounded like Monteverdi. The voices soared up to the fluted vaults as though on wings. The morning autumn sun was driving through the stained-glass windows throwing colours on to the floor of the nave, the whole building was a psalm in stone. It all made me aware of the indescribable joy derived from beauty.

'Cor, it's bloody big, ain't it?' said Smudger Smith. He was right. It was bloody big.

There was a beer-up that night, and another dance. After 2343 hours I don't remember anything. Next day we returned to that jewel of the south coast, Bexhill.

DETENTION

October 1942. We were alerted for a practice shoot at
Sennybridge Camp in Wales. Burdened down with kit, I
decided to hide my rifle in the rafters of the hay-loft. 'That's
a good idea,' said patriotic Edgington. The short of it was
several other patriots did the same. And it came to pass, that
after we had gone thence, there cometh a Quarter Bloke,
and in the goodness of his heart he did inspect ye hay-loft,
and woe, he findeth rifles, and was sore distressed, whereupon he reporteth us to the Major, who on Sept. 14th, 1942,
gaveth us fourteen bloody days detention. For some reason
all the other 'criminals' were sent to our RHQ at Cuckfield,
but I was sent to Preston Barracks, Brighton, alone, no
escort, Ahhhh, they trusted me. At Brighton station, I tried
to thumb a lift; I got one from an ATS girl driving a
General's Staff car. She dropped me right outside Preston
Barracks. As the car stopped, the sentry came to attention,
then *I* got out. I reported to the sergeant I/C Guardroom.
'Welcome to Preston Barracks,' he said.

'You're welcome to it too,' I replied.

'Now,' he said, 'from now on you keep your mouth shut
and your bowels open.'

Then he gave me a cup of tea that did both. He stripped
me of all kit, leaving essentials like my body. The cell, my
God! it must have been built in anticipation of Houdini.
Seven foot by six foot, by twenty foot high, stone floor,
small window with one iron bar, up near the ceiling,
wooden bed in the corner. The door was solid iron, two
inches thick, with a small spy-hole for the guard. No light.
'You go to sleep when it gets dark, like all the good little
birdies do,' said the sergeant. 'Make yourself comfortable,'
he said, slamming the cell door. Every day, a visit from the
orderly officer, a white consumptive lad who appeared to be
training for death. 'Got everything you want?' he said. 'No,
sir, I haven't got a Bentley.' I grinned to let him know it was

a joke, that I was a cheery soul, and not downhearted. It wasn't the way he saw it. He pointed to a photo of my girl by my bed. 'That will have to go,' he said.

'Yes sir, where would you like it to go? I think it would go nice on the piano.'

'Put it out of sight.'

'But it's my fiancée sir.'

'Photographs are *not allowed*.' He was starting to dribble.

'What about statues sir?'

He lost his English 'cool'. 'Sergeant – put this man under arrest.'

'He's already under arrest sir,' said Sarge.

'Well give him extra fatigues for being impertinent!'

I planned revenge. I cut my finger-nails. On his next visit I placed them in a cigarette lid.

'What are those?'

'Finger-nails sir.'

'Throw them away.'

'They are my fiancée's sir.'

'Throw them away.'

'Very good sir.'

The next time he visited I had cut a small lock of my hair, tied a small bow on it and placed it on my bed.

'What's that?'

'A lock of hair sir.'

'Throw it away.'

'It's my fiancée's sir,' etc. etc.

The last one I planned was with an artificial limb, but the officer never visited me again. He was drafted overseas, and killed during an air raid on Tobruk; a NAAFI Tea Urn fell on his head.

My duties were not unpleasant.

1) Reveille 0600. Make tea for the Guard. Drink lots of tea.
2) Collect blackberries along the railway bank for Sergeants' Mess Tea.
3) In pouring rain, shovel two six-foot-high piles of coke

into 'One Uniform Conical Heap'. (A Bad Day.)

4) Commissioned to draw a naked Varga Girl for Guard Room. (A Good Day.)
5) Trip to beach to collect winkles for Sergeants' Mess Tea.
6) Weed Parade Ground by hand. (Bloody Awful Day.)
7) Commissioned to draw Varga Girl for Sergeants' Mess. (Another Good Day.)
8) Oil all locks and hinges at Preston Barracks, sandpaper door of cell, prime, undercoat, and paint gunmetal black.
9) Drive Major Druce-Bangley to Eastbourne (his driver taken ill with an overdose of whisky) to have it off with his wife in house on seafront.

After fourteen days I was sent back to Hailsham – I arrived to find the whole Battery boarding lorries – yes! 'Prepare to move' again! With my kit I jumped into a fifteen hundredweight, making it a sixteen hundredweight.

'Where are we going?'

'I don't know, it's another secret destination,' said Sergeant Dawson.

Three hours later, we were back to square one. Bexhill.

'I wish they'd make their fucking minds up,' said Sergeant Dawson.

'Look Sarge, they're moving us about to make us look a lot,' said Gunner Tome.

'We look a lot,' said Dawson, 'a lot of cunts.'

'Give us a merry song, Sarge,' I said, running for cover.

After the war, in 1968, I was appearing at the Royal Theatre, Brighton. I took a trip to Preston Barracks. All changed, the Old Guard Room with my cell had gone – everything had changed – except the large parade ground, that was still there; did I really weed it by hand in 1942? We must have all been bloody mad.

DECEMBER 1942–JANUARY 1943 – EMBARKATION LEAVE

As the monkey-keeper at the Zoo said, when a new trussed-up gorilla arrived, 'It was bound to come.' We were going overseas. Of course we should have gone yesterday. Everything had to be packed into everything else yesterday. Somewhere great wooden crates appeared yesterday. 'Good God,' said Edgington yesterday, 'they're sending us by parcel post!' The crates were filled, nailed down and stencilled 'This Way Up' at all angles. Vehicles had to be waterproofed. Oh dearie me! This smacked of a beach landing. Everything was camouflaged black and dark green so it couldn't be the desert. All our missing clothing was replaced. We then ran straight down to the town and sold them. One issue was a large vacuum-sealed tin of 'Emergency Chocolate', only to be eaten in the event of, say, being surrounded by the Enemy. That night, in bed, surrounded by the Enemy, I ate my Emergency Chocolate.

The news had been broken by the Old Man in the NAAFI hut, the dear old NAAFI hut. In it we wrote letters home, drank tea, played ping-pong, banged tunes out on the piano, or, when we had no money just sat there to keep warm. It was in this hut that I first heard the voice of Churchill on an old Brown Bakelite Ecko Radio. On the day of the official pronouncement, we were marched in and sat down. Enter Major Chater Jack, 'Eyes Front!' Chater Jack acknowledges Battery Sergeant-Major's salute. 'At ease Sergeant-Major.' At ease it is. 'You can all smoke,' said Chater Jack, 'I'm going to.' (Light laughter.) Smilingly, he starts to speak. 'You may have been hearing rumours that we were going abroad.' (Laughter. Rumours had been non-stop.) 'We are, finally, going overseas. It's what we've all been trained for, so, it shouldn't come as a shock.' He cut out all unnecessary gas and told us dates and times. A very Scots voice from the back, 'Where are we going sir?'

'Well, I know it's not Glasgow.' (Roar of laughter.) 'Embarkation leave will start immediately, married men first . . . they need it.' (Laughter.) A voice from the back, 'Don't we all.' (Loud laughter.) He told us that there would be a farewell dinner dance at the Devonshire Arms. He finished 'Good luck to you all.'

I arrived at Victoria Station during the rush-hour. The crowds were a weird mixture of grey faces carrying early Christmas shopping. I was wearing my new red artillery forage cap, and felt rather conspicuous. I took the crowded tube to London Bridge, and from there a train to Honor Oak Park. The faces of the commuters were tired and pinched. Occasionally one would steal a look at me. I don't know why. To break the boredom I suppose. A man of about fifty, in a dark suit and overcoat, leaned over and said 'Would you like a cigarette?' 'Thank you,' I said, and like a bloody fool smoked it. A bloody fool because, dear reader, I had just gone through three weeks' agony, having given up the habit. As I walked from the station down Riseldine Road a raid was in progress. It was very, very dark, and I had to peer closely at several doors before I arrived at Number 50. The family were about to have dinner in the Anderson Shelter. 'Ah son,' said my father, in that wonderful welcoming voice he had, 'you're just in time for the main course.' Holding a torch he showed me down the garden. 'Put that bloody light out,' said my brother in a mock ARP warden voice. The voice was in the process of breaking, and I swear in speaking that short sentence he went from Middle C to A above the stave. By the light of a hurricane lamp, called 'Storm Saviour Brand', I squeezed next to my mother. They had made the shelter as comfortable as possible, with duck boards and a carpet on top, an oil heater, books, and a battery radio. Mother said grace, then the four of us sat eating luke-warm powdered egg, dehydrated potatoes, Lease Lend carrots and wartime-strength tea. I felt awful. So far I hadn't suffered anything. Seeing the family in these miserable circumstances did raise a lump in my throat, but they seemed cheery enough. 'Got a surprise for you son.' So saying Father put his hand under the table and produced a bottle of Chateau La Tour 1934. 'It's at Shelter temperature,' he said. We drank a toast to the future. The next time the family would drink a toast together was to be ten years later.

Mother related how the week previously the whole family had nearly been killed. It was nine at night; Father, wearing aught but Marks and Spencer utility long underwear and tartan slippers, was heavily poised in the kitchen making a cup of tea, strength three. He was awaiting that jet of steam from the kettle that signals the invention of the steam engine. In the lounge, oblivious of the drama in the kitchen, were my mother and brother. This room had been modified

Picture, taken at the insistence of my father to show the Milligan family at war, on my embarkation leave

into a bedroom-cum-sitting-room, double bed in one corner and the single for my brother in the other. This arrangement made my brother's night manipulations extremely difficult. However, Mother was seated on an elephantine imitation brown mochette couch with eased springs, knitting Balaclavas for the lads at the Front. My brother, Desmond, a lad of fourteen, was sitting on his bed, looking through his wartime scrap book, reading aloud sections on Hitler's promised invasion. A two-thirds slag, one-third coal fire smoked merrily in the grate. Suddenly, an explo-

My father appeared at the door clutching a kettle. (Drawn by my brother, who was there at the time)

sion, arranged Luftwaffe. Mother was blown six feet up in the sitting position, then backwards over the couch. My brother was shot up against the wall, reaching ceiling level before returning. The fire was sucked up the chimney, as were mother's C & A Mode slippers. The Cheesemans of Lewisham's imitation-velour curtains billowed in and the room was filled with ash. It was all over in a flash. My mother was upside-down behind the couch. My father appeared at the door. 'What's happening?' he said. He presented a strange figure, clutching a steaming kettle and smoke-blackened from head to foot. He said, 'Wait here,' went to the back door and shouted 'Anybody there?' He then returned and said, 'It's all right, he's gone.' Despite the activities of German Bombers I was determined to sleep in my old bed. Sheets! Sheer bliss. Lying in bed I realised that the family was finally broken up – the war had made inroads on our peacetime relationship, I was independent, my brother no longer had my company. All was changed. For the better? We'll never know. We had been a very close-knit family, something not many British families were.

My week's leave was spent in 'sitting in' with local gig bands, seeing people from the Woolwich Arsenal (where I had worked before the War), drinking, and walking home bent double with sexual frustration from 45 Revelon Road, Brockley.

I arrived back off leave, and, I quote from my diary, 'Returned back at billets to find every. ody drunk, jolly or partially out of their minds.' The knowledge that at last we were going overseas had given the Battery the libertine air of the last day at school. It was impossible to try and sleep. Everyone was hell bent on playing practical jokes. Beds crashed down in the night, buckets of water were fixed over doors, boots were nailed to the floor, there were yells and screams as thunder-flashes exploded under unsuspecting victims' beds. The Battery was in a state of flux, most were on leave, others were about to go, others were on their way back, some couldn't get back, others didn't want to. One night the barracks were full, the next they were empty, God knows who was running us, certainly all the officers were on leave, what one good Fifth Columnist could have wrought at that time doesn't bear thinking about. I remember very well, one rainy night, Harry and I lay in bed, talking, smoking, unable to sleep with excitement.

'Let's go and have a Jam in the NAAFI.'

It seemed a good idea. It was about one in the morning when we got in. For an hour we played. 'These Foolish Things', 'Room Five Hundred and Four', 'Serenade in Blue', 'Falling Leaves' and the inevitable Blues. In retrospect it wasn't a happy occasion, two young men, away from home, playing sentimental tunes in a pitch black NAAFI. Oh, yesterday, leave me alone!

Friday, December 18th, 1942: the place? The Devonshire Arms; the occasion? the Farewell Dinner and Dance for D Battery. It was Chater Jack's idea, and I think I'm right in saying that he paid for the whole evening, because I overheard Captain Martin saying to him, 'You'll pay for this.' For the first time D Battery band didn't play, the music was provided by Jack Shawe and His Band. We would have liked to have played, but Chater Jack insisted that we had the 'night off' for once.

It was a marvellous evening. We all enjoyed the dinner despite the frugal wartime fare. The enthusiasm of the occasion was terrific. In retrospect I don't suppose many of the lads had ever been to a dinner dance on this scale. It was the eve of what for most of us was the greatest adventure of our lives.

The dinner over, the dance got under way, some lads had brought their wives down for the occasion, the local mistresses and girl friends were all present, everyone knew everyone else. I picked up with a WAAF Corporal, her name was Bette. I forget the surname. I ended up in bed with her, somewhere in Cooden Drive. I always remember a woman looking round the door and saying 'Have you got enough blankets,' and I replied something like 'How dare you enter the King's bedchamber when he's discussing foreign policy.' This sudden late affair with Bette flowered rapidly and we did a lot of it in the last dying days prior to Embarkation. Actually, I was glad when we left, I couldn't have kept up this non-stop soldier-all-day–lover-all-night with only cups of tea in between. I was having giddy spells, even lying down. I don't suppose there's anything more exciting than a sudden affair; it is the sort of thing that defeats the weather, and gives you a chance to air your battle-dress. When I went overseas, Bette wrote sizzling letters that I auctioned to the Battery lechers.

THE TRAIN JOURNEY (BEXHILL–LIVERPOOL)

The date was January 6th, 1943, the time just before midnight. An army on the march. Weather, pissing down. Standing in a black street, the hammer of the Germans stands silent in full FSMO. With arms aching from typhus, typhoid and tetanus injections, Edgington and I had been detailed to carry a Porridge Container. 'Quick march!' Shuffle, shamble, slip, shuffle, scrape. Nearing the station, a voice in the dark: 'Anybody remember to turn the gas off?'

'Stop that talking.'

'Bollocks!'

'No swearing now Vicar!'

The rain. It seemed to penetrate everything. We reached the station soaked. My porridge-carrying arm was six inches longer. Down the stairs we trooped on to the platform where the train was now not waiting in the station. Permission to smoke. An hour went by. We struck up a quiet chorus of 'Why are we waiting?', followed by outbreaks of bleating. At 2.14 a.m. the train arrived. Ironic cheers. All aboard! and the fight for seats got under way. A compartment packed with twelve fully-equipped gunners looks like those mountainous piles of women's clothes at Jumble Sales. Once sat down, you were stuck. If you wanted to put your hand in a pocket, three men in the carriage had to get up. The train started. As it pulled fretfully from the station, I suddenly realised that some of us were being driven to our deaths! Edgington and I in the corridor decided to look for somewhere special to settle. The guard's van! It was empty save for officers' bed-rolls. Just the job. Removing our webbing, we lay like young khaki gods, rampant on a field of kitbags.

January 7th, at 2.45 that afternoon we arrived at Liverpool Station. We detrained. Chaos. Non-commissioned officers kept running into each other shouting orders. Captains bounded up and down the platform like spring-heeled Jacks shouting 'I say!'

Dawson clobbered Chalky White and self. 'You two! See the officers' baggage into the three-tonner.' Great! We didn't have to march. Gradually the Battery drained out of the station. We had to wait hours for the lorry. We loaded the officers' kit on, and drove through the black gloomy streets, with their grey wartime people, but it was still all adventure to us.

It was dark when we arrived at the docks, which bore scars of heavy bombing. Towards the New Brighton side of the Mersey, searchlights were dividing the sky. Our ship was HMTL15, in better days the SS *Otranto*. She'd been converted to an armed troopship with AA platforms fore and aft. Her gross was about 20,000 tons, I could be a couple of pounds out. Just to cheer us up she was painted black. Loading took all night; there were several other units embarking. We got the officers' bed-rolls into the cargo net, then boarded. A ship's bosun: 'What Regiment?' he said, 'Artillery? Three decks down, H deck.' H deck was just above the water line, the portholes were sealed and blacked out, such a pity, I wanted to see the fishes. Along each side were tables and forms to accommodate twelve men at a time.

Fore and aft were ships' lockers with hammocks, strange things that some said we had to sleep in. Ridiculous! Long about ten o'clock. The lads were wandering freely, exploring the ship. Some had dodged ashore and were standing at the dock gate chatting up late birds. It was their last chance. Other more honourable men were furiously writing the last V-mail letter before sailing. I went on the top deck, aft, smoked a cigarette and watched reflections in the dark waters below. So far it had all been fun, but now we were off to the truth. I don't know why, but I started to cry. 11.30! There was to be a demonstration of how to live in a hammock. I arrived in time to see an able-bodied seaman deftly put one up between two hooks, then vault into it without falling out. It looked easy. Nobody wanted to sleep. I worked out we were waiting for the tide. About one o'clock the ship took on an air of departure. Gangways were removed. Hatches covered. Chains rattled. The ship started to vibrate as the engines came to life. Waters swirled. Tugs moved in. Donkey-engines rattled, hawsers were dropped from the bollards, and trailed like dead eels into the oil-tinted Mersey. We were away. Slowly we glided downstream. To the east we could hear the distant cough of Ack-Ack. The time was 1.10 a.m., January 8th, 1943. We were a mile downstream when the first bombs started to fall on the city. Ironically, a rosy glow tinged the sky, Liverpool was on fire. The lads came up on deck to see it. Away we went, further and further into the night, finally drizzle and darkness sent us below. I set about putting up my hammock. It was very easy and I vaulted in like an old salt. No, I didn't fall out. Sorry. In the dark, I smoked a cigarette, and thought . . . We were going to war. Would I survive? Would I be frightened? Could I survive a direct hit at point blank range by a German 88 mm? Could I really push a bayonet into a man's body – twist it – and pull it out? I mean what would the neighbours say?

ALGIERS

On January 18th, 1943, I wrote in my diary: 'Arrived Algiers at Dawn.' Harry and I got up early to enjoy the sight of Africa at first light. We saw it bathed in a translucent pre-dawn purple aura. Seagulls had joined us again. A squadron of American Lockheed Lightnings circled above. The coast was like a wine-coloured sliver, all the while coming closer. The visibility grew as the sun mounted the sky; there is no light so full of hope as the dawn; amber, resin, copper lake, brass green. One by one, they shed themselves until the sun rose golden in a white sky. Lovely morning warmth. I closed my eyes and turned my face to the sun. I fell down a hatchway. 'Awake!' said Harry down the hole, 'for Morning in the Bowl of Night, Has flung the Stone that puts the Stars to flight. Omar Khayyam.' 'Get stuffed, Spike Milligan.' The convoy was now in line ahead making for the port. Gradually the buildings of Algiers grew close. The city was built on a hill, and tiered, most buildings were white. We were closing to the dockside. Activity. Khaki figures were swarming everywhere. Trucks, tanks, aircraft, guns, shells, all were being off-loaded. Odd gendarmes looked helpless, occasionally blew whistles, pointed at Arabs, then hit them. They'd lost the war and by God they were going to take it out on someone. Now we could see palm tree lined boulevards. We made the last raid on the canteen, stocked up with fags, chocolate and anything. In full FSMO (pronounced Effessmmmoh) we paraded on deck. I tell you, each man had so much kit it reminded me of that bloody awful Warsaw Concerto. A Bombardier came round and distributed little booklets saying: 'Customs and Habits of French North Africa. How to behave. The Currency. Addresses of Post-Brothel Military Clinics. And a contraceptive. Only one? They must be expecting a short war. Harry Edgington was horrified. 'Look at this,' he said, his lovely face dark with rage, 'putting temptation in a man's hands.' Whereupon he hurled it overboard. Others blew them up and paddled them ashore shouting 'Happy New Year'. Down came the gangplanks and the 56th Heavy Regiment, ten days at sea, heavier than it had ever been, debouched.

We marched through the palm-lined streets, into a vast concrete football stadium. On the pitch were scores of tents. It must have been half-time I thought. But no! They were the bivouacs of a Scots Battalion, just back from the front. Hanging on the washing lines were battle-scarred kilts. It must have been hell under there! It was a vast concrete football stadium. I mention that again in the nature of an encore. All the action was around a field kitchen. Several queues all converged on one point where a cook, with a handle-bar moustache, and of all things a monocle, was doling out. He once had a glass eye that shot out when he sneezed and fell in the porridge so he wore the monocle as a sort of optical condom. He doled out something into my mess tin. 'What is it?' I asked. 'Irish Stew,' he said, 'Then', I replied, 'Irish Stew in the name of the Law.' It was a vast concrete arena. We queued for an hour. When that had passed we queued for blankets. Next, find somewhere to sleep, like a football stadium in North Africa. We dossed down on the terraces. After ship's hammocks it was murder. If only, if *only* I had a grand piano. I could have slept in that. Anything was better than a vast concrete arena. At dawn my frozen body signalled me, arise. I stamped around the freezing terraces to get warm. I lit up a fag and went scrounging. There were still a few embers burning in the field kitchen. I found a tea urn full of dead leaves from which I managed to get a fresh brew.

Gradually the sun came up. There was no way of stopping

it. It rose from the east like an iridescent gold Napoleon. It filled the dawn sky with swathes of pink, orange and flame. Breakfast was Bully Beef and hard tack. I washed and shaved under a tap, icy cold, still, it was good for the complexion. 'Gunners! Stay lovely for your Commanding Officer with Algerian Football Stadium water!' I stood at the gates watching people in the streets. I made friends with two little French kids on their way to school, a girl and a boy. I gave them two English pennies. In exchange they gave me an empty matchbox, with a camel label on the top. I shall always remember their faces. A gentle voice behind me. 'Where the bleedin' 'ell you bin?' It was Jordy Dawson. 'Come on, we're off to the docks.' And so we were.

Arriving there we checked that all D Battery kitbags were on board our lorries, then drove off. The direction was east along the coast road to Jean Bart. We sat with our legs dangling over the tail-board. Whenever we passed French colonials, some of them gave us to understand that our presence in the dark continent was not wanted by a simple explicative gesture from the waist down. We passed through dusty scrub-like countryside with the sea to our left. In little batches we passed Arabs with camels or donkeys, children begging or selling tangerines and eggs. The cactus fruit was all ripe, pillar-box red. I hadn't seen any since I was a boy in India. The road curved gradually and the land gradient rose slightly and revealed to us a grand view of the Bay of Algiers. Rich blue, with morning sunshine tinselling the waves. Our driver 'Hooter Price' (so called because of a magnificent large nose shaped like a Pennant. When he swam on his back, people shouted 'Sharks') was singing 'I'll be seeing you' as we jostled along the dusty road. It was twenty-six miles to our destination, with the mysterious name 'X Camp', situated just half a mile inland at Cap Matifou. X Camp was proving an embarrassment to Army Command. It was built to house German prisoners of war. Somehow we hadn't managed to get any, so, to give it the appearance of being a success, 56 Heavy Regiment were marched in and told that this was, for the time being, 'home'. When D Battery heard this, it was understandable when roll-call was made the first morning:

'Gunner Devine?'

'Ya wol!'

'Gunner Spencer?'

'Ya!'

'Gunner Maunders?'

'Ya wol!'

The march of the Regiment from the ship to Cap Matifou had been a mild disaster. It started in good march style, but gradually, softened by two weeks at sea, and in full FSMO, two-thirds of the men gradually fell behind and finally everyone was going it alone at his own pace. A long string of men stretched over twenty-six miles. I quote from Major Chater Jack's recollection of the incident in a letter he wrote to me in 1957. 'Perhaps some will remember the landing at Algiers and that ghastly march with full kit, for which we were not prepared. The march ended after dark, somewhere beyond Maison Blanche, and was rather a hard initiation into war – a valuable initiation though, for it made many things thereafter seem easier!' To top it all there was a tragedy – Driver Reed, who flaked out on the march, tried to hop a lift but fell between the lorry and trailer and was squashed to death. The only way to unstick him from the road was by pulling at his webbing straps. Tragedy number two was Gunner Leigh, thirty-six (old for a soldier); as he arrived at the camp he received a telegram telling him his wife and three children had been killed in a raid on Liverpool. He went insane and never spoke again. He is still in a mental home near Menston in Yorkshire.

Sanitary Orderly Liddel was learning the trade of maintenance on the outdoor hole-in-the-ground latrines. The lime powder that is normally used to 'sprinkle' the pit, had not arrived. He, being of an inventive turn of mind, mixed petrol and diesel and used that. Dawn! Enter an RSM pleasure bent! He squats on pole. Lights pipe, drops match. BOOOOOOOOM! There emerges smoke-blackened figure, trousers down, smouldering shirt tail, singed eyebrows, second degree burns on bum – a sort of English loss of face.

He was our last casualty before we actually went into action. Next time it would be for real.

VOLUME TWO

ROMMEL:
Gunner Who?

January–February

ALGERIA

The ground was like rocks. The nights were rent with gunners groaning, swearing, twisting, turning and revolving in their tents.

Temperatures fluctuated. You went to sleep on a warm evening, by dawn it dropped to freezing. We had to break our tents with hammers to get out. Dawn widdles caused frost bitten appendages, the screams! 'Help, I'm dying of indecent exposure!' We solved the problem. I stuffed my Gas Cape with paper and made a mattress. Gunner Forrest wrapped old *Daily Mirror*s round his body, 'I always wanted to be in the News,' he said, and fainted. Others dug holes to accommodate hips and shoulders.

At night we wore every bit of clothing we had, then we rolled ourselves into four blankets. 'We look nine months gone,' said Edgington. 'Any advance on nine,' I cried.

We slept warmly, but had overlooked the need to commune with nature, it took frantic searching through layers of clothing to locate one's willy, some never did and had to sleep with a damp leg. Gunner Maunders solved the problem! He slid a four foot length of bicycle inner tube over his willy, secured it round his waist with string, he just had to stand and let go. Jealous, Gunner White sabotaged it. As Maunders slept, fiend White tied knots in the bottom of the tube.

CONFINED TO CAMP

It is night, Gunner Simpson is darning something which is four-fifths hole and one-fifth sock, 'I wonder when they'll let us into Algiers.' 'You gettin' randy then?' says Gunner

White, 'because, we've all had our last shag for a long time.'

'Are there French birds in Algiers?'

'Yer. They're red 'ot. Cert Crumpet.'

'You shagged one then?'

'No, but my dad told me abaht 'em in the first world woer.'

'They're not the same ones?'

One by one the soldiers would fall asleep. I lay awake, thinking, dreaming young man's dreams, jazz music would go through my head, I could see myself as Bunny Berrigan playing chorus after brilliant chorus in front of a big band surrounded by admiring dancers. Suddenly, without warning, 'Strainer' Jones lets off with a thunderous postern blast, he had us all out of the tent in ten seconds flat.

One freezing dawn we were awakened by a Lockheed Lightning repeatedly roaring over our camp. 'Go and ask that bastard if he's going by road,' says Edgington. I got outside just as the plane made another dive. I shouted 'Hope you crash you noisy bastard,' the plane raced seaward, hit the water and exploded. I was stunned. The gunners emptied from their tents to watch the flames burning on the sea. 'Poor sod,' said a Gunner, and he was right. Reveille was sounding. 'Listen,' said Edgington cupping an ear, 'they're playing our tune.'

PART TWO ORDERS

'Disciplinary action will be taken against other ranks responsible for the stamping and groaning on route marches.'

I noted Frangipani everywhere, but not yet in flower, magenta coloured Bougainvillaeas were in full bloom. Towards evening the air filled with the cloying perfume of Jasmine. Belisarius was said to have placed one in his helmet at Tricaramaron saying, 'If I die, I will at least smell sweet . . .' Generals! Going into battle? Then use Perfume of Jasmine! Hear what one General says:

General Montgomery: I use Jasmine – I couldn't have won El Alamein without it. Get some today.

Marches took us through timeless Arab villages, Rouiba, Ain-Taya, Fondouk, when we halted I'd try the Arab coffee; piping hot, sweet, delicious. I watched Gunner White sip the coffee then top it up with water! I explained the water was for clearing the palate. 'I thought it was for coolin' it down,' said the descendant of the Crusaders.

Lieutenant Joe Mostyn was Jewish, five foot six, on bad days five foot two, and, no matter how frequently he shaved, had a permanent blue chin; 'try shaving from the inside' I suggested. His forte was scrounging grub. One route march he bought a hundred eggs for twelve francs. Having no way of transporting them, he made us carry one in each hand till we reached Camp. Puzzled wayfarers watched as British soldiers marched by, clutching eggs accompanied by mass clucking. Water was rationed but we were on the sea. At day's end we plunged into the blue Med. I watched gunners, unfamiliar with salt water, try to get their soap to lather. 'Something wrong wiv it,' says Liddel. 'Nuffink can go wrong wiv soap,' replies Forrest, who plunges into a furious effort to prove his point. 'You're right,' he finally concedes. 'This soap is off.' NAAFI Managers tried to understand how some fifteen gunners all had soap that wouldn't lather. No one mentioned salt water, dutifully they exchanged the soaps. Next morning the soap lathered beautifully. 'This is better,' said Forrest. That evening, at swim parade, I watched Forrest and Liddel arguing about what had gone wrong with the soap since morning. We all bathed starkers, the lads gave wonderful displays of Military Tool-waving at passing ladies with cries of 'Vive le Sport' or 'Get in Knob its yer birthday'.

It was all good stuff and bore out Queen Victoria's belief that 'Salt Water has beneficial effects on the human body.'

There were dreadful gunners who floated on their backs playing submarines. At the approach of a maritime phallus, Gunner Devine shouted 'Achtung! Firen Torpedo!' and threw a pebble, and the hit 'periscope' would sink with a howl of pain. Another nasty trick was invented by Gunner Timms: Tie rock to piece of string, make noose at other end, next, dive under unsuspecting happily swimming gunner, slip noose over end of his Willy, let go rock; retire to safe distance. Mind you some gunners *liked* it. You can get used to anything I suppose.

We had received no mail. 'They've forgotten us! Out of sight out of mind!' says Gunner Woods scratching himself in bed.

'You're always moaning,' says 'Hooter' Price. 'I got a wife and two kids, and I bet they haven't forgotten me.'

'With that bleedin' great nose, I don't suppose they can.'

'Look, a large nose is a sign of intelligence. The Duke of Wellington had one.'

'Yer, 'e 'ad one, but you look like you got two, and,' I added, 'how come you're only a bleedin' driver eh?'

'I chose to stay with the men,' said Price with great indignation. In the dark, a boot bounced off his nut.

To help kill boredom in the Camp I started a daily news bulletin posted outside my tent.

January 23rd. Bombardier Harry Baum, nicknamed 'Hairy Bum', told us 'You lot are to be allowed into Algiers and let loose on the unsuspecting women therein. The Passion Waggon leaves at 13.30 hours, and you will all be back at 23.59, like all gude little Cinderellas.' Fly buttons flew in all directions.

We set about cleaning up. Boots were boned, web belts scrubbed, brass polished and trousers creased. It made little difference, we still looked like sacks of shit tied up in the middle. A three tonner full of sexual tension, rattled us to

---

X Camp 201 PoW
MILLI-NEWS

Libya: *Last night, under cover of drunken singing, British Commandos with their teeth blacked out, raided an advance Italian Laundry, several vital laundry lists were captured, and a complete set of Marshall Gandolfo's underwear, which showed he was on the run.*

China: *Chinese troops are reported in the area with their eyes at the slope.*

Syria: *It is reported that Australian troops have taken Coscara. They are trying to keep it dark but it is leaking out in places and the troops are evacuating all along the line.*

Rome: *Il Duce told the Italian people not to worry about the outcome of the war. If they lost, he had relatives in Lyons Corner House, from whence he would run the Government in Exile.*

Local: *Sanitary Orderly Liddel takes pleasure in announcing his new luxury long drop Karzi.* Secluded surroundings, screened from the world's vulgar gaze by Hessian. Plentiful supply of Army Form Blank. Book now to avoid disappointment in the dysentery season.*

* From the Zulu word M'Karzi, meaning W.C.

Algiers Docks. Most others were looking for Women and Booze. Not Gunner Milligan, I was a good Catholic boy, I didn't frequent brothels.

No, all I did was walk round with a permanent erection shouting 'Mercy!', in any case, I was in the company of 'Mother Superior Edgington', who shunned such practices. Was he not the one who threw his army issue contraceptive into the sea where it was later sunk by naval gun fire? So we entered Algiers, with pure minds, and the sun glinting on the Brylcreem running down our necks. We were joined by

Bdr Spike Deans and Gunner Shapiro. Along the main tree-lined Rue d'Isly, we entered a small café, 'Le Del Monico'. 'That means "The Del Monico",' I explained. Inside we were shown to a table by an attractive French waitress. We perused the menu.

MENU
Moules Marinières
Homus
Spigola al Forno
Sole Niçoise
Scampi Provençale
Poulet Rôti
Carré d'Agneau
Courgettes

'Eggs and chips four times,' we said. 'Make mine Kosher,' added Shapiro.

'There's no such thing as Jewish Chicken,' I said.

'And I'll tell you why,' said Shapiro, 'there's no money in it.' The eggs arrived sizzling in round copper dishes. 'Where's the chips?' says Shapiro. 'She's forgotten the chips.'

'Don't be so bloody ignorant,' rebukes Edgington, 'in French cooking le chips are served separate! Patience!' So we sat in patience. We sat a long time in patience. She had forgotten 'le chips'. The mistake rectified, we ate the meal with quaffs of Thibar Rosé.

'You'd never think there was a war on,' said Dean.

'I think there's a war on,' said Shapiro.

'I notice,' said Edgington, 'you dip your chip into the yolk first.'

'True,' I said. 'I cannot tell a lie.' We finished the meal.

'What now?' says Milligan.

'Let's go to the pictures,' says Shapiro.

'PICTURES? We come all the way from England to Africa and you want to go to the bloody PICTURES?'

'I like the pictures,' he says, 'they make me forget.'

'Forget what?'

'I can't remember.'

We decided to wander through Algiers, it was amazing how boring it could be. 'Isn't this the place where Charles Boyer screwed Hedy Lamarr?' said Deans. 'Yes,' I said. 'I'm not surprised,' said Edgington, 'there's nothing else to do.'

By 23.15 hours we were all in the Passion Waggon. The noise was incredible, talking, singing, farting, laughing, vomiting. Versatility was going to win us the war. It was horrible, but there was a kind of mad strange poetry to it, that is, ask any one why they were like they were at that moment and they'd have a rational answer.

An hour later we settled in our beds, listening to the lurid exploits of Driver 'Plunger' Bailey, 'Plunger' because he had a prick the size and shape of a sink pump. He had entered the forbidden Kasbah in the search of his 'hoggins' and gained entrance to an Arab brothel. 'They wouldn't let

Drunks being loaded into 'Passion Waggon' after first visit to Algiers

me in till I took me boots off,' he said. He had been shown a room where a naked Arab girl had entertained him with a belly dance, feeling he should reciprocate he sang her a chorus of 'The Lambeth Walk' and then 'got stuck up her'. From now on, all my illusions of the Arabian Nights were dead.

THE LONG HAUL TO THE FRONT

One day, there was the long awaited news on the notice board.

0600 11 FEB. 1943. Regiment will prepare to move etc. etc.

Great excitement, packing, renewing kit, selling kit, buying fruit for the journey, writing 'Farewell for ever' etc. to sweethearts, etc. The day before the move I developed toothache. It started at two in the morning, the pain shot up my head down the back of my neck, disappeared down my spine then reappeared in my chest sideways up the tent pole. How could one tiny hole neutralise a whole man? Will-power! *That* would stop it. I did will-power till three o'clock. It got worse. Old wives' recipe! Stuff tobacco into the cavity. I lit the lamp. Edgington woke, he saw what appeared to be Gunner Milligan splitting open cigarettes and poking the tobacco down his throat. 'Look mate,' he said, 'you're supposed to smoke 'em.'

Next morning, I drove to the Dental Surgery, in a villa on the sea at Cap Matifou. The dentist, a young fair-haired Captain sat me in the chair, and drove his prodder down till it got through to the collar bone.

'OWWWWWWWWWWWWWWWWWWWWWW sir,' I said.

'You scream very well.'

'Yes sir, I'm practising for the front line.'

I drove back with the left side of my face frozen dead. You may ask, what use is half a frozen face? Well, it keeps longer. To this day, the left side of my face is two hours

*Part of the Regimental Convoy on its way to the front
— Jan. 1943*

younger than the right. We were to fill in our wills in the
back of our Army Pay Books. I had no possessions, no
money, two cheap fifty shilling suits, a second-hand evening
dress, a few Marks and Spencer shirts, and a mess of ragged
underwear. My trumpet was my only bounty, so I wrote 'I
leave my trumpet to my mother and the HP payments to my
father.' Others made lavish entries, Gunner White 'I leave
my Gas Stove to the Sgt Major,' etc. To some it wasn't
funny. Reg Griffin said 'When millions of perfectly healthy
young men have to make their wills out, there's something
nasty going on in the world.'

'This tea tastes funny,' I said.

'It's Bromide,' said Gunner Devine. 'It stops you havin'
improper thoughts while you're in action and causing you to
lose your aim.'

Dawn, February 11th 1943. Yawning, I threw back the tent flap and felt the chill air run over me in the pre-dawn light, I hadn't been able to sleep, the excitement of the coming adventure had got to me. I had risen first, dressed and started packing my kit. As the morning grew my comrades started to stir, the odd voice commenced to break the silence in the camp. After breakfast I loaded my kit on to the Humber Snipe Wireless Truck.

At 8.30 a.m. the transport of the Regiment was lined up pointing due East. Edgington, late as usual, was swearing. A squadron of Bell Aircobras roared over.

'I hope you bloody well crash,' I shouted instantly.

'Any luck?' said Harry.

'No.'

'Your power is waning.'

'Rubbish! I've got the lowest wain-fall in the Battery.'

'Get out before I laugh,' said Harry pointing upwards.

Driver Shepherd and I had been detailed to drive Lt Budden, in the Wireless Truck. We had been standing by vehicles for an hour and nothing had happened but it happened frequently. Despatch Riders raced up and down the column shouting 'Fuck everybody' but that was all. We started to brew tea, when Lt Budden's Iron Frame Glasses appear round the truck, 'You're supposed to be standing by your vehicles.'

'Sorry sir, I'll say three Hail Marys.'

'Give me a cup and I'll say no more about it,' he said producing a mug from behind his back.

Lt Budden flags down a DR. 'What's the hold up?'

'I'll tell you sir. I'm the DR who follows the DR in front with a message that cancels out his message.'

A cloud of dust is approaching at high speed. From its nucleus formidable swearing is issuing. It's our Signal Sergeant Dawson, 'Get mounted, we're off,' it bellows as it goes down the line, followed by mocking cheers. I jump in, engines are coming to life, the hood is rolled back so

Budden can stand Caesar-like in the passenger seat. Shouts are heard above the sound of the engines revving, 'Right Milligan,' says Lt Budden. 'World War Two at 25 m.p.h.' He looked back at the long line of vehicles. 'My God, what a target for the Luftwaffe.'

'Don't worry sir, I have a verbal anti-aircraft curse, that brings down planes.'

'Keep talking Milligan. I think I can get you out on Mental Grounds.'

'That's how I got in, sir.'

'Didn't we all.'

There was a throttle on the steering column, I set it to a steady twenty m.p.h.

'I said twenty-five,' said Budden.

'Trying to economise, sir. The slower we go chances are by the time we get there it might be all over.'

'Oh it *will* be all over Milligan,' he said, 'all over bloody Africa.'

Next day, according to my diary, I sat in the back of the truck with a 'Huge pink idiot youth from Egham', who I don't seem to be able to recall. Egham yes, him *no*, but Egham yes. Perhaps I was sitting in the back with a huge pink Egham? I passed the time testing the wireless set; when I got 'This is the Allied Forces Network, Algeria' a stentorian American voice said, 'Here for your listening pleasure is Tommy Dorsey and his Orchestra.' Great! I listened all day. I lit up a cigarette, now this was more like war.

A sign, Sik-en-Meadou, 'Sir,' I called to Budden, 'we've just passed a sign saying someone's been Sick-in-the-Meadow'; there was no reply, just silence, but dear reader, it was a *commissioned* officer's silence, of course, if you were a Brigadier you could command a brigade of silence, there was no end to it. I could feel it getting chilly at nights and made a mental note where my balaclava was . . . In the drawer of a cupboard in 50 Riseldine Road, Brockley, SE26. 'You'll never need woollens in Africa,' my father had said. The movement of the truck had lulled huge pink faced idiot from Egham to sleep. When we staged for the night I woke him up.

'Where are we?' he said.

'Africa,' I replied.

'Oh,' he said, 'I thought it was Egham.' What he needed was a direct hit.

The Arabs of this village looked better off than the plain Arabs. (Two plain Arabs and one with chocolate sauce please.)

Feb. 13th 1943. This morning, tired of those coughing, scratching reveilles, I took my trumpet and blew a swing bugle call. Chalky White appeared from under a blanket with a severe attack of face and eyes with blood filled canals. 'Whose bloody side are you on!' he groaned. Odd silent soldiers, hands in pockets, eating utensils tucked under arms were making their way to the Field Kitchen. Our Cook, Gunner May, a dapper lad with curly black hair and Ronald Colman moustache was doling out Porridge. He spoke with a very posh voice and Porridge.

'Where'd you get that accent Ronnie?' asked Gunner Devine.

'Eton old sausage.'

'Well I'd stop eatin' old sausages,' says Devine.

With a flick of the wrist, May sent a spoonful of Porridge into Devine's eye. 'Good for night blindness,' he says ducking a mug of tea.

From Setif the road to the front ran fairly straight. During a halt, along comes a pregnant American staff car that gave birth to an American called Eisenhower. The driver was a tall girl with a Veronica Lake hair-do. Eisenhower approached and spoke to – I can't remember who – but I recall him saying 'What kind of cannons are these?' (Cannons!? CANNONS!? That's like calling the HMS *Ark Royal* a boat.) Eisenhower got back in the car, struck his head on the roof, said 'Oh Fuck' and left. He had shaken hands with Sergeant Mick Ryan who didn't know *who* he was. Ryan! Oh what a ruffian that man was! One night, back at Bexhill, he made for the fish and chip shop, as he reached the door the proprietor closed it.

'Sorry,' said the proprietor, 'we're closed.'

'No, you're bloody not,' said Ryan, punched through the glass door and laid him out.

We were pressing on down the dusty road towards Souk Arras a hundred miles from the front. At Oued Athmenia, we got into a secondary road. We were on a high plateau, the sun overhead, the endless jolting finally made you numb. At the next break Driver Shepherd took over. Budden emerged from behind a tree, shaking off the drips. 'Right Milligan, off we go.'

'I'm not Milligan sir,' said Shepherd, in a hurt voice.

'Oh it's *you* Shepherd, good!'

Voice from back of truck. 'It's the Good Shepherd sir.'

19 Battery was now to part from the main body of the Regiment. *They* went to spend the night at Guelma (the dirty swines) while *we*, the lilywhite boys, went on half the distance again, into a night bivouac outside Souk Arras.

Meantime at No. 10 Downing Street.

Churchill in bed sipping brandy. Enter Alanbrook.

LORD ALANBROOK: Prime Min. have you seen the bill for Singapore?
HON. W. CHURCHILL: I know – those Japa-bloody-knees – why couldn't they come round the front?
LORD ALANBROOK: They're Tradesmen. Any news of Randolph?
HON. W. CHURCHILL: He's out in Yugoslavia with that Piss-Artist Evelyn Waugh.

Now read on:

15 Feb. en route to Le Kef. Souk Arras lay along the head waters of the Mejerda River which later swept down and watered the vineyards of the great Mejerda Valley. Thought you'd like to know. Everywhere this dusty light sand-coloured soil reflected the sun's glare so we used our anti-gas goggles. Everywhere seemed parched, and on this the fourth day of driving, our faces were sore. The horse flies! These buggers would break the skin and suck your blood, given 2 minutes they could give you anaemia. You had to hit them the *moment* they landed, a split second later was too late. Men with slow reflexes suffered, like Forrest, who was covered in bites and great bruises where he had hit at them and missed. The more he missed, the harder he hit. 'I wish I was Jordy Liddel,' he moaned. 'When they bite him, they fall off dead.'

'It's all that shit he works with.'

About 12.15 Mr Budden said, 'Milligan, we have just crossed the border into Tunisia.'

'I'll carve a statue at once.'

On the border was Sakiet Sidi Youseff, where there was some kind of mine. A few donkeys and Arabs were at a pit head or shaft out of which ran a narrow rail, from inside the hole a tipper truck would appear with the powder produce which they shovelled into sacks on the donkeys.

'Where did you spend your last holidays Milligan?' Mr Budden broke in.

'I went with some friends to Whitesand Bay in Cornwall.'

' . . . . Cornwall? Cornwall.' He put his binoculars up.

'You can't see it from here sir.'

'I'm not *looking* for Cornwall.'

The journey had covered us all in fine white powdery dust giving us the appearance of old men. Sid Price started to walk bent double like an old Yokel, within seconds the whole battery were doing it, Africa rang to the sound of 'Oh Arrr! Oi be seventy three oi be in Zummerzet.' At the head of the column Major Chater Jack sat watching us. 'It's going to be a long hard war,' he was saying. I can still see his amused smile, especially as Woods, his batman, *was* from Somerset.

'Lot o' daft idiots zur,' he said to the Major.

'Yes Woods, a lot of daft idiots, but I fear you and I are stuck with 'em. The thing to do is keep them well camouflaged.' We were off again, and owing to a laundry crisis I was living dangerously, no underwear!

17th Feb. Dawn. Yawning, I slipped the Humber into gear.

'Rendezvous Map Reference 68039,' said Lt Budden. 'You holidayed in Cornwall you say?'

The road was difficult. Come to think of it, so was I. It was marked camel track and it took us to El Aroussa, a small wayside railway station, now a smoking ruin. Around it were the blackened skeletons of a dozen or so lorrics. Inside shattered buildings were blood spattered walls, blood soaked battle-dress jackets and trousers. An old Arab, all that was left of the station staff ('Toute morte') described how it happened. Stukas had come yesterday, in a few minutes it was all over.

'Christ,' says Bdr Sherwood. 'What's happened?'

'Don't worry, these are only the cheap seats,' I said.

'He must have been a bad driver,' said Chalky White. The humour was a bit forced. None of us were sure what to say. The officers were grouped around a map, and appeared more excited than is good for English gentlemen.

'What are they on?' said Chalky.

'Vitamin B,' I said.

Up the line comes Chater Jack's truck. 'Prepare to move! Lads, Yoiks, Tally Ho!'

We followed him towards Bou Arada. Half a mile on he turned left across the railway lines, down a bank, over a dusty wheat field towards a small farm nestling at the foot of the Djbel Rihane (nicknamed 'Grandstand Hill'). Behind, the great khaki guns rolled like fat babies as they negotiated the bosomy terrain. The silence was broken by the sharp crack of artillery.

'They sound like Mediums,' said Lt Budden.

'Too small sir,' I said. 'I take Outsize.'

Sergeant Dawson raced past on his motorbike; when we arrived at the farm, he was waiting with the Major, soon the area was a mass of frenetic action.

'Scrim Nets on!'

'Disperse Wireless Trucks under those trees!'

'Monkey trucks prepare to lay ten-mile telephone line!'

'All guns in that Wadi there!'

'Bombardier? Form OP Party!'

'For God's sake,' I said, 'There's more orders than men.'

Edgington joined in, 'All Gunners stand on one leg and lean eastward.'

The guns were towed into a Wadi. Command Post tent appeared to have been put up by trainee Wolf Cubs. Bren guns were mounted against aircraft. 'Lucky sods,' said White, 'all they got to do is scratch their balls and look up.'

The 200 lb mustard coloured shells were being unloaded and stacked. Signallers were lugging communications equipment into the Command Post, specialists were putting up Artillery Boards and all those fiddling instruments that computed which German the shell would hit. Of course they could have put all the names in a hat. A trestle table was erected for the Tannoy Control. Next to it were the telephone and the wireless set. Cables were run to the gun positions, loudspeakers at each sub-section connected and tested. It worked like this. Place loudspeaker near gun, connect wire from Command Post, press button on top of loudspeaker at Gun Position. Immediately light flashes in Command Post control panel.

'Hello B Sub. You're flashing, can you hear me?'

'Yes, but we're not B Sub, we're A Sub.'

'Oh fuck, can you flash again?'

'I'm not going to become a flasher fer anybody.'

Signallers are laying a line to the Waggon Lines, the place for vital supplies, vehicles, cowards, and Porridge. It is important to appear busy. Gunner White was cunningly going round with an empty DDT tin, when questioned, he would spring to attention and say 'Delousing Sah!' and he got away with it.

BATTERY DIARY:

19 Battery moved into action, north of Bou Arada.
Map Ref. 6006.

By nightfall guns were dug in, and living quarters constructed. In my mud hut I took out my trumpet and played 'Lili Marlene'.

The Signallers were all inside the Arab hut which now glowed yellow with improvised oil lamps. I checked my Tommy gun for the night. I had continually worked out in my mind the precautions I would take if confronted by Germans. It was a simple but highly effective plan, I would raise my hands above my head and say, 'I surrender.'

A 7.2 howitzer being made ready for its first time in action
– Bon Arada Feb. 1943

Through our door came Sergeant Dawson! Grinning evilly he removed the blankets from my weary body.

'We're looking for our first hero casualty. We're laying a line to the OP.'

'Tonight?'

'Yes.'

'I was just going to bed, it's Rita Hayworth's turn.'

'Get yer bloody boots on.'

'I must get my rest Sarge – people are saying I'm finished.'

'I'll tell you when you'll be finished. Four o'clock tomorrow morning.'

I pulled my boots on, got my pliers, Tommy gun, and slid into the dark. The detail was, L/Bdr Sherwood and his Bren Carrier, Sgt Dawson, Gunners Hart, Webster, Milligan and Bdr Fuller, who knew where the OP was. Dawson told us 'Silence is imperative.' We set off being imperatively silent which couldn't be heard because of the noise of the Bren Carrier. We walked behind with a cable drum that went clinkety-clank. Why? The 'hole' in the cable drum was *square* but the spindle was round. We all spoke in hysterical whispers. God knows why, to communicate we had to shout above the engine. As this charade went on, we started to giggle, then outright laughter. 'Stop the bloody Bren,' shouted Dawson, himself on the verge of laughter. There was a suppressed silence. Unable to stand it, we all burst out laughing again.

'Stop it at once!' said Dawson through his own laughter. We stopped. 'Now stop it, or I'll kill the bloody lot of you.' A white star shell lit the night.

'What's that?' said Ernie Hart.

'That, Ernie, means that a child has been born in Bethlehem,' I said.

'Well, he's two months late and the wrong bloody map reference.' Another two star shells.

'She's had triplets,' said Ernie. After an hour we reached the OP hill.

'This way,' said Bombardier Fuller. Birch and I followed with reel.

'Stop that fokin' noise,' hissed an angry Irish voice, 'you'll get us all fokin' mortared.'

We took the spindle from the drum and unwound by hand. More flares, suddenly a rapid burst of automatic fire. It was a Spandau, a return burst, the unmistakable chug, chug, chug of a Bren gun. A flare silhouetted us beautifully for the whole Afrika Korps to see. 'Freeze,' hissed Fuller. I had one leg raised when he said it. Somewhere a German OP officer was saying 'Himmel! zey are using one-legged soldiers.' The flares fade. Fuller says 'I'm lost.'

'I thought you'd never say it,' I said.

We groped our way back to the party who were inside the Bren practising fear and smoking. Dawson attached a phone to the line.

'Hello, Gun Position here.'

'This is Sergeant Dawson. Tell Major Chater Jack we can't find the bloody OP, will it be all right tomorrow?' We waited. 'Yes,' Chater said, 'OK tomorrow, but before first light.' 'Let's bugger off,' said Dawson.

We piled into the carrier. I looked up. What a sky! The heavens encrusted with stars, the Milky Way hung like a luminous veil across the firmament.

'Halt.' Two sentries loomed in the dark. 'Friend or Foe?'

'Friends,' we all screamed from the grovelling position.

'What's the password?'

Dawson tried explaining in a thick Geordie accent, 'Why mon, we doant noe. Weaire Gooners from 56 Artilury, weaire layin a lyine.' The accent was sufficient for us to pass. About one o'clock we arrived at the GP. Our guns were firing. What a bloody noise. What in heaven's name did they think they were doing – it was past midnight! What would the neighbours say? Soldiers needed rest. They have to get up every morning looking lovely for their Regiments.

I got to bed. Yawning, I pulled the blankets over me,

The first round in anger – 19 Battery at War

doused the lamp and slid into dreamlit hours of dark
freedom. To sleep under the ear shattering blasts of our
guns seemed impossible, yet as they thundered in the night
towards Medjez el Bab, we slept like babes. It seemed I had
just put my lovely head to pillow when the boot of the
sentry delicately kicked me conscious.

'Milligan.'

'Mmmm? Arggggg Schmatter Gwanpizorf.'

'You and Fuller have got to connect the OP line.'

'Whassermarrer? Ahhhhhhhbalztoyer alllll.'

'There's early breakfast laid on for you.'

'I don't like people laying on my food!'

It was 0500 hours, it wasn't fair! Who invented early?
The late people were much happier, like the Late King
George, or the Late Rasputin. I didn't bother to wash or
shave. Red-eyed I ambled to the Cook House. 'How long
you been dead?' said the Cook. The morning air was cool,
light blue mist cast a hazy veil over the landscape. The dawn
peace was shattered by the Fifth Mediums laying down a
barrage. Breakfast was a surprise. The new Compo K

rations had arrived, cases of tinned and dehydrated foods. We had scrambled egg, sausages and Ahhha Porridge.

'They're just fattening you up for the kill,' said the Cook.

0600: Bombardier Fuller and I set off. We skirted our guns to avoid the muzzle blast and Porridge. The ground was covered with a very light dew that was now drying out. Every twenty yards we stapled the wire to the ground.

The sun came up, it was going to be a lovely day. Reaching the foot of the hill Bdr Fuller suddenly 'remembered' where the OP was, 'We was too far to the left.' (We?) 'You (You?) go and bring it this way.' I walked to where we'd dumped the cable. Unbeknown, I was under enemy observation. WHOOSH-BANG! Behind me a purple and red explosion. WHOSSH-BAM another one; I didn't like it, dropping the cable drum I made a tactical withdrawal to the foot of the hill.

'They must have seen you,' says Fuller, a master of the obvious. Two more burst behind the crest, half a dozen more, they were searching for us. Then all quiet.

'Look,' I said, 'this is bloody dangerous work. I'm going to put in for a rise.'

'I (I?) must get this bloody line finished,' says Fuller, 'OP is straight up to the right of that tree.'

I played out the line as he went forward. Nearer the crest he started to crouch and finally disappeared into the scrub. Now and then I'd feel a tug on the line as he freed it from some obstruction. I was holding the line when two Bren carriers of infantry passed down the hill to my right.

'Fishing, mate?' said a laconic voice. I made a time honoured gesture. Fuller re-emerged.

'Everything OK?' I asked.

'Yes.'

'Who's up there?'

'Lt Goldsmith and Bdr Edwards.'

'Let's get back,' I said. I now produced my new pipe,

which I had bought to try and avoid smoking those bloody awful Vs. Having a pipe clenched in your teeth seemed to make you feel calm, thoughtful, unflappable.

Major Chater Jack: I see Milligan is smoking a pipe.
Sgt Dawson: Yes sir.
Major Chater Jack: He looks very good smoking it.
Sgt Dawson: Yes sir.
Major Chater Jack: He looks manly.
Sgt Dawson: Very manly.
Major Chater Jack: Unflappable?
Sgt Dawson: Definitely unflappable!
Major Chater Jack: What's he like as a soldier?
Sgt Dawson: Bloody awful sir.

Rather than go back to the gun position we hung around at the foot of the OP hill yarning and smoking. Finally, towards evening, we started back.

'It was all a bit of an anti-climax,' Fuller said.

'Yes. I wonder which bit it was?'

I felt my chin. I had a three day growth. A dust storm was starting to blow up, I couldn't decide whether it was German or one of ours. In the middle of it, a staff car emerged from across the fields.

Me: Look Frank! In the middle of it, a staff car has emerged from across the fields!

It was General Alexander with some staff officers. They got out, pointed in all directions, leaped back in the car and shot off at speed. The rich have all the fun! Dusty and tired we arrived at the gun position. Lt Joe Mostyn had just returned from a meal with an Arab sheik. 'I had to eat three bloody sheeps' eyes!'

'Really?' I said, 'Bend down and you should be able to see out the back.'

Poor old Joe! He was not particularly good at Gunnery! On his first day at an OP he scored ten direct hits – on a field. I pointed out there were no Germans in it.

'Ah,' he said, 'they may fall in the holes.'

'Of course,' I said, 'German Division surrenders with twisted ankle.'

'You've *got* to miss sometimes,' he said, 'it's good for business! What a war! There I was just doing well in the Schmutter Trade, and this Schmoch Hitler comes along so I have to switch from outsize blouses to battle-dresses. I'm just starting to do well again when *I* get called up. *Me* a soldier? This major says "Mostyn, with your head for figures you're ideal for the RA." So here I am wasting shells, *ten* shells, that's see . . . nearly £400 quid, *wasted*, for that I could have made three hundred and ten battle-dresses.'

Dawn 20th Feb. 1943. A khaki creature was shaking me. 'Come on Harry James stand to . . .' 'Stand Two? I can't stand one.'

It was 0400 hours. 0400 hours? There was no such time, it had been invented by Hitler to break us. I staggered out into the chill morning darkness. Bombardier Edwards posted me in a trench directly outside the officers' hut.

'Get in, keep your eyes open, stay in that hole. If you get killed, just lay down and we'll fill it in.'

'Very funny,' I said to him. 'With your sense of humour you should be on the other side.'

I was alone in the hole in the ground in Africa. It was very quiet. All the guns had stopped firing. They usually did in the small hours, even wars get tired. There was the distant yapping of Arab farm dogs. I wondered when the bloody animals ever slept. As eyes focused to the dark I could see the black shapes that were the block outlines of the huts, the Bren carrier, the wireless trucks, the tracery of the scrim nets. Above, the heavens with stars glittering in the traverse of the sky. The officers' hut door opened, I saw the outline of Major Chater Jack followed by Goldsmith. Seeing the top half of a human in a hole he said 'My God, who's that?'

'Gunner Milligan sir.'
'What's the matter? I thought you were taller!'
'I'm in a hole sir.'

Hitlergram No. 3086142

With our Führer behind the Enemy Lines

GNR. HITLER: Ach! I hate zese stand-toos! I shouldn't be doing zat, I should zer Sergeant be in zer kip!

GNR. WHITE: Arsoles!

HITLER: You say arsoles to *me*? In Germany I am Leader of zer Turd Reich! You are lucky I only ask you for ein Fag!

GNR. WHITE: I thought you didn't smoke?

HITLER: Zat is silly bugger Goebbels propaganda — he says you must never be seen wiz zer fag on! I smoke zeben-und fünfzig fags a day! I have to hide in zer cupboard, in zer Karzi, it is not easy. I am human like anybody else, I may burn ein Jew or two, but nobody's perfect I tell you.

GNR. WHITE: What about sex?

HITLER: I make mit zer shag ten times a day.

GNR. WHITE: Poor Eva Braun.

HITLER: Oh, not her, I screw her in zer night, she is der greatest, we screw in zer shape of a swastika! Zen ven she plays die Valkyrie on zer Beckstein I make vid zer Back Scuttle. Zen we are dansing de Tangogerstein with ze Berlin Novelty Trio.

GNR. WHITE: You look shagged out — if you're goin' ter win this war you better get some sleep.

HITLER: Ha! you little Kakhi foolen! How can I loose? Look at zese good conduct passes — 1st prize Five String Banjo at Gratz country fair! Three times Last Tango Champion in Paris — admit defeat Tommy!

I heard Chater Jack chuckle. He said something to Goldsmith and they both returned convulsed with suppressed laughter.

I was again alone in a hole in Africa. At this moment among the warring nations there were literally hundreds of thousands of little men, all standing in holes, in France, Germany, Poland, Russia. What a lot of bloody fools we must look! The door of the officers' hut opened again. The mountainous figure of Chater Jack's batman, Woods, loomed towards me. He handed me a cup of tea 'With the Boss's compliments,' he said. I sipped the tea – there must be some mistake! It had *whisky* in!! I'd better hurry. I gulped it down and as I finished Gunner Woods returned. 'Were there whisky in thart tea?' he said. I nodded.

'Well bugger oi down dead,' he said, 'that were Major's tea.'

Woods had approached me with the mind of a boy of twelve and left with one of thirteen. Experience ages a man. The first light was quickening the morning sky. Ghostly outlines were gradually turning into detailed reality as the covers of night fell off, we were all thinking, breakfast! Loudspeakers crackled into life. 'Take Post!' Gunners dropped their food and ran to the guns, to cries of 'Fuck our luck.' I discovered that some swine had stolen my shaving brush, so I stole someone else's. I had an early breakfast, and was detailed to check the OP line. I liked going. It took me away from the mob and gave me a sense of freedom. I told Shapiro I wanted him to come with me.

'Oh no,' he said, 'I can't come, my tin hat doesn't fit properly.'

'You're a hat cutter, it's your own bloody fault.'

'OK,' he grinned.

MY DIARY: 23 FEB. 1943

Up at dawn. To OP with Shapiro and Webster. Shapiro

reports someone has stolen his shaving brush. This is the 5th day he's reported it. Anything rather than buy one. This will be my fifth continuous day as OP linesman. Arrived midday. Shelled . . .

The blast threw me to the ground. Webster and Shapiro doubled for cover, like idiots we ran *up* the hill, and jumped into a trench. Help! A mortar pit knee-deep in mortar bombs! Sitting quietly in the corner smoking a pipe was an old Irish Sergeant. I tapped Shapiro.

'Ask him if he wants to sell his fags.'

Several more shells fell around us. Christ! if one landed in this pit! . . .

Gunner Milligan (22) after only five days in action

'Let's get out when it stops,' said Shapiro.

'Oh, youse will be safe in here lads,' said the Sergeant.

'Safe? In a pit full of bombs? Only the Irish . . .'

It went quiet. 'Right! *now*!' I said. 'Not me,' said Webster. Two of us crawled out and down the hill, then Whoosh Kerboooommm. Christ, we were caught in the open! 'Our father who art in heaven . . .' I started. A German smoke bomb dropped fifty yards to our left, it was a repeat performance of yesterday. The Stukas tumbled out of the sky. 'We're in the bombing zone,' I shouted. 'You think I don't know,' says Shapiro. One by one the Stukas peeled off. 'Are you insured Shap?'

'For everything but this,' he said.

The first stick of bombs fell along the crest of the hill, right in the middle of the London Irish again. I couldn't resist looking up and watching the slow almost lazy majesty of the Stukas as they went on their nose for the final dive. It was all over as quickly as it started. We got up and ran, to the bottom of the hill, seeking safety in a wadi. I tapped into the line in case the bombing had damaged it. It was OK. Webster appeared. 'You lousy buggers! You pissed off and left me.'

'Rubbish,' I said. 'You stayed behind and left us.' After a smoke, we limbered up and set off back. I remember we didn't talk much this time. Perhaps that built-in countdown had started to tick in our heads; each shell that missed you brought the one that killed you one shell nearer.

FEBRUARY 26TH

The storm broke at about 9.30 a.m. Our troops pushed off OP Hill, Lt Goldsmith and OP Party came back. Sergeant Dawson set up an OP directly on the hillock in front of our guns. Position now called 'serious', 'How do you feel now Milligan?' 'Serious sir, very serious.' Sporadic fighting all around in isolated groups. Infantry manoeuvring for position.

Major Chater Jack was anxiously awaiting orders from Div. HQ to move. By three in the afternoon it hadn't come, so Chater Jack took the initiative and gave the order, 'Move and Quick.' I packed everything in two minutes, piled it on

Sherwood's Carrier which was moving out with Lt Goldsmith aboard.

'What's happening sir?'

'We're moving Milligan.'

'Somewhere cheaper?'

'No, quieter . . . If you see a milkman tell him no milk tomorrow.'

We were the first vehicle out. Here is an excerpt from Edgington's letter with his version of that occasion:

'Monkey-Two was bumping out of a wadi and gathering speed as I came at it, with Bill Trew, Pedlar Palmer and Jack White reaching anxiously out over the half-up tail-board (all the equipment had just been slung in), and I finished my run with the most blood-curdling hurdle-jump to clear the tail-board sufficiently for Bill, Pedlar and Jack to grab enough of me to hold on to, and nearly tearing me cobblers off.'

I watched as the Battery pulled out. We were retracing tracks we had originally taken from the El Aroussa road, when we reached it, Bdr Sherwood, swerving, braked his left track and turned onto the tree-lined road leading towards Bou Arada. A company of infantry were digging in along the railway bank. They were second-line defence, this was the direction Jerry wanted to come. The guns were now well across the field but, as they turned onto the road, 88 mm shells started to burst among the convoy. It was deadly accurate and miraculously they didn't hit men or charges. I watched fascinated as scarlet and purple flashes exploded under the lumbering lorries and guns.

It was a lovely warm clear day – pity someone was spoiling it. Up the line comes Sgt Dawson on his motorbike.

'I was in the middle of that bloody lot,' he said.

'It suited you,' I said.

'Anyone hurt?' said Goldsmith.

'No sir,' said Dawson.

'Well anyone annoyed then?'

The shelling stopped, we had gone half a mile when Sherwood turned right off the road, into a copse of Acacia trees, the first thing I saw was a grave, a crude cross on top, a helmet with jagged shrapnel holes. A 15 cwt truck is leaving the site, the driver stops. 'You're not staying here are you? We bin shelled out, Jerry's got this place zeroed so he can drop 'em in yer mess tins.'

'Oh good, I'll get mine ready,' I said.

The guns hove to, gunners grinning, giving thumbs up signs, behind comes Major Chater Jack, unruffled, smiling, and returning the stopper on his whisky flask. 'I'm sorry we had to move gentlemen.'

While all this had been happening, at Waggon Lines a critical situation had arisen. 'I say Soldier what's that arising over there?'

'That sir is a Critical Situation.'

Orders for them to move had arrived at the same time Jerry tanks infiltrated from 'Tally Ho' corner; to give the vehicles a chance to get away, Captain Rand, BSM McArthur and Bdr Donaldson went north to a crest to hold off a tank attack, with pick handles. Lucky for them, as the Panzers came into view, Churchill tanks of the Derbyshire Yeomanry came through the waggon lines at speed, counter attacked, knocking out 7 Mark IIIs.

MY DIARY: FEBRUARY 26TH

'Waggon lines evacuated south of El Aroussa.' Telephone contact with Waggon Lines was down, so I was sent to open up wireless contact. I threw my gear into Doug Kidgell's lorry (who was up with the rations).

'Mind if I drive Doug?' Of course he didn't, I took the wheel, put my foot down.

'What's the bleedin' hurry?' says Kidgell hanging on grimly.

'I want to live,' I said raising one eyebrow like John Barrymore and crossing my eyes. 'I'm young! Lovely! I want to feel the wind of this giant continent blowing through my hair,' I laughed. 'Happy darling?' I said as Kidgell shot two feet up, hitting his nut on the roof.

'Slow down! Fer Christ sake!!!'

'*He's* not in the back is he?'

'Milligan, stop! Or the child will be born premature.'

'If you saw Jerry's artillery back there, you'd realise I'm not doing this for fun!'

'I didn't say it was fun,' he raged.

We hit a large pothole, Kidgell goes up, while he's up we hit another pothole, so while he's on his way down the seat is on its way up to meet him, this time he does a semi-somersault, I have to brake suddenly and there on the floor in the shape of a granny-knot is Kidgell.

We raced past El Aroussa station – now we were safe from Jerry's artillery, I slowed.

'Who taught you to drive?' said Kidgell.

'Eileen Joyce.'

'She's a pianist.'

'That was the trouble.'

We arrived at Waggon Lines at five o'clock, too late to bivvy, so I kipped down in the back of Kidgell's lorry.

MARCH

Germans launched an offensive called 'Ocksenkopf'.★ It went from 26 February to 5 March. They nearly broke through at Hunt's Gap, but an incredible resistance by 5 Hampshires and 155 Bty RA for over twelve hours (the latter were finally overwhelmed), decimated the Bosch so much – he had to stop.

★ 'Ox Head'. With names like that for a major offensive, they just couldn't have had a sense of humour.

Driver Kidgell, sans tin helmet, showing utter contempt for the Germans whilst fifteen miles from the front

12 March 1943. Q Bloke, Courtney says: 'We've got to move to a place called "Beja".' Soooo, we all start this bloody kit packing again. Finally the convoy lined up. It was 44 miles to Beja, en route we passed a glut of POWs; without fail, we gave them Nazi salutes and morale sapping raspberries. The Germans looked baffled. Was this rabble the Army they were fighting? And what was this strange farting noise they made?

A mile outside Beja, on the verge of a tree-lined dusty road, we parked our vehicles, draped scrim nets over them. Flanking us were fields of ripening corn that rittle-rattled in the afternoon breeze. The afternoon was good drying weather; I had to wash my denims and battle-dress trousers because they pleaded with me to. I hung them to dry, and repaired in my shirt and socks to sleep in Kidgell's lorry. I awoke to find the lorry a mile away at an Ordnance Depot about to be loaded with blankets. I was hoiked out of the back accompanied by wolf whistles from soldiers.

An RSM spotted me. 'Oi! *Yew*, 'ere, and double!' It was a rare sight, me running across a busy square. I came to an unclassic attention.

'Wot the bloody 'ell you think you're doing?'

'It was an accident sir.'

'What kind of accident?'

'Dysentery sir – I'm excused trousers during an attack.'

'If the A-rabs sees you they'll think we're all bloody queer.'

He took me to the Quarter Master's Store.

'Fix this nudist up with trousers.'

Kidgell was bent double with laughter as we drove back. 'You swine, Kidgell, I hope on your honeymoon your cobblers catch fire and roll down the bed.'

March 13th. The mail had arrived. Everyone went mad! I had one from Mum and Dad, one from Lily, and Ohhh ArGGGGHHHHHHHH! Three from Louise of Bexhill. AHGGGGHHHHHHHHHH. Help! I'm going blind. My father had rejoined the Army as a Captain in the RAOC. He was over fifty, but using glazier's putty, and blacking his bald head with boot polish, looked forty-nine. My brother Desmond was working as a runner-cum-slave to a press photographer in Fleet Street, and was in the middle of all the fire raids and frequently came home smoke blackened, but whistling cheerfully. This caused mother to worry. She got Doctor O'Brien to prescribe whisky to 'relax her'. Every evening she would open the front window, sip whisky, and listen for Desmond's whistling. By the time he arrived mother was so relaxed she was stretched out in the passage.

March 18th. We were to take returnable salvage to the RASC Depot at Souk El Khemis, Kidgell, Edgington and I, a perfect trio, all barmy, and none of us queer. On the way we stopped to exchange old battle-dresses and see-through blankets with Arabs, for bunches of dates. The stickiness! By the time we got to the Depot we were stuck to each other. Kidgell had to prise his hands off the steering wheel. It was even on our boots, six feet away from the eating area!

A stark white sign with the red letters BEJA, no admission, TYPHUS.

'I wonder what Typhus is like,' said Edgington.

'Typhus is an Arab village,' I said.

'Then wot's Beja?'

'Beja is a dread disease that has struck down the people of Typhus.'

'You notice that the Wogs don't have these diseases until we arrive.' We drove along in silence.

'What did one date say to another?'

'I'm stoned.'

Midday. Arrived at Service Corps Depot. Stopped at gates by small redcapped, two striped, military Hitler.

'Wot is yourn business?'

'I'm a Vicar's Mate but the war has spoilt it.'

'We want to play a little game do we? Gude. I like little games, now we are going to play a little game called Vicar's Mate waiting at the gate for one hour.'

'Where do they find people like him?' says Edgington.

'You take a pig's offal,' said Kidgell, 'and make it a Corporal.' Finally allowed in we drove to the salvage bay, unloaded our junk – got a receipt for it.

'Why does anybody have to sign for a load of crap like that,' says Edgington.

'Why? It puts the responsibility for all that crap onto someone else. Life is all bits of paper. You don't exist until you have a birth certificate, you are nameless unless you have a baptismal certificate, you have never been to school without a school leaving cert, you can't get insurance without a clean bill of health certificate, and you're not legally dead without a death certificate.'

'You can't do a crap without one,' added Kidgell.

Before departing I spied a pile of American two-man

pup-tents. I approached them respectfully, saluted, placed one under my arm and said 'This is for Wounded Knee, it's also for Wounded Teeth, Wounded Ear and Ulcerated Tongue,' one pace back, on the lorry, and away. A brilliant tactical move, and my first blow against General Patton. The wind blew pleasantly through the lorry window. 'Did you know,' said Edgington now covered in date-sticky, 'there's a man in St John's Road, Archway, who's kept a whole egg in his mouth for a year without taking it out?'

'He must be bloody mad,' I said.

'Maybe, but he's still a civilian,' he said, sliding dates down his throat. We finished the dates and felt sick.

That evening, I erected my new tent, and invited Edgington to share it. Suddenly the rain. 'Oh Christ,' said Harry, 'I'm on guard in five minutes,' he moaned. 'Right,' I said, 'off you go and stand in the pissing rain for your King and Country.' He went off groaning, and rustling in his Gas Cape. I lit the oil lamp. Now! Where were me old pornographic photographs . . . ('It's all lies officer! I bought them as art studies, I am a keen art student of twenty-one' etc.)

Pouring rain, everything was damp, cigarettes went out – matches wouldn't ignite. I was asleep when Edgington returned.

19 March, 1943. I awoke in the wee small hours, but not for a wee, no! *something* was crawling on my chest, my first thought was it must be an eleven foot King Cobra, it was moving slowly down towards where women affect you most, if he bit me there, some twenty women in England would take the veil. I called very softly 'Harry . . . Harry . . . Harry . . .' He moved and mumbled something like 'It's all right mother, I've known her three years.' 'Pay Parade!' I said. This got his eyes open. 'Now listen! There's something on my chest.'

'They're called blankets.'

'I'm serious, it's moving downwards, can you carefully take the blankets back and get it? He lit the oil lamp, and very carefully peeled off the blankets, he gasped.

'Cor bloody hell!'

'Never mind that, what is it?'

'A black scorpion.'

'Rubbish, it's an eleven foot King Cobra!'

'It's a two inch scorpion. I'm going to knock it on your side.'

'What's wrong with yours.'

With a sweeping movement he whisked the scorpion off, smashed the tent pole, collapsed the tent, extinguished the light, spilled the paraffin, and set fire to the blankets. From then on the evening lost its splendour, we stood in the pouring rain amid smouldering blankets, trying to avoid the scorpion, and to retrieve our kit. The night was spent in the gay carefree interior of Kidgell's lorry.

'You clumsy bugger you wrecked our little love nest.'

'Thank you very much, next time you knock your own bloody scorpions off.'

'It was an eleven foot King Cobra!'

March 22nd. The morning of March the 22nd dawned. The rain had stopped. Sol ascended. We strung our damp gear on a makeshift clothes line. 'Milligan! pack your kit, you're going up the line,' said BQMS Courtney.

'But me kit's soaking wet!'

'Stop the war, Mr Milligan's kit is wct.'

I massaged my steaming belongings into my kitbag, and boarded the Ration Truck with Driver Wilson.

'Where you taking me?'

'Munchar.'

'Munchar?'

'Munchar. It's a bombed village.'

So it was. I was to relieve L/Bdr Wenham at the Command Post. He'd come up in strange splotches and was reporting sick. Munchar was a French Colonial Farming village now deserted. The whole village lay in the shadow of Djbel Munchar, a gigantic razor-backed rock, looking like a fossilised Dinosaur, cast by nature in grey-white granite, it reflected the colours of the day, pink at dawn, blazing white at noon, scarlet at sunset. By moonlight it looked awesome, like the hump of a colossal white killer whale, beyond it, waiting, lay the enemy. I arrived about 9.30 a.m., the truck waited to take the ailing Wenham back, he was covered in dabs of some purple medicine. 'It's lurgi,' he grinned throwing his kit in the back. 'You'll like it here,' he said, 'we've done fuck all for 3 days, and it's been pissing down.'

'Now the bad news?'

'I've tested the set, the Dags are charged, the Don 5 is working, all you got to do is play with yourself and drink tea.'

The billet was a bombed farmhouse, minus a roof, but the first floor kept off the rain. I entered the building. Inside was a room about 20 ft × 20, to the left a burnt staircase. Lying on the floor were two of the flowers of English manhood, Gunner Arthur Tume and Gunner Payne.

'Hello Spike,' says Tume, 'I'm just reading the *Daily Mirror*.'

'You always were a daredevil.'

'You'll be glad to know that they've evacuated all our lads safely from Dunkirk.'

'Thank God, one of them owes me money.'

I dumped my kit in the corner. 'Who's on duty?' I said. 'I am,' said Payne, 'I've got my tin hat on.' He was cleaning his nails with a small hammer. 'As you're both lying down I think I can break the news, I am now Lance Bombardier Milligan.' Tume lowered his newspaper, 'Oh Christ no.' The 'phone buzzed, 'Hello,' said Payne, '19 Battery-all-action-packed Command Post. What? Yes, he's arrived, and he says he's a Lance Bombardier.' There was a howl of laughter from the other end and Payne hung up.

The overcast sky was clearing and the sun shone. I reported to Lt Budden, who had one of the 'rooms'.

'Ah Gunner Milligan.'

'It's Bombardier Milligan now sir.'

'Bombardier?' He turned and looked out the window. 'Oh dear,' he said. 'I'll put you in the picture. We're in support of the OP,' he laid out a map, and indicated the spot, 'Lt Goldsmith and Bombardier Deans are up there, where the tea stain is, they're pissed out of their minds. *We* are the carrying party for food, ammo, mail, fresh batteries, line testing and relief.'

'Do we have to take the dog for a walk as well?'

The floor was the bed, and while I was down there I did a rough pencil drawing that survived, though it's so faint I've had to ink it over.

I spent the morning exploring the house, burnt stairs (still strong enough to support one), to the First Floor, pitiful traces of happier days, a lady's slipper, a burnt doll, some women's magazines, a prayer book in French, and of all things, still hanging on the wall, a picture of M. Renaud. But lo! and behold in the room at the back was a piano, still playable but the floor adjacent had given way, so, I made no effort to play my attractive version of Chopsticks, which is not better than any other version, except I do it blindfolded standing on one leg with my trousers down. Oh I know it would mean nothing at a Chopin recital, but it had been well received in the NAAFI Canteen on Christmas Eve 1942, and who's to say, during those long nights at the Carthusian Monastery in the Valedemosa, Chopin didn't drop his trousers to compose the E Minor Nocturne? It was common knowledge that when he played in the relative minor of C, his legs over-heated, at one time George Sand's hands were a mass of burns.

One afternoon the line-laying truck (M2) halted by the door, and a long thing called Harry Edgington drew nigh, giving our special 'choked scream'. I greeted him in my drawers cellular. (I was counting my legs to see how near to Chopin I could get.) 'And why,' he said, wriggling his fingers in the air, 'are you in a state of dishabillé?'

'I'm practising to be Chopin's legs.'

'Good, I'm training to be George Sand's teeth.'

I told him about the piano, gleefully he ascended the blackened stairs. As I dressed, I heard Edgington plunge into the keyboard, Big Fat Romantic chords G aug 9th + 11th + 13th – then, the music stopped, and started but now, very sad, I climbed the stairs and found him with the burnt doll propped on the music stand.

'Blimey, this *is* sad,' he said taking the burnt doll in his hands. 'It says the whole war. Ahh!' he said, 'you've brought your trumpet, great, what is it? Honey Suckle?' I nodded. As I drew near the piano it became apparent the sagging would not take our combined weight. So! There was the strange scene of Edgington and piano in the far corner and me in the doorway blowing a trumpet. We played a few of our favourite tunes. 'What's new', 'Have you met Miss Jones?' A loud beeping from M2 Truck signalled the call for Edgington's return. 'Come on Paderewski!' came the irreverent voice of 'Pedlar' Palmer. 'Hitler wants you to tune his piano!'

Monkey 2 truck bumped and bounced away. Harry in the back, hat on sideways, posed eyes crossed, shouting –

'I *am* Napoleon, I tell you I *AM*.'

'You know Milligan,' said Lt Budden, 'one of these days someone's going to believe him.'

'I believe him sir.'

From the back room came the most terrifying tearing of wood, falling masonry and the most God-awful crash, followed by swearing and twanging. The piano had fallen thru the floor into the Batman's room, *just* missing Gunner Pill who was polishing his boots when the instrument arrived at his side.

We rushed in to see him covered in dust, a gaping hole in the ceiling – the ruins of a French Colonial Piano on the floor.

'Cor, bloody hell,' said the astonished Pill.

'You never told me you were musical,' I said. Under the circumstances his reply was remarkably controlled, 'Just missed my fuckin'' 'ead!'

It's not often we had been detailed to:

'Clean up that mess of French Colonial Piano.'

The area abounded with hot springs. To utilise this resource we dug a huge hole, dropped a canvas gun sheet in and diverted the waters thereto. One day, I observed a Gunner bathing in it, when it rained, at which he rushed from the water to take shelter. Early one sunny morning, some fifty yards from the billet, skulking in the long grass was a canine-like creature, 'Are there any wolves in Tunisia sir,' I asked Budden.

'There are *no* wolves in Tunisia Milligan,' said Lt Budden looking at me very strangely. Through binoculars I saw it was a dog, a cross between an Alsatian and a Something Hairy. He was very thin, but then by God so was I. Every night I put some bully beef on a plate and left it out for him, and every night he would eat it, save for the nights I went out and ate it myself, I got hungry too. After a few days the dog had enough confidence to let us all touch him. He was nervous about coming into the house so I knocked up a kennel for him. I made it so nice, Gunner Tume asked if he could sleep in it and the dog sleep in his room. We named him Havelock Ellis, don't ask me why.

Lt Budden enters from his room, his face almost obscured with shaving soap.

'Is today the 26th or 27th?' he said.

'It's the 25th sir, you are at this moment shaving, your name is Lt Cecil Budden and – I know there are no wolves in Tunisia.' He peered at me. He had cut himself in several places, 'Am I bleeding,' he said, 'Yes sir,' I said, 'you are

bleeding awful.' He walked vaguely round the room pouring blood and humming a Bach air, then exited. Between snatches of Bach he was speaking to Havelock, 'There, did darling like that biscuit?' This was followed by growling, 'Milligan, this dog is still half wild.'

'Well only stroke the other half,' I said. 'In any case your Bach is worse than his bite.'

29 March. Night. Loaded with supplies, I drove the Bren Carrier in torrential rain towards our OP on Frenchman's

Hill. Next to me, a sodden cigarette in his mouth sat Lt Budden. 'I'm not looking forward to relieving Tony,' he said. I did not like driving at night because I suffered with night blindness. I kept walking into things, falling down holes and treading on sleeping comrades. I had trodden on Gunner Maunders so many times he asked me, should he change his name to Axminster, but this night I didn't tread on Gunner Maunders, no, I just drove straight into a minefield. 'Don't worry,' I said, 'It's one of ours.'

'For God's sake Milligan,' said Budden, 'you've only just been promoted.'

'I'm sorry sir, a wolf ran across the road.'

Using the massed cigarette lighters of the occupants, I backed out of the danger.

'I see where I went wrong . . . I should have stayed a civilian.' With everyone praying for Divine guidance we arrived at the foot of Frenchman's Hill. 'If this is his foot, he must be a big feller, ha ha ha ha ha ha,' I said. We loaded ourselves with rations and batteries and set off along a goat track. The rain had temporarily stopped, inviting Verey lights into the sky. We were all soaked to the skin and bloody miserable. 'Someone up there doesn't like us very much,' said Ernie Hart. 'Someone down here doesn't like him very much,' I said, 'I think it's on the cards that God is a German.'

'Who ever he is, he's got a weak bladder.'

We stumbled and fell, sometimes we fell and stumbled which is exactly the same only the other way around (Eh?) We reached a swollen stream and crossed it on a narrow plank of wood, with Hart halfway across the plank started to wobble, but by using his superb balancing skill, he fell in.

We toiled up the final slopes and eventually arrived at the OP trench covered with a tent and camouflaged with brush. We hammered on the tent pole.

'Who's there?' said a voice.

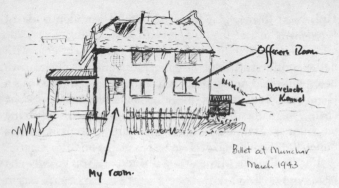

Officers Room

Havelocks Kennel

Billet at Munchar
March 1943

My room.

'A band of Highly Trained Nymphomaniacs.'

The tent flap flew open and an unshaven face that appeared to belong to Bombardier Deans appeared. 'Ah. You must be the one that goes round frightening little children,' I said.

We all squeezed into the tiny dug-out. Hart, saturated, sat quietly steaming.

'I see you brought your own water with you,' said Lt Goldsmith. He opened his new bottle of whisky, took a swig, passed the bottle saying 'Anyone for gingivitis?' We sat cramped, passing the bottle to and fro, I was on the fro side and didn't see much of it. We passed what little news we had, smoked our cigarettes, waited for the rain to stop but no, out into it we slithered, retracing our steps to the Bren, by midnight we were back at the GP billet with a very weary Lt Goldsmith and a pissed Bdr Deans who were welcomed back by a snarling 'Havelock Ellis'. 'Who does he belong to,' said Deans, 'Himmler?'

APRIL

The war was now an accepted daily routine, we had 'periods of utter boredom then bursts of sudden excitement', as Colonel Grant had told us, from then on we went about saying 'Hello Dick, are you in an "utter boredom period"?'

'Oh no. I'm right in the middle of a "sudden burst of excitement".'

The night of April 4th the rain was thundering down, we heard Havelock suddenly barking and snarling, there was a pistol shot. I doused the light, grabbed Tommy Gun, got out the back door, Jerry patrols were famous for throwing grenades into rooms. A long figure at the front door was saying 'Pleese open ze door.' Someone said 'It's Charles Boyer!' It was the French farmer who owned the house, he had come back to ask us if we'd seen his dog, which was in fact Havelock Ellis who in the dark had attacked him, and the Frenchman had shot him.

We found Havelock in his kennel, a bullet in his head. God knows how he managed to get back, it's the homing instinct, even if it's only made from charge cases. We were all broken up about it. The Frenchman had brought us a bottle of wine. We drank it and cheered up a bit. Lt Goldsmith invited us all into his room, where he opened up his whisky. Alf Fildes got his guitar out, and I played 'Parlez-moi d'amour' on my trumpet. A strange evening, but then, weren't they all? Next day we buried Havelock. I washed the blood off his face. We lined a large charge case with an old blanket, dug a respectably deep grave. Over it we mounted a board, and I wrote,

> Here lies the body
> of Havelock the Dog
> Shot in the head
> And dropped like a log
>
> He was a very Good dog.
>
> April 1943

I suppose he's still there.

APRIL 6TH 1943. BATTERY DIARY:

Battery Command to Sidi Mahmoud OP as CRA Dep for 71 Field Arty: Group.

Munchar CP. 0800 hours. Pouring rain, and other things. Sgt 'Georgie' Dawson's motor-bike arrives which he drives straight into the room. 'There's going to be a big party tonight,' he grinned.

'A party?' I said, 'I can't go, I haven't a thing to wear!'

'Good, it's for nudists.' He proceeded to give details:

Major Chater Jack, Gunner Woods, Gunner Tume, L/Bdr Milligan (oh shit), Bombardier Edwards, OPAck* and Bombardier Andrews from the recently arrived 54 Heavy Regiment. 'He's coming along for the experience,' said Dawson. He grinned evilly. It was deluging. The rain dripped in from every crack and seeped over the door sill.

'The wireless truck will collect you at 1900 hours.'

'1900?' I said. 'That's a pity, my watch only goes up to 12.'

MY DIARY:

6th April on this thing. Howling gale, intermittent rain. Gnr Tume, Bdr Andrews from 54 Heavy RA left at dusk. 'Chater' in high spirits (Johnnie Walker), asks me how 'Highland Laddie' goes.

Me: It goes Dum-de dum-dum-dum with intermittent rain.

Major Chater Jack: Thank you, I can manage on my own now.

We moved off at dusk into the approaching darkness, the noise of the wind making conversation difficult. I switched

* Observation Post Assistant.

on the set, the red contact and the working light came alive. I donned headphones, tuned into battery network, the interference was appalling, the voice of Shapiro at the Command Post was barely audible, the mud a foot deep with the differential constantly coming in contact with rocks. I tuned in BBC News, passed spare headphones into the cab. 'Very bad reception,' shouted Chater. 'Yes sir, shall I write and complain?'

He said something, but was drowned out by the elements, 'At *once* sir!' I said smartly. Two miles on we reached Sidi Mahmoud and started up hill. Driver Robinson puts his stamp on the evening, he lands us in a minefield. 'Sorry sir,' his squeaky voice was saying. 'I didn't know what Achtung Minen meant.'

'It means instant bloody death man!' explained Chater Jack with remarkable control. Hanging over the tailboard I directed him back on our tracks and my face was spattered with yellow mud. 'You've got mud on your face, ha ha ha ha,' said Bdr Edwards who was not noted for his wit. 'It's not mud,' I explained, 'this is what happens when the shit hits the fan.'

'How does it go again?' called Chater. I re-sang the opening bars with intermittent rain.

'Doesn't he know any other tunes?' said Edwards.

'Any *others*? Christ, he doesn't know this one, he only brings me along as an amanuensis.'

'Amanuensis?'

'It's what Eric Fenby was to Delius.'

'The dirty sod,' said Edwards who was not noted for his wit.

When we arrived at the OP, the rain stopped but the war didn't. Chater Jack ensconced himself in a splendidly roofed OP, on the forward slopes of Sidi Mahmoud, reached by a communication trench. There to meet him were three artillery officers from 71 Field Artillery Group, holding maps. The truck was 50 yards behind the OP. To avoid detection, we had to run the wireless remote control to the OP while I stayed on the truck to relay the orders. Meanwhile Tume and Andrews dug a trench.

Midnight, the wind almost a gale. In the back of the truck we sipped tea and played twilight pontoon, me with headphones listening on the Infantry network. A silent attack was to go in and take their objectives by 04.00, we were standing by if they called for fire. At 03.50 hrs. on our right, an Artillery barrage was to support the 78 Div. attack on the Munchar–Medjez-el-Bab front. As the hour came I thought of those young men going forward into darkness towards death or mutilation. At 03.50 the sky sang with flashing lights, a thunder of iron artillery rolled through the night, my wireless came alive with urgent voices, 'Hello Baker Charlie 2, we're pinned down by mortars at Wog-Dog Farm,' every call was a life and death affair, and here I was in comparative safety.

'Hello Milligan?' it was Chater Jack. 'Yes sir – it goes Da-da-die —'

'No, no! I want to speak to "Sunray".'*

I moved the dial towards our own net, as I did the opening bars of Bach's Toccata and Fugue filled my headphones, it was too much, I burst into tears. 'What's the matter,' said Driver Robinson.

'It's a piece of music.'

'Must be fucking 'orrible to make you cry.'

The music soared, the barrage raged on, turning the night red, green, orange, purple . . . Gunner Tume relieved me on the set. 'There's tea in the OP,' he said.

I stumbled along the communication trench, the wind had dropped, I looked up, the sky was clearing.

In the dim light of the OP Chater Jack and three Officers were sipping tea. I saluted. To a man they ignored me. Two

---

* Sunray: Code name for Battery Captain.

signallers squatting on the floor clutching telephones, writing messages and handing them to the officers who, to a man, ignored them. Gunner Woods, slaving over a hot primus, filled my mug. The officers were talking, 'I don't like hybrid strains,' one was saying. 'Too much like having a queer in the garden. Ha ha ha.' 'What a crowd of bloody fools,' I thought. 'You should have come earlier,' whispered Woods, 'they were on about the price of tennis shoes.' Chater was passing his whisky flask around. Suddenly, at 04.59 the Barrage stopped. The phone buzzed. 'For you sir,' said a buck-toothed Signaller. 'Hello?' said Chater, 'Right.' He put the phone down. 'Gentlemen, the North Irish Horse are going in,' he looked at his watch. 'Dead on time,' he grinned.

'How's the attack going sir,' I ventured.

'I haven't had one yet Milligan,' he ventured. The junior officers laughed – they had to. They peered thru the slits into the night, where a myriad permutations of muzzle-flashes told their story. Woods grinned at the sight of officers staring into the darkness with binoculars. 'They're our leaders,' he whispered, tapping his head. Dawn was emerging from our right, which was a good arrangement. Soon the battle panorama was revealed; in front, a large valley, on the far slopes, tanks of the North Irish Horse were fighting their way up Djbel Kachbia. To our left the 2nd Hamps. were attacking the slopes of Djbel Mahdi. 'We've got to get the set out of the truck,' says Tume hurriedly, 'it's got to pick up something.'

'Oh shit!'

'It could be that.'

We unloaded the set. Blast! The remote control cable wouldn't reach the slit trench. 'Oh shit II.' So we had to leave it on open ground, then, the bad news, a series of 88s burst around us, we moved at considerable speed into a trench and huddled in the bottom, I let out a yell as a piece of red hot shrapnel fell on to my hand.

'There's bloody luck!' said Tume, 'hit by the enemy and no blood.'

'My Blighty one and it didn't work,' I moaned.

Bombardier Andrews was sweating and pulling at his lower lip – I don't know why, it looked long enough.

'How long does this go on?' he said.

'Until the war is finished,' I said.

'Don't take any notice of him,' said Tume, seeing that Andrews was frightened. 'Sometimes a few minutes, sometimes an hour, it depends which *German's* on duty.' The wireless came to life, bravely Tume crawled out and put the headphones on – bravely I watched him do it. Luckily the shelling stopped. The battle was moving away. Sgt Dawson

𝕳𝖎𝖙𝖑𝖊𝖗𝖌𝖗𝖆𝖒 𝕹𝖔. 27

ADOLPH HITLER: You realise soon zer Englishers people
    will be *crushed*!
ME: It must be rush hour.
ADOLPH HITLER: Zere is no need to rush!! Soon it will
    all be over.
ME: Hooray! back to Civvy Street.
ADOLPH: Civvy Street is no more! It was destroyed by
    zer bombs of mine Luftwaffe.

had arrived, he dismounted and let off. 'Ah, that's better,' he said. 'Only for you,' I said running clear. 'Come back you coward,' he shouted. 'It's one of ours.'

The rest of the day was a bore save for sudden rushes to hide from ME 109s and periodic visits to watch the Battle. We dined well on hot stew brought in vacuum containers. By sunset the battle had left us behind, we packed up and returned to Munchar.

APRIL 11, 1943

I awoke to a sunny morning, 9.00 a.m., a lizard was sunning himself on the window ledge. Gnr Pills did a noble thing, he brought me breakfast in bed! 'Why did you do it? You're not queer are you?' 'I don't know,' he said, 'waitin' on orficers is a dooty, well, I was orf dooty, and I fort I'd do a good deed for the day and I seed you sleepin' and I fort, he's 'ad an 'ard time or 'eed 'ave gotten up for 'ees breakfast, so I'll get it for 'im,' then added, 'You won't tell anyone will you, or they'll all bleedin' want it.'

A bath! Ten minutes later I stood naked by the thermal spring soaping myself, singing, and waving my plonker at anyone who made rude remarks about it. 'With one as big as that you ought to be back home on Essential War Work.' It was nice to have these little unsolicited testimonials. The animal delight of sitting in a rocky pool of running warm water, under a blue sky and a brilliant sun, is one of life's bonuses.

I dried myself on what had once been a towel against what had once been a body. I was a wiry nine and a half stone. I tried to think of myself as a suntanned lean Gary Cooper but I always came out dirty-white skinny Milligan. 'You look like a bag of bones held together by flesh coloured tights,' said Spiv Corvine. 'Don't go,' I said, 'stay for my description of you, you short-arsed little git!'

LETTER HOME:

My dear Mum, Dad, Des,

   Thanks for the parcel, don't put soap in with fags. Out of action for the day, hence letter. Weather is hotting up, about 70°, it's shirt sleeves. And how silly we all look, naked except for 2 shirt sleeves! I believe they are shortly to issue Tropical Kit, or KDs (Khaki Drill) which will bring back memories of Poona. I still remember those boyhood days with remarkable clarity. I think if you enjoy a childhood, it is indelible for life. Clearest are memories of hearing the strident Bugle, and Drums of the Cheshire Regiment playing 'When we are marching to Georgia', and the Regiment swinging by, so impeccable, bayonets and brass buttons flashing light signals in all directions, the blinding white webbing, boots like polished basalt, trousers crackling with starch, the creases with razor edges, the marks of sweat appearing down the spines of the men, the Pariah dogs slinking from the path of the column, and the silent resentment of watching Natives. I don't think we can retain it as part of the Empire much longer. I give it until say 1950. Can't tell you much because of Censorship; so far miraculously, no one in this Battery has been hurt by enemy action. Not much chance to play Jazz at the moment, but listen regularly to AFN Algiers. I hope my records are O.K. I put them in a box under my bed with a cardboard sheet between each record. If you move, please be very careful of them. We're billeted in a war-damaged house, it's in a bad state, and we are trying to get a reduction in our rates. I hear a distant scream saying 'Lunch will be served in an empty cowshed,' or is it 'Cows will be served in an empty lunch shed,' so I'll be off.

> *Love to you all,*
> *your loving son,*
> *Terry.*

P.S. Send more cake, chocolate, fags, Pile ointment, but for Christ sake no more holy medals.

LAST DAY MUNCHAR

'Fresh flowers from the fields of Tunisia sir.'

'Oh Milligan how nice,' beamed Lt Budden, his solemn face journeying to a smile.

'I don't like plucking flowers, but' – I recalled Lady Astor visiting Bernard Shaw, remarking it was summer yet he had no flowers in his house. 'No mam,' he replied. 'I like flowers, I also like children, but, I do not chop their heads off and keep them in bowls around the house.' A great man. She was a twit. She filled Parliament with Bons Mots, and put progress back a hundred years.

'Put them in this,' said Lt Budden filling a broken jar with water. We placed the flowers on a rough square wooden table.

'They do brighten up the place,' said Lt Budden standing back to admire them. Christ, I thought, the English are so bloody civilised, and I made a mental note to forgive them for the dispossession of my family's farm in Ulster during The Plantation.

'I think they are Ranunculus.'

'Oh? I thought they were flowers.'

The phone rang. I beat Budden to it.

'Hello, Bdr Milligan.'

'Want any chicken shit?' said a voice.

'Who's that?' I said.

'Rhode Island Red,' a gale of laughter, then click. I suspect the joker was Bdr Sherwood, who was given to such pranks, he was one of five brothers, a first class driver, a very clean soldier, a good footballer, and a bloody awful pianist, I think it was the beer.

I yawned one of those yawns that makes the back of your head touch your shoulder blades and push your chest out. Tomorrow the new Gun Position. Oh no! *not* tomorrow . . . *at midnight* we were beaten awake with rifle butts, our erections smashed down with shovels. We were to move *now*.

'This isn't war,' screamed Edgington, 'it's Sadism. S-a-d-e-s-e-a-m' etc. The convoy crawled along in pitch darkness, the moon having waned. 'Where are we going sir?' I asked.

'It's a place called Map Ref. 517412,' said Lt Goldsmith.

'They don't write numbers like that any more sir.'

We passed the bombed shattered village of Toukabeur, full of Booby Traps. Seven Sappers were killed during clearing. Outside the village was our new position. At night it looked like the surface of the moon, or Mae West's bum the moment the corsets came off.

In front of us was a rocky multi-surfaced outcrop 80 feet high and a hundred yards long, behind us a ledge dropping sheer 50 feet to a granite plateau 50 yards long, then another 30 foot drop into a valley, in fact two giant steps. The canvas command post erected, I pitched my tent on the edge of the first drop, because shells falling behind me would drop 50 feet down and I would avoid being subdivided by the Third Reich. However, if shells landed in front of me, I'd suffer the quincequonces. The guns were

Gunner Milligan showing his unflagging belief in his King and Country

pulled, heaved and sworn into position. Wireless network opened with 78 Div. HQ and 46 Div. OP line laid and contact made. Jerry dropped an occasional Chandelier flare. Kerrashboom-kerak! Our first rounds went off at 2200 hours. I was on Command Post duty all night.

In between fire orders a running argument developed between Lt Beauman-Smythe, Gnr Thornton and self.

Thornton: There's been heavy casualties on Bou Diss.

Me: I'm glad it's not me.

B-Smythe: That's a selfish view.

Me: Selfish sir? All I said was I'm glad it wasn't me that died.

B-Smythe: That's not something to be *glad* about!

Thornton: I think –

Me: Sir! You want me to say 'I'm sorry it wasn't me that got killed'?

B-Smythe: It's better than being *not* sorry. Someone's got to get killed in wars.

Me: Well, someone *was*, it's just that it wasn't me.

Thornton: I think –

B-Smythe: I still say your attitude to death was selfish.

Me: Look sir, mother went thru a lot of pain to have me, I was a 12 lb. baby, 11 lbs. was my head, me father spent a fortune for a Sergeant on my education, some days it was up to threepence a day, I'm not throwing all that away. My father still goes round with a begging bowl.

Thornton: I think –

B-Smythe: I still say your attitude to death was selfish.

Milligan: Shellfish?

Thornton: I think –

Me: Sell? What *do* you think?

Thornton: . . . Oh Christ – I've forgotten.

Me: Well be a good boy, go outside and get killed to cheer up Lt Smythe.

Off duty at 0600 hours, went straight to bed and I think I died.

April 14. Wednesday. 1943. Midday, guns didn't wake me but Lunch did. In daylight our newly painted green and yellow guns stood out dangerously against the chalk white surroundings, but, by ingenious draping with dark and light grey blankets they blended in splendidly. 'It would have been better if we'd painted the bloody rocks yellow and green,' said crazed voices who had to wait all day to get their blankets back and then rise at dawn to give them up again. Our OP was in a dodgy position on Djbel Chaouach being under mortar fire, hence the small sign by the OP trench. 'For sale – no reasonable offer refused, owner forced to sell, apply Fear and Co.'

At short notice I was rushing up to Chaouach OP to collect some dead batteries, idiot driver Cyril Bennett parks wireless truck in full view of Jerry, mortared to hell before we drove to safety.

'Why did they shoot at us,' said Driver Bennett, 'they could *see* we wasn't armed.' Today that driver is Anthony Barber MP. Another parcel from home! Fruit cake, holy medals, and soapy cigarettes. I divided the cake among the poor of the parish, we ate the lot in 20 minutes, it was a question of getting as much down you as soon as you could before the word got round. Chater Jack had got wind of it and entered the CP to find men with cheeks bulging.

'What are you eating?' he said, his voice slightly strained. Lt Beauman-Smythe said, 'Wegge eaghting schom of Milligan's Chake Suh,' sending out a stream of air borne crumbs in the Major's face. Chater Jack scanned the cake flecked maw. 'Any left?' he said hopefully but with dignity. I held up the empty tin. Chater Jack paused, clenching and unclenching his fists. 'Next time Milligan . . .' he never concluded the statement, like a Napoleon at Waterloo he turned, and left.

15 April 1943. Hooray! I discovered a hand hewn room in the face of a cliff below our Command Post. Safety at last! I moved in. I awoke at 3 a.m. to the patter of tiny feet, I was crawling alive with fleas. I suppose delousing by the light of a candle could be considered 'non essential war work'.

0600: On duty again, a mass of bites and scratches.

'What in Christ's wrong with your face?' said Gunner Thornton.

'Nothing *wrong* with it,' I said thru a thousand blotches. 'It's the new Helena Rubenstein Gunners Dawn-Kiss make up, it will soon be the rage of the 1st Army.'

'What's it called?'

'Stage One Leprosy.' Let me describe Thornton, 36, old for a Gunner, but young for an Englishman, 5 foot 11 inches, about 11 stone, the removal of his boots brought him down to 8 stone. A handsome face in the Gregory Peck mould but obviously there wasn't room in the mould for him. Blue eyes with an honest frank look, even honest Jim, he smoked a briar pipe that only rested when he washed or slept, he never laughed out loud, primarily because his teeth shot out, he had a habit of scratching the back of his left hand whenever he was thinking, that's why he never scratched the back of his left hand. The phone buzzed. 'Command Post Answerin',' I said. It was the OP. 'Action Stations, Moving Target, Range 11,500! . . . Angle of sight 45°! HE 119! Charge 4, Fire!' The guns burst into shuddering iron monsters, just as the dawn in all its majesty was coming up like thunder, but I couldn't have cared a fuck less. I returned to my rocky room with a tin of DDT, put in fresh straw. Later that day, I arranged to allow Gnr Shapiro to move in with me during air attacks, at 2 fags a raid.

Through the hot afternoon we lay in our cool stone bower playing battleships. Suddenly an air raid explodes on the area, '2 fags!' I said. Guns were going off in all directions, the sky a mass of explosions, shouts and yells, sounds of men running like the clappers. 'It must be hell out there,' said Shapiro calmly. We looked at each other, the thought of all that shit flying about outside, with everybody crashing into each other was too much, we cried with laughter. I loaded my captured German rifle and loosed off a few rounds at a plane. It was one of ours. 'Never mind,' said Shapiro. 'You tried.' Our safe arbour soon became known, the next air raid there was a thunder of approaching boots, and 20 gunners dived into my tiny hideaway, 'Two fags a time!' I shouted from underneath.

Friday April 16th. April the 16th. My birthday. I'm 25 years old. I requested the guns to fire a 21 gun salute, they said 'Happy Birthday, piss off.' My family had sent me a birthday card and another 3 holy medals, I now had 103 – I used them as currency with the Arabs.

There was bitter bloody fighting on Djbel Tanngouch, Heidous and Djbel Ang, all of them changing hands several times throughout the terrible day. In support of them, we fired continuously, the Gunners were out on their feet, but knew their lot was easy compared with the PBI so they never complained. There was, however, an occasional cry of 'Fuck this for a livin''. Lt Tony Goldsmith at the OP did some deadly accurate shooting, and remained stoically calm through the most blistering mortaring. In between shoots he would 'phone command post.

'Hello Milligan, I'm going to have a nap, would they turn the volume down on the guns.' He has eight days of his young life left.

Saturday April 17th. I'm 25 and one day old and I smoke soapy cigarettes. Gunner Edgington is out on M2 Truck laying a line to the OP. They stop for tea, it was infusing to a nicety when down came a black bird to peck off his nose in the shape of half a dozen MEs all taking it in turns to bomb, and straff. As one man, our brave lads, pop-eyed with fear and nicotine stained shirt tails, are on the truck which goes from nought to sixty miles an hour in three seconds.

Edgington, showing the phlegm of his Island race, runs *back* for the tea, he is overtaking the truck when the MEs let him have bullets thru the seams of his trousers, at which moment Edgington removes tin hat and places it over the tea. Save shrapnel pitted mudguards and flattened tyres they escaped unharmed, questioned later about his heroic action, he replied, 'I didn't want any bits to get in.'

Sunday 18 April. Weather getting very warm, all stripped to the waist. Gunner Woods and Driver Tibbs digging trenches.

Woods: 6 foot 2 inches. How far you down?

Tibbs: 5 foot 3 inches. Three feet.

Woods: 6 foot 2 inches. That's no good you want to go down 8 feet.

Tibbs: 5 foot 3 inches. How the bloody hell am I going to get out?

Woods: 6 foot 2 inches. Dig another hole coming up.

19 April 1943. On duty at CP from 2200 hours till 0200. Awakened at dawn by German planes dive bombing 25 pounders in valley behind us. We all sat and enjoyed it very much.

Up front the fighting raged for the peaks dominating the way to the plains before Tunis. Boston Bombers, 60 at a time, went over and blasted the peaks, so much explosives were rained on Longstop, it changed the contour of the summit.

24 April. Fighting on Longstop at a Crescendo all day. OP under murderous fire – support group at bottom of hill also under heavy shell fire. Gunner Collins hit in hand. At about 11.10 I heard the dreadful news, Lt Goldsmith had been killed. Alf Fildes noted in his diary 'Learn with regret we have lost our best officer.'

I went back to my cave and wept. I remember calling his

name. After a few minutes I straightened up, but the memory of that day remains vivid. Apparently, he and Bdr Edwards were sheltering in a fox hole. *'We were under mortar attack, we sat facing each other, our knees touching. Tony had the map board on his chest, his arms folded round it. Suddenly, I was blown out of the trench. I went to get back in and I saw that Tony had been hit by a mortar bomb in the chest, he died instantly . . .'* All the boys came back very shaken. Bdr Dodds was so 'bomb happy' he went to hospital and never came back. For someone as splendid, kind, intelligent and witty as Tony to be killed outraged my sensibilities. His friend, Terence Rattigan, wrote a personal Obituary in *The Times*. I remember his last words to me. He was about to leave for Longstop.

'It won't be long now, I'd say Tunis in 10 days,' he was patting his pockets, 'Blast I'm out of cigarettes.' I gave him 5 of mine, 'Here sir, have 5 of my soap-saturated Passing Clouds, a holy medal in every packet . . .'

He took them, smiled, tapped the driver on the shoulder and said, 'To battle!'

Hitler chalking slogans in Downtown Berlin Gents Toilet after hearing of the fall of Longstop

The evening of the 25th April. The Major called us all around his tent, he was well disposed to the world and his fellow men via a distillery in Kirkintilloch in Scotland. In contempt of the Hun he ordered a bonfire to be lit, gathered us around and told us, 'The last battle is nigh, Alexander has offered the Bosch "Unconditional Surrender", or a watery grave, we'll give him Dunkirk without the evacuation facilities. Now let's have a song.' We sang, there was the smell of victory in the air. Next day, we heard that the 8th Argyle and Sutherland Highlanders had taken Longstop at Bayonet point in one incredibly heroic charge, led by Major John Anderson, who was awarded the VC. Three days of slaughter for the peak had ended.

Almost immediately we got orders for a hurried move to take up new positions somewhere on Longstop. In the rush Edgington hands me a piece of paper. It read:

> Stalin's Order of the day,
> (a) Two Lagers.
> (b) Packet of Crisps.
> (c) Stalingrad.

'This is vital information, comrade Edgington, this must never fall into enemy hands, it must also not fall into enemy feet, teeth, legs or ears, this must be burnt and you must swallow the ashes,' I said, whereupon he snatched the paper, and ate it!

'Delicious,' he said.

'That's called the Readers' Digest,' I said.

26 APRIL

Gunner Driver Alf Fildes writes in his diary:

'Spike kindly sleeps all day, while I use match sticks, 5 hours sleep in 2 days. I think I'll hand my blankets in for the duration.'

Now for the love of me I don't remember sleeping all day! *My* diary says,

'Fildes kindly sleeps all day, while I use match sticks, one hour's sleep in eight weeks, I can't go on like this! Worse still last night I caught Alf Fildes copying something from my diary. In the morning I'm going to tell teacher.'

OP reported a five-hour tank battle, some using flame throwers. 6th Armoured vs the X Panzers. ME 109s bombed vehicles using the Medjez-el-Bab–Tunis Road, but ran into well concealed Beaufort Guns that shot two down in flames amid whoops of jubilation from the lads. Part II Orders: *'The sheikh from Medjez-el-Bab has complained to General Anderson that chickens are being stolen by Allied Troops, this practice will stop forthwith. Any one seen in possession of a chicken will be questioned, and will have to show proof as to how he came by it.'* 'Oh Fuck!' says Chalky White. 'There goes two months' free dinners.'

A swelling had started on my knee. I said so to Lt Budden.

'A swelling has started on my knee.'

'It's got to start somewhere,' he said.

'True,' I said, 'I hope it's nothing trivial.'

I hobbled about dropping hints, 'Oh dear, *there* it goes again, tsu! tsu! . . . I hope it does not get any worse, or dearie me, I will have to stop serving my King and Country and he will have to serve himself!' The knee got worse, I reported to the MO, a laconic Canadian who looked like Charles Boyer and dribbled. 'Yur, you've got some kind of infection, I think it's a blind boil.'

'Does this mean an optician?'

He wrote something on a bit of paper that looked like 'Asparagus tetani-scrotum.' To a Field Hospital I went, a series of tents on an arid plain near Beja. A man, disguised as a female nurse said 'Undress, lie on that bed, and die!' I pulled on blue military pyjamas that had remained unchanged, and I suspect unwashed, since the Crimea. The tent was a hundred feet long, beds lining the walls, filled with various 'non combatant' ailments, i.e. boils, piles, flat feet, dandruff, varicose veins and cowardice. To my left a Grenadier Guardsman with bunions, to my right a Corporal with Mange. Nurses go around every morning at 4.00 and stick thermometers in your mouth or up the anus. I had mine orally, I prayed every morning I'd get it *before* the first of the rectums. A red-faced pissed sandy-haired doctor stopped at my bed, looked at my chart.

'You're shuffering from Milligan?'

'No sir, that's my name.'

Next day he said, 'Bad knee I shee!'

Next day, 'We must have a look at it.'

Next day 'What's the matter with you?'

'I'm suffering from a recurring amnesiac sandy-haired doctor.'

I was given massive doses of the new drug, Penicillin. The knee subsided, but I started to swell, my temperature soared. What luck! I was allergic to Penicillin! I spent three wonderful days in clean bedsheets, and visits from the WVS ladies.

'What are you ill with?'

'Penicillin poisoning, mam.'

'You brave boy. Your parents must be so proud of you.'

'No, they think I'm a silly bugger.'

She smiled. She was deaf. The ground temperature was 100° as she gave me a woollen pullover, scarf and gloves. 'It gets very chilly in the evenings,' she added. A kind old dear, but the wrong kind, I think her name was Trowler, she was about a hundred and sixty, and always carried a shovel. There was one magnificent nurse, Sheila Frances. She had red hair, deep blue eyes and was very pretty, but that didn't matter! because! she had big tits. Everyone was after her, and I didn't think I had a chance, but, she fancied *me*. I got lots of extra, like helping me get her knickers off in her tent and she eased my pain no end. It was all very nice but had to end, one morning I was loaded on to a truck and driven back to the regiment for a well-deserved rest. Every night after that I would face in the direction of the hospital, take all my clothes off and howl.

BATTERY DIARY

May the 1st. Battery still engaged on Counter Battery Targets. The Offensive launched at end of April has ground to a halt. What now?

I didn't have to wait long for an answer. On the Medjez plain to our right appeared the vehicles of the Eighth Army, all painted sandy yellow, tanks, half tracks, Brens, transports, the lot, the dust they raised was like a sand storm. At night they lit bonfires and the scene looked like Guy Fawkes night on Hampstead Heath. What was happening? Alexander had moved the 4th Indian, the 7th Armoured Div. (The

Terrible effect of Mepacrin on Gunner Woods

Desert Rats) and 201 Guards Brigade on to our Front, to build up for the final Battle (STRIKE).

The accumulation of Eighth Army Units went on until the 3rd of May. A new officer has arrived to replace Tony Goldsmith, one Lt Walker, dubbed 'Johnny', blond, blue-eyed, a cavalry moustache, 5 foot 8 inches, quiet, funny – i.e. lying on a hill in the dark at a dodgy OP, I heard him draw his Colt Automatic and put a round in the breech. 'What's that for?' I whispered. 'Academic reasons, Milligan,' he said. Away from his Bivvy, he left a notice – 'This is a forward office for a Dewar's Whisky Agent, who is authorised to taste any whisky to verify that it is of the required standard. For this service – there is no charge.'

The arrival of hot weather brought an issue of Khaki Drill. The sight of white knobbly legs plus voluminous shorts brought forth howls of laughter. We looked like ENSA comics trying to look funny.

'What are you writing inside your trousers?' said Edgington.

'It says, "these shorts must never be worn in sight of the Enemy . . .".' The sun never sets on the British Empire – with these shorts it would never set on their knees either.

'Bloody mosquitoes! I thought they'd all been killed by the British Army in India,' said heavily bitten Smudger Smith. Indeed they hadn't. Fortunately we were taking anti-malarial Mepacrin tablets three times a day, with unfortunate results, for some gunners turned yellow. Gunner Woods went to sleep an Anglo Saxon and woke up a Chinaman.

'Oh, look, chop-chop,' I said. 'You fightee Jelly Soldier disgluised as Chinky Poo.' Poor Woods, a simple man, went into a depression. 'It'll wear off,' I consoled. 'It won't, I been tryin' to wash it orf all morning, I rubbed the skin orf and it's still yeller underneath.'

'What you need,' said Lt Joe Mostyn, 'is a solicitor. In your condition you could sue the British Army for altering your nationality without your permission.' Fortunately for the Chinese race the effect of Mepacrin wore off after a week. It was about this time that I saw something that I felt might put years on the war. It was a short Gunner, wearing iron frame spectacles, a steel helmet that obscured the top of his head, and baggy shorts that looked like a Tea Clipper under full sail. He was walking along a gulley behind a group of officers, heaped with their equipment. It was my first sight of Gunner Secombe; what a pity! We were so near to Victory and this had to happen. I hadn't crossed myself in years, and I remember saying, 'Please God . . . put him out of his misery.' I never dreamed, one day he, I, and a lone RAF clerk called Sellers, at that moment in Ceylon imagining he could hear tigers, would make a sort of comic history, not that we were not making it now; oh no – every day was lunatic. What can you say when Gunners taking mobile showers get a sudden call to action? Imagine the result – the sight of a gun team in action, naked, in tin hats and boots, all save Bombardier Morton who holds his tin hat afront of that part which only his 'loved one should see.' As I stood there I thought 'My God, what havoc one determined German could wreak on this lot with a feather duster.'

MAY 2ND BATTERY DIARY:

BC to OP. Enemy Battery observed active 62356 engaged by 19 Battery and silenced. Enemy guns active from DJBEL GUESSA, Favourable Meteor brings them within range of 19 Battery, effective observed, fire continued till last light, one enemy troop silenced, the others out of range.

Well, that took care of May the 2nd. The third and fourth continued as both sides jockeyed for positions for the final round. 'Bloody 'ell,' says an alarmed Gunner Forrest rushing into the Command Post. 'There's bloody black soldiers fightin' on our side.' I explained they were the Fourth

Indian Div. 'I didn't know they let 'em fight for us, I thought they was never allowed out of India, I mean can you trust 'em, they're all bloody Wogs. My dad said they were lazy buggers and you couldn't trust 'em.' I explained that nearly a fifth of the Eighth Army was made up of 'Wogs' and all that lay 'twixt him and the Jerry at this moment were in fact Wogs. That night I heard he slept with a loaded rifle by his bed. 'I hope the Germans give 'em a bloody good hiding,' he said. Today that man is Alf Garnett.

We continued various firing tasks, then!

0300 hrs. on the 6th: At that hour, on a very narrow front, 600 guns in two hours dropped 17,000 rounds atop the Baddies. The Infantry moved forward. By 7.30, 6th Armoured started to move forward through a mine-free gap prepared by the 4th British Div., but alas the job had been botched and this slowed up the armour. Overhead there was an unending umbrella of British and American aircraft that bombed and straffed anything that moved, including us. Our battery continued firing at targets chosen by our OP. The ammunition expenditure was enormous. 'This is costing us a fortune,' said Lt Mostyn. 'Honestly, in the last three hours we've spent enough to have opened two hat shops in Whitechapel, with a hundred pound float in the till.' I calmed him, 'Would it help if we fired slower, sir?' He shook his head, 'It's too late now, if I had been running this war I could have done it at half the price, I mean what's Churchill know about business? Nothing! Give him a dress shop and in two weeks he'd be skint!'

A gown shop in Whitechapel:
CHURCHILL: Good morning modame.
SHOPPER: I'd like to see a black velvet evening gown with a plunging back.
CHURCHILL: Is that a dress?
SHOPPER: Yes.
CHURCHILL: In two weeks I'll be skint.

A lucky escape by Sergeant 'Maxie' Muhleder whose gun prematurely exploded at the muzzle but no one was hurt. Lt Mostyn rushed to congratulate Muhleder on his escape – at the same time trying to sell him an insurance policy.

In the heat of the final battle, the intense use of artillery never gave much time for anything except moaning.

'If this is bleeding Victory, I prefer stalemates.'

'Even if we win the war, the bloody Germans won't admit defeat, they'll say, "Ve came second".'

DIARY MAY 7TH, 2.45 A.M.

On the Command Post wireless I picked up the electrifying message – '6th Armoured and 7th Armoured Units on outskirts of Tunis!'

I threw the headphones in the air. It was round the battery in minutes, everybody was grinning – this was it!

'The Major wants us to look out our white lanyards for the Victory Parade,' said Lt Walker. 'Just this once,' I said.

'Prepare to move, we've got the bastards holed up in Cap Bon,' said Sgt Dawson. The great chase started. We passed swarms of prisoners and gave them the usual treatment.

We raced along the dust choked road to Grich el Oued. Across the great baked plain of the Goubellat we thundered in concert with Infantry and Tanks, all shouting and yelling with the excitement of the kill. 'The Kill!' for that's what it was. Here was I, anti-war, but like the rest of us feeling the exhilaration of the barbarian – it's just under the surface folks, so watch out! BSM MacArthur almost mummified in dust goes down the column. 'It's all over!' he's shouting – and it was! We camped at Oued Melah, told to 'stand alert for a call.' It never came. On May the 12th the fighting ceased. The war in Tunis was over. 'Cup of tea?' said Edgington, 'Ah, cheers,' I said. 'Let's tune in to Radio Algiers.' We did.

VOLUME THREE

MONTY:
His Part in My Victory

Subject:- Artillery Equipment   141F/2373/11/RA
Comd. 1 A.G.R.A.,   27 June 43
Comd. 2 A.G.R.A.

   I would be grateful if you would congratulate all
ranks in 54 and 56 Hy Regts through their
Regimental Comds. on the sentence in D.A.D.A.,
First Army Report dated 22 June 43 (in reply to
HQRA A.F.H.Q. 191/RA of 5 June 43) 'The
pieces and recoil systems of howitzers held by units
are in very good order'.
   Knowing how splendidly 7.2″ How detachments
performed in the March–April and May battles, the
tribute is well earned.
   The effect of 200 lb shells on enemy morale can
be summed up in one remark by a German officer
taken prisoner North of LONGSTOP 'The fire of
your 24 Heavy guns on my Regiment was quicker
and more accurate than any fire previously
experienced by my men'. Only four 7.2″ Hows
fired on this unit. They were manned by personnel
of 56 Hy Regt and fired 800 rounds in 24 hours.
The impression appears to have been indelible.
                        (Sgd)   J.W.L. Pratt Brigadier,
                            Royal Artillery,
                            HQ Force 141

In the Field.
PWHP/VDS.
Copy for:- Comd. 54 Hy Regt.,
          Comd. 56 Hy Regt.,
          C.C.R.A. 5 Corps (late Comd 1 Hy Regt
          1938–1939)

Officers Commanding,   H.Q.14
R.H.C., 15, 17, 18 & 19 Btys 56 Hy Regt. R.A.

   The above copy of letter is forwarded for
information.
                        S.N. Rand, Captain, R.A.
                        Adjutant, 56th Heavy
                        Regiment, R.A.
Field
30 June 43. W.P.

       Copy to Major Chater Jack, R.A.

OUR FIRST VICTORY

May 7th 1943. In a tent, dripping with rain, battery clerk, L/Bdr Mick (I think I'm ruptured) Haymer, rattled a dodgy typewriter and printed 'Tebourba ¾ reported % clear of ½ enemy, @ leading elements of Armoured Div., dntering etc Tunis & ¾.' That day fighting reached maximum intensity, and at 3.20 Tunis fell. 'We got to engage pockets of diehards holding out on Djbel El Aroussia,' said a man claiming to be a Sergeant.

'Wot's die hards?' asked Gnr Birch.

'Well, when you die you go 'ard,' says White, 'like gangsters in cement.'

'That's why they're called hardened criminals,' says Birch.

'You're a cunt,' says Devine.

'Tunis fallen?! Ups a daisy!'

Had we ordinary layabouts beaten the formidable German Army?

'Dear Fuhrer, beaten ve haff been by zer Ordinary Layabouts, signed Formidable German Army.'

'We won,' said White, as though it had been a game of football. Gunner Lee parts his hair, the comb clogged with a six months pâté of Brylcreem and dust. 'I bet the victory cost Ladbrokes a fortune, we was 100–1.'

'I hear there's fighting in Cap Bon.'

'You must have good hearing, that's 20 miles away.'

We gathered round the Cook House in a gulley adjacent to the now silent guns. Looming behind us is Longstop Hill, a blood drenched salient taken at Bayonet point by the Argylls. In the twilight our ground sheets glistened with rain.

'What's for the victory feast?' says a cheery voice.

Something that went 'Splush!' was dropped in his mess tin.

MP booking a 17-pounder for parking on the wrong side of the battlefield

May 9th 1943. Dawn. Rain stopped. I prod Edgington.

'Awake! for morning in a bowl of light, has cast the stone that puts the stars to flight.'

'Bollocks.'

'No it was Fitzgerald.'

'Fitzgerald's bollocks then.'

The sun rose, angering the morning sky, and Edgington was none too pleased either.

'Wassertime?' he said, as he unstuck his tongue from the roof of his mouth with a spoon.

'It's hours 0600 darling.'

'It's hours too bloody early "darling".'

He opened his eyes with a sound like the tearing apart of fly papers.

Driver Fildes rapped on the window. 'I'm driving to Tunis.'

Edgington sits up. 'Can I come too?'

'It's about time you came to,' I chuckled. The boot missed me, landed in the mud and sank slowly out of sight.

'It's one legged marching from now on,' I tell him.

We set off across the Goubellat Plain to Tunis, following the wake of the victorious 6th and 7th Armoured. We passed smouldering tanks, dead soldiers in grotesque ballet positions, Arab families emerging from hiding, baffled and frightened, and the children, always the children, more baffled and frightened than the rest.

In the Tunis streets the milling throng are thronging the mills. At a café, two German officers drink coffee. Lt Walker asked what they were doing. In perfect broken English they replied, 'Ve are vaiting to be took prisoners old poy.'

We motored slowly through the crowded streets, being kissed several times by pretty girls and once, by a pretty boy.

'No one's kissed me,' complained Gunner Holt, his face like a dog's bum with a hat on.

'Never mind – 'ere comes one now, I'll stamp on her glasses!'

A fat lady with revolving bosoms shouts 'Vive les Americains.'

'She thinks we're Americans,' says Holt.

'We'll slip one up her, then blame them,' says Devine.

A group of 'Eyeties' insist they be taken prisoner or they'll surrender.

'Sorry –' I explain, 'We British Army prisoners.'

The day passed with the drinking of wine and the ogling of women. We were well oiled when two Gunners, The Pills (twins), cadged a lift. 'Either I'm pissed – or he is,' said Devine referring to the twins. The Pills told us the Battery had 'rejoined Regiment on t'other side T'Oued Melah', by sheer luck we found it in t'dark.

'Have you caught it yet?' greeted Bombardier Deans. He held up a half empty bottle. I recognised the gesture at once.

I must have got pretty stoned. When I awoke next morning I was fully dressed, face downwards, on the roof of a lorry, with a severe attack of face.

'On yer bloody feet,' said a fiend sergeant. We were going into action again!! 'He's bottled up in Cap Bon, so no Tunis tata's today.'

Chater Jack consults his map.

'Milligan,' he says, 'we're going into Cap Bon to establish a suitable OP.'

'What's wrong with Lewisham?' I said.

'I've just written home saying – stop worrying, fighting has stopped – now I got to send a telegram saying – Ignore last Letter,' says Driver Shepherd.

'If you want to drive 'em really mad,' I said, 'send a telegram saying – Ignore last Telegram.'

Driver Shepherd has a large boil on his neck covered by a circular plaster. While he slept some artist had drawn a bell push with the word 'press' on it. And they did.

MY DIARY:

'*Motoring inland towards Djbel Bel Oueled. Stop to ask Jerry prisoners the way. Chater Jack takes shortest route twix himself and whisky flask and flags down Mercedes carrying German officers, point blank asks them "Haben ze Schnapps." He gets 3 bottles!*'

A message from RHQ. 'Return to base.'

'What!?' said Chater. Snatching the mike, he shouts 'We've only just bloody arrived, who's buggering us around? We've been up since 0600 will you make up your bloody minds, what is the situation . . .'

All was wasted as he forgot to press the transmit button.

'They're all bloody deaf back there. Drive on, Shepherd.'

The road is a mixture of Allied and Axis transport, groups of Germans talk with British soldiers. It's all very strange. 'Have you any of that fruit cake left, Milligan?'

'No, sir.'

'Just asking, Milligan. It's a hot evening, I don't see why we shouldn't indulge in a dip, got your costume?'

'No sir, I've learnt to swim without it.'

Adjacent to a POW Camp where a brass band played Tyrolean Waltzes, we enjoyed a delicious swim in the Med. starkers, save Chater who wore his knee length 'drawers cellular', something to do with an officer being 'properly dressed'. The sky turned the colour of a cut throat that bled onto the sea.

I swam out about 300 yards then, to my horror, I saw a mine floating towards me. I yelled a warning – 1 part salt water – 2 parts swearing.

British sergeant selling his lorry to an Arab

Chater Jack shouts 'Quick! explode it with small arms, it's ruining the holiday.' We blazed away, and soon a hundred of His Majesty's soldiers were showing what bloody awful shots they were. Finally, with a roar, the monster exploded.

'I hit it!' said Major Chater Jack, 'It was *me*! If anyone contradicts me he'll be on a charge. Now let's get back, it's time for the cooks to poison us.'

MAY 13, 1943

Bright, sunny. Warm. Breeze: Some Gunners go with Chater Jack to see the results of our counter battery work. A conducted tour of shell holes?? Not for me! We bagged a scout car, Fildes, White, Devine and me (not Edgington, he was kneeling in his tent pointing to it and saying 'Down boy'). We stopped outside Tunis, to dust ourselves, then plunged into the streets; at an outdoor café an Eyetie POW trio played Neapolitan songs, then go round with the hat, 'It's yer own bloody fault for losin',' shouts White.

On this day I met a girl in the street. 'Good morning, would you like me to take you home to have some food?' she said. Food? She took me home to 16 Rue de Lyon, and I met her (wait for it) *family*! 'Vive l'Armée Premier' they said, which is no substitute for sex. The girl was Daisy Setbon, 17, Jewish-French, about 5 foot 5, olive skinned, with raven shoulder-length hair. She showed us the sights of Tunis; mostly consisting of drunken British soldiers kipping in the gutter.

I wrote to her for 10 years after the war, when suddenly her letters stopped. All enquiries brought no response. Of course! Plunger Bailey! So! the waiting game had paid off.

That evening we were given a dinner at the Setbons' home as Alf Fildes notes in his diary, *'Had swell meal of spaghetti and beans topped with best red Italian wine.'*

Our truck is missing! We follow a trail of wine and dog

ends and find it in the middle of a square; standing in the driver's seat is another square, Gnr White. A truck full of Tunisians were taking it in turns to wear his hat.

MY DIARY: 14 MAY 1943. AFTERNOON TO 15 MAY.

Try to get watches off Eyetie POWs.

I approached Eyetie POW.

'You got Tick Tock,' I said and did a superb mime of a watch. He took off his boots. 'No. No – Tick Tock – watch . . .'

I got one for forty stale 'V' cigarettes. They must have killed him within the week; I hope so, the watch didn't work.

We got back to camp late, woke the sentry up and said 'Good night!'

May 15th 1943. Off to Tunis again! The Arab drains!!!

'Corrr Christtt,' said Edgington, 'they're worse than Maunders' feet.'

'True!' I said, 'it takes a thousand years of Arab culture to build up a pong like this, sniff it all up, tourists pay for this.'

'How do they know which one's theirs,' said Devine observing women in purdah.

'Easy, outside every wog house there's a weighing machine, and the husbands just check. "Ah it's darling 16 stone 3 lbs."'

'They must have stamina, having twenty wives,' said Devine.

'They don't do 'em all in one go.'

'Ah! but it must be a temptation, I mean, say you have it away with two, you doze off and wake up at, say, 3 o'clock, you get up for a glass of water and well, it would be silly to go back to sleep when there's another eighteen of 'em crawling up the wall. That's why the men wear those long night shirts in the day time, they got to be ready.'

Approaching are Gunners Musslewhite, Roberts and Wilson, riding donkeys and stoned: days later they were found in Sousse with no recollection of anything. Up before Major Chater Jack, the answer to his question, 'What's your excuse?' was 'Pissed sir'.

'Such honesty cannot go unrewarded,' said Chater Jack, 'case dismissed.'

OUDNA

13 May 1943. History of the Regiment says we moved to OUDNA, I won't argue. I was to drive the Major. 'I chose you Milligan because you've never driven me before, and it's time I had another accident.' It was a brief journey.

Oudna was a must for suicides, a barren plain, bisected by a Roman Aqueduct. Observing the ruins Gunner Collins remarked, 'Cor, Jerry didn't 'arf bomb that.' He was never commissioned. We arrived in a great cloud of dust which improved the place. Each soldier's features were obliterated.

I could, however, tell many by the shape of their boots.

OUDNA IDYLL

2.20 p.m. I lay in my tent, the heat was terrific, flies and minute dive bombing insects were at large, on the outside of the mosquito net they hung, waiting . . . occasionally I displaced them with jets of cigarette smoke. Why should I suffer alone. In the next tent was Gunner White.

'Wot you doin'?' I said.

'I'm laying on me back smokin' a Woodbine with me left hand, and scratching me balls with me right.'

'Say hello while you're there.'

'I was thinkin',' he said, 'at this time back in England on a Saturday afternoon, you know what I'd be doing?'

'No.'

'I'd be in my bedroom, layin' on me bed, smoking a Woodbine with me left hand and scratching me balls etc. Wot'd you be doin'?'

'I'd mow the grass in the garden and my father would sit in a deck chair and encourage me with cries of "It does you good lad", and I'd say to him "Why don't you do it then?" and he'd say "Because it doesn't do *me* good, I've tried it".'

'This is a waste of bloody time, my life is going past, time is on the march and here I am on me back in bloody Oudna doing sweet FA. This isn't living! This is . . . this is . . .' he fumbled for a word, couldn't find it and settled for 'fucking terrible . . . what I need in life is variation, something *different*!'

'Right, try smoking with your *right* hand and scratching your balls with your *left*.'

In his tent Edgington starts a tune. 'Lada da da de de' which emerged as 'Red Sails in the Sunset, Way out on the Sea . . .' I joined in harmony, this was taken up by Gunner White and in the next tent to Edge, Gunner Tume. One by one the entire tented camp joined in. I got up. I was the only person visible; from the sea of tents the great chorus 'Oh carry my loved-ed oneeee, home safeleeeee to meeee' soared over the sunbaked plain. No one would have believed it. I didn't.

16 May '43. 'Good morning, Bombardier Milligan,' said Syd Price, fiddling with a camera.

'What do you want?'

'I wish to take a photograph of the Oudna landscape.'

'There isn't one.'

'I know,' said Price, 'therefore, would you and a few like silly buggers care to pose in the foreground to relieve the monotony?'

The result is the only picture ever taken of Oudna to

prove there's no such place. If you are wondering why I'm playing the trumpet, so am I.

'There's a battle scheme starting at 0600 hrs tomorrow.'

We were divided into opposing sides, Ack and Beer – by midday thunder flashes kept exploding everywhere, referees would rush up, chalk you with a white cross and say 'you're dead'. I asked Lt Budden permission to throw a thunder flash under our vehicle so that we could play cards.

'Let's have lunch first.' He pointed to a cool conglomerate of date palms.

A crowd of black faced lunatics jumped us from behind bushes.

'You're all prisoners of Ack Army.'

Says Budden, 'We *are* Ack Army.'

The attackers lowered their rifles, grinning sheepishly and retreated.

'I thought we were Beer Army sir,' I said.

'We don't want *everybody* to know,' said Mr Budden.

A referee roars up. 'You're all casualties,' he said, and marked us with white and red chalk. 'Sign here,' said the referee, 'three dead and two wounded.'

Dutifully Budden signed, the Sgt saluted, mounted his bike, kicked the starter which failed, he kicked again, then several agains, the starter kept sticking, suddenly, when he

(left to right):
Gunners White,
Milligan, Fildes
J. Jnr, Fildes Snr.
Note ack-ack shells
bursting overhead

wasn't ready, it shot back. With a scream he clutched his shin, and well he might, he'd broken it. He lay on the grass, and we radioed up an ambulance.

'Which one is hurt?' said a soppy RAMC orderly.

'I think it's the one on the ground screaming,' said Budden.

As they put him on the stretcher, I marked him with red chalk.

'You bastard,' he said.

We returned to base at the prescribed hour, where dusty and weary, the Battery took tea.

'We must never go to war again,' said Gnr Devine, 'we've lost the knack.'

The great Edgington gave forth: 'Ohhhh,' it says, 'Ohhhhhh,' the sound was from his trembling tent. 'I'm ill. I and my tent are very, very ill.'

He was sweating, steaming, shivering and groaning, a versatile man. He thought me strange for contracting a cold in this climate, now he'd gone one better, he'd got pneumonia. No! he'd gone *two* better, it was *double* pneumonia. We waved as they took him off to dock in a lorry, one man in an empty three tonner, the army were like that. Dutifully we rifled his tent for fags.

VICTORY PARADE

20th May. 'There's to be a Victory Parade!' Vigorous activity followed the announcement, some of it productive. 'A' subsection gun was chosen for the occasion, men swarmed over the piece, the result was a masterpiece of spit and polish, the 7 point 2 looked beautiful. 'My God, we'll never be able to fire that again,' said Sgt Ryan, 'we'll have to get permission from the Pope.'

May 20 1943. The 'Beauteous Artillery Piece' is limbered up and driven under wraps to Tunis. The Parade! Not since

Tunis Victory Parade march past Derbyshire Yeomanry. Our battery's gun in left-hand corner. Note 1st Army shield

*General
Eisenhower
saluting*

Armistice Day, Poona, had I seen the like; on the saluting base were Generals galore! Alexander, Eisenhower, Anderson, Giraud, Admiral Cunningham, Mr Macmillan.

Past the rostrum marched an incredible mixture of soldiers, Camel Corps, Spahis, Americans, Scots, the Irish, The Guards, Goumiers, Greeks, Poles, Czechs, Gurkhas, Rajputs, tanks, armoured cars, in the van came the Free French with that exciting sound of Bugles and Drums, all followed by a small black dog. Pity I didn't have a camera. I'd have taken a picture of myself.

CARTHAGE

22–23–24 May. Our long weekend leave was about to start. Friday till Monday! Where to spend it?

'Edgington,' I said, as I shaved with a thousand year old blade, my face a sea of cuts, 'All my born days I've wanted to see the ruins of Carthage.'

'I think you've only got a pint of blood left,' says Edgington.

'I must hurry.'

'What's a Carthage?' said Doug Kidgell.

'A great archaeological site.'

'Oh?' said Kidgell, 'Why we goin', you got friends there?'

'It's to improve my education.'

'Can't we go to the pictures?' said Kidgell. 'There's Bing Crosby in *The Road to Bali* in Tunis.'

That evening, excited as schoolboys we drove off along the Tunis–Bizerta road, it was as though the war didn't exist, eventually we pulled up on a sandy beach for the night.

There was no moon, but the sky was a pin cushion of stars. Great swathes of astral light blinked at us across space. We made a fire, glowing scarlet in cobalt black darkness, showers of popping sparks jettisoning into the night air. Tins of steak and kidney pud were in boiling water, with small bubbles rising to the surface.

'Gentlemen, a surprise!' I produced a small bottle of Schnapps. 'It fell off the back of a Major Chater Jack.'

'That is a spoil of war,' said Edgington, striking a dramatic finger-pointing pose.

'Well, it's not going to spoil mine,' I said, pouring out the white liquid.

Alf sipped and grasped his throat. 'Christ! If they drink this, they *are* the master race.'

It was fiery stuff.

'It'll kill us,' said Edgington.

He spat a mouthful on the fire, it exploded in a sheet of flame. 'See? When you go to the bog, for Christ's sake don't strike a match.' We mellowed. Harry got hiccups.

Edge: I wonder – hic – what's going to hickhappen to – us next –'

He didn't have long to wait for the answer – a spark shot out of the fire and burnt him.

We sat close to the fire. The smoke kept the mossies away – an occasional brave one would die under hand as it landed.

'Silly sods. I wouldn't risk my life to pass on malaria,' said Fildes. 'I think I'll turn in.'

Through the night a 3 ton lorry, with a mosquito net across the back, was home to four lads from London, who slept sounder and safer than those *in* bomb ridden London. It seemed all wrong, but it was all right to me.

We awoke at first light, and played 'Who's-going-to-make-the-tea?' By ten past 9 no one had given in, finally Edge arises, bent double, bladder bursting. 'I'll make it.' 'He'll only *just* make it,' I thought.

We heard him tinkering about outside, he broke into a little tune.

Don't blame me,
For falling in love with you.
I'm under your spell
But how can I help it don't blame – *BUGGER!*

'How's he going to rhyme that,' I thought. He'd burnt
himself. With Edgington, striking a match could lead to
anything. Edgington tying a boot-lace could end up with a
broken arm. Edgington cutting his toe nails could mean an
amputated leg.

'Come and get it!'

We got it, fried eggs and sand. It was just after 10 a.m.
when Doug put the lorry in gear and started following the
signs.

'What happened at the Carthage?' said Doug, who was
still puzzled.

'It was a great Naval Power! Had a war with Rome, I
forget the score. The Romans razed the city, and ploughed
the ground with salt.'

'How did you know all that?'

'Chambers Encyclopaedia,' I said, 'as a kid I loved
reading. Given a chance I could have been a great scholar,
even University.'

'You could have been a great University?'

'Everyone ought to get a university education,' said Alf.
'I reckon if Harry had been through a university, he might
be writing concertos instead of burning himself makin' the
tea.'

'I think he'd burn himself writing a concerto.'

'Chambers Encyclopaedia?' said Harry. 'I thought that
was the history of Piss Pots.'

We were doing 15 miles an hour, at that speed you could
say 'Look at that', but, at modern speeds it's 'Did you see
that?' Finally, CARTHAGE! We parked by a clump of
trees, and walked to the ruins of the amphitheatre.

It was almost featureless now. What a sight it must have

presented, clad in marble, as high as El Djem, the sun of Africa reflecting its white surface, the roar of crowds, the blood, the mangled remains, like Celtic vs Rangers.

'Is this it?' said Doug.

'Yes.'

'*This* is what I missed Bing Crosby on the Road to Bali for? It's terrible, it's like Catford.'

'One minute you're allying yourself with Nelson and when you see history you say it's Catford! You short arse, I only brought you here because the ruins were low enough for you to see over.'

'Well,' said Kidgell, 'I still say a Carthage is not as good as Bing Crosby in *The Road to Bali*.'

We brewed our tea on the floor of the arena, it was hard to believe blood spilled here 2,000 years ago.

We upped anchors and drove on, finally Doug picked a spot adjacent to a heavily bombed French maritime repair docks.

'Ah!' says Kidgell, 'This looks more like a Carthage.'

He backed the truck under a large tree – a small group of Arabs with 3 donkeys and a camel are passing towards

A postcard I sent home at the time. It shows the amphitheatre at Carthage that Kidgell objected to

135

Tunis. They sell us oranges, eggs, dates and things that look and taste like Pistachio nuts, mainly because they were.

After a day of swimming, we are in bed smoking and talking.

'Got to be back by midday tomorrow – sod it,' said Doug regretfully.

'Good night lads,' yawned Edgington.

'Steady,' I said. 'You haven't had an accident for an hour.'

BACK TO THE BATTERY

We arrived back dead on time, 6 hrs late. What's *this???
Move* at dawn???

'Where to?'

'Somewhere else,' we were told.

'We're already somewhere else,' I said.

'This bloody moving,' said White, 'I should write to my MP.'

'Why don't you?'

'He's a cunt, that's why; he's in the Navy – 2nd Class stoker.'

'If you voted him in you're all cunts.'

'No, we're not, Huddersfield is a very intelligent town.'

Then why did you say it with a small h?'

'Pardon?'

'Huddersfield? They're at the bottom of the third division!'

'Because all their players are in the Kate.* You know how old the current goalie is?'

'No.'

'68. He had 13 own goals and two heart attacks last season.'

* Kate: Kate Carney = Army.

May 30/31 1943–1st June. 'We're here,' said someone. 'We're here' was a place called Ain Abessa. We all leapt enthusiastically from our lorries to be confronted by another desolate plain with a slight rise in the middle.

'That rise, gentlemen,' said Lt Budden, 'is home.'

One afternoon Edgington and I were practising post-war sleeping when the distant voice of L/Bdr Sherwood was heard. 'Oi, you in there.'

'Hello?' (me)

'I bet you I can get you out of that tent in minutes 2.'

'Balls –'

'10 francs.'

'Done.'

'Right – minutes 2 starting *now*.'

We doze on.

'Minutes 1 and 40 secs,' shouts Sherwood.

I hear a combustion engine approaching. I have a nasty feeling: I raise the tent flap. A Bren Carrier is nearly upon us. The bastard! He'd put it in bottom gear, pointed it at our tent and let it loose unmanned!

'Fuck! He's going to win,' says Edgington.

'No, he's not, grab that tent pole, I'll take this one.'

'That was cheating,' said Sherwood as he unscrews his wallet. He had to run 400 yards after the Bren and we had to reset up our tent. All for 10 francs. We were bloody mad.

The Arabs had rifled the tombs of the Pharaohs, now it was our turn. Chalky White was asleep. A brown hand came under the tent flap, White hit it with a pick handle, and there was an agonised, 'Ow fuckin' 'ell.' It was Gunner Devine feeling for White's fags.

FRENCH CONCERT PARTY

Fri. 18th June 1943. 'Milligan? Band is to report to 74 Mediums, music playing, for the uses of.'

At 74 Mediums camp we were greeted by a humptey-

EXTRACT FROM BATTERY ORDERS
by
MAJOR F. CHATER JACK, D.S.O., M.C., R.A.

COMMANDING 19/56 HEAVY REGT, R.A.
FIELD.   11.6.43

---

1. INFORMATION.
   The Battery will be interested to learn that they hold the record for the greatest number of 7.2″ rounds per gun fired in 24 hours.
   The figure is 220 on 23rd April '43 and these, as will be remembered, were on the targets involved in the fight for 'LONGSTOP': the Battery positions being then at TOUKABEUR.
   The next highest figure is 134 r.p.g. fired by two other Btys of 56 Heavy Rgt, during the final attack on 6th May '43 when the two Arm. Divs broke through to TUNIS and the Peninsula.
   Third comes a figure of 80 r.p.g. also fired by 19 Bty on 24th Apl '43 during the final assault on and capture of 'LONGSTOP'.
   During the final battle of MEDJERDA Valley between 22nd April and 6th May, 19 Bty fired a total of 2340 rounds the next highest of any 7.2″ Bty being 1564.

F. Chater Jack
Major, R.A.

COMMANDING 19/56 HEAVY REGT, R.A.
FIELD
11.6.43
AGP

'2,340 rounds? No wonder we were shagged out.'

backed Captain who appeared to be training for death.

'I'd like you to do your turn in the miggle of the show.'

'When?'

'The miggle of the show.' He definitely said mi*ggle* – so! he couldn't pronounce his Ds. 'How woulg you like to be announceg?'

I paused. 'D Battery Dance Duo and Doug on Drums.'

Carefully he wrote it down.

Would we like drinks? OK. The stage consists of trestle tables covered with blankets. I am a trumpet player covered in battle-dress. A charabanc arrived with the Algiers Opera Company. First to alight was Soprano Mlle Beth Villion, she must have been 15 stone, the charabanc rose 3 ft when she got off. 'Cor,' said Harry, 'there's enough for all of us.' She was followed by a petite soprano, Mlle Garcia. 'You're mine, all mine,' says Doug clutching his parts, next came a crazed mop-headed French Algerian Pianist.

A tent had been erected for the ladies to change in. Gunner Liddle detected a hole in it . . . what he saw set his testicles revolving, Mlle Villion was sitting on a stool, naked, making up; Liddle was a sporting man, spread the word. My God! the size! She could sit in one spot and still be several other places at the same time.

The concert started, and finally it was our turn. The Captain announced 'I have great pleasure in announcing G Gattery Gance plus Goug on Grums.' Got 'im! We belted through our numbers, got a great reception, and then cleared for Mlle Garcia. During the interval a human being dressed up as a Gunner approached me. 'You don't know me from Adam,' he said. I told him he must be better dressed. The stranger was Gunner Snashall (Snatch) from the 8th Survey Regiment, he said he played the violin and could he sit in on the next session. OK, we said. It turned out that he was great, a real good Jazz violin player, though the fact that he appeared with a garland of wild flowers around his head was a bit disconcerting.

Mlle Villion in a black silk dress was approaching, her bosoms going on ahead of her by ten seconds.

'You play zee jazz verre good, you naughty boy,' she said.

'Help! massage,' I said weakly.

We listened spellbound as she sang the Habanera from Carmen, her voice was pure silver. In the warm African night, it was an unforgettable experience, with the moon shining down on those lovely white boobs. She stopped the show, but then she was big enough to stop anything. The show over we waved the French artiste and her boobs goodbye. A letter from Snashall reminds me how the evening concluded, 'I remember the French ENSA chara-banc disappearing into the night, then afterwards, Harry, Alf, Doug and I in the back of a 3 tonner with a quarter moon, palm trees, you on guitar playing and us singing, Come Rain . . . Come Shine . . .'

21st June 1943. It was a great day for Alf Fildes. He won 195 francs on Nasrullah in the Derby. He felt good, and decided to buy the lads drinks. It cost him 200 francs.

22nd June 1943. Suddenly came the Bad News. Major Chater Jack was being transferred to another regiment. Sadly he told us, 'I'm leaving you all. I don't want to, but it's promotion, and you know what that means.'

'More lolly,' says a voice.

Sgt Griffin chirps up, 'We're sorry to see you go, sir and we wish you the best of luck,' or something like that. It didn't matter, with his going the Battery was never the same again, we'd never been the same before, but now we were never going to be the same again.

THE NEW MAJOR

His name was Evan Jenkins. His physique? He didn't have one. The nearest description? Tut-an-Khamen with the

Men of the 7th Batt. Black Watch, almost out of their minds with boredom, recreate a Busby Berkeley musical happening

bandages off. His neck measurement would be 11 inches, including shoulders. When a strong wind blew he had to hold his head to stop it from snapping off. His Adam's apple stuck out like a third knee and when he swallowed, it disappeared down the front of his shirt and made him look pregnant. His arms must have been sent from Auschwitz; they were for all the world like two pieces of string with knots tied where the elbows were. His legs were like one of Gandhi's split in two. His eyes were so close together that to look left or right one of them appeared to cross the bridge of his nose. He had a pair of outsize ears which attracted flies. It got him the nickname Jumbo, but despite his comic appearance he was a real bastard; he had us taking our bootlaces out and ironing them so that they were 'nice and flat'. He made us use tooth-paste on our webbing to make it 'Nice and White' while our teeth went black. At night he'd sit in his tent and play 'Whistling Rufus' on a clarinet, and every morning he could be heard gargling with TCP then spitting it back into the bottle, the mean sod. He insisted on giving us cultural lectures. A Sergeant, who shall remain nameless, said 'H'eyes front! now then, today the Major will be talking about ' – (here he referred to a piece of paper) – 'Keats, and I don't suppose one of you higgerant bastards knows what a Keat is.'

23 June 1943. With trees spaced its length, the road to Setif curved hither and thither – we were at a thither part.

'Are those Poplar trees?' said Kidgell.

'Very,' I said. We were bumping our way to the first rehearsal of the Concert Party.

We had been 'talent-spotted' the night of the French ENSA do by L/Bdr Bennett – he had told L/Bdr Carter, 'You must hear these lads.'

Outside the Municipal Theatre, there are posters advertising: GRAND CONCERT. 2 AGRA CONCERT PARTY PRESENTS THE JOLLY ROGERS IN STAND EASY, IN AID OF THE ROYAL ARTILLERY BENEVO-LENT FUND.

It's thirty-two years since then, and so far no benevolence has reached us. The stage was alive with scruffy Gunners hanging up scenery; tuning the piano with a pair of pliers is the MD Gunner Sabin. Edgington confronts him.

'Are you a trained piano tuner?'

'No, that's why I'm in Africa.'

Ken Carter is on stage. 'Up here,' he said, and led us back stage. 'These are your dressing rooms.'

'We don't need 'em. We come ready dressed,' I said.

FIRST NIGHT OF THE CONCERT

Diary of Driver A. Fildes: July 28 1943. 'First night excited but OK.:'

We heard that the French ENSA concert party had gone over a cliff on their way back to Algiers and had been in dock for three weeks, I prayed Mlle Villion's boobs were all right.

The Opening Night was attended by top brass and high ranking local French officials whose sole purpose in life was neither to laugh at, nor applaud anything. Back stage was alive with last minute crises.

Carter is hurrying in all directions, his hair falling out in handfuls, Lance Bombardier Reg Bennett is saying 'Fuck Show Business' over and over again. We four are being made up; blue eye shadow, rouge, lipstick, powder . . . Kidgell looks up, 'Give us a kiss,' he said. I nearly did.

'It looks a good programme,' said Edgington, 'not a spoon player in it.'

Fildes comes up. 'The theatre's packed.'

'Well for Christ's sake unpack it – we're due to start in 10 minutes,' I said.

A vast Gunner, in a vaster vest and shorts, is calling down the corridors,'Beginners please', and spitting out grape pips.

The pit band strikes up a tune which I recognised as 'The King' though I doubt if the Queen would; there follows a strangled version of the Royal Artillery March Past that suggests Gunners are cripples. The curtain rose, crashed down and rose again, the whole cast appear singing 'Kiss the Blues Goodbye'.

The show was away . . .

PROGRAMME OF CONCERT

When our turn came I announced 'Now! from the fabulous star studded 56 Heavy Regiment! the 19 Battery Jazz Quartet!' We started by my putting my trumpet through the curtains, beginning on a low C then dinging up to play 'Softly as in a Morning Sunrise' . . . very loudly . . . Then Kidgell sings 'Tangerine', we feature 'Snatch' on violin in 'Stardust', we round off with Nagasaki (Back in Naga-saki where the fellers chew tobaccy and the women wiggy-waggy-woo).

You can't *describe* a show, you have to *be* there at *that* time with *that* audience, *that's* what made it come alive. Come alive it did; troop audiences went into hysterics at the antics, and we got the sort of applause that would usually only be heard at a Promenade Concert.

A pencilled note at the foot of Part II Orders read: All ranks from now on will walk on their hands to keep their boots clean for parade.

NAVY DANCE BOUGIE

6th July 1943. 'The Navy are holding a dance tomorrow, and they want you to play.'

'How much?' said my Jewish side.

'Sweet FA but all the booze you want.'

'OK.'

'Admiral Cunningham's coming.'

The 'do' was in the huge, school dining-hall. The Navy, with a flair for such occasions, put up coloured bunting. We had finished our show by 9.00; the dance started at 10.00.

The top of the piano was lined with whisky and gin.

'They're for you,' said a snotty.

'I told you we should have joined the bloody Navy,' said Kidgell.

By 10.30, the hall was packed with dancers, the heat of the African night was unforgettable, it was like a gigantic sauna bath. We were getting through the grog. By 11.30 our KDs were black with sweat; still we drove the jazz along. Edgington went into a trance.

'What key are you in?'

'B.'

'I'd better come up ½ a tone and join you.'

We'd start a number but he'd have to wait a few bars to realise what it was. 'Go on,' he'd say, 'I'll catch you up.'

The Wrens looked unbearably attractive in white uniforms and with tanned limbs. Oh the heat! the heat! the limbs! the limbs! by 1.30 I was stoned and making announcements like 'Schel-tage you're parlis for – ha! ha! ha! yes!'

'We're out of fags,' they're saying behind me.

'OK.' I approached Admiral Cunningham who was, despite the 3/4 tempo, dancing in 5/4.

'Excuse me sir,' I said.

'It's not an "Excuse me", soldier.'

'Excuse me sailor then, I wonder if you've got any fags.' He was about to have me flogged but, realising I was the life and soul of the party, produced a packet of ships' Woodbines.

Someone had turned the light out to cool the place – shafts of moonlight lit up the interior.

By 2.00 several Wrens had been molested, several men had been molested, all the booze had been drunk, red whisky-filled faces staggered past, some with partners, sailors were dancing together. At 0230 hrs I've had enough because there was no more. Leaving Harry, Doug and Alf still playing, I pushed through the sweating bodies up the stairs, along the long stone verandah to the classroom where we slept. I'd lost my mozzy net so I emptied my palliasse and got inside. Later: THUD! GROAN! It had to be someone with a big head hitting a stone floor. Harry! of course! it was time for his accident, I got up, forgetting I was in a mattress and crashed to the floor. I pushed my feet through the bottom, and made for what was a huge drunken semi-conscious groaning figure – Sgt Hulland and Kidgell appeared, both naked. We stood round the slumped creature.

'It's Harry,' said Kidgell. 'He's shit himself.'

We dragged him by his lovely legs towards the shower at the end of the corridor.

'Orrgggg Arwagfff,' said the dragee. Standing him on his head, we slid the body from the trousers and reversed same for his shirt; we propped the dead shit-covered body under the shower and turned it on. He slept there all night. I heard a groaning thing approaching. It was 4.30 a.m.

'Let me in,' it said.

'There's no door,' I told it. It walked in, fell onto the bed, which splintered. We heard the head go thud for the second time, and he slept like an angel with a baby smile on his fizz.

There had been a time, when he was but three, his mother tucked him in and gave him his bottle. He'd come a long way since then.

ALF FILDES' DIARY

Alf Fildes' Diary. Wed. 7 July 1943. Sorry to leave Bougie. 60m to Djelli. Rehearsed in Glacier Cinema where we give show. Few civilians here. After short rehearsal we take truck with band and posters to advertise show, funniest thing ever. Afternoon show fair, evening a wow! Standing room only. Crazy gang ad lib bits hilarious.

ON THE ROAD

We packed up and set off to Djelli, 60 miles from Bougie. We drove along the spectacular Gulf of Bougie Road, which hugged the coast. The scenery made mince-meat of tourists' valhallas like Nice, Costa Blanca and Blackpool. We were billeted in rooms back stage. The matinee was not too well booked, but the evening shows were a sell-out, and, of course, the show was forever improving, more and more gags being fed in. It was tending to become a 'Hellzapoppin'. In the show, Sergeant Hulland sang 'Jerusalem', and during this we took up positions behind the curtain, all joining in harmony. Just for fun, Ernie Evans pulled the curtain to reveal the 'Holy Chorus' standing in underpants, towels, with some holding beer mugs.

'If that's the promised land, I don't want to know,' said Carter.

'I've just heard that the invasion of Sicily started at three this morning,' said Alf Fildes in the interval.

At the end of the show we announced the news. The audience cheered. At last things were going *our* way.

Back at Ain Abessa mail is waiting. 'What's this? – Income Tax demand 1938–9?'

'Sir, it has been brought to our notice that in the year 1938/9 you received payments of money as a professional musician (see Sub. d. 3, para. 9, section 76). Will you please remit immediately a list of payments received, dates and by whom the payments were made.' I send the following reply.

Date	Place	Band Leader	Tune	Payment		
				£	s	d
1st Jan. '38	Scrabble Rupture Appliances Ltd Annual Hernia Dance.	Tom Danger.	Sweet Sue (2 chor.). Little Dutch Time Bomb Tick-Tock. Boom.	0	10	1½
				0	14	3
May 6 '39	Dagenham District Ramblers Club.	Eric Knotts.	Honeysuckle Rose.		3	6
Aug. 23 '39	Leeds Cat Crematorium Social.	Sir Henry Wood.	God Save the King.			gratis
June 6 '40	Dunkirk	Gen. Alexander.	The Retreat.			gratis
			Total	£1 – 7 – 10½		

Tuesday 10th August 1943. My Diary. Since the Concert Party terminated, there had been unending demands from all Regiments for its return, so lucky lucky lucky, we start re-rehearsing. We are to do two more shows then fini. It's much the same as the old show except a few changes. Beryl Southby, a girl-friend in Norwood, sent a new tune 'Happy Go Lucky' which we used for the finale.

Sept. 5th 1943. Battery Diary: All light vehicles left for Phillipville staging at Ain Milia.

This means we lost Alf Fildes. We said goodbye, 'see you somewhere some time'. He gave us a thumbs up and a smile as he drove off with the convoy. It was all happening. We were given no rest. Intensive signal training. We had to learn new Signalling Codes, we had to adopt the American phonetics. A used to be Ack, it was now Able, B used to be Beer, it was now Baker and so on. We were told to replace all our old kit, for most of us that meant everything, our KDs were so threadbare the Arabs refused to steal them, my underwear on a line looked like distress signals from shipwrecked tramps.

8th September 1943. Italy have surrendered!

9th September 1943. 5th Army lands at Salerno; there is heavy fighting. 8th Army lands in the South unopposed.

The days that followed were all focused on the wireless news about Salerno, it was obvious that it was pretty tricky going, with the 8th Army hurrying up the coast to link up with the 5th.

On the 13th of September Alexander signalled Churchill, 'I consider situation critical,' of course I didn't know that at the time, no, I had to buy Alexander's Biography in 1973 to find out and by then it was too late for me to worry. It was a near thing! All our vehicles are being waterproofed, it looks like a beach landing.

'Oh yes, waterproof the bloody vehicles, what about us?' says Gunner White, 'it doesn't matter if we drown.'

10th September 1943. Loading party return from Phillipville, where they have been loading vehicles onto cargo ships, we're all puzzled, if we were waterproofing vehicles why are they on cargo ships????

'Somewhere, Harry,' I said, 'there is a lunatic. Every day

Churchill listening as troops of the 1st Army address him

he's taken from Colney Hatch, locked in a room with a phone at the War Office, he phones through a series of orders and these are transmitted directly to us.'

Edgington nodded his head and laughed. 'It's something like that,' he said.

Now dear reader, a blank appears in my memory, all there is in my diary is the word PISSED. This happened between Sept. 10th and the 11th. But I recall arriving back in a lorry with Edgington to Ain Abessa to discover the Camp deserted.

'They've deserted without us,' said Edgington jumping down.

'Wait! an oil lamp glows in yon Nissen hut,' I said.

A figure filled the doorway. It was Bdr Fuller. 'Where's everybody?' I said.

'They've gone to secret destination 397,' says Fuller donning his crash helmet.

He gave us 15 minutes to pack any gear we had left in the

Nissen hut. We were all a bit dazed by the change of events, here we were looking forward to a good night's sleep, and now we were off to somewhere.

'This is an outrage,' said Edgington as he strained, lifted and hurled his kit onto the lorry.

'It's also an inrage,' I said, carefully mixing my kit with his.

'We've got to catch up with the main convoy,' said Fuller, 'they're 10 hours ahead.'

'Australia's only 8.'

'Let's chase that – it's nearer.'

'Hurry up,' shouts Fuller, 'we're keeping Adolf waiting.'

'Fuck 'im,' said a voice under some strain.

'Right away.' Edgington slams the tailboard, and bangs on the side.

Sept. 11/12 1943. My Diary. Caught up with main convoy at 0500 hrs just outside Ain Milia. Breakfast amid olive groves. Bought delicious green grapes in village. Convoy is waiting for a lost truck to turn up, by midday no sign of it, so we all push on again:

I spent the whole day asleep in back of truck only waking for food. By nightfall we had arrived at Ghardimaou, it was so dark I've no idea what the place looked like. I went on sleeping as fast as I could so we could get there quicker, I slept all night and only awoke when Gunner Edgington said ''Ere Rip Van Watsit' and gave me a cup of tea.

We walked to the Wireless Truck for the 7 o'clock news about Salerno. The announcer was saying, 'Three attacks by Panzers were thrown back in the night.' It all sounds dodgy.

A huge formation of Baltimore Bombers passed overhead in the direction of Sicily. 'That ought to cheer the lads up,' said Ben Wenham. 'If they're American, they're as likely to drop the bloody lot on *us*,' said White.

Drivers are warming up their engines, they are dispersed

among the olive trees, affording ideal camouflage for the vehicles which are painted black and green.

'Prepare to move!' The order rings through the camp. Diesel fumes turn the air blue, gradually the convoy pulls onto the 'road', the leader raises his hand, drops it, and we pull away. This was a slow convoy pulling heavy guns, the speed averaged thirty miles an hour. We had crossed the border into Tunisia and were passing familiar battle grounds where the skeletons of German tanks lay rusting. In the fields, amid grazing sheep, Arabs are re-working the land, ploughing round the shell holes. We passed acres of cork trees and groves of eucalyptus trees, it all seemed so peaceful, yet here we were, obviously headed for Salerno and bloody hell! We passed Sidi Nsir where the gallant 155 Battery had made their stand against General Lang's 10th Panzer and Mark VI Tanks of 501 Heavy Tank Bn17, the guns were fought to the muzzle, only 9 Gunners survived but they put paid to the German advance.

Sept. 14. Thank God! Pay Parade! What's this? It's in lire? So it is Italy for sure. We are given a small booklet. Customs and language of Italy.

'It says the Italians are very jealous of their women, and in the South they are usually chaperoned . . .'

'Wot's chaperoned.'

'Means they orlways got someone wiv 'em.'

'Oh? What 'appens if you want to 'ave it away wiv her.'

'Well the chaperon 'as to be done as well, otherwise they won't let you do it at all.'

The daily routine: Morning Parade with Small Arms.
Maintenance and training.
Lunch.
Afternoon off.

The afternoon was spent doing laundry and writing letters in the NAAFI. Usually a lorry went down to a great surf beach at Cap Blanc just outside Bizerta, which was crowded with American troops. The sea here has huge breakers and great fun was had by diving into them, or coming in surf-board style.

From the 15th to the 20th we passed the time as best we could, and it wasn't good enough. Apparently we were waiting for landing craft from Salerno; they had stayed longer than anticipated, as at one stage it seemed as though they would have to evacuate the beach-head. We played football games that went on for hours with sides of up to 50, scores like 63 goals to 98 were not uncommon. Our MO described the camp as the only lunatic asylum run by the inmates. I wrote home to my brother

Dear Hairy,

Don't ask me what is happening. It's whispered that the war is over and no-one has the nerve to tell us. The American troops don't know what we are, they drive past in Cadillacs, throw us

The Afrika Korps having lost North Africa try to play their way back to favour with the Führer

*sweets and ask where our sisters are. We play 500 a side
football, it's the only way one can get a game. The NAAFI
queue is nine miles long, the men at the front are from World
War One. Our major wants us to invade Italy so he can see
Vesuvius 'before it goes out'. He is a brilliant soldier and can
almost dress himself. It's a very trying time. Try it. Love to
Mum and Dad.*

Ever loving Brother known as 954024

*22 September 1943: Battery Diary: First Party embarked (Part
of HQ, 17 and 19 Batteries).*

In terms of the physical it started when a crowd of our
officers started to run at high speed in all directions crashing
into one another and finally disappearing into the HQ Tent,
shoe sides bulged outwards with the combustion of Commissioned Ranks within. Suddenly the tent flaps burst
open, and out thunder the officers. Lt Pride says, 'We're off
lads, as usual it should all have been done yesterday,' a great
scramble ensues, and by ten o'clock we are on the way to
whatever it was we were on the way to, which turns out to
be Bizerta Docks. Some Hundred LST are lined up, jaws
open, waiting to devour us. Through the stifling day, in that
peculiar muddled British style, we load our vehicles onto
the HMS *Boxer*, we watch her sink lower and lower in the
water, as hour after hour we pile our gear aboard.

'There's no bunks, sleep wherever you can,' said Lt
Pride.

We are issued with seasick pills. I never suffer from this
so I threw them over the side where fish ate them and were
immediately sick.

'It's all very exciting,' says Kidgell. 'Wonder what they're
going to do with us.'

'First make us sea sick, and when we are vomiting at our
limit, land us on a beach in Italy under shell fire.'

The ramp is being winched up. ''Ello, we're off then,' the

HMS Boxer, *the LST that took us to Salerno*

engines throb into 'Hard Astern', we hear the ring of the ship's telegraph. We pull away from the jetty, we are all lining the railing. It's six o'clock as we pull into the middle of Lac de Bizerta.

'Well,' says Doug Kidgell, rubbing his hands with excitement, 'we're off at last,' whereupon we drop anchor.

'You were saying?' I said.

There's a cool breeze from the sea. 'Grub up,' we all troop down to the galley where containers of hot stew are opened and doled out with a mug of ship's cocoa.

'Like a fag?' A sailor, short and squat, holds out a fifty tin of ships' Woodbines, in those days a luxury. 'Ta,' I said with a certain amount of surprise.

'Take a handful,' he said. 'This is a trap,' I thought.

'You're not queer are you,' I said.

His name was Eddie Hackshaw. As darkness fell there was a feeling of frustration on board, so I got out me bugle and, down on the mess deck, blew some tunes. Eddie Hackshaw was so pleased he gave me a silver Arab ring.

'It will bring you good luck,' he forecast.

'Good luck?' I said. 'What's that.'

He wangled an extra mug of cocoa for me before we all

settled for the night. Doug Kidgell and I slept on top of his Scammell. It was incredibly quiet. We could hear the lap of waves against the ship.

As I lay, stretched out on top of the huge Scammell lorry, believing I would surely die at Salerno, I started to cogitate on my Will, the last one I had made out was when I was due to get killed in the North African landings, however, we had arrived too late. My most expensive possession was my trumpet, I wanted that buried with me in case I am buried alive, I could blow a few bars and they would dig me up again. Second most expensive item, twenty Wills Woodbines in an old tobacco tin. Then there were the women . . . 'Listen to this Kidgell – I want you to be a witness, it is my last Will and Testament.'

'You making it out on top of a lorry?' he said in disgust.

'No better place – listen, my women – I leave Ivy Chandler and three Woodbines to Gunner Chalky White. I leave Kay of Herstmonceux to Gunner Devine, I leave Betty Ormsman and one Woodbine to Gunner Kidgell.'

'Is that the one with the big boobs?'

'Yer.'

'Smashing . . . but only one Woodbine?'

'That's all you'll have time for with her! . . . Now to Gunner "Plunger" Bailey, I leave Shirley Wright, Mrs Eileen Leech and Molly Parkinson.'

'That's not enough for 'im.'

'It'll have to do . . . this is an emergency . . . Now to my mother, I leave my brother, to my father I leave my mother.'

'Wot you going to leave your brother?'

'I'm going to leave him alone . . .'

Those were the last thoughts as I dropped into a sleep that would terminate in Volume IV . . . what time will Bombardier Milligan arise, what will be his first words to the dawn . . .? Read all about it in Volume IV, order your copy to-day. I need a reason to start writing it.

'I wonder why we're waiting?' I said as I threw my stub-end over the side.

'We're waiting for the tide,' says Kidgell.

'That's the best news I've had.'

'Why?'

'The Med's tideless.'

VOLUME FOUR

MUSSOLINI:
His Part in My Downfall

SALERNO

THURSDAY, SEPTEMBER 23, 1943

My Diary: Still at war! Early closing in Catford, read letter from mother saying Chiesmans of Lewisham are so short of stock, the manager and staff sit in the shop miming the words 'sold out'.

Dear Reader, the beds in the Dorchester Hotel are the most comfortable in England. Alas! neither Driver Kidgell nor Lance-Bombardier Milligan are in a bed at the Dorchester – no! they are trying to sleep on a 10-ton Scammell lorry, parked on the top deck of 4,000-ton HMS *Boxer*, inside whose innards are packed 19 Battery, 56th Heavy Regiment, all steaming in the hold; from below comes the merry sound of men retching and it's all from Gunner Edgington. We are bound for Sunny Salerno. For thirteen days since the 5th Army landing, a ferocious battle had ensued on the beach-head. Even as we rode the waves we knew not what to expect when our turn came. The dawn comes up like Thinder. *Thin*der Yes, that's Thin Thunder. 'Shhhhhh,' we all shout. The chill morning air touches the khaki somnambulists sleeping heroically for their King and Country. We are awakened by Gunner Woods in the driving cab, who has fallen asleep on the motor horn. A puzzled ship's Captain is wondering why he can hear the sound of a lorry at sea. Kidgell gives a great jaw-cracking yawn and that's him finished for the day. He stretches himself but doesn't get any longer. Deep in his eyes I see engraved the word, 'TEA'. 'Wakey wakey,' he said, but didn't. The ship is silent. The helmsman's face shows white through the wheel house.

'It is Dawn,' yawns Kidgell.

'My watch says twenty past,' I yawned.

'Yes! It's *exactly* twenty past Dawn,' he yawned.

We yawned. Like a comedy duo, we both stand and pull our trousers on; mistake! he has mine and vice versa. The light is growing in the Eastern sky, it reveals a great grey convoy of ships, plunging and rising at the dictation of the sea. LCTs. LCTs, some thirty of them, all flanked by navy Z-Class destroyers. The one on our port bow is stencilled B4. Imagine the confusion of a wireless conversation with it.

'Hello B4, are your receiving me?'

PAUSE

'Hello B4 answering.'

PAUSE

'Hello B4, why didn't you answer B4?'

'Because we didn't hear you before.'

In the early light the sea is blue-black like ink. Kidgell is carefully folding his blankets into a mess, 'I haven't slept that well for years'.

'How do you know?' I said. 'You were asleep.'

He chuckled, 'Well it *feels* like I slept well.'

'Where did you feel it, in the legs? the elbows? teeth?' I was determined to pursue the matter to its illogical conclusion; I mean if *sane* people are going around saying 'I slept well last night', what would lunatics say? 'I stayed awake all night so I could see if I slept well'?

The Tannoy crackles. 'Attention, please.'

A Gunner faints. 'What's up?' we ask.

'I thought I heard someone say please.'

'Attention . . . this is the Captain speaking . . . (What a good memory he had) . . . In three minutes the Ack-Ack guns will be firing test bursts . . . this is only a practice, repeat, practice.'

Soon the sky was festooned with erupting shells, black puffs of smoke with a red nucleus from the barrels of the multiple Pom Poms. The Tannoy again.

'Hello this is your –' a burst of amplified coughing follows.

'It's the resident consumptive,' I said.

The coughing ceases. 'Attention, that practice firing will be repeated every morning at –' coughing – coughing – 'at' – coughing . . .

The helmsman's face showed white through the wheel house.

'I feel a sudden attack of roll-call coming on,' I said.

I was right. Sgt King lines us up on deck. We answer our names and anyone's that isn't there; even if they called 'Rasputin' a voice answers 'Sah.'

'Milligan?'

'Sah!'

'Devine?'

'Sah!'

'Edgington? . . . Edgington?'

From the deck below comes a weak voice 'Sah!' followed by retching.

Britannia rules the waves, but in this case, she waives the rules. A roar of engines, the Spitfires return, we all get up again. They repeat roaring back and forth through the day, we get used to it, we get so used to it that when a Focke Wolfe shoots us up, we're all standing up, aren't we?

SEPTEMBER 24, 1943

Regimental Diary: HMS Boxer landed first party on Red Beach, Salerno Bay at 0940 hrs.

The ship touched the beach very gently, so gently I suspect it's not insured. 'Sorry about the bump, gentlemen,' said a chuckling Navy voice on the Tannoy. A cheer arose from the lads as the landing ramp was lowered. Another salvo from *Warspite*. At the same time an American supply ship starts to broadcast Bing Crosby singing 'Pennies from Heaven' over its speakers. To our right, over the Sorrento peninsula, a German plane is flying very high; pinpoints of high bursting Ack-Ack shells trace his path.

*Lorries and guns coming ashore at Red Beach, Salerno. Note
the man in the foreground with two broken forearms – now going
for broken legs to get his ticket*

Time 9.30. Sea calm.

The Tannoy crackles. Another coughing demo? No.

'Hello, is it on? – Hello, Captain Sullivan speaking.'

'Give us a song, Captain,' shouts Gunner White.

'Attention, will all men without vehicles, repeat, without
vehicles, please disembark first?'

'I think I'm without vehicles,' I said to Harry. 'How
about you?'

'No, I haven't got vehicles, but they might be incuba-
ting,' says Edgington, who is, now that the sea is calm, back
to his cheery self; the roses haven't come back to his cheeks,
but he tells me they're on their way. 'They have reached my
knees and are due in me navel area this afternoon.'

The Tannoy: 'Will men without vehicles disembark now?'

'We've been spoken for, Harry,' I said as we trundle down the gangways to the 'Floor' of the *Boxer*. We were about to set foot on Italy. The jaws of the *Boxer* are opened onto a sunlit beach.

'I could never have afforded all this travel on my own,' I say. 'It had to be the hard way, World War 2. I've always wanted to see Russia, I suppose that would mean World War 3.'

I don't believe it, we were walking down the broad ramp onto the Salerno beaches, no bullets! no shells! and I didn't even get my feet wet, as I leave my first footprint in the sand. I shout loudly 'TAXI', and point in the direction it's coming from. 'The woods are full of them,' I add.

We move in a milling throng on to the beach. I start the sheep bleating and soon we are all at it, much to the amusement of the seamen watching from top deck. The scenery by L/Bdr Milligan: the beaches are a mixture of volcanic ash and sand, the colour of milky coffee, it stretches left and right as far as the eye can see. Strewn along the beaches is the debris of a battle that had raged here; an occasional German long-range shell explodes in the bay. There are no hits. The beaches vary from twenty to thirty yards deep. Back from this is a mixture of pines, scrub, walnut trees and sand hillocks mounted with Tuffa grass. Bulldozers have made clearways flanked by white ribbons denoting them mine-free. There is activity the length and breadth of the shores. Great ammo dumps are, as we watch, getting higher and bigger. Just inland, Spitfires are refuelling and about to take off from a makeshift airstrip. American Aero-Cobras are revving their engines, turning into the wind and taking off in the direction of Naples.

We all stand well back far away from any work, and watch the confusion of unloading the vehicles. Officers and Sergeants are weaving back and forth saluting, shouting.

'What *are* they doing?' says Edgington.

'I think they're trying to win the war,' I said.

'Why?' he said. 'I'm satisfied with it as it is.'

Kidgell's Scammell lorry is emerging from HMS *Boxer*. I ponder the logic that gives a driver of five foot five inches a giant lorry to drive that necessitates him putting an orange box on the seat before he can see out. Gunner Devine has taken his boots and socks off and is paddling in the sea; an irate officer shouts at him, 'Hey, you! What do you think you're doing?'

'I think I'm paddling, sir,' was the reply.

'Paddling? This isn't bloody Blackpool.'

'I know that, sir, Blackpool's in England.'

'Get dressed at *once* and report to me!'

Nice Lt Budden is approaching.

'Hands up all the men who want to go to war!'

There is a massive negative response. He points at me.

'*You*. Milligan.'

This was victimisation!

'There must be some mistake, sir. I'm eighty-six and a cripple.'

Salerno Beach. Soldiers treasure-hunting

He points. 'Over there, 25-year-old liar.'

I clamber on to Sherwood's bren carrier to be taken to a premature death. The carrier is overloaded, I perch on top. Budden sits in the passenger seat looking at maps. We roll across the sand hills; it's not easy for me to stay on, so with consummate skill I fall off.

'Stop being silly now, Milligan,' says Mr Budden.

I remount. This time I jam myself between two kitbags. We reach a secondary road and – here comes the bonus – we pass the Temple of Neptune and Cerene, at Paestum, both looking beautiful in the sunlight. Strung from the Doric columns are lines of soldiers' washing. At last they had been put to practical use. If only the ancient Greeks had known.

'We are to establish an OP, somewhere up there,' Budden points to the mountainous country ahead.

I hated OPs; when they were quiet they were quiet, but when the shit was flying it was a dicey place. We pass several burnt-out tanks, mostly ours; that's the trouble, Jerry had better tanks. We were trying to get away with superiority in numbers, very unfair on our tank crews. We never had any armour to match the Tiger, or the Jag Panther. The shades of night were falling fast as we went through Battapaglia past the ruins of the Tobacco factory that had been a bloodbath for both sides.

My Diary: Got on to narrow road to Mango. Road jammed with vehicles, two trucks ahead struck by jerry mortars. Study for nearly two hours.

Progress is slow, road jammed with vehicles, very dark now, ahead is a glow of a large fire. Lt Budden dismounts, he is coming towards us with a face that says Confusion Unlimited, and he appears to be the Managing Director.

'That's the mountain there,' he points to a mountain that is so big it doesn't need pointing to. Still I take his point. 'We've got to get up that.'

'We need a ladder, sir.'

18 Battery negotiating a difficult road near Sipicciano; note sergeant in foreground, hoping lorry will run over him

'How we going to get a bloody bren carrier up there?' says Birch.

'Post it.'

He tried to hit me.

A Despatch Rider is riding up from down behind us calling out 'Any 19 Battery here? . . . Any 19 Battery here? . . .'

Birch says 'Yes.'

Silly sod! *Never* answer anything in the Army, too late now. It's Don R. Lawrence. He tells us we have to take the bren carrier and go back to pick up a wireless set which has just arrived from the beach, and Captain Sullivan on another truck is going to the OP, so we breathe a sigh of relief, we start extricating the bren carrier from the congestion, marvellous, when we've almost got it out the bloody thing breaks down, we struggle and manage to push it onto its side to allow the traffic through. Budden tells us, 'We'll have to walk to HQ and get fresh orders.'

I tell him I don't need fresh orders, I'm perfectly satisfied with the ones I've got.

'Please, Milligan,' say's Budden, '*try* and be a soldier.'

We finally reach RHQ. It's off a walled lane in an Italian farmhouse, built around a forecourt two storeys high; an exterior staircase leads up to the first floor, which is surrounded by a balcony. The farm is blacked out except the room where *our* HQ is, that is a mass of light chinks coming from windows and doors like an early *Son et Lumière*. Several vehicles are parked in the forecourt. The drivers are asleep in the back. Twenty minutes pass. Mr Budden appears, he smells of Whisky, the khaki after-shave for men. He is much happier.

'We are not needed, Milligan,' he says.

'Does that mean for the duration?'

We both walk back to the gun position, which is easily found. We just followed the loudest bangs.

SEPTEMBER 25, 1943

I awoke, sat up, yawned. I felt as tired as though I had not slept. A morning mist is rapidly disappearing. It swirls around the head of Monte Mango.

A voice is calling across the land, 'Bombardier Milligan.'

'Bombardier Milligan is dead,' I call in a disguised voice.

The voice replied, 'Then he's going to miss breakfast.'

Good God! it's nearly nine! I just get to the cookhouse in time to have the remains of powdered eggs, bacon and tea that appears to have been all cooked together.

'You slept late,' says Edgington.

'I'm training for sleeping sickness.'

We are now gathered around the Water Waggon doing our ablutions. Edgington is at the lather stage, peering into a mirror the size of a half crown propped on a mudguard. He was moving his face clockwise as he shaved. I had stripped to the waist, which brought cries of 'Where are you?' I had my head under the tap enjoying the refreshing cascade of chlorinated cold water, at which time, twelve FW 109s are enjoying roaring out of the sun, guns hammering, there's a God-awful scramble, we all meet under a lorry. I caught a glimpse of the planes as they launched their bombs on the 25-pounder regiment behind us.

'Look out,' warns Edgington, when the planes were half way back to base. He hurled himself face down. 'All over.' We stand up, Edgington presented a face, half lather, dust and squashed grapes.

What was I laughing at? One moment I was well. Next moment I was on my knees vomiting. It was unbelievable. I became giddy, kept seeing stars and the Virgin Mary upside down.

'Report sick,' says Bombardier Fuller.

'You're so kind,' I said.

They took me to the Doc, who said I had a temperature of 103.

'What *have* you been doing?' he said.

'I was washing, sir.'

Having a temperature of 103 allowed you to stop fighting. No but seriously, folks, I was ill! Oh I *was ill*!! The war would have to go on without me! In a bren carrier they took me shivering with ague to the Forward Dressing Station. It was a small tented area off a rough track; a Lance-Corporal, tall, thin with spectacles, took my details, tied a label on me, I think it was THIS WAY UP.

'That stretcher there,' he said.

So, they were going to stretch me! I felt a bit of a fraud. Around me were seriously wounded men. Some were moaning softly. A chubby Catholic Priest, about forty-five, red faced, blond hair going grey, walked among us.

'What's wrong with you, son?'

'I got fever.'

'Fever?'

'Yes. Disappointed, father?'

*Loading a 7.2 – to the right, Monte Stella; to the left, Monte
Mango*

He grinned, but it didn't wipe the sadness off his face. He
told me they were awaiting the arrival of some badly
wounded men from the Queen's.

'They were trying to take that.' He nodded towards
Monte Stella.

Three jeeps arrived with stretcher cases. Among them is a
German, his face almost off. Poor bastard. There was a
trickle of wounded all afternoon, some walking, some on
stretchers, some dead, the priest went among them carrying
out the last rites. Was this the way Christ wanted them to
go? The most depressing picture of the war was for me the

blanket-covered bodies on stretchers, their boots protruding from the end. For my part I kept falling into a delirious sleep, where I told General Montgomery to sing 'God Save America' with his trousers down. When I awoke it was evening. I'd been lying there about four hours.

It was four stretchers to an ambulance; in between with his back to the driving cab sat an orderly. The inside was painted white. The vehicle smelt new. A blood plasma bottle was attached to the soldier on the lower bunk, his chest swathed in bandages. The orderly constantly checked the flow of the plasma. The German kept groaning. It all seemed to be coming to me through a heat charged mist. I was hovering twixt delirium and reality. I doze off.

The ambulance stops, near-by artillery are banging away, the doors open, it's dark, voices mixed with gunfire, I am being unloaded. I'm on the ground, from there a large municipal building with a flat roof is silhouetted against the night sky. Covered with ivy, it looks like the setting for *Gormenghast*. I am carried up stairs along corridors, more stairs, and finally into a dim-lit ward of about thirty beds, all with mozzy nets down. I am placed on the floor.

'Can you undress yourself?' says an overworked orderly.

Yes, I can.

'The pyjamas are under the pillow,' he points to a bed.

My God, it looked good, already turned down, white sheets and pillows, TWO PILLOWS, being ill was paying dividends. I pulled on the standard blue pyjamas.

'Where's the karzi?' I said weakly.

He pointed out the door. 'Dead opposite.'

I wasn't quite dead but I went opposite; that journey over, I pulled my body under the sheets. I was desperately tired and feverish, but stayed awake to enjoy the luxury of sheets. Another orderly; they all wear gym shoes so you don't hear them coming, he took my pulse, temperature, entered them on a board that hung on the foot of my bed.

'Like some tea?' He spoke Yorkshire.

'Aye,' I said in Yorkshire.

'Anything to eat?'

'Yes, anything.'

He came back with a plate of tomato soup and bread. On the tray were four white tablets.

'Take these when you dun, they'll help bring temperature down.'

'I don't want it down, I want it up for the duration.'

I gulped it down. Took the tablets, brought them all up. Who said romance was dead? So much for my first forty-eight hours in Italy.

THURSDAY, SEPTEMBER 30, 1943

BRILLIANT RECOVERY FROM SANDFLY FEVER BY HUMBLE L/BOMBARDIER

So the headlines should have run, all I got was a Lance Corporal suffering from incurable stupidity, who said, 'Bombardier Millington?'

'That's almost me,' I said.

'You are to be discharged tomorrow.'

'I understand that my name is now Millington and I am to be discharged as fit.'

'Yes, RTU★.'

RTU? That had me, so I sang it to a Novello tune 'RTU again whenever spring breaks through.' (Groans).

He blinked and made me sign a piece of paper that in as many words said, 'We have tried to kill this man but failed.'

'You will be ready by 0830 hours and take the unexpired portion of your day's rations.'

Unexpired rations? The mind boggled. I started a series of farewells and looked deeply into the eyes of all the nurses with a look that said quite positively, 'You're lucky I never screwed you,' and they looked back with a smile that said,

★ Return to Unit.

'When you've been promoted to Captain, knock three times.'

OCTOBER 1, 1943

It's a mixed day, a soufflé of sun and cloud. Outside the 76th General a 3-tonner truck is waiting like a wagon at the Knacker's Yard. A short squat driver with a squint in his left eye 'finds' and calls our names out from a bit of tacky paper. 'Lance Bombardier Mirrigan?'

'Yes, that's me,' I said. 'Lance Bombardier Mirrigan.'

He calls out the names of several more soldiers of the King, who at the sight of them would abdicate. I enquire where we are being taken.

'Corps Reinforcement Camp.' He pronounced the word 'Corpse'. An Omen.

The journey seemed endless. 'Where in God's name are they taking us?'

'I tink,' said the Mick, 'dey are just querying us.'

As quick as it started the rain stopped, the sun came out. Soon we were all steaming like wet laundry. At midday the lorry arrives at a field of tents, fronted by a farmhouse; there is a sign: Corps Reinforcement Unit. We are shown into the HQ office. A Corporal seated behind a desk:

'Name? Number? Religion? Regiment?' He tells us, 'You are here to await pick-up by your regiments.'

'How long will that take?' I said.

He frowns. I've broken the code! 'Well, I don't exactly know, so far no one has picked up anybody, we've only been 'ere for a week, so it will take a while for 'em to find the location. There are tented lines, two men to a bivvy. Part 2 Orders are posted on the board outside.'

We walked along the line of muddy tents. I find an empty one. I see men walking rapidly with empty mess-tins; food! I follow. We arrive at a field kitchen. Food??!! Two slices of cold bully beef, a carrot, a boiled potato. A mug of tea, two biscuits. No mess tent, eat where you stand.

We squat in our tents, smoke and talk. At this camp there was a morning roll-call at 7.00, breakfast from 7.30 to 8.30, then Parade at 9.00, the rest of the day you did what you could with a muddy field and two hundred tents. There was no transport, no entertainment, no money. The boredom was unbelievable. I mean, if a man sneezed, it was considered entertainment. The camp was about three hundred yards from Red Beach, Salerno. For the next three days Arrowsmith and I just foraged around, collecting walnuts and looking for war souvenirs. We had the occasional bathe, but the water was getting that first autumnal chill that made swimming nippy.

The Pioneer Corps were on the beaches collecting war salvage, all middle-aged men. We talked to them. Why did they join up?

'Anyfink ter git away from the bleedin' wife.'

They are all old soldiers, some from World War I, they are well organised. At lunch they light a fire on the beach, and are soon frying eggs and bacon.

'Like some grub?' says their Sergeant.

'Christ, yes,' I said.

The Sergeant is a Londoner, he's about fifty, big, burly and used to be a fish porter at Billingsgate.

'I wos gettin' fed up, so I fort, 'ave a go in the Pioneer Corps. When they knowed I bin a sergeant in World Woer I, they makes me a sergeant right away, so strite on I'm orl rite fer lolly.'

He tells us about the 'perks'.

'The CO 'e says, go orf and get some salvage, so we takes a day's rations, bully bread cheese an' all that, we piss orf somewhere and swop the bully and cheese fer Eyetie eggs or chickens, an' we live like fightin' cocks, but', he giggled, 'we don't do no fitin'.'

For two days we met them on the beach and gave them a hand picking up empty ammo boxes, shell cases, and were rewarded with marvellous grub; the last day they brought three bottles of white Chianti, we got back to the camp that evening very merry. We had also solved sleeping in the mud. Three hundred yards east of our camp in a field, I spotted a small hut on legs; these are apparently farmhands' resting places during the hot harvesting season, made of straw, with wooden slats for the supporting skeleton. It was lovely! dry and warm.

Suddenly, with no warning we have to move. A back-breaking twenty-four hours loading stores on to lorries, again in the pouring rain. The Major (his name escapes me, but I think it was Castle) must have felt pity, for as the Bombardier and I sat in the empty storeroom, soaked, he brought in a bottle of whisky, and poured a liberal amount into our tea mugs.

'You've worked very well, Millington, I appreciate it, it's been a bloody hard boring time setting up this unit, we've had bugger all co-operation, all the stores, etc., have all been rushed up to the front lines, that's why the food's been so bloody awful, but this place we're moving to, things will be much better.'

OCTOBER 10, 1943

WE MOVE TO A NEW DEPOT

The new depot was at the north end of a coastal town called Castellammare di Stabia. We were to occupy a great railway repair depot, now deserted. It had been hammered by our planes, but two-thirds remained intact. There were plenty of empty goods wagons which we immediately used for store-rooms and billets; they were ideal, about six men to a wagon. Now it was hard to go 'off the rails'.

I spent two days putting up shelves and organising the stores. The Major's promised improvement in living standards never materialised, it got worse, no guarantee of our seven a day cigarette ration, I went four days without a cigarette, I got withdrawal symptoms. The pupils of my eyes dilated to pinpoints; my night manipulations increased until the skin was rubbed off and I spoke in a high strained voice on the verge of a scream.

OCTOBER 15, 1943

Thank God!! 'You are being transferred,' said the RSM, whose name was Death. (What happened if he was killed in Action? We regret to announce the death of Death?) 'You are being transferred to the CPC.'

I envisaged another endless lorry journey, but no!!! It was in the same marshalling yard. I wrote home and told my folks I was now serving under Marshal Yard. This time I was billeted on the edge of the Complex. It was a building, one-time offices, I was in a basement with windows at ground level. Outside, the River Sarno ran past the window, looking left I could see the beach, and offshore the Isola Revigliano with the remains of a Roman lighthouse. Just what I needed!

Towering above the countryside, with vines growing on its lower slopes, was the ominous shape of Vesuvius, like me it smoked heavily. At night, from my bed, I could see the purple-red glow from its throat, it looked magnificent. At one time it had looked so to those doomed people, the Pompeians, but I wasn't a Pompeian, I was Irish, how could Vesuvius wipe out Dublin? No, I was perfectly safe, but Vesuvius wasn't. I discovered that Pompeii was but three miles as the crow flies. This incredible relic of a Roman city free of camera-clicking tourists was a situation I had to thank Hitler for. Thank you, Hitler!

HITLER: You hear zat, Goebbels? Milligan is visiting Pompeii. Keep all tourists out, and zer ruins *in*!

After roll-call, accompanied by a Private Webb, we

hitched and walked till we arrived at the gates. There was no one about, save a sleepy unshaven attendant, who said he had no tickets and charged twenty lire to go in, which he put straight into his pocket. It was a day I shall treasure, a day I met the past, not only the past but the people from it, be it they were now only plaster casts. I had read Pliny the Younger's account of that terrible day of destruction, *Gells Pompiana* and several text-books, so I was reasonably well informed. We had gone in the entrance that opened onto the amphitheatre and the Grande Palestra on our right. The excitement it generated in me was unbelievable, and it stayed with me all day. I don't think there are many sights as touching as the family who died together in the basement of their home, off the Via Vesuvio, the mother and father each side of three little girls, their arms protecting them this two thousand years. There were the lovers who went on banging away even though being suffocated. He *must* have been a Gunner. What a way to go!

All through that warm dusty day I wandered almost in a dream through the city, now almost deserted save for an occasional soldier.

It was late evening when we finally arrived at the Porta Ercolano that led into the Via de Sepolcri. We sat in the mouth of one of the tombs and smoked a fag. Webb was knocked out.

'Bloody hell,' he said. 'I never heard of the place, I never knew it existed, they don't say a bloody word about places like this at school. Alfred the Great, Henry the Eighth, Nelson, Queen Victoria and that's the bloody lot.'

I discovered that the Americans had actually bombed it! They believed German Infantry were hiding in it! Not much damage had been done, museum staff were already at work trying to repair it. Bombing Pompeii!!! Why not the Pyramids, Germans might be hiding there? Or bomb the Astoria Cinema, Wasdale Road, Forest Hill, that's an ideal hiding-place for Germans? Or bomb Mrs Grollick's boarding house, Hagley Road, Birmingham?

Webb afforded me amusing incidents during the day; we approached the front of a house in the Via de Mercurio, another shabby unshaven attendant was standing outside. He looked like a bag of laundry with a head on. He indicated a boxed partition on the wall. '*Vediamo questo?*' he said, and the innuendo was that of something 'naughty'.

'*Si*,' I said fluently.

We gave him ten lire each, and with a well-worn key he opened the door. It revealed a male figure dressed as a Roman soldier; holding up his kilt, from under it was an enormous phallus that rested on a pair of scales, the other scale held a bar of gold. Very interesting, but the point of it all escaped me.

'Wot's 'ee weighing 'is balls for?' said Webb, the true archaeologist.

'I think it's something to do with wartime rationing.'

The Italian explains the message, the man is saying, 'I would rather have my prick than a bar of gold.' Wait till he's sixty, I thought.

Another diversion is the Lupanarium.

''Ere, isn't that a man's prick sticking out over the door?'

'Well, it certainly isn't a woman's.'

It was a monster made of concrete and about a foot long.

'What's it doin' up there?' says Webb.

I demonstrate by hanging my hat on it.

'A hat-stand? Get away.'

'Well, it's a stand of some kind,' I explained, 'and this is a house of ill repute.'

Webb grinned from ear to ear. 'Ahh, that's why they got that bloody great chopper sticking out, then.'

'You should have been a Latin scholar,' I said.

The Lupanarium: around the walls were paintings, or rather a catalogue of the various positions that the clients could have; there was everything but standing on the head.

I observed that the cubicles the ladies had to perform in were woefully small, one would have to have been five foot four or a cripple. It must have been an interesting sight that day of the eruption, all fourteen cubicles banging away and suddenly Vesuvius explodes, out the door shoot men with erections and no trousers followed by naked screaming tarts. You don't get that stuff in the film versions.

The sun was setting when we retraced our footsteps. I was loath to leave but I was to return here again in exciting circumstances. We hitched back on several lorries including one American with a coloured driver, yellow.

'Ain't you limeys got any fuckin' transport?' he said.

'Yes, we have lots of transport, trams, buses, but they're all in Catford.'

'Screwsville – Pompeii': when we got there the girls had gone

He didn't know what I was talking about and he said so. 'What are you talkin' about, man?'

He hated me. I hated him. It was a perfect arrangement. We were just in time for dinner. I took mine to the billet (the walk did it good) and ate it in the semi-reclining position; when in Rome . . .

OCTOBER 19, 1943

I was getting twitchy, doing nothing positive for so long. I had started talking to myself, and I wasn't satisfied with the answers. I had rearranged my billet so many times that my bed had been placed in every position except the ceiling, and I was working on that. There were days when I'd try and see if I could get both legs into one trouser leg, and both feet into one sock. I was carrying out this exercise when Percival comes in.

'There's a bloke in a truck waiting fer you.'

'Is he wearing a white coat?'

'He looks bloody daft so he must be from your mob.'

I couldn't believe it. I packed my humble belongings and dashed outside. There was my Cinderella's coach in the shape of a 15-cwt truck. The driver is Ted Wright, a short, very dark, good-looking lad with large brown eyes, and eyebrows so perfectly arched that they looked as though Jean Harlow had drawn them on him.

'I've come to take you home,' he said with a grin.

In sheer delight I gave him five cigarettes.

'What's this for?'

'That's for picking me up, Ted.'

'I must pick you up again.'

'You saved me from going mad.'

We ride in silence. We go through the Salerno Gap, and are soon nearing the outskirts of Naples. Lots of pretty girls. Soon we are in the thick of the Via Roma traffic, we move at a snail's pace. People are as thick as flies, some thicker. It takes us nearly an hour to get through the chaos.

'Never think there was a war on here, would you, shops full of stuff, all the squaddies buying knickers for their birds, mind you the prices are going up like lightning. It's the Yanks, they pay anything for stuff, they're loaded with money.' He stopped, and said, 'Cor, I forgot,' he started to feel in his map pocket. 'Got some mail for you.'

Mail! MAIL! I hadn't had any for a month. It was like being five years old on Christmas morning. Ten letters! I read my mother's first. My father has now been transferred to the Command RAOC Depot, Reigate, where he has decided that the standard Infantry ammunition pouches are useless. They helped win Alamein but that's not good enough for Father. He has designed some strange things that are strapped round the leg that, my brother later told me, made it impossible to walk or run. In other words you could carry twice as much ammo but had to stand still all the time.

Thank God he wasn't running the war like he wanted to. My mother was apparently doing little for the war effort except pray for the death of Hitler. If he didn't die soon, her knees were going to give out. My brother has won the South London Poster Design prize, for which he got a certificate saying 'You have just won the South London Poster Design Prize'. After six dusty hours we arrive at an Italian farmhouse near the village of Cancello just across the Volturno on the 46 Div. front. It's dark and I can't get a picture of the layout, looming around are vehicles draped with camouflage nets, looking like strange grotesque monsters. It started to drizzle. The Waggon Lines are billeted in various buildings, the central one being the farmhouse. I noted in my diary, 'People living in and about look nervous and strained.' I was very happy to be back with the lads, though my real pals were at the Gun Lines where I would journey on the morrow.

I reflected, as I lay in bed, that I'd had a cushy few weeks behind the lines, but from the stories the war was not going to be a gentleman's one like we had in North Africa. Since those distant days I have actually met one of the German lads who was in the line opposite us in North Africa, Hans Teske. In fact, I organised a small reunion at the Medusa Restaurant in December '76 for those who had been involved in fighting in and around Steam Roller Farm, February 26, 1943. An officer present, Noel Burdett, hearing Teske and me stating that we must have actually fired at each other that day, said, 'Your survival indicates you must both be bloody awful shots.'

Later Hans Teske dispelled the belief that Germans had no sense of humour by inscribing my menu 'Dear Spike, sorry I missed you on February 26, 1943.'

As I lay dreaming, an unbelievable experience happened. In the dark a farm dog had got into our room. I heard him sniffing around. I made friendly noises and in the dark his cold nose touched my hand. I patted him and left it at that, the next thing the dirty little devil piddled on me. Was he Mussolini's Revenge?

My Diary: 0600 A.M.: Driven from waggon lines to gun position.

It was sunny, but everywhere wet, damp and muddy. Cancello is a small agricultural town on the great plain that lies on the North bank of the Volturno. I'm in a three-tonner with Driver Kit Masters. At seven we arrive at the gun position, the guns have gone, and all that is left are the M Truck Signallers who are to reel in the D5 lines.

'This is it,' said Driver Masters, pulling up in a morass of mud.

I leap from the vehicle and land knee-deep in it.

'It's all yours,' says Masters, and speeds away like a priest from a brothel.

Emerging from holes in the ground are mud-caked troglodytes. I recognise Edgington.

'Why lawks a mercy,' he said in Southern Negro tones, 'welcome home, massa Milligan, de young massa am home, praise de Laud and hide de Silver.'

'Good God, Edgington, what are you wearing?'

'Mud, it am all de rage.'

'I can't tell how good it is to be back, mate,' I said.

'Oh what a pity – now we'll never know.' I offered him a cigarette.

'You must be mad, why in God's name did you come back?'

'I ran out of illness.'

'Get out! All you got to do is a pee against a Neapolitan karzi wall and you get crabs.'

'Where's the guns?'

Edgington countenanced himself as a Red Indian. 'White men gone, take heap big fire-stick and fuck off.'

More mud-draped creatures are issuing from what had been the Command Post. I suddenly remembered!

'Where's all my kit?'

'We had to auction it off – it started to smell.'

'Don't bugger around, everything I treasure is in my big pack.'

Harry shook his head. 'Sorry mate, yer big pack has gone AWOL★, but yer kitbag's safe in G Truck with Alf Fildes.'

'Where's Alf Fildes?'

'He's at the new gun position, last time I saw him he had the shits, anyhow your kit's in his truck.'

My big pack, lost! It was a major disaster.

'You can report it missing killed in action,' says Edgington.

All that I held dear was in there, things close to a soldier's heart, like socks, drawers cellular, worst of all my Nazi war

★ Absent without leave.

loot, a dagger, an Iron Cross, an Afrika Korps hat, and a set of pornographic photographs taken lovingly from a dead Jerry on Longstop. I was going to send them back to his home. Now never would his mother hold those photographs of three people screwing close to her heart and say, 'Oh mein dear son'. Bombardier Fuller is approaching.

'You're just in time, we've got to reel in the OP cable.'

'Oh,' I groaned, 'I can't do that, I'm convalescing from sandfly fever, they've got all the sand out but there's still a lot of flies left.'

He shoves me forward. 'On that bleedin' truck.'

There was no escape. The M Truck signallers start to reel in the line. We travel North along a tree-lined road; ahead in the distance lie a range of mountains, some snow-capped: these are the ones we will have to cross to gain access to the Garigliano plain. Jerry has pulled back into them and is waiting.

'He knows a good thing when he sees it,' says Fuller, looking at them through his war-loot binoculars.

BSM Griffin, seen here with a broken arm caused by over-saluting and drink

OCTOBER 22, 1943

I glanced at my watch, 0700 hours, the sun is shining like a spring morn. It had a cheering effect, so I gave three cheers. I arose from my straw bed and was soon at the cookhouse for breakfast. The mosquitoes return to the attack. We eat with Gas Capes draped over our heads.

'Where'd you kip?' said Edgington.

I pointed. 'Over there.'

'Jerry slung over a dozen in the night.'

'I didn't hear them. Did they have silencers on?'

'Poor old Bill Trew, he was havin' a crap in the field, the first one landed behind him. He set off and ended up in the ditch, with his trousers still down.'

'I heard that Captain Richards of 17 Battery has got the MC.'

'What for?' I said.

'I dunno,' said Edgington, 'it arrived with the rations so he pinned it on, and our Johnnie Walker's been mentioned in despatches.'

'Oh, what did he do?'

'Drinking a whole bottle of Scotch under heavy mortar fire, and never spilled a drop.'

We all realised as we drank our tea that the guns were silent.

'Is it a strike?'

'No,' says Bombardier Fuller. 'There's Jerries in the area supposed to be massing for an attack, and so we don't give our position away, we been ordered to stay silent.'

'Oh,' I said, 'are we talking too loud?'

'He's up there,' said Bill Trew, emerging from under his Gas Cape long enough to point to a hill about 4,000 yards away.

'You mean he can see us?' I said.

'Yer,' says Trew.

I gave a cheery wave at the hill. 'Hello, lads,' I called.

It was amazing, Jerry could see us but wasn't doing anything about it, a strange uneasy feeling; anticipating a Stonk* by Jerry, we set to and dug a funk hole into the side of the ditch. A plume of black smoke is ascending from the Jerry position.

'He's still got fags then,' said Edgington.

We made a floor out of bits of wood that kept us off the mud. At the same time we were also involved in digging an alcove for the Telephone Exchange; also along the ditch was the Command Post, Cookhouse, Officers' Mess and Battery Office. It looked very much like a World War I trench. An incredible find by Edgington, a huge cupboard that we wedge into our funkhole – we sit inside with the door closed to avoid the mozzies.

At about 0930 the guns open up again and we could see our shells bursting on the hillside behind Sparanise. The siting of our guns was obviously good, behind a bank of trees that hid them from view, but we gunners walked about the fields in full view like the silly sods we were.

A big attack is going in tonight. The Grenadiers and Scots Guards are the poor bastards. They've got to take the hill to our immediate right to deny Jerry observation and put our OP on it. The sirens have gone and an air raid starts on Naples. 0430: the Artillery opened up and fired non-stop until 0624, then a silence. From the distant hill we hear the dreadful sound of Spandaus and Schmeisers that are spraying the early morning with bullets, and I can't but wonder at the courage of these lads in the Guards Brigade going forward into it. What a terrible, unexplainable lunacy. There must have been a lot of casualties as there was talk of us having to send gravedigging parties. In the end they sent some Gunners from the Waggon Lines. When they came back they spoke of Italian civilians being shot out of hand

* Concentration of Artillery fire.

by Germans. There must be a lot of needle between these two nations. I should hate to be a German prisoner thrown to an Italian mob . . . The mosquito-bites and the scratching have turned our faces into what from a distance look like uncured bacon. In desperation I had rubbed Sloane's Liniment on my face, and lo! it kept them away!!

'I've done it, Harry,' I said, rushing into the Command Post with bottle in my hand.

'What have you done?' said Edgington, turning from the Telephone Exchange, 'and if you have done it in that bottle, don't empty it in here.'

'I've stopped the mozzies biting me,' I said.

'How?' said the great man.

'Sloane's Liniment,' I said.

'How in God's name did you get 'em to drink it?'

Even as he spoke I regretted the new-found repellent, my face started to sting and then burn as though it was on fire. I had to plunge my head repeatedly into a bucket of cold water. It was hours before the stinging stopped, wasn't *anybody* on my side?

During the day there was a story that suddenly, on one of our wireless sets, a German had been heard asking for information. The Signaller recognised the accent and said, 'Fuck off, Fritz.' The answer was instant, 'All right, English bastards, Off.'

OCTOBER 23, 1943

Today non-stop firing. In the Command Post there's hardly time to light a fag in between Fire Orders. A party of our linesmen have nearly been driven mad; they have been reeling in what was an old telephone line. They went on reeling in for two miles only to discover that another battery was in fact reeling it out. Harry comes back on M truck and says, 'We're all bloody mad, fancy two bloody miles of reeling in a line and another sloppy lot are laying it out.

Good job we caught 'em up, otherwise we'd be the other side of the bloody Alps by now.'

The mosquitoes are so bad that an official complaint has been made to the MO and now three engineers with spray guns are going round squirting the countryside and our dinners; it helped a little, but far too late. The mosquitoes had left, why?

'They couldn't find any space between the bites,' says Fuller, whose face resembled a side of beef with scabs on.

Some of the lads' scratches went septic and they were daubed with some pink stuff that made them look like Indians in war paint. They came dancing from the MO's tent with war whoops.

OCTOBER 25, 1943

Morning. Medium day, cloudy, chilly, occasionally bursts of sun. Good breakfast. Drank three mugs of tea on the trot with three Passing Cloud. Most of us are fed up with the new Major, 'Jumbo' Jenkins. 'He is a pain in the arse all over,' says Arthur Tume. He is finicky, difficult to contact. You can never get near him. He is the product of a spoiled or deprived childhood, and is playing at soldiers; every minute he is on fault-finding missions, you never see him smile. From his driver, Sherwood, we discover that he's a hypochondriac and carries a medical chest around with him. Driving along, he suddenly shouts 'Stop'. Sherwood jams the brakes on, out leaps Jenkins, lies on the bonnet and squirts drops up his nose, directly behind rolls up an American General bleeping his horn. Sherwood puts the car into gear and drives off the road, the American witnesses a British Major lying on his back putting drops up his hooter and wonders why we are Allies.

Bodies of the German aviators have been found. They are buried by 18 Battery.

'See? 18 Battery again,' says Chalky White. 'They get all the fun.'

Gunner Devine is passing with a bandage on his hand.

'There's a curse on 19 Battery,' he says solemnly.

'A curse?' queries Edgington. 'What is it?'

'Fuck 'em,' said Devine, a great Liverpudlian grin on his unshaven face.

'That is indeed a terrible curse,' says Bombardier Milligan. 'I wonder who put it on us.'

'It's "Jumbo" Jenkins, 'ees the bleedin' curse on us,' said White.

'Fuck him,' said Devine.

'See? There goes that curse again,' says Edgington.

Edgington borrows Fildes' guitar, and off duty, we have a little sing-song in our dug-out.

'Ahhhh! There you are,' says a voice followed by the body of Sgt-Major Griffin. Our much-beloved Welshman has that half evil, half benign smile on his face. Before we can dive for cover, he says, 'You, you, you, and you,' all the while pointing at me, 'we're moving, lads.'

A great groan rents the air.

'Oh, cheer up now,' he says in a mock cheery voice, 'the King is going to let you all have a nice shovel on loan for the day.'

More terrible groans.

'We are going to make some nice little holes in the ground for our guns.'

We are all packed off in a three-tonner. We drive through Sparanise, badly shelled and bombed, some buildings still smouldering. The inhabitants are in a state of shock, women and children are crying, men are searching among the ruins for their belongings or worse, their relatives. It was the little children that depressed me the most, that such innocence should be put to such suffering. The adult world should forever hang its head in shame at the terrible, unforgivable things done to the young . . . despite all this the lads strike up a song.

'Bang away Lulu, Bang away Lulu, Bang away good and strong. What you gonna do when you want a blow through and yer Lulu's dead an' gone' . . .' A line of German prisoners go past, our wheels splatter them with mud, as usual we give them the full treatment of raspberries, two fingers and Heil Hitler salutes. They don't even bother to look back, they trudge on, all in step.

Jam-Jar Griffin alone and unafraid, his BO having driven the Germans from the Volturno Plain

OCTOBER 26, 1943

No sleep. Feeling tired. During the day the guns arrived and spread themselves about in their unexplainable pattern, two were ahead of us and two behind us with their backs to the wood. The Command Post was not to the liking of the Major.

'He doesn't like it,' said Chalky White. 'Nobody *likes* a Command Post, you don't see soldiers goin' around sayin' "I like Command Posts".'

'He says it's not big enough.'

All hell is let loose, Ack-Ack start blazing away, we all go head-first to the deck, a swarm of MEs roar over the position at nought feet. We hear the Major shouting, 'Tommy Guns . . . Tommy Guns.'

A laconic voice, 'Tommy Guns is on leave, sir.'

Edgington first to rise to his feet. 'Any questions?' he says.

He knelt over me, made a sign of the cross and then started to feel my pockets for fags. I am notoriously ticklish, and using one hand to tickle and convulse me, the other had withdrawn my fags. There followed a friendly struggle during which Major Jenkins appears and says, 'What is going on, this isn't a nursery, Bombardier, you ought to know better. Get these men on with the digging.'

I jumped up and Yes-sirred him on his way. He's back before we stop giggling. 'Did any of you men fire at those planes?' he said.

We admit we didn't. I explained. 'It's not easy to shoot down planes with shovels, sir.'

'You will keep your side arms within reach, next time I expect to hear a volley.'

'Very good, sir.'

In an hour the planes flew over, and we let fly. The Major is running up, waving his arms. 'No, no, bloody fools, they're ours.'

'Don't worry, sir, when they fly back again, we'll apologise,' I said.

He didn't know how to take me, he stood there clenching his fists, his face a mask of frustration.

OCTOBER 27, 1943

Regimental Diary: Infantry pushing forward all day, we are bombarding and firing Y targets. Some slight enemy retaliation but not much.

Good news! We are allowed to write home and actually tell our families that we are in Italy. Oh hooray.

> Dear Mother,
>   I am in Italy.
>   Your loving son,
>   Barmy Fred.

Rumours of yet another 'big attack'. The rain has stopped, a wind is blowing, so I will hang out my laundry that now lies reeking at the bottom of my big pack. Diving into those dark depths I pull out dreadful lumps of congealed mildewed clothing. Soon I am boiling a tin of water. Whhheeee Boom! an air-burst shell. It stops, I arise and see that the water is boiling, I drop in my clothes, then half a bar of soap and start stirring the lot with a stick. My idyll is shattered by another air burst; was Hitler trying to range on my laundry?

German Op Officer: Three rounds on to zer underpants Milligan. Fire! Ach Vonderschoen! a direct hit on zer soap! For you Gunner Milligan, the laundry is over.

NOVEMBER 1, 1943

Regimental Diary: (I can't resist reporting this entry!)
Had orders to move from 083857 by 10.00 hrs as 'X' Corps want to come into the area. The orders from 2 AGRA were vague and they were unable to indicate any hide area for us to go. They could not tell us where the enemy were, they could not tell us whether we were to go into action that day. So we aren't doing anything.

Any questions folks?
Ted Lawrence, our Don R., comes up and says, 'Jerry's

retreatin'.' He ought to know, he's just stamped his bare foot on a dog-end and comes hot-foot from HQ. We've all got to be ready to move at a moment's notice. A mad rush as we start hurling our crappy clobber into big pack, small pack kitbag, cardboard boxes, brown paper parcels all held together by miles of knotted string and bits of bent wire. It was really terrible to see what a once immaculate Battery looked like. No longer did we appear as Conquerors, no, we looked like families of impoverished Armenian refugees fleeing the Turkish slaughter. Bundles of canvas, tea-chests and waterproof sheeting were piled on the roof, obliterating the outline of the lorry which, in silhouette, appeared to be an extinct dinosaur. So we all started to slither and slide to the main road. My God! What a mess! Vehicles were everywhere, all pointing the wrong way, the giant Scammell lorries with guns in tow had 'jack-knifed', red-faced Sergeants were yelling abuse at the drivers, who in turn yelled abuse at the gunners, who pointed accusingly at the Sergeants. The signallers (us) are all OK. We are sitting in our trucks and have managed to get to the main road known as Route 6, facing the *right* way. We have brewed up. Great steaming mugs of tea are jamming the roadway. American trucks with coloured drivers are racing past shouting, 'Out of the way, Limey white trash', and we shout back, 'Fuck Joe Louis.' We drank tea till our bladders were crippled and the tannic acid showed red through our skin, by which time the great guns had finally been extricated from the mud.

By eleven o'clock, we were in convoy, looking like Council Dustcarts on the move.

'Oh! *look* who's coming up the road! It's our leader, General Mark Clark! God bless 'ee zur!'

I was babbling on like this when the beckoning face of Sergeant King appears. 'Ahhhhh,' he leers, ''oo 'as been 'iding from 'is nice Sergeant?' He's looking at me. 'You are to go with our dearly beloved Major Jenkins forward, in search of (a) the Enemy, and (b) an OP.'

Ted Lawrence, with his pistol pointing in a direction that could ruin his marriage

Soon I am in G truck with Spike Deans, Vic Nash and Lt Wright. I am not actually with Major Jenkins, he's in H truck. Behind us is X truck; what had happened to all the numbers? In the back of the truck the ever-inventive Bombardier Deans opens the pontoon school.

A voice is calling, 'All personnel over here.'

It's Lt Wright, who is standing outside the mouth of a cave which looks like it's going to swallow him. With great urgency on our faces we amble across. Mr Wright waits patiently.

'Now,' he says, looking at some orders pinned to his map.

'We are now at San Marco, here,' he taps the map, his papers fall in the mud. 'Blast,' he says.

I bend down to pick them up; he is now clutching a handful of muddy papers. 'I was saying we are here, and we've temporarily lost touch with the Bosche – so we will carry out maintenance of wireless sets, small arms and vehicles until further orders, that is all.'

I clutch Bombardier Deans' arm dramatically, and whisper, 'He's going to leave us. What are we going to do?'

A rattling sound reveals Sherwood's bren carrier loaded to the gills, with Lt Walker, Gunner Ben Wenham, Gunner Pinchbeck and Lt Budden followed by Don R. Lawrence – *they* are going forward to look for Jerry.

'May God go with 'eee,' I said, striking a dramatic pose, one hand clutching my heart.

Ben Wenham grins and says, 'Who's a silly bugger then!'

We wave them goodbye as they disappear over the brow of a hillock. Indeed the Germans had pulled back, quite a distance.

'They must be suffering withdrawal symptoms,' I told

'Group looking for Jerry'. Left to right are Don R. Ted Lawrence, Lt Walker, Ben Wenham, Gunner Pinchbeck, Lt Budden and Bdr Brookes

Mr Wright. 'It's a sort of wartime coitus interruptus.'

That night was wonderful. I remember it was crisp, cold, clear, starlit, that's if I remember: if not, it was raining.

SATURDAY, NOVEMBER 6, 1943

Very cold. 'We must be high up,' Edgington is announcing.

'Why must we be high?' I enquire, because we were sitting down.

'The rations, *that's* why.'

'What about the Russians?'

'*Rations!* You silly Gunner, *rations*. Haven't you noticed that in addition to our ration we now get little round vitamin pills?'

'I thought they were concentrated Plum Puddings to save shipping space.'

For the millionth time we are in the back of a lorry lumbering through a muddy cold landscape, winter black trees line our route like dying sentinels. I trace our position as we progress. The town we are passing through is Teano! I tell Edgington, 'This is where Garibaldi invented spotted biscuits and reunited Italy for King Emmanuel the umpteenth.'

'I am thrilled,' says Edgington.

'It was Garibaldi that caused the Bourbons to flee over the Rocky Alps.'

'Ah, thereby hangs the phrase, a Bourbon on the Rocks.'

Groans. We have halted. 'Look what I've rescued.' Vic Nash has come to the tailboard of our lorry. He holds a small wriggling black puppy; this was to be christened Teano, and was to become part of the Battery. We stroked him, petted him, gave him a bit of cheese and handed him back.

'Hide him from Driver Kidgell, won't you?' I said.

'Why?'

'Because he'll eat him.'

Vic Nash giggled, the pup is furiously licking his face, so it can't have long to live.

'Get mounted,' calls an important voice from up front.

'Get stuffed,' comes the reply.

We move off in fits and starts, the lorry starts, we have fits.

We are on a mountain road with a gradient of one in four. We halt. 'Dismount!' We climb out. On the right side of the road is a Church, semi-Gothic style. Just behind it is the Vicarage. The road opposite flanks a high bank with several footpaths leading up to a cave set in a sort of browny-red sandstone.

'That's it,' says Bombardier Fuller, riding up on his mo' bike. 'That cave; get all the Command Post stuff in there.'

We struggle and strain with all that bloody stuff we've carried so many times before. Edgington has developed the oriental carrying posture, balancing a battery on his head. We all copy and march Indian file up the slope chanting, 'Sandy the wise, Sandy the strong.'

'How long is this going to last?' he says.

'With time off for good conduct by the time you're eighty-three the future is yours.'

Lieutenant Budden hoves to. 'Has anyone seen Mr Wright?'

'Yes, sir,' I said, 'I saw him yesterday.'

He looks at me in despair and says, 'Can't you take anything for it, Milligan?'

Out of politeness I asked where the guns were.

'They're in the woods somewhere.'

'Where are the woods, sir?'

'Ah! That's another question.'

'Get the vehicles off the road and under cover.'

We walk around muttering, 'The woods are full of 'em!'

The lethal voice of Major Jenkins is penetrating the air. We drive up the slope and onto a small muddy plateau with numerous trees. We follow a small trail to the high bank.

Under the trees we camouflage G truck.

'Jerry's been shelling the area, better dig in,' says Bombardier Deans.

Dig? One thing I don't dig is digging. I'm not the first to spot the possibilities of sleeping in the church.

I move my kit in that evening. In the aisle is a catafalque mounted on a trestle. The catafalque is all black velvet with a great black cloth to cover the whole thing. What the hell! It looks great inside, so I make my bed in it. If I get killed in the night, I'm all ready. Great fun, I am asleep in my catafalque, Bombardier Trew comes in to wake me up for my spell of duty. He is unaware of my macabre resting place. Gradually I arise from my box with the black velvet cover over my head. I let out a terrible howl and Bombardier Trew screams 'Ghosts' and runs for his bloody life, and I find him gibbering in the Command Post to Lt Budden.

An OP has been established on Monte Croce. Not again! Rain!!! Where does the stuff come from??? There's to be a big attack on Monte Camino, it's the 201 Guards Brigade to do the dirty work. I can't lie here, I must do something to help the war effort. I do. I go to the cookhouse for dinner. What's this I hear? That hungry bugger Kidgell, he's been having one dinner here, then running across to the American Battery next to us and scrounging another. He must have hollow legs.

'The attack goes in tomorrow night,' so speaks Major Jenkins, who for once has deemed to tell us what's happening. I am on Command Post duty up till 11.30. Mr Wright is duty officer. In between firing he reads the *Daily Express*. At 1100 hours the thing called Edgington comes in, it carries a mug ahead of it.

'Good news,' he says, he looks very merry, he should, there's been a rum ration and he's had his and a little more. 'I've got yours here.' He poured a measure into my mug.

'A Merry Christmas to you all,' I said.

He empties a pocket full of chestnuts, soon they are

roasting on our fire, and splitting open with a little bang. They taste delicious!!

'Alf Fildes is feeling groggy,' he tells us. 'He's got a sore throat so has gone to bed in the back of his truck.'

There is nothing like a 15-cwt truck for a sore throat. Vic Nash is coming on duty. 'Oh my poor guts,' he says.

'He's got the shits! Keep away,' we all say and cringe in the corner.

The guns report difficulty with the platforms, mud is making it increasingly difficult; each time they fire, the gun slithers in a circle. We can hear the swearing from the Command Post. But it's imperative they keep going as the attack is about to go in, they need help up there, so the back-breaking work of manhandling the guns back on target continues.

TUESDAY, NOVEMBER 9, 1943

What's this? Edgington has made an incredible find. A free-range harmonium! It's in the Vicarage and the priest says we can use it, so the morning is spent playing jazz; as a mark of respect I play my trumpet muted, Alf plays guitar and the priest and his lady cleaner sit and listen a bit amazed, jazz under Mussolini had been banned as decadent; well, the music wasn't, but we certainly were. It was an unusual morning, the priest giving us an unexpected blessing before we departed.

'What was he doing then?' said Edgington.

I explained. 'It's a blessing.'

'What good does it do?' he said.

'Well, it's supposed to be a solemn occasion on which he, as a minister, fortifies your soul by sprinkling holy water over you.'

'It only made me bloody wet,' said Edgington.

Grim news of the fighting on Monte Camino, the Guards are attacking but Jerry has reinforced his position with

1st/104 Panzer Grenadiers, and fighting is raging all over the peak.

THURSDAY, NOVEMBER 11, 1943

Armistice Day. Ha ha ha.

Lt 'Johnny' Walker is at an OP on Monte Croce. He is suspicious that a white farmhouse is harbouring the enemy, so he drops a few 200 pounders around it; as they get closer a door bursts open and out rush a Jerry patrol who run like hell to a farmhouse a hundred yards away. Walker then shells that place, out runs Jerry back to farmhouse one, he does this till the Jerries are shagged out and finally double back to their own lines. 'When I fight an enemy, I like to keep them fit,' says Walker.

That night fairly quiet in the Command Post, Lt Stewart Pride not feeling very well. 'I must report sick in the morning,' he says. 'Any music on the wireless?'

I fiddle with the knobs. We are surrounded by hills and the reception is very bad. I get what sounds like someone singing in Yugoslavian.

'I don't understand, Milligan,' says Stewart Pride, 'you can't get our bloody OP, which is only half a mile away, yet you can get some idiot singing in Yugoslavia.'

'That's because he's singing very loud, sir. If our signallers at the OP could be given training in opera, it would be easy.'

SATURDAY, NOVEMBER 13, 1943

Because of the OP's field of view, and a thousand feet height added to the guns' range, the targets are never ending. Despite the cold the gunners are actually sweating. A casualty! my boots are leaking. I examine them seated in the back of G truck. White passes by sipping tea.

He stops. 'What's on?'

'My boots are leaking.'

'Oh? Outwards?'

'Outwards my arse, the bloody water's getting *in*, Jerry's got the right idea. Jack Boots, no lace holes. Great.'

'Have you tasted the apples here?'

'Not yet.'

'They're bloody marvellous, better than English ones, full of juice.'

Army conversations were unique, from leaking boots to apples in one line. I reported to the Quarter Master Courtney for new boots, he makes me take mine off and examines them. 'Like a jeweller's glass,' I said sarcastically.

'Well,' he says, 'we haven't got your size, see; you take an eight, we've only got twelves.'

'Twelves? TWELVES? Christ!'

'Take it or leave it.'

A choice! Size twelves or bare feet. It was like wearing landing barges. I used to haul myself around in the mud walking like Frankenstein's monster, my feet kept coming out of the bloody things, and I had to stand on one leg trying to tug the monster boot out of the mud. It was impossible, I told the Quarterbloke and he relented. 'I'll send a truck to Base Depot and get you a pair of eights.'

The new size eights arrive and are like iron. They have been in store since World War I. I have to attack them with a hammer to break them down. I cover them with great loads of dubbin, put them near the fire; I watched those boots absorb two pounds of dubbin, with a noise of Glug Glug. 'The bloody things are alive,' said Gunner White, watching fascinated as the boots devoured the dubbin. After half an hour's battering with a Tent Peg Mallet I tried them on. Great! they were as soft as buckskin.

We have news that 17 Battery has had a premature. No one killed but one gunner injured. This was strange as the gun had just come back from workshops, where it had been repaired for a previous premature.

WEDNESDAY, NOVEMBER 17, 1943

The BBC News: 'Heavy rain in Italy is slowing the Allied advance.' (Advance? What advance?) Today was a crisis day, the drivers tell us of chaos on the roads: flooding and cataclysmic subsidence has all but brought traffic to a halt. A Recce party return with the news that we have a new gun position at 966976.

Sgt J. Wilson, Bdr Sainsbury and gun-crew filling in football coupons, Monte Santa Maria, apple orchard position, November 17, 1943

THURSDAY, NOVEMBER 18, 1943

Today was, as Sean O'Casey said, 'A state of Chassis'. Everything is now mud brown – men, machines, trees, mountains, apples. I hear Edgington singing 'It's a Brown World without you' to the tune of 'It's a Blue World without you'. I try and match it with 'When the Brown of the Night meets the Brown of the Day, someone waits for me'. He tops that with 'When you hear that serenade in Brown'. I go on with 'Brown Moon, I saw you standing alone'. I sing 'Am I Brown', he sings 'St Louis Browns' then 'In my dear little Alice Brown Gown'.

'Brown Skies.'

'Brown Birds over the Brown Cliffs of Dover.'

We have to be ready by mid-day. The only way to get the guns out of the mud is tractors. We are to try the Americans.

'Americans?' gasps our Major. 'No, we must never sink that low.'

'We *are* sunk that low, that's why we need them,' we informed him. To our aid came three giant American tractors.

We are off at a snail's pace. God knows how drivers can cope.

'Can you see where you're goin'?' calls Hart through to poor Driver Masters.

'No,' comes the reply, 'I'm driving in Braille.'

It's about midday, or if you go by the light, midnight. We have been halted on a road; to our right, looming over us are Monte Santa Croce and Monte Mattone, both over 600 to

Muddy conditions

1,000 feet. They run east to west on a range that ends up near the coast with Monte Massica, 800 feet. 'They ought to keep the draught out,' says Hart. All that day we were truckbound by rain; if and when the bloody stuff stopped, we debussed and stretched our legs. There is no sign or word of the cookhouse.

'I think under the circumstances we should surrender,' I said.

NOVEMBER 20, 1943

The morning of November 20 burst cheerily on us with an exciting cold downpour. Gad! It was good to be alive, the question was, were we? We are concluding the finishing touches on the Command Post, a sandbagged blast wall on the open side of the dug-out. There are many brilliant minds at work in the war, Radar, Infra-Red Telescopes, Mulberry Harbours, but no bugger has invented how to get wet mud into a sandbag. We are almost pouring it in. When we seal the sandbag the mixture starts to squeeze through the hessian like thin spaghetti! We fill them to bursting, yet when we lay another bag on top, it flattens like a wafer.

'This isn't a job,' moans one miserable Gunner. 'This is a bloody sentence!'

17 Battery tell us they have managed to fire twenty rounds in the afternoon.

'The bloody fools,' says Alf Fildes, 'if we all kept quiet Jerry would pack up and go home.'

GUNNER EDGINGTON'S PUBLIC APPEARANCE

'Crabs! They've got crabs!' the cry runs through the serried ranks.

The 'Theys' were the crew of Monkey 2, it was the first mass outbreak of crabs in the Battery, how proud we were of them, at last the label dirty bastards could be added to the Battery honours. The only other mass outbreak of crabs was Gunner Neat in Bexhill. He told the MO he got them off a girl in Blackpool. 'I brought them south for the sun, sir,' he said.

Among the crab-ridden is Gunner Edgington. Let him recount the grisly details.

We hadn't had our clothes off for some considerable time, much less our underwear, such as it might have been, and as I've said, a bath was something we only vaguely remembered from long ago. My hair was a matted lump. The whole world we knew at that time was to get phone lines out and keep them going – all else was sleep and food and a good deal of the latter was often scrounged from strange outfits we encountered while out on the line.

Not surprisingly we began to smell strongly and then to scratch: the irritation became incessant and something obviously had to be done: I don't think Bentley came to us . . . it was just arranged by phone calls, that we go over to RHQ.

I think there *must*'ve been more than the M.2 team, for the 'crab-ridden' were taken in a three-tonner to where some showers had been erected in the corner of a field. The showers were a Heath Robinson contraption mounted under a tin roof on angle-iron supports, but they were thoroughly efficient.

Capt Bentley, keeping a distance, called down instructions from the safety of his room on an upper floor of an adjacent building.

'Strip off!' he called to us, and this was just the Monkey 2 gang at this point. 'Have a thorough washdown all over as hot as you can possibly stand it.'

In the middle of this field, in full view of civilians and soldiers alike, we disported ourself joyously under four very efficient jets of steam and near-boiling water to the accompaniment of screams, yells and cackles.

'Blimey, you can see the bloody things! See 'em moving under the skin? Those little bastards.'

Sure enough, I could see my collection in the skin of my belly just above the 'short-and-curlies'.

Some five minutes, and Bentley calls:

'OK, that's enough – get up here like lightning!'

Away we went in a tight bunch for the steps which led up the side of the building; these being only wide enough to permit one at a time, it meant some of us had to ease back to create a single-file rush up the stairs, all naked and freezing. Into a small bare room we thundered, its only furniture a bare table, on which stood in a row seven empty cigarette tins, and a large dob of cotton wool alongside – no sign of Bentley though.

Looking round puzzled, we see his grinning face peering round a distant door at the far end of the room – he had no wish to get near us. The legend 'crabs can jump six feet' still lingered on.

'Right! Each man grab a tin and a blob of cotton wool. Dip the cotton wool into the tin and dab it generously all over the affected parts . . . quickly now, quickly!' He slammed the door, in case any escaped.

Looking in my tin I saw a clear mauve liquid. The lads were all still chortling and crying in mock agony – 'Unclean! Unclean!', the war-cry we had been bellicosely hollering from the lorry that brought us – and ringing imaginary handbells.

The fluid was liberally applied – backs, balls and bellies as well – not one of us having guessed what it was, it took about ten to fifteen seconds to act. Then everyone's balls caught fire. It was raw alcohol.

The first 'Cor-mate!' was rapidly echoed all round, followed by a growled 'Awww! Gawd blimey!!' Faces were transfixed with pain and cross-eyed agony, they yelled, they screamed, they fell and rolled, they jumped, they ran back and forth, they twisted, cannoned into

The terrible crab-ridden M.2 team

walls – each other – they fell over the table. At the height of the chaotic fandango I was sat on the floor, knees drawn up, left arm wedging my trunk half upright, right hand fanning my 'wedding-tackle', when through the mêlée of flailing arms, legs and prancing bodies I saw the inner door open again slightly and Bentley's face appear in the narrow gap. 'Merry Christmas,' he said and was gone!

For Edgington to remember that occasion in such detail thirty-five years after the event is quite a feat of memory. Mind you, one doesn't get crabs every day, not even at the fishmonger's.

NOVEMBER 23, 1943

'Milligan? Fildes?' a voice of authority calls. It tells us we are to take twenty-four hours' rations, drive to the top of Monte Croce and set up the wireless relay station.

'They say the reason for the bad reception is adverse metals,' said Fildes.

Adverse metals? I thought. 'What are adverse metals?'

'Fuck knows,' he said.

'Do you think it's the metal rings on the laceholes in our boots?' Fildes shrugged.

Fildes has put chains on the wheels of the truck. Does he think they're going to escape? We wave goodbye, and take the road that travels round the rear of our position skirting the foot of Monte Croce, we get onto a rough mountain road slippery as grease. The road finally disappears. 'It's come to something when the road can't get up the hill,' I said. By steady driving Fildes gradually makes it to the top; we pull up just below the crest. The slopes are slightly wooded, with a scrubby grass floor. We look down into the valley at our gun positions; so skilful is the camouflage that we can see everything as though under a magnifying glass. Cautiously we peer over the crest into enemy territory. The view is obscured by drizzle and mist. Comfort! *that's* the thing. Brew up! Hot water boiled for dinner. Make up beds in the back of truck. We stow our spare gear in the driving cab. Attempts are made to contact the OP, no luck, we report this to the Command Post, they say stay up there on listening watch, we put the set to 'receive' and put the earphones in a mess-tin, to amplify the sound.

NOVEMBER 24, 1943

My Diary: Up very early to contact our gun position. Reception strength 9, but the OP strength 1. I will try and put up very long aerial.

'I'll try and put it up this tree, Alf,' I said, with good intentions.

'You should look good in a tree. I always thought, in your paybook where it says place of birth it should say Tree.'

'Hold this aerial, Alf,' I said, 'and I will climb up and insult you from a great height.'

The words rang clear on the morning air, also clear in the morning air was my lone scream as I fell ten feet.

'You all right?' said Fildes with a whimsical smile.

'Of course, don't you know falling ten feet from a tree is always all right?'

Clutching and swearing, twigs snapping around me, I managed to get up to the lower branches and let out a Tarzan call.

'Pass me up the aerial, Alf,' says Milligan.

It would appear I have climbed too high for him to reach me.

'You'll have to come down a bit,' he says.

The tree is winter-green and slippery; in various contortions that are only done by a man with strychnine poisoning, I get to a lower level and give a Tarzan cry.

'Here, grab 'old,' says Fildes, holding up the aerial. I firmly grab one of the Windmill antennae, it snaps off.

'Never mind, there's still three more.'

I try and haul the thing through a complex of branches

Bombardier Syd 'Butcher' Price wearing whitewashed boots for locating in the dark

and boughs; now, a twenty-foot-long pole is no manoeuvrable item. It was like trying to thread a giant darning needle and I wasn't trained for that. I gave another Tarzan call, it got to the stage where I was trapped between the branches and the aerial.

'Shall I chop the tree down?' said Fildes, giggling.

'It's the antennae that's in the way,' I said. 'I'll unscrew them.'

I soon have three loose antennae in one hand, and I find the other hand insufficient to climb *and* hold the aerial.

'Catch,' I said, and dropped the antennae. Looking up, Fildes loses his balance, and starts to slide back down the muddy slope. So smooth is his progress that he doesn't realise he's moving; gently the back of his nut collides with a tree. I gave the Tarzan call, and a lot of bloody good it did. The antennae are now slopped in the mud. I, in contrast, am covered in the green moss of the tree trunk and covered in scratches. This is called modern wireless communications.

We hear a 'Heloooooo' from further down the slope. Was this the spirit of Arcadia? There, amid the greenery we see a clutch of muddy gunners in various stages of climbing. They are Bombardier Syd Price and his merry ration carriers.

'Come down here,' he calls.

'Why?'

'Because *we* can't get up *there*.'

'If *we* come down *there* where you can't get up from, *we'll* be down *there* as well not being able to get back up *here* where we are *now*.'

'It's yer bloody rations, take 'em or we'll eat 'em here.'

A desperate situation. Alf and I slither down the hillside.

Rations are rations and we'll do anything to get them. Along with them we find 'Two bloody great batteries for the wireless.' We manage to get the rations up, but the weight of the batteries is too much, so we leave the things on the mountain. Syd Price puffs his pipe as he and his 'porters' slither backwards down the mountain.

'When are we going to be relieved?' I asked as a parting question.

'Use a tree,' he calls.

We are alone again in our little heaven in the clouds. A small group of silent Infantry men are leaving their position. They pass us in silence. We've had a belly full of wireless.

'Let's pack it in,' I said, 'I feel a bit feverish.' I bed down and Fildes prepares an evening meal. I had fallen asleep before he served it.

NOVEMBER 26, 1943

It was like a spring morning. 'I don't believe it,' said Fildes. 'The sun.' It changed everything, colours once brown were now green, green, green. Today I would shave. Today I would organise my life anew. No more slobbed in bed all day, today I would do things. What those things were I didn't yet know, but it would be 'things', the first 'thing' would be breakfast. I build a fire and soon make the bacon sizzle. The smell is wafting through the morning air. A string of mules accompanied by Cypriot attendants come from the left and pass slowly by. They are a little amused seeing us in nothing but socks, boots and shirts. Fildes is shaving.

'Marvellous what the sun will do,' he says.

He whistles in between strokes of the blade. I will do the shave 'thing' after the breakfast 'thing'.

'After this I'm going to have a look over the hill "thing" at Jerry's positions,' I declared.

'I'm beginning to wonder how long we'll be up here,' said Fildes. 'It's been four days now, we were only supposed to be here for twenty-four hours.'

Someone in the valley below is trying to attract our attention with a mirror.

'I wonder what they want.'

'We better switch on the set,' said Fildes.

We get through and the message is 'Come in. Position being closed down.' We take our time. I stroll to the top of the mountain ridge for a last look, a marvellous view meets the eye, 1,000 feet below us is the great Garigliano plain, with the snow-mottled Aurunci Mountains on the far side of the river. To the left is the Gulf of Gaeta. In the distance at the curling point of the bay is Gaeta itself. Even as I watch, a great plume from an explosion starts skywards, Jerry carrying out demolitions. Why can't I get a fun job like that? The last of the infantry are leaving their foxholes, and wearily making their way back down the mountain.

Whistling merrily, we pack all our gear and prepare the

Alf Fildes writing cheques for his wife Lily

descent. The ground was like grease, Fildes drives down at one mile an hour, engaging four-wheel drive. I have to walk ahead and scout out the least dangerous bits, gradually the gradient became more acute. The truck starts to slide down with a gathering momentum. All I could think of saying was 'Goodbye, Alf, I'll tell the missus.' Alf doesn't want to die. He remembers an old bus-driver's trick. He puts the truck into reverse, and the counteraction of the wheels slows the vehicle up and it gradually comes to a halt. He looks out the cab and grins.

'Cor bloody hell, I want more money for this job.'

'That was brilliant! *Brilliant*, do you hear me, Fildes! I won't let this go unnoticed . . . you see, by tomorrow morning you'll be on the honours list and an extra egg for breakfast, a present from a grateful nation, God bless you, young Alf, you and your see-through underwear. England isn't finished yet . . . it'll be finished tomorrow.'

Together we gradually slither down the hill, and with perfect timing arrive back as Bombardier Deans is making coffee.

'It's the men from the hills,' announces Nash.

'Yes, we bring good tidings, Jerry is blowing up Gaeta.'

Fildes has raced to the battery office and returned with mail.

'You always get more than anyone else, Milligan.'

'Well, you unimaginative buggers only write to one bird, I wrote to ten; you're paying the penalty for monogamy.'

NOVEMBER 29, 1943

'Wakey, wakey.'

My watch says 0500 hours.

'Wakey, wakey my arsey, why don't you fuckey wuckey offey?' is my clear language reply.

Oh dear, it's no use, it's Sergeant King, he says, 'You are goin' hup the Ho-Pee – it's only for twenty-four hours.'

'That's long enough to get killed,' I said.

In Sherwood's bren carrier I travel a fifteen-mile road to Sipichiano. At times we are in full view of Jerry. He doesn't shell us. But you have that feeling that any minute he will and that's like being shelled.

'How come they picked you?' said Sherwood.

'I wasn't quick enough.'

Whee-crashhh!

'He's spotted us!' shouts Sherwood.

He drives off the road behind a deserted farmhouse. Whee Crash. Whee Crash. 88s! Is he going to drop one behind the farm? No, he just goes along the road. Five more rounds and then stop. Is he waiting for us to come out? Only one way to find out. Sherwood revs up and then rushes out on to the road. I cringe . . . nothing, soon we're safe behind covering ground. The OP was manned by Bombardier Eddy Edwards, Signaller 'My brain hurts' Birch and a Lieutenant from 18 Battery whose name I can't remember and a face that's left an indelible blank on my mind. The trench was in low scrub on a forward slope, interspersed among the infantry and to our right an OP from 74 Mediums which I, muggins, had to crawl to, linking them up to us by phone. At the bottom of their trench grinning upwards is L/Bombardier Ken Carter. Little did I know I was looking at the man who would one day produce *Crossroads*. Had I known I would have killed him there and then. During the night I spoke to him on the phone. I'd heard he was putting together a new show. 'Yes, it's a pantomime . . . *Ali Baba*.'

'Same cast as *Stand Easy*?'

'Bigger, much bigger . . . about a hundred.'

'Hundred? Christ, who's left to fire the guns?'

'I want it to be really big, West End stuff, the lads must be fed up with all those skinny bloody six-handed ENSA shows.'

'Think you'll be allowed to do it?'

'Yes, I've already spoken to Brigadier Rogers.'

'Did he speak to *you*, though?'

'Yes.'

'Another class barrier has fallen! Headline! Bombardier addresses Brigadier and lives.'

'Silly cunt,' said Birch.

A soft lush pink mounts the heavens and I watched over-awed as it turns almost crimson, then pales into the lucidity of daylight. Hello, who's this approaching on his stomach?

'Sorry I'm late,' it says, as it slithers into the trench.

Ah, I recognise those brown teeth, it's Thornton, my relief. What a relief!

'Sherwood's waiting behind the hill to take you back in his little Noddy car.'

I collected my small pack and crawled back, always conscious that a bloody German might spot me and riddle my arse with metal, but no! I'm safe and riding back in the bren carrier.

'It's dodgy along here,' says Sherwood.

'It's your own bloody fault for coming in daylight.'

'Couldn't help it,' he said. 'Thornton was late seeing the MO.'

'Excuses, bloody excuses, this bloody army is made up of them.'

'Keep moaning,' said Sherwood. 'It's the only way to promotion.'

Heeemmm Bammmmm! Wheeem Bamm! It's the same bloody 88mm from yesterday! Luckily he has only spotted us as we go round a hairpin bend out of view.

'We're not safe yet,' said Sherwood. 'Those bloody things can fire round corners.'

They couldn't. What they *could* do was wait for you to reappear, and when we did, he was waiting. Wheeeem Bammm! Wheeem Bammm! He was getting too close, we'd have to take evasive action. Sherwood pulls the carrier off the road down a very steep gradient, it takes us out of view but puts us at a perilous angle. We wait, listening intently. We know what to do, it's a terrible trick, you wait for a vehicle going in the opposite direction, and while Jerry is following him, you scoot out the other way. This we did, some poor bastard in a recce car came by and got the lot, and Whoosh! the khaki cowards were gone!

DECEMBER 1, 1943

Regimental Diary: Supported fire continued through the night.

Fildes' Diary: The 'do' begins tonight.

My Diary: Rain, bloody rain.

'And, on the fifth day, he divideth the land from the waters.' Not any more he didn't, for 'On yer umpteenth day, he mixeth the land and the water and lo! he maketh mud, and he putteth his beloved son, Gunner Milligan, up to his neck in it.' Command Post very busy all day, preparations for fire plan for attack at 0200 hours.

Ammunition is being dumped by the guns, through the day the pile of mustard-coloured shells mounts up. Mud is everywhere. Are they going to attack in this weather? Up a mountain? At two in the morning? I couldn't help but recall Siegfried Sassoon's World War I poem:

> He's not a bad bloke
> Said Harry to Jack
> As they humped their way forward
> With a rifle and pack
> But he did for them both with his plan of attack.

(I *think* that's right.) Did that thing still happen? To add to our emotional confusion we are issued with Christmas Air Letter Cards. They have no particular artistic merit, done by a run-of-the-mill artist. Most certainly I wouldn't let him run my mill.

0200. BARRAGE STARTS
After preliminary fire orders are given to the guns, the fire plan takes over and we just sit and wait for targets from the OP. There are nearly a thousand guns savaging the night.

0400. THE ATTACK GOES IN
Like a miracle the rain stopped just before zero hour. Is God on our side?

DECEMBER 2, 1943

We were very busy all morning, a total of 587 rounds were fired in support of the Camino Battle. On the Infantry network I hear a new map reference: 'Bare Arse Ridge'. How it got its name is hard to conceive. Lt Walker said it was during a previous attack, the Guards had come upon several Jerries squatting down having a 'Pony'. One would be hard put to it to find a memorial that said 'To the Fallen of Bare Arse Ridge', and yet that was the case.

We came to a slack period. I start writing seasonal letters, and some poetry which was crap. I read it to Lt Wright. 'What do you think of it, sir?'

'I'm afraid, Milligan, I shall never think of it,' he said.

The rain had let up, a weak silver sun strained to make itself felt. Suddenly, from what seems directly above me, comes the roar of aero engines, oh God! are we for it?, a long burst of machine-gun fire. We all rush out, there are shouts of alarm, men are running and looking up. There, at about 500 feet, are a squadron of American Kittyhawks; the leading plane appears to be coming straight for me. I don't understand, I hadn't ordered one. His machine guns are blazing away, a figure hurtles from the cockpit, a parachute mushrooms, the fighter flashes past and hits the ground a hundred yards to our left. There is no explosion, so! Hollywood had been lying to us. The pilot is floating down onto an adjacent field. Our idiot Major appears.

'Follow me,' he says as though we're the Light Brigade. He leads, holding out his pistol, he doesn't run straight for the pilot, no: we follow the track plan, we skirt the edge of the field in Indian file, the pilot is extricating himself from his chute and wondering why we are circling him, the Major bounds up, he points his pistol at a man chewing gum, wearing a red flying jacket with the words HANK, THE KID FROM IDAHO on the front, and a yellow bird on the back inscribed FLYING EAGLES, he is taking a cigarette from a packet of Camels.

'Hands up! English or German,' says the looney Major.

The American went purple. 'You're fucking lucky I'm anything, it's your trigger-happy fucking Ack-Ack, why don't they make up their minds whose fucking side they are on.'

The Major was a little taken aback, steadied himself and said, 'Consider it a gesture in return for the number of bloody times you've bombed us.'

This was great fun – Christmas, not only fighting Germans but each other. After being entertained at the officers' mess with a cup of tea, he was whisked away by a USAAF jeep driven by a coloured private wearing a white bowler hat. Don't ask me why. We waved them goodbye.

'Come and crash on us again some time,' we called.

Edgington is stumbling from his cave. 'What happened?' he said. 'I was writing to Peg.'

I grabbed his arm dramatically. 'Writing to Peg?' I echoed. 'You missed the crash? Wait, I'll see if I can get him back.'

They all go across to see the remains of the Kittyhawk. The thieving bastards make towards the wreck with chisels, hacksaws, screw drivers, I call, 'Leave a bit for me.'

Circling the wreck Edgington had said, 'I wonder if there's anyone underneath.'

White bends down and shouts: 'Anybody underneath?'

DECEMBER 8, 1943

This day the battle was won. Jerry pulled out and Monte Camino was ours. I don't think a battle could have been fought under worse conditions. The pace now slackens, I manage a wayside bath in a tin. It's so cold you keep the top half fully dressed while you do the legs, then on with the trousers, strip the top half and do that.

We are all fed up with being in the same position, and rumours are flying. We're going home, etc., and the best one of all – the war is going to finish in eight days!

Soldier and Italians trampling on a German soldier in back of lorry

DECEMBER 9, 1943

I can't take much more of this bloody rain. It's time we had a rest. I must have been depressed because on this day my diary is empty.

Fildes' Diary: I'm getting fed up with myself here and will be glad when we move or go for a rest.

Regimental Diary: Body of soldier reported lying dead in passage in RHQ.

It wasn't mine. It turned out to be an engineer who had committed suicide. 'Lucky bastard,' said Nash. I think we were all feeling like that. At 1530 hours came orders that might have saved his life. '17 and 19 Batteries will move to rear position for refitting and rest.' The news fell like a bombshell, it galvanised smiles back onto our faces. We were walking around and saying like Mr Barrett to Elizabeth, 'You must *restttt*, my dear.'

I give the order from the Command Post to all Guns, 'Cease fire – prepare to move.' We could hear the cheers come back over the headphones. The tempo changed as though we'd all been given a shot of adrenalin. I got radio AFN and plugged it through to all the gun-pit Tannoys.

We danced with each other all day.

DECEMBER 10, 1943

We were ready to move. We stand by our vehicles, all smiling, and as I say, ready to move. We warmed the engines up, ready to move, cleaned the windscreens, ready to move. Oh yes, we were ready to move. I said so. 'I'm ready to move, aren't you?' I said to Edgington and he said, 'Oh yes, I'm with you on that, as sure as I'm 954022, I'm ready to move.'

For three hours we were ready to move, then four, five and six hours. We were all falling silent. On the seventh hour Bombardier Deans said, 'I think somebody's fucked it.'

Lt Walker is passing with a bemused smile on his blond face, he turns and says, 'What are you waiting for?'

'Anything,' I said.

He paused then walked on towards his truck, where he turned and shouted, 'If it's any consolation, I'm as pissed off as you are.'

'There's a big hold-up on the Teano Road,' said BSM Griffin, trying to help.

'There's a bigger fucking hold-up here,' said Jam-Jar Griffin. 'I'm going to see a lawyer!'

'Give him my love,' said Griffin.

All night we sat and froze with only tea and bread scrounged from the cookhouse truck as relief. In painful positions we tried to sleep out the rain-filled night. It was like being tied up in sacks and thrown in the Bosporus. The growling of empty stomachs rings round the valley. At the sound of a snore a sleepless voice says, 'Lucky bastard.' I have had my legs in every position except behind my neck, and I'm saving that for an emergency. I am just dozing off with my legs behind my neck when the truck jolts.

'Mummy, mummy.' I shake Deans gently by the throat. 'Get the bucket and spades, we're off.'

Along the dawn-haunted roads we slush along. By now, life has so little interest, an announcement that the world was coming to an end could only have cheered us up. I am dozing, dozing, smoking, dozing . . .

'Wake up! We're 'ere.'

Deans is clambering out the truck, sleepily I follow, and where are we? It's a farm. We are in a large courtyard flanked by a large four-storey redbrick Victorian Gothic building with a circular Camelot-type tower, along with numerous other utility buildings. The courtyard was knee-deep in crap. We donned our 'Wellies'. We are all assigned a building, the Specialists and Signallers are given what is a shed being used as a coal-bunker.

'You'll have to clear it up if you want to get comfortable,' said Sergeant King. I dumped my kit on the coal dust-laden floor.

'Can't we burn it and start again?' I said.

There was the 'sorting-out-where-to-kip' time-lag, and then at 10.30, BREAKFAST! By which time most of us had forgotten how to eat. Hard on that we parade for Captain Sullivan.

'As you can see, this yard has been crapped in for the last hundred years by chickens, cows, sheep . . .'

Was he going to say, 'now it's our turn'?

'If we've got to spend Christmas here, we don't want to spend it up to our neck in shit, so we've got to set to and clear it up, the sooner the better.'

He then left us to clear up the shit, while he went away not to. The lads set to with shovels, but I could see that it was going to take days. I put the great Milligan brain to work and I came up with the answer. Some large squared-off timbers lay around, the thickness of a tree trunk; they were about twelve feet long by about four feet square. To these we attached dragging ropes and by pulling them along the yard up a slope, we deposited the crap into an adjacent canal. Any chicken that tried to crap here now got a brick on the back of the nut. Clouds of black coal dust swirled in the air as we set about our shed. We got so black that soon the strains of 'Swannee Ribber' were heard, and what appeared to be Negro gunners doing the cakewalk.

'I don't think this was always a coal-bunker,' said a blackened Deans. 'It's been used as a garage at times.'

'Oh what a relief,' I said. 'These little bits of unsolicited information do wonders for us.'

It was a weary bunch of gunners that bedded down that sooty night.

With the usual ingenuity, each man had concocted a bed of sorts, the most painful was Gunner Devine's. He slept on a sheet of corrugated iron, it made the most devastating clanging noise every time he moved.

DECEMBER 20, 1943

'Looking forward to Christmas, Harry?'

Edgington looks up from his mess-tin. 'I'm not sure, mate, in one way yes, in another no, the no part is spending it away from home. You can't help feeling homesick, and it's worse at Christmas.'

There is no place to be at Christmas except home. I thought of the Christmasses I remembered from boyhood days in Poona. I remember the little room I slept in at the back of the house in 5 Climo Road, the indescribable excitement of waking at four in the morning, with the world of adults all silent, finding the pillow-case full of boxes and toys, and the magic as you unwrapped each one . . . I remember waking up at the very moment my mother and grandmother were putting the pillow-case at the bottom of my bed, explaining how 'Father Christmas had just gone', and when I asked which way he went, they pointed at the window; as it was covered with chicken wire, I worked out that he was magic, had got through the holes and was now a jig-saw puzzle. All that and more was moving in the memory bank of my past, and I too knew that Christmas on a farm in Italy could never be the real thing.

WEDNESDAY, DECEMBER 22, 1943

Battery Orders: the following men have been chosen for GOS's Parade. Santa Maria La Fosse.

Breakfast	0630
Parade	0730
Embuss	0745

                    Arrive   0815
                    Parade   0830
                    March Past.

Best battle-dress. Lanyards will be worn. All webbing to be blancoed. Full FSMO less small and big pack. Rifles will not be carried.

As each one saw his name on the roll he gave a groan and slumped away like a broken man, the one word that destroyed, BLANCO!, it struck terror into all.

In disbelieving voice Sergeant King reads, 'Concert Party *excused guard* in lieu of Rehearsals!'

Morning Parade has gaps in the ranks. 'It's the Concert Party, sir,' comforts BSM Griffin.

'There's SIXTY men missing,' says Major Jenkins. 'What are they putting on . . . *Aida*?'

We have sent for Driver Kidgell in Naples. The Guns and the Scammells are at workshops being overhauled; *he's* not being overhauled, no, he and his oily bloody mates are sitting on their fat arses saying 'Phew' as they exhaust themselves playing Pontoon, and only move for meals and selling petrol. Half of them are freezing to death as they've sold their blankets, some of them are already in the Mafia.

On the morning of December 22, his lordship Kidgell arrives in a stately three-tonner lorry, he's waving from the window like Royalty and the subjects are returning it with certain signs from the waist down. He drives up to Edgington and I who are trying to make one cigarette do the job of twenty.

Short-arse Kidgell is preparing to leap from the cabin, for this he really needs a parachute.

'It's an insult,' he said, 'why didn't they send the Rolls?'

'Rolls? You *still* bloody hungry,' I said. 'Let me take the Royal Big Pack, and count the Royal Cigarettes.'

He'd done all right for fags in Naples. 'I bought 'em on the black market,' he said, as I unearthed ten packets.

Edgington is walking behind, holding up Kidgell's overcoat like an ermine cape. Bombardier Deans spots the entourage, runs forward with his groundsheet and throws it before the dwarf driver.

''Tis the Virgin Queen,' he chortles.

He's timed his arrival well. Lunch.

'Where's the cookhouse?' he said, forming a queue on his own. The sight of our well-prepared stage had impressed him. 'Bloody marvellous,' said he, 'can you eat it? Where's the cookhouse?'

We watch as Kidgell devoured a third helping of duff as though he'd been adrift with Captain Bligh. Kidgell licks his knife. 'My motto is, today I live, tomorrow I die.'

'Well, it won't be from bloody starvation.'

Meanwhile, back at the stage, Sid Carter and a group of minions are performing miracles, using coloured crêpe paper and bunting; the stage looked splendidly seasonal, even front curtains on runners. 'Mangelwurzel' Wenham had installed footlights.

'Watch this,' he said, and lowered the lights.

'Cor,' said appreciative Kidgell, 'nearly as dim as you.'

'You bugger,' said Wenham.

The piano has arrived. It is an aged black upright. Edgington supervises the unloading as though it were a Bechstein, however it was to sound more like a Franken-stein. As he struck the first chord the response was like running an iron bar around the spoke of a bicycle.

'What bloody fool chose this?' gasped Edgington.

'I did,' said Lt Walker. 'Isn't it satisfactory? I mean . . . it looked all right.'

'Oh, it looks all right, that's all you can do, look at it.'

'Oh dear.' Lt Walker was obviously distressed, after all, he was an officer, and here he was being told he was a musical ignoramus. 'That piano has set me back to the tune of 800 lire.'

'Well sir, that's the *only* tune you'll get out of it.'

CHRISTMAS DAY, DECEMBER 25, 1943

Alf Fildes' Diary: Sgt-Major Griffin and Sgts wake us with tea and rum and we're off!

My Diary: Late reveille, don't have to get up. BSM and SGTS bring us tea and rum in bed.

It was all too much. 'Give us a kiss, Sarge,' I said as Mick Ryan filled my battered tea mug.

'You'll kiss me arse,' he says. An unbearable thought.

All around, smiling gunners are sitting up like old ladies in Geriatric Wards, grinning. 'Merry Christmas,' they say to each other. We linger over the Rum-laden tea.

'There's a carol service at RHQ, at 11.00, if anybody wants to go.'

Why not? It's Christmas, the season of goodwill? Nobody went. A Regimental Parson in a barn merrily sang 'The First Noel', all by himself. Fried Eggs and Bacon for breakkers! Wow!!!

The morning was spent fiddling around with the stage and props. All seemed set; we then concentrated on thinking about Christmas dinner.

'I will eat mine *very, very* slowly. I want it to last as long as possible,' said Gunner White.

'They say there's tinned turkey on the menu,' I said.

'How do you know?' said Kidgell, his stomach revolving at the thought.

'I heard a rumour.'

'Look, mate, said Kidgell, 'I don't want a *rumour* of a turkey, I want a *real* bloody one, parson's nose and all.' So saying, he ran off to practise eating.

A detail of layabouts had been rounded up and a long makeshift table laid out in an adjacent barn. It consisted of long planks resting on trestles, blankets for tablecloths; someone with a soul had stuck thorn-leaves into some tins to resemble holly. BSM Griffin's voice rings on the air.

225

'Come and get it!'

We take off like sprinters and collide as we try to squeeze through the door. Thundering ahead is Kidgell, his legs barely touching the ground; pounding behind him is Gunner White, his tongue dragging along the floor. The cry goes up, 'For God's sake stop Kidgell before he gets there or we'll get bugger all.'

Like a jig-saw puzzle we all fit into place around the table. We sat on an assortment of chairs, stools, tins, logs. We are served, as is the tradition of the Royal Artillery, by the Officers and Sergeants. Lieutenant Walker is the wine waiter; himself having partaken of several pre-lunch drinks he is missing the glasses by a substantial amount. Gunner Musclewhite has a lap full of white Chianti, and Gunner Bailey is getting red wine among his greens. The Sergeants are ladelling out tinned turkey, pork, beef, roast potatoes, sprouts, carrots and gravy. None of our 'waiters' are quite sober and there is an overlap at the end of the dinner when Sgt Ryan is pouring custard over the turkey. As the wine takes effect, the chatter and laughter increase. For duff we have Christmas pudding and custard.

''Urry up, you buggers,' said Sgt 'Daddy' Wilson, 'we're waitin' to 'ave ours.'

There seemed endless helpings and unlimited supplies of red and white wine, but it was a long way from the Dickensian Christmas around a log fire in the parlour, with Grandma and Grandpa present.

The Sergeants and Officers are returning, carrying makeshift trays laden with bottles of beer, oranges and nuts. Smudger calls for a toast to 'the Orficers and Sarnts'. There follow more toasts to the Regiment, the King, and in fact anybody. I distinctly heard, 'Gentlemen the toast is Anybody.'

We gave the Sergeants and the Officers a cheer and in that order. We left the table looking like Genghis Khan's horsemen had galloped over it. I felt as though they'd galloped over me. There was aught but sleep it all off. We washed our mess-tins in the three separate troughs – WASH, RINSE, DISINFECT, for those interested in detail – these were made from oil drums sawn in half and filled with the requisite liquid. In fact there was to be a 'Quickie' in the concert where 'Brutarse' stabs Julius Geezer, then proceeds to Wash, Rinse and Disinfect the murder weapon.

Those who had thoughts of getting into Naples were frustrated, as the city was declared out of bounds due to typhus. 'Merry Typhus,' some of them were saying. The great moment is drawing nigh, the Concert! The audience are arriving early, most of them with bottles of beer stuffed in their coats.

'THE SHOW'

The 'artistes' are hidden from view behind a screen of blankets that have run the length of the hall. Behind it all the secrets of showbiz are poised to hurl on an unsuspecting audience. The building reverberates to the buzz of conversation. We open with a chord behind the curtains, then I shout:

'Ladies and Gentlemen! the 19 Battery Christmas Show!' The Band swings into 'We're the Boys from Battery D', then switch to our two ocarinas for the Rocamanfina Rhumba. In the absence of a good finish the band all shout HOI! Curtain down, we dash off to change. We hear Gunner Joe Slater in his strangled tenor singing *As Time Goes By*. Edgington is left behind to accompany him on piano.

'Harry will have to be quick,' said Fildes. 'He's only got "The Green Eye of the Little Yellow God" to change in.'

Edgington rushes in while Slater is still taking his applause. 'Where's me beard?' he gabbled. We help him into his gear and soon he looks like Zeke MacCoy of Coon

County. Sgt King is on and getting a hard time from the lads.

'He was worshipped by the ranks.'

'Was he fuck!' came an authoritative cockney voice from the back.

'You're on,' says Jam-Jar Griffin.

Fildes, White and Kidgell set themselves up on the stage. Edgington and I wait in the wings.

'Ladies and Gentlemen, the Royal Horse Hillbillies.'

Boos, etc. Curtain up. The scene, three hillbillies, seated, drinking Racoon Juice and 'Barr's Sweat' from our rum-ration jugs. Gales of uncontrollable laughter. Why? Gunner White is showing a pair of testicles hanging in full view from under his nightshirt. Fildes is paring his toenails with a jack-knife; in his hands a dozen three-inch bolts that he drops as his toenails are pared. Kidgell swigs his 'Racoon's Piss', spits, and from the back of the hall comes a Danggggggggg! as BSM Griffin hits an empty 25-pounder shell-case. BANGGG! BANGGG! Edgington and I let off our blank cartridge muskets. We had never tried them before, so loud was the explosion that a great gasp of 'Corrr bloody hell' ran through the audience. At the same time two tin plates dislodged from the roof and covered us in a patina of rust.

'Don't fire any more,' said a terrified Sloggit, who was working the curtains.

Enter Edgington and Milligan.

Kidgell: War yew tew bin? (SPIT AND DANGGGGGG).

Spike: We dun just kilt a barrrr (SPIT AND DANG).

Edgington: Beegest Barrrr I ever seed (SPIT . . . LONG PAUSE SMALL TING!!!).

Spike: That barr, when I seed him he dun growl, so Ahhh growls back, he leans ter the laift, so Ahh leans to the laift, he scratches his balls, so Ahh scratch me balls . . . then that barrrrr dun a shit, and I said Barrrr yew got me there . . . I dun that when I fust seed yew . . .

A few more gags like that, then we all sing 'Ah Like

Mountain Music', Fildes on the guitar, me and Edgington on ocarinas, Kidgell on the 'Racoon's Piss' Jar. The music was interspersed with rhythmic spits and distant Dangsssss!!! in tempo, and we went off a treat.

'Gunner Shipman will now sing "Shipmate of Mine",' announced Jam-Jar Griffin. ''Ees never seen a bleedin' ship,' heckles a voice.

The curtain goes back to reveal Edgington at the piano in bare feet, dressed as a hillbilly. Shipman has a pleasant baritone voice inaudible in the low register; he insists on walking about as he sings, causing numerous clink-clanks from the stage. His song is frequently interrupted by hissed whispers from the wings, 'Keep still.' He stops in mid song to ask the voice what it is saying. 'Keep still, the floor's squeaking when you walk about.' He then continues except that his last position was on the extreme right of the stage, so we have a spectacle of a piano one side, an empty stage, and a singing gunner on the extreme right. He is well received.

Jock Webster follows with a series of hoary old Scottish jokes. 'Is anything worn under the kilt? Nai man! everything's in perfect working order,' etc. etc.

To the great mock fight twixt Deans and Robinson. They appeared in Long Johns and plimsolls. They had been rehearsing this mock fight for a week, but it was all pointless, as in the first few moments Deans took a right hander to the chin that had him groggy, and from then on Robinson had to nurse him along. The crowd barracks, 'Kill 'im . . . call a priest . . . send 'im 'ome . . .' The 'fight' went the whole distance and they were given an ovation, especially Deans who now had blood running down his chin. His parting remark, 'You want blood, you bastards, well, you got it.'

Next, I and the mob in community singing. American officers were baffled by songs like

> I painted her,
> I painted her,
> Up her belly and down her back
> In every hole and every crack
> I painted her,
> I painted her,
> I painted her old tomater over and over
> again.

It's BSM Griffin now, and he's had quite a skinful and does a conjuring act that to this day neither I nor anyone else understands. *He* doesn't even remember it; he sat hidden under a blanket pushing cards out through the slit asking 'What is it?' A member of the audience would identify it: 'Ace of Spades.' He would take it back inside the blanket and from his obscurity say, 'So it is.' I think he got booed off, and seemed well pleased with it.

Kidgell next, his old favourites, 'Sweet Mystery of Life', 'Drigo's Serenade'. He has a very good voice.

'He ought to have had it trained,' said Edgington.

'To run errands,' added Fildes.

Kidgell had announced himself, 'I will sing songs you all know and love.'

Voice of horror from the back, 'Ohhhh Nooo.'

When Doug had finished the same voice said, 'I didn't love or know any of 'em.'

Behind the stage Sid Carter has opened a few bottles of wine to celebrate the show going well.

'We should wait till the end really,' he said, 'but with this mob there might not be any bloody end.'

Edgington is at the piano playing his own tunes with that grim bloody look on his face, as if he expected a shot to ring out from the audience. One of the notes went dead on him and he brought forth laughter whenever he came to the missing note, as he stood up and sang the note himself. Next, from Liverpool, we have a real 'Scouse', Joe Kearns.

He tells lots of Liverpudlian jokes like 'My owd man's got a glass eye, one night he swallowed it, he went to see the doctor, doctor said drop 'em, bend down, and he sees this glass eye lookin' at him out the back and he says, '"Wot's the matter, don't you trust me?"''

After him the Band are on again. We play a favourite of ours, 'Tangerine', and what in those days was a red-hot number, 'Watch the Birdie'. We didn't go that well because the boys had heard us so many times at dances. The Finale was a send-up of Major 'Jumbo' Jenkins in Command Post Follies, in which we took the piss out of him in no uncertain fashion. He was fuming, but put a fixed grin on his silly face. We conclude with the cast singing 'Jogging Along to the Regimental Gallop' to the tune of Jenkins' own favourite, 'Whistling Rufus', and by God, we got a mighty ovation at the end.

The officers came backstage to congratulate us, and with consummate skill drink all our grog. We all got pretty tanked up; long after everyone had gone to bed Harry and I sat on the stage drinking and re-running the show. It had been a great night.

'Now what?' said Edgington.

Now what indeed.

SEARCH FOR AFN NAPLES

January 2/3, 1944. I wanted to get the Band a broadcast; with this in mind I skidaddled to Naples, hitching all the way. After much searching, I finally located the offices of the Allied Forces Network. They were located on the first floor of the San Carlo Opera house. I passed along a corridor of Baroque doors. Signs – 'Cappo de Ballet', 'Maestro del Orchestra', 'Prima Ballerina', and 'Vietato Ingresso'. Finally a piece of true British enterprise, 'AFN Liaison Officer', written on a piece of cardboard with a three-inch nail through it. I knocked politely – the door was opened by a tubby ATS girl who greeted me with 'Yes?'

'I'd like to speak to someone about doing a broadcast.'

'Oh yes?'

'Yes . . .'

She stood there like a dummy.

'Well – could you tell me who to see?'

'Well, there's only Lieutenant Mondey.'

'Can I see only him?'

'Does he know you're coming?'

'Not unless he's an extra-sensory perceptionist.'

'I'll tell him you're here.'

She waddled off to a door directly behind her. Her bottom wobbled as though operated by an invisible hand. She reappeared blushing as though she had been interfered with. If this was the case her molester must be blind.

'Lt Mondey will see you now.'

I walked into a room that had obviously once been a broom cupboard. The desk took up most of the room, the walls were barren save for a nail with a hat on. On the desk was the stub of a pencil, a telephone and a copy of the *Union Jack*. Behind it sat a minute, sallow-complexioned man; he was either a dwarf or sitting on a milking stool. If the latter was the case, the pained expression suggested the stool was inverted. He looked at me as though I had come from Mars.

'Yes, what is it?' he said, shifting his seat.

His demeanour gave me the same feeling Edith Cavell got on the dawn of her execution.

'I'm Lance Bombardier Milligan, sir, 56th Heavy Regiment.'

He received this announcement as though it was an eviction notice.

'Oh yes,' he said.

'I'd like to get a broadcast for a Jazz Quartet.'

An eviction notice plus seizure of all assets. This was all new to him; by the silly look on his face, *any*thing was new to him. He squirmed and said, 'I see.' He didn't really. 'Are you professional musicians?'

I thought the answer 'Yes' a good one.

'Do you earn your living as a musician?'

'No. I earn it as a Lance Bombardier.'

'I'd better make a note of the Band's name,' he said. 'It's – er? – er?'

'It's – er D Battery Dance Band.'

'E Battery?'

'D sir.'

'What?'

'It's D, sir.'

'D? D what?'

'D Battery – you were writing E.'

'Oh,' he scribbled out the E and wrote D. 'There,' he said as though he'd climbed Everest. 'Now!' He placed his pencil tidily on his desk. 'Anything else?'

Anything else? What was he talking about?

'Yes, sir . . . when?'

'When what?'

'When can we broadcast?'

'Broadcast? Well . . . we don't know what you sound like, do we? ha ha ha.'

'Well, how about an audition?'

'Audition?' It was like checkmate. 'Ah yes – an audition – now when?'

'Any time.'

'Any time – when would that be?'

God! there was only one way he became an officer, he was baptised one.

'I think my boys could make it day after tomorrow – the afternoon.'

'Let me check my diary.' He opened a drawer which was empty, he pretended to write something, closed the drawer. 'Well, that's that,' he blinked.

I saluted, he didn't. I don't think he knew how to. I walked out past the ATS girl, who was preparing for the next groping session.

Outside I rubbed my hands with glee. (I always kept a tin handy.) Wait till the lads hear the news!

'Now what songs will I sing?' were Kidgell's first reactions. 'I'll be a hit on radio – for a start they can't see what a short-arse I am.'

'It took a bloody war to get us on the air,' Fildes says, 'we owe it all to Hitler.'

'Gentlemen,' I said, 'will you all stand for Adolf Hitler.'

JANUARY 4, 1944

My Diary: Night of fourth. News that we are about to move 'somewhere' at 'short notice'. This has flattened any hopes of the band playing on the AFN network in Naples. Bugger! Bugger! Bugger!

It was a coldish night, so most of us were in bed, some with bottles of vino, some reading old newspapers, some writing those feverish letters home. I was reading letters from Bette, Beryl, Lily, Ivy Mae, Madge, and for some inexplicable reason, Jim. I would read all the best bits out to the most frustrated Gunners. White is sitting up in bed, with Happy New Year chalked on his tin hat.

Enter Bombardier Fuller. What's he doing up? He is fully dressed, looking very alert, and bearing down on us. It looks bad. It is bad. He says, 'Listen fer yer names.' He calls out, 'Nash, Milligan, Deans', he drones on for about ten more. My God, they've found us, we were going to war again – a new position. We are the advance party to dig gun-pits, Command Posts, cookhouse, shit house, etc. etc.

'You've got to be packed and ready to leave at 0530 hours.'

Christ. Breakfast at 4.30. Bloody hell!! Why don't they make sleeping a crime and have done with it?

JANUARY 5, 1944

By eleven, we arrived at the hill village of Lauro – through it ran the road to the 5th Army west front.

THURSDAY, JANUARY 6, 1944

On the job at 8.15. Bitter cold. Through the bushes masking our positions we can see the snow on the hills across the Garigliano.

We were supposed to dig a Command Post, but No! No, we find a super cave right near the gun positions. So, instead we have to dig a cookhouse; this took most of the day. We dug into a bank under the supervision (Super?) of Vic Nash. There is nothing so invigorating as an ex-Old Kent Road pastry cook tellin' you how to dig a hole.

Hands and feet are freezing, the only way to get them warm is dig. By five o'clock it was too dark to see. We returned to the billet and luxuriated in the warmth inside provided by an old Italian device, a large stone the size of a millstone, with a countersunk hole in the middle filled with charcoal, that burnt brightly with the minimum of smoke. It was all very quiet here, but at night we hear how close our infantry were by the night exchanges of machine-gun fire, just over the brow of a hillock behind us. At night we would hear the grumble of vehicles bringing supplies for the 'build up', and a sound that always made me feel ill, infantry men coming up the line, the unending trudge of what sounded like hollow boots and the occasional clank or clink of some metal equipment, and most distinctive, that ring of an empty metal tea mug. I used to wonder how in God's name the High Command could keep the movement of a quarter of a million men secret . . . I always had the feeling that Hitler knew exactly where I was all the time.

On this the coldest day of the year, we hear that bitter fighting is going on for Vittori, and we are now only five miles from Cassino.

The days that followed were all the same, digging. To speed up the process more gunners arrive to dig at night! Mail is slow in coming up here owing to the traffic congestion and the one-way road system.

JANUARY 11, 1944

My Diary: Digging finished. Swearing stops.

At last. We could relax, but still all movement had to be minimal and carried out under cover. Nash used to hold a piece of cardboard over his head. He was desperate for an officer to ask why, but it never came to pass. One fine morning he says, 'I must have a look at Jerry's lines. It's a nice clear day, the view ought to be good.'

He was right, the view was so good he got a Jerry bullet over his head, and a terrible telling off from Sgt Jock Wilson.

'You want tae giv awa' oer position? You stoopid little cockney cunt!'

We had done all the digging and were now to evacuate our own G truck billet. Down a small bank we find an ideal spot, and start to dig. We make it almost a room-size excavation, we roof it with corrugated iron, prop it up with poles, some canvas to waterproof it, a camouflage net on top along with dressing of bushes and branches. With loving care *I (me)* tunnelled out a large chimney, and had a fire going to dry out the interior. What I needed for a bed was a good piece of wood. Now, Gunner Nash had mentioned a ruined church across the road.

'There's catacombs, you can see 'em through the floor.'

Yes indeed, Nash saw Milligan disappear down that hole; soon hurling upwards were numerous bones, skulls, rocks, etc. as I searched for a coffin lid. Eureka! I got three, and soon I was lying on it in grand style; the others I gave to Deans, and one to the telephone exchange for the duty signaller to lean against.

SATURDAY, JANUARY 15, 1944

I woke up with a feeling of foreboding, had it all day, I remember on duty in the Command Post. In the darkness men, machines and guns are moving, moving, moving, an occasional mule brays out a protest; this luxury is not afforded the men, it's uncanny how we hear no utterance from them. It's as though they are struck dumb. To add to the depressing atmosphere a lone piper wails in the rain-filled dark 'The Skye Boat Song'.

'It's the London Scottish, they're burying their dead,' said Bdr Fuller, who had come in to replace the batteries in the telephone. 'Poor bastards, buryin' 'em in the bloody rain, their graves are 'alf full of bloody water.'

The air above the gun position is an overlay of Jerry shells. 'They're after something behind us.'

We hear the shells exploding, and I wonder if they're on target. Grapevine says No. 0350 hrs, more fire orders, no one sleeps tonight. 0500 hrs. The rain has stopped. Through the cave mouth I see the trees growing in the morning light; among them I see the muzzle bed. In comes Tume.

'Oh, here we bloody go again,' he puts his mug of tea down, no time to drink, more fire orders. I leave the cave; outside it's guns guns guns! There's a frost. I feel it crunching underfoot. I descend the ladder to our dug-out. Deans is asleep . . . the fire is just alive, I throw a handful of wood on, the noise awakens him.

''Ello,' he yawns, 'what's the time?'

'Just gone five . . . bloody cold.'

I automatically prepare my bed. I'm off to collect grub, I wobble across the hard ground, balancing my dixies, powdered egg and mashed potatoes; as I walk I sip the life-giving tea – why do we dote on tea? It tastes bloody awful, it's only the sugar and milk that makes it drinkable. It's like fags – we've got hooked. Weary, I climbed into my bed, three dark blue blankets, and one grey, funny how I should still remember the colours . . . As I closed my eyes, the sun was streaming above my sand-bagged wall; it cut a golden swathe into our dug-out, illuminating Deans' legs. He was shaving into a metal mirror and humming a tune.

'Sorry mate,' Sgt King is peering down on me, 'we're fresh out of signallers, you'll have to go back on Command Post at eight.'

What was it now? 6.40. 'OK, Sarge, I'll kip till then. You'll wake me, won't you?'

No he won't. I sleep fitfully, casting glances at my watch. I'm back in London – no I'm not, I'm in Italy. My mother is making banana sandwiches. I'm off to work – no I'm not, I'm in Italy at five to eight. And I was washing in Spike Deans' dirty water; a fag, and I'm back in the Command Post. Lt Stewart Pride is duty officer. Christ, I'm tired.

'I'll get you a relief at mid-day,' said Bombardier Fuller; the bugger looked clean-shaven and fresh. He'd been getting his quota of kip.

MONDAY, JANUARY 17, 1944

Regimental Diary: Regimental OP established at 882960 and line laid by 10.30.

Fildes' Diary: This was the hottest time I've ever had when we crossed the Garigliano. Shepherd and I in jeeps were two days behind the advance carrying party, who footslogged to the river then crossed in boats. We joined them at 167 Brigade HQ.

My Diary: Breakfast at 0800. OP party foregather at 0900. We are issued with Arctic carrying packs. We have a 'dress rehearsal', fully loaded, then break off till further orders, in which time I am writing this.

I had made a note in my diary at this point saying, 'I died

for the England I dreamed of, not the England I know.' I had a terrible foreboding of death. I'd never had it before. We hang around all day. The waiting is the worst part. I oil my tommy gun, I don't know why, it's already oiled. Word that our Major and his OP party are at 167 Bde HQ at Santa Castrese.

'I suppose', says Fuller, '"ees the patron saint of Castration.'

'They make a damn fine stew,' I said.

'What do?'

'Bollocks.'

I had a great urge to go to the ballet. I had always loved ballet, and was forever in love with ballerinas; it's something I still suffer from. Somehow I couldn't see myself going to the ballet today. Going to the Major, under fire, crawling forward to him and saying, 'Excuse me, sir, could I have a 24-hour pass to see Coppelia?' It wasn't on.

'You're not going, Milligan, you're wanted on the WT

Lt Stewart Pride awaiting a call to stand in for James Mason

at the Command Post.' Bombardier Fuller gives me the news. Birch is to go in my place. Christ, what game are they playing? That's twice! This will drive me bloody mad. Still I was going to be safe. Why was I grumbling? It's still evening. It's sunny, and, it's good to be alive.

'Christ! You back again,' said Deans.

'Is it bothering you?'

'No.'

'Well, it's bothering me.'

I flopped on my bed and dumped my small pack down. Five o'clock. Time for Command Post. I've got a sore bottom. The dreaded piles!

The evening in the Command Post was enlivened by some Coon-type singing. Lt Stewart Pride, Edgington, Deans and I were given to spirituals. Our programme was 'Swing Low, Sweet Chariot', 'I looked over Jordan', 'Old Man Ribber'. At eight o'clock I flopped onto my bed. I knew there was a barrage going over at 2100 hours. I didn't want to miss it, so I read a collection of *Tit-Bits* and *Tatler*s. I must have dozed off but I was awakened by the Boof boof boof of Beauforts blazing away about four hundred yards from my dug-out. In my diary I write, 'Barrage not very intense. Beauforts using one in five tracer, I think it's more a marking barrage for the infantry. Better get my head down, I'm on at 0500! Piles giving me hell.'

JANUARY 18, 1944

Somewhere in the small hours I heard explosions in that distant sleep-ridden way; I heard Spike Deans say in a sing-song voice like Jiminy Cricket, 'Oh Spikeeeee, we're being shelleeddd.'

I remember my reply, 'Fuck 'em', and dozed off but then . . . my diary tells the story:

0220 hrs: Awakened by someone screaming coming from the guns, pulled back the black-out and could see the glare of a large fire, at the same time a voice in pain was shouting 'command post, for god's sake somebody, where's the command post?' It was someone with his hair on fire coming up the path, he was beating it out with his hand, I jumped from my bed sans trousers and ran towards him, it was bombardier Begent. I helped beat the flames out. His face and hands were badly burnt, I helped him up the ladder to the command post and I blurted out to those within, 'There's been a direct hit on the guns.' I realised then I was late with the news, wounded gunners were already being attended to. Everybody looked very tense, behind me flames were leaping twenty feet in the air, I rushed back to my dug-out, dressed in a flash. Took my blankets back to the command post to help cover the wounded. I then joined the rest of the battery, who were all pulling red-hot and burning charge-cases away from those not yet affected. They were too hot to pull by hand so we used pickaxes wedged in the handles. Lieutenant Stewart

Spike Deans waiting to steal a lorry

Pride was heaping earth on them with his hands. Gunner Devine seemed to be enjoying it, he was grinning and shouting, 'This is the first time I've been warm today.' It never occurred to me that some of the boxes that were hot might still contain unexploded cordite charge, fortunately they didn't go off and that's why I'm able to write this diary today.

It was a terrible night, four Gunners died and six were wounded. All suffering burns in varying degrees. The work of subduing the fire and tidying up went on until early dawn. It was terrible to see the burnt corpses. There was little Gunner Musclewhite, he'd been killed sitting up in bed. He was burnt black, and his teeth showed white through his black, fleshless head. Sgt Jock Wilson too, Gunner White and Ferrier . . .

A burial party under BSM Griffin were starting to dig as dawn came up. I went on duty at the Command Post. I wondered where Edgington was and wondered if he was a victim.

'No, he's on Exchange duties,' said Chalky White.

I had to run over to him just to verify. I pulled back the black-out that covered the little cave that the Telephone Exchange was; I could see he was visibly shaken by the affair.

'Just seein' you was still alive,' I said and rushed back to the chaos.

What had happened need never have been so bad had we all not become careless. The Gunners had dug themselves a dug-out and covered it with a camouflage net, but they had surrounded their dug-out with Charge Boxes. The first shells must have hit the charges, which blew up and ignited the camouflage net that then fell in flames on top of those trapped underneath . . .

1650 HRS: Lauro dive-bombed by seven enemy fighters. The all-night standing had made the piles worse. They started to bleed, it's all I needed for a perfect night.

Yes! I have what is called the curse of the Milligans –
piles! My father had them, my grandfather had them, I was
born with them. I thought they came along with legs, arms
and teeth. They were bloody painful, and mine were
bleeding down my legs.

JANUARY 19, 1944

*My Diary: Fildes arrived back from OP with Ernie Hart all
badly shaken, Hart is all in and crying. 'Those poor bastards up
there,' he says.*

Lt Wright calls the few remaining signallers together.
'Look,' he sounds uneasy, 'they need a signal replacement
up at Tac HQ . . . any volunteers? . . .'
There is an embarrassing silence, I can't stand it.
'I'll go, sir,' I heard myself say; I was the only NCO
there, I *had* to say it, example and all that. 'So, Mr Fildes,
you have come to take me for a nice little ride.'
Alf Fildes smirks. His eyes tell a different story.

GOING TO DIMIANO OP

January 20, 1944. I get into the jeep next to Alf and we set
off; he didn't say much until we got through Lauro and then
on to the railway track, now denuded of rails and used as a
communications road. It was a lovely day, sunny. Suddenly
Alf said, 'This is beautiful! Sunshine – birds singing, I
could do with more of this.'
He told me the OP and the Major's HQ were both in
'dodgy' positions. Hart had been up the OP, and it had
finished him – Jerry was ramming everything onto them. It
all sounded grim, and I wondered what my lot would be.
The sounds of Artillery faded as small arms, automatic
weapons and mortars increased. We were passing a steady
stream of ambulances; one I noticed had shrapnel holes in
the sides.

We turned off the railway embankment on to a country 'road', really a cart track; a one-mile sign read 'Castleforte 5 kilometer'.

'How's Jenkins been behaving?' I said.

Fildes smirked. 'He sends everyone up the OP except himself. I think he's shit scared, that or barmy.'

Off the road to our right is a cluster of farmhouses, some shelled, some intact.

'This is it,' says Fildes, as we turn right into them.

We pull up in front of the centremost one. A two-storeyed affair – all around are dead Jerries. MG bullets are whistling overhead as we duck and run inside.

It was a large room. On a makeshift table was a 22 Set. There was Jenkins. Lying down at the far end of the room, 'Flash' Gordon, Birch, Fuller, Howard, Badgy Ballard, Dipper Dai – all looked as gloomy as hell.

'It isn't the war,' said Birch, 'it's Jenkins.'

'Milligan – you can get on the set right away,' says Jenkins.

I took over from Fuller; immediately, Jenkins sends RHQ a series of pointless messages. 'It's very stuffy in the room.' 'There are eight ORs, two NCOs and myself.'

Alf Fildes on the path just outside our dug-out in Lauro. His hands are tied behind his back to stop him going blind

'Thornton coming back.' 'The Germans are shelling us.' 'The Germans have stopped shelling us.'

I don't exactly know what his job was supposed to be. The people who were taking the stick were Lt Budden and party, who were being 'stonked' unmercifully. In the room, save for a direct hit, we were comparatively safe. From the time I arrived (about 4pm) the bastard kept me on the set all night, a total of seventeen hours with the headphones on. It was my third night without sleep, just the noise of the interference was enough to drive you potty. To get a break I said, 'Do you think, sir, under the Articles of War, I could be relieved, so I can relieve myself?' Even then he said, 'Well, hurry up.' I felt like saying, 'I will piss as fast as I can, sir – would you like someone to time me in case I loiter?'

Outside a young Lieutenant was talking to a Sergeant. ' . . . Then why didn't they stay inside. I mean those inside didn't get killed.' I presume he was referring to the unburied dead who lay without the walls. It was dark. A stream of MG bullets whined over the roof, God knows what he was aiming for – there was nothing behind us.

Dawn came. I was almost numb with fatigue, and my piles had started to bleed. I should never have volunteered. One of the lads makes breakfast – while I'm eating it Jenkins tells me, 'Bombardier, I want you to take Gordon, Howard, Birch and Ballard to the OP with fresh batteries and a 22 set.' Great, all I have to do is carry a 50lb battery to the top of a mountain, anything else? Like how about a mile run before in medieval armour?

Ballard apparently knows the way. At 9.00 we put on Arctic Packs and strap on one battery each. We set off single file on the road towards Castleforte, which sits in the near distance on a hillside full of Germans. We turn left off the road into a field; we pass a Sherman Tank, a neat hole punched in the turret; a tank man is removing kit from inside. Lying on a groundsheet is the mangled figure of one of the crew.

'What a mess,' says the Tankman in the same tones as though there was mud on the carpet.

I grinned at him and passed on. Above us the battle was going on full pelt; coming towards us is Thornton, dear old 36-year-old-Thornton; he looks tired, he has no hat, and is smoking a pipe.

'Hello, what's on?'

He explains he's been sent back. 'I'm too old for that lark. I kept fallin' asleep.'

I asked him the best way up. He reaffirms, 'You go up a stone-lined gully; when it ends start climbing the hill, it's all stepped for olive trees. Of course,' he added, 'if you're in the gully and they start mortaring, you've had it.

'Thanks,' I said, 'that's cheered us up no end.'

He bid us farewell and we went forward, we reached the gully. In a ravine to the left were Infantry all dug into the side; they were either 'resting' or in reserve. So far so good. We reach the end of the stone gully and start climbing the stepped mountain – each step is six foot high, so it's a stiff climb. CRUMP! CRUMP! CRUMP!, mortars. We hit the ground. CRUMP CRUMP CRUMP – they stop. Why? Can they see us? We get up and go on, CRUMP CRUMP CRUMP – he can see us! We hit the deck. A rain of them fall around us. I cling to the ground. The mortars rain down on us. I'll have a fag, that's what. I am holding a packet of Woodbines, then there is a noise like thunder. It's right on my head, there's a high-pitched whistle in my ears, at first I black out and then I see red, I am strangely dazed. I was on my front, now I'm on my back, the red was opening my eyes straight into the sun. I know if we stay here we'll all die . . . I start to scramble down the hill. There's shouting, I can't recall anything clearly. Next I was at the bottom of the mountain, next I'm speaking to Major Jenkins, I am crying, I don't know why, he's saying, 'Get that wound dressed.'

I said, 'What wound?'

I had been hit on the side of my right leg.

'Why did you come back?' He is shouting at me and threatening me, I can't remember what I am saying. He's saying, 'You could find your way back but you couldn't find your way to the OP', next I'm sitting in an ambulance and shaking, an orderly puts a blanket round my shoulders, I'm crying again, why why why? Next I'm in a forward dressing station, an orderly gives me a bowl of hot very sweet tea, 'Swallow these,' he says, two small white pills. I can't hold the bowl for shaking, he takes it from me and helps me drink it. All around are wounded, he has rolled up my trouser leg. He's putting a sticking plaster on the wound, he's telling me it's only a small one. I don't really care if it's big or small, why am I crying? Why can't I stop? I'm getting lots of sympathy, what I want is an explanation. I'm feeling drowsy, and I must have started to sway because next I'm on a stretcher. I feel lovely, what were in those tablets . . . that's the stuff for me, who wants food? I don't know how long I'm there, I wake up. I'm still on the stretcher, I'm not drowsy, but I start to shiver. I sit up. They put a label on me. They get me to my feet and help me to an ambulance. I can see really badly wounded men, their bandages soaked through with blood, plasma is being dripped into them.

When we get to one of the Red Cross trucks, an Italian woman, all in black, young, beautiful, is holding a dead baby and weeping; someone says the child has been killed by a shell splinter. The relatives are standing by looking out of place in their ragged peasants' clothing amid all the uniforms. An older woman gives her a plate of home-made biscuits, of no possible use, just a desperate gesture of love. She sits in front with the driver. I'm in the back. We all sit on seats facing each other, not one face can I remember. Suddenly we are passing through our artillery lines as the guns fire. I jump at each explosion, then, a gesture I will never forget, a young soldier next to me with his right arm in a bloody sling put his arm around my shoulder and tried to comfort me. 'There, there, you'll be all right mate.'

We arrive at a camp. I was put into a tent on a bunk bed. An orderly gave me four tablets and more hot tea; in a few seconds they put me out like a light. I had finished being a useful soldier. I've had it.

I wake up, it's very early, am I now stark raving mad? I can distinctly hear a brass band, right outside the tent, they are playing 'Roll Out The Barrel' at an incredible speed. I get up, look outside. There in a circle stand a collection of GIs, all playing this tune; they are in a strange collection of garments, some in overcoats with bare legs and boots, some in pyjamas, others in underpants, unlaced boots and sweaters, an extraordinary mixture.

I looked at my watch. It was 0645. This I discovered was the American Reveille; the tune finished, the men doubled back to their beds. But where was I? It was a large hospital tent, full of bunk beds with sleeping soldiers. I was the only one awake, and was still fully dressed save my battle-dress jacket. For the first time I felt my right leg aching. I sat on the side of my bed, took the plaster off my leg to look at the wound. It was a wound about two inches long and about a quarter of an inch deep, as though I had been slashed with a razor blade. Today you can only see the scar if I get sunburnt. It wasn't hindering me, so what was I here for? I lit up a cigarette. It was one of my five remaining Woodbines, now very crushed. Two RAMC Orderlies enter the tent, young lads, they go around the beds looking at the labels; they woke some of the men up, gave them tablets. They arrived at me. I asked them where I was. They told me it was 144 CCS, I was labelled 'Battle Fatigue'. I was to see a psychiatrist that evening. Meantime there was a mess tent where I could get breakfast. I told them I didn't have my small kit. 'Don't worry, lad, they've got knives and forks there.'

Lad? So I was Lad now. It was a wretched time. No small

kit, no towel, no soap, no friends. It's amazing what small simple things really make up our life-support system, all I wanted was for some cold water on my face. I went across to the American Camp and from a GI (of all things smoking a cigar) I scrounged a towel. He was more than generous, he took me to his Quarter Master, who gave me two brand-new khaki-coloured towels, soap, and a razor. I'm afraid I was still in a terrible emotional state, and I started to cry 'Thanks' but apparently they were aware that the Camp next to them were Battle Fatigue cases.

I wandered through a mess of tents till I found the Ablutions. It was still only 7.30, but the place was full; there was the terrible silence of a mass of people who don't know each other. I washed in silence, and the cold water made me feel a little fresher. The seat of my trousers is all sticky. Oh God, what a mess, blood, the curse of the Milligans is still working. What I really want is a bath. I'm given two different-sized pills. I ask what they are, the orderly says, 'I don't know, chum.' (I'm Chum now.) He knows all right, but it was early days for tranquillisers. 'Take them after breakfast.' I have absolutely no recollection of eating breakfast, I think that I took the tablets right away; next thing it was evening time, I'm very dopey.

'You got to see the "Trick Cyclist",' says the young orderly. I had no idea what 'Trick Cyclist' meant. I asked. Psychiatrist? That was for lunatics. Was I one? I was to find out. In a small officer-type tent, behind an Army folding-table covered with a grey blanket sits a stern, or rather attempting to look stern, officer. He is a Captain. Middle-aged, a small, almost pencil-thin, moustache. He asks me all those utterly boring questions, name, religion, etc. . . . He asks me what happened. I tell him as much as I can recall. He is telling me that it takes 100,000 shells before one soldier is killed, he ends with (and in a louder voice than before), 'You are going to get better. *Understand?*' Yes, I understand. I'm back in my tent, still a bit airy-fairy in the head. I've never had mind drugs before.

I get an evening meal. There's no lighting in the hospital tents, the orderlies come round with a Tilly Lamp, and I get more knock-out pills. Next morning, 'Roll Out The Barrel'; it's a great place for Battle Fatigue, a week here and it would be 'Roll out the Battle Fatigue'. I am to be sent back to the Regiment. I suppose they know what they are doing. Time was to prove that they didn't.

How I got back to the Battery I don't know, this was a time of my life that I was very demoralised. I was not really me any more.

BACK TO THE MOB

January 27, 1944. The Battery are still at Lauro in the same position.

The first things I notice are the graves of those who died on the night of the fire. BSM Griffin is pottering around the graves tidying them up, they have white crosses, and the names written on them.

The tradition of putting the deceased's steel helmet on the cross still persists. One suspects that it happened at Thermopylae. I am so miserable, the spring that made me Spike Milligan has gone. I'm a zombie. Anyone can do or say anything to me. I hear that those who had been with me on the OP fiasco had all been given seven days' leave. Why not me? As soon as our guns start to fire, I start to jump. I try to control it, I run to my dug-out and stay there. I suddenly realise that I'm stammering. What a bloody mess! The Major thinks I'm a coward, perhaps I am? If so why didn't I run from the line the first day in action in North Africa? I am aware that the date is January 27. A whole week? Where have I been? I'm on duty in the Command Post and I really shouldn't be. I manage to stop crying, but I am now stammering very badly, so I can't be of any use

Grave of gunner killed at Lauro

passing wireless messages or Fire Orders; I just copy down Sit-reps. Then they put me on the Telephone Exchange.

To add to my misery I am 'Court Martialled' by the Major. I am marched into his tent by Sgt Daddy Wilson, and I'm told I had been due for a second stripe but owing to my unreliable conduct I am to relinquish my stripe. I suppose in World War I the bastard would have had me shot. Mind you, he had had it in for me for a long time. I didn't represent the type of empty-minded soldier he wanted. I had been a morale-booster to the boys, organising dances and concerts, and always trying to keep a happy atmosphere, something he couldn't do. Now he was letting me have it. So I was Gunner Milligan, wow, what a world-shaker. All this despite the fact the discharge certificate from the 144 CCS had stated that 'This man must be rested behind the lines for a period to stabilise his condition.' I was also taking some pills that they had given me. I suppose they were early tranquillisers, all they did was

251

make me into a zombie. I am by now completely demoralised. All the laughing had stopped.

JANUARY 28, 1944

The whole week is still very bitty in terms of remembering it. I had been told to report to the MO every morning. When he saw me, and heard the incredible stammer I had, I knew he was going to send me away from the Battery for good. In retrospect, if the idiots had just sent me back for a few weeks in the first place, I'm sure I would have been all right, but the Major, who was an unthinking bastard, loved playing God. What did he know about 19 Battery? He was a regular – a regular bastard. We weren't regulars. He was used to a life of Regiment hopping. I suppose in his career he'd been in hundreds of units, one was very much the same as the others, but for us this was not so, we'd always been in one Battery right from the start. The feeling of togetherness was something he never participated in, but we still have it. We have two reunions a year. No other mob has that going for them; we were unique. We've never heard from Jenkins. After the war, he's never been to a reunion, he didn't really belong to us. We're still together. I doubt if he is. I remember at the time thinking I'd like to order a Council steam-roller to drive over him, instructing the driver to go as slow as possible.

He lived on that one narrow plane and everyone had to be judged by that; he didn't know of deeper or higher feelings, those were areas that he could never enter. The bloody fool had got rid of someone who was deeply attached to the Battery and the lads, yet the bastard had made *me* stay at the gun position. 'The noise of the guns will boost your morale,' the bloody fool said. It didn't, the noise drove me mad. Came one of the saddest days in my life, I had to leave. I got up very early, I didn't say goodbye to anyone. I got in the truck, alongside Driver Wright. As I drove back down that muddy mountain road, with the morning mists filling the valleys, I felt as though I was being taken across the Styx. I've never got over that feeling.

'Do you know where I'm going?' I asked Wright.

'Yes, it's the 865 FDS.'

FEBRUARY 10, 1944

My Diary: Landed up in No. 2 General Hospital, Caserta.

This was a real hospital, or rather they had made it so. The weather was sunny, and I was shown into a long ward with lots of windows to let in the light and air. It had a polished stone floor, the walls and ceilings painted white. Beds along the walls. Down the centre were trestle tables with books, and a few pots of flowers. Very pleasant. I was soon in bed, dressed in blue service pyjamas. This was a Psychiatric Ward with about fifty patients in. About two-thirds were under drugs, and slept most of the day. The remainder were very silent and morose. No one spoke to anyone.

All day and every day I just sat on the bed and read. I wondered if I did anything apart from that. I've checked my Letter list. I noted that I wrote to my father on January 22, to Lily Dunford on January 30, then a note 'Acknowledged all mail on 30 Jan.' By chance one of those letters still exists, the one to my father. I don't mention my ordeal, but say 'I pass the hours reading poetry.'

By now my parents had been informed of me being a casualty. They were living at Orchard Way, Reigate, when the telegram arrived. It was stamped 'OHMS. War Office'. My mother had opened the door, and when she saw it she called to my father, 'I can't open it.' They said they felt I had been killed. Parents must have spent a lifetime of anguish as they opened the telegrams not knowing the contents.

I was to see a Major Palmer, a Psychiatrist, whom I

believe invented the revolutionary deep narcosis for the treatment of Battle Fatigue. My turn came for the interview; I told him that being in hospital I was only taking up a bed space. What I needed was a job to occupy me. He looked up and said, 'I appreciate that. A lot of the bastards like to malinger here as long as they can.' He was a rugged-looking man with a broken nose, a relic from his amateur boxing days. I was told of a Scottish soldier who had to see him because of an 'ungovernable temper'. 'So you lose your temper, do you?' 'Aye, and I lash out.' 'Would you hit me?' 'Yes, I would.' 'Well, go on and try.' The Scot had lashed out, Palmer had parried and riposted with a right to the jaw, felling the Scotsman.

A novel form of Psychiatry. I wonder if it cured him. He had me posted to a Rehabilitation Camp north of Naples.

VOLUME FIVE

WHERE HAVE ALL THE BULLETS GONE?

AFRAGOLA

What *is* an Afragola? An Afragola is a small grotty suburb of Bella Napoli. Named after a Centurion who performed a heroic deed against Spartacus and Co: he hit one of them and in return was killed. A grateful Emperor named this spot in his honour. It was a spot I wouldn't give to a leopard. A field adjacent to this 'spot' is now a transit camp for 'bomb-happy' soldiers and I was now 'bomb-happy', having been dumped here, along with some untreated sewage, following treatment at No. 2 General Hospital, Caserta. After several medical boards, I was down-graded to B2, considered loony and 'unfit to be killed in combat' by either side. My parents were so disappointed.

It's a bleak misty day with new added drizzle for extra torment. Mud! How did it climb up your body, over your hat, and back down into your boots? The camp's official title is REHABILITATION. *Oxford Dictionary*: Rehabilitation: Dealing with the restoration of the maimed and unfit to a place in society. So! *Now* I was maimed, unfit, and about to be restored to a place in society! The camp was a mixture of 'loonies' and 'normals'. One couldn't tell the difference, save during air-raids when the loonies dropped everything and ran screaming in the direction of away, crying 'Mummy'. Today mud and men were standing around in huddled groups or sitting in the tents with the flaps up; our camp emblem should have been a dead hippopotamus. A Sergeant Arnolds appeared to be 'running the camp' . . . into the ground. He was to organisation what Arthur Scargill was to landscape gardening. Would I like to be a unit clerk? Why? He had spotted a pencil in my pocket. The job has advantages – excused parades for one, and I sleep in a large marquee, which is the office. Having a tilly lamp put me in the 'that rotten bastard can read in bed' category.

At ten of a morning, a lorry would arrive bearing the latest intake of 'loonies'. I would document them on large foolscap forms that were never asked for, nor ever seen again. The weather is foul, or more, duck. The damp! Matches, like Tories, wouldn't strike, fags went out and never came back, paper wouldn't crackle, blankets had the sickly sweet smell of death. Men took their battle-dresses to bed to keep them dry and, sometimes, for companionship.

FEBRUARY 30

The war seems to have stopped, the weather and casualties have ground our advance to a halt. If no news is good news, we must all be delirious with happiness.

92 GENERAL HOSPITAL NAPLES

Mud and trench foot have triumphed! We move to 92 General Naples! Here we are in warm dry billets and for a time the administration was taken over by the hospital, so Jock and I were 'spare wanks' but were told to 'Stand by'. We did. We 'stood by'. What we were standing by for we knew not, but whenever we were asked 'What are you men doing?' we replied 'Standing by, sir', and it sufficed.

MARCH 1944, TORRE DEL GRECO

Torre Del Greco was a dust and rags village astride the Salerno–Naples Road on the south side of Vesuvius. It was adjacent to this that a new tented camp had been erected for our 'loonies'. A short journey by lorry saw us settling in. It was life as per Afragola. The warm weather had come and we watched as the sun dried out our mud-caked men, making them look like fossilised corpses of Turkish Janissaries. The office tent is in among olive groves, yes. Olive

Groves, the diva that sang with Ivor Novello. Who could christen a child Olive Groves? Why not Walnut Trees?

THE NEW BROOM CWEEPS SLEAN

The camp is to be run by a loony officer; he's been blown up on the Volturno and blown down again at Cassino. Captain Peters of the Queens. Tall and thin, large horse-like face, pale blue eyes with a rapid blink and a twitch of the head; all done with a strange noise at the back of the nose that goes 'phnut'. He is balding and has a fine head of hairs. Speaks very rapidly due to an overdraft at Lloyds.

To date one had the feeling that the Rehabilitation Camp was totally unknown and unrecorded in the Army lists. With the coming of Captain Peters all that changed. The camp went on being unknown and unrecorded, but now we had an officer in charge. The camp had a turnover of about a thousand men, all in a state of coming and going, unlike me who couldn't tell if I was coming or going. Under Peters the food improved. He indented for twice the amount, and sent scrounging parties to buy eggs, chicken and fish, all of which the cooks dutifully boiled to shreds. 'I think they put it in with the laundry,' said Peters. He also allowed men out of an evening, but the effect of alcohol on some of the loonies who were on tranquillisers was alarming. It was something to see the guard commander and his men holding down a half naked, shit-covered, wine-stained loony alternately being sick, screaming and singing. Some loonies tried to climb Vesuvius. God knows how many fell in. A resident psychiatrist arrived. He immediately dished out drugs that zombified most of the inmates, who walked around the camp staring-eyed, grinning and saying 'Hello' to trees.

VOLCANOES, THEIR USES IN WORLD WAR II

Yes, Vesuvius had started to belch smoke at an alarming

rate, and at night tipples of lava were spilling over the cone. Earth tremors were felt; there was no more inadequate place for a thousand bomb-happy loonies. An area order: 'People at the base of the Volcano should be advised to leave.' Signed Town Major, Portici, a hundred miles away. Captain Peters is telling me that as I speak the 'Eytie' to 'take the jeep and tell those people,' he waves a walking stick out to sea, 'tell them it's dangerous for them to stay!' Bloody fool, it was like telling Sir Edmund Hillary: 'I must warn you that Mount Everest is the highest mountain in the world.'

It was evening when I set out in the jeep. Due to the smoke, it was dark before sunset. A strange unearthly light settled on the land, reminding me of those Turner chiaroscuro paintings. Up the little winding roads, through fields of dark volcanic soil. I did it, but I felt bloody silly shouting out 'Attenzione! E pericoloso rimanere qui!'

I stopped at the last farm up the slopes. It was dark now,

the mountain rumbling and the cone glowing scarlet like the throat of a mythical dragon. A yellow glow in a window. A little short weathered farmer is standing at the door. At my approach he waves. I give him the message. He appears to have got it already: 'Vesuvio, molto cattivo.'

'Si,' I said. I was fluent in 'si's.

Would I like some wine?

'Si.'

He beckons me into his home. Accustomed to the gloom, I see a humble adobe room. An oil lamp shows simple things, a table, chairs, a sideboard with yellowing photos; a candle burns before the Virgin, possibly the only one in the area. In the centre of the room is a large circular stone, hollowed out and burning charcoal. Around it sit the farmer's twin daughters.

As I entered, they stood up, smiling; identical twins, about five foot four, wearing knee-length rough black woollen dresses, black woollen stockings to the knee and wooden-sole sandals. Madre? 'Madre morta. Tedesco fusillato.' Killed by a stray shell which he blamed on the Germans. The girls were fourteen, making a total of twenty-eight.

We sat and drank red wine. Motherless at fourteen, a war on, and the mountain about to blow. It was worse than Catford. The girls sat close together, heads inclined towards each other, they radiated sweetness and innocence.

The farmer is weather-beaten. If not the weather, then *someone* has beaten the shit out of him; he has hands like ploughed fields. He is telling me his family have been here since – he makes a gesture, it's timeless. I could be talking to the head gardener from the House of Pansa at the time of Nero. His trousers certainly are.

I drove back by the light of Vesuvius, it saved the car batteries. The lava was now flowing down the sides towards the sea, the rumbling was very loud. The camp was all awake and in a state of tension. Men stood outside their tents staring at the phenomenon, their faces going on and off in the volcano's fluctuating light. It was all very exciting, you didn't get this sort of stuff in Brockley SE26.

The volcano claimed its first victim. A forty-year-old Private from the Pioneer Corps dies from a heart attack. Captain Peters was not a man to worry about such things. 'He'll miss the eruption,' he said, under great pressure trying to calm the camp of loonies. 'Keep calm,' he shouted to himself, popping pills all the while. Men were running away from the camp. It presented a problem.

Earth tremors are coming up the legs and annoying the groins but nothing falls off. Naples is in a state of high anxiety; church bells ringing, Eyties praying, dogs barking, alarmed birds chirping flitting from tree to tree; some of the camp loonies are also chirping and flitting from tree to tree.

DIARY: MARCH 21

Very dark morning, heavy rumblings. Is it Vesuvius? No, it's Jock. It was my day off. I hitched a ride to Naples and the Garrison Theatre to see Gracie Fields in 'Sing As We Go'. Having never sung as I'd been, I was keen to see how it was done. It was terrible, so terrible that I thought that at any moment she would sing the bloody awful Warsaw Concerto. She was on to her hundredth 'Eee bai gum' when the shit hit the fan. The whole theatre shook, accompanied by labyrinthine rumblings. Vesuvius had blown its top. The audience became a porridge of screams and shouts of 'What the fuck was that?' all the while hurtling towards the exit. It coincided with Gracie Fields, followed by spanner-clutching extras, marching towards the screen singing 'Sing As We Go'. It looked as if the screaming mass were trying to escape from her. I alone was in hysterics. Outside was no laughing matter – the sky was black with ash, and Vesuvius roaring like a giant monster.

Rivulets of lava, like burst veins, were rolling down the

seaward side. The streets were full of people walking fast with the shits.

I thumbed a lift. 'Torre Del Greco?'

'You must be bleedin' mad,' said a driver.

I assured him I was.

'That's where all the bloody lava's going.'

'Yes,' I said, 'lava come back to me.' Not much of a joke in 1985, but at the time I was an amateur soldier, not a professional comic, and it wasn't a bad joke for an earthquake.

No lifts, so I walk; it starts to rain a mixture of ash and water, bringing with it lumps of pumice the size of marbles. So this is what Dystopia was like. I trudge wearily down the road to Pompeii. But wait! This was the very road trod by Augustus, Nero, Tiberius, even the great Julius Caesar, and I thought 'Fuck 'em' and was well pleased. All the while people are running in and out of their homes like those Swiss weather clocks.

A black American driver pulls up: 'Wanna lift?'

I don't need a lift, I need a lorry and he has one. Yes, he's going to 'Torrey Del Greckoe'. He offers me a cigarette, then gum, then chocolate. I wait for money but nothing comes. The fall of ash has turned his hair grey. He looked every bit like Uncle Tom. I stopped short of asking how little Eva was, or how big Eva was now. When we arrived at the Loony Camp it was pitch-black and so was he. 'Goodbye,' said his teeth.

The camp was in a state of 'chassis'. Half the loonies had bolted, and the Eyeties were looting the camp. Captain Peters has organised the sane, issued them with pickaxe handles, and they were somewhere up the slopes belting the life out of thieving Eyeties. The guard were alerted and roaming the perimeter with loaded rifles.

'Captain Peters told us to shoot on sight,' they said.

'Shoot what on sight?' I said.

'Oh, he didn't go into details,' they said.

There was nothing for it but to lie back and enjoy it. What am I waiting for? – there is the jeep unoccupied. I put it in gear and drive off, headlights full on to penetrate the viscous gloom. I stop to purchase two bottles of Lachrymae Christi, and on to the gates of Pompeii Vecchia, La Scavi! A short walk to the Porta Marina, down the Via Marina, the Via Abbondanza, then square on in the Strada Stabiana and there at the end pulsates Vesuvius! I swig the wine. It's all heady stuff. I'm in a time warp, this is AD79, the streets are rippling with fleeing Pompeiians, except, I recall, the plaster cast of the couple screwing. What courage, banging away with red-hot cinders bouncing off your bum. What courage, the first case of someone coming and going at the same time. The roar of the mountain is blanketing the countryside. More wine. I make my way to the house of Meander, the wall frescos dancing in the fibrillating light, Fauns, Nymphs, more wine, Leda, Bacchus, more wine, Ariadne, Lily Dunford, Betty Grable, someone with big boobs. I finish the wine and it finished me. What a night! For three hours I had been Pliny. I had also been pissed.

I drove back to the camp in great humour. The camp guard is Polish. He gets it all wrong. 'Health my friend! What goes on there?'

'The green swan of the East meets the grey bear,' I said.

'Pass it up,' he said.

I'm told that Captain Peters has gone to the Portici to 'An Officers' Dance'. 'What is it?' I said. 'Firewalking?'

I fell asleep knowing I'd never have another day like that.

I was wrong. I awoke and it *was* another day just like that. The cooks had 'buggered off'. We raided the cook-house and made breakfast, porridge and volcanic ash. The grey powdery fall-out was everywhere. It looked like a plague of dandruff.

Captain Peters approaches, waving his stick and cracking his shin in the process. 'Ah! Milligan, I'm putting you and phnut! Rogers in charge.' Why? There isn't anybody else.

'I'm off to the Town Major's. If any of the cooks come back, phnut! put them under arrest.'

'Is that for cooking or deserting?'

The eruption reached its zenith that day, and then all was quiet; but the breakdown of all organisation at the camp must have reached the ear of someone who decided that loonies need peace and tranquillity to recover, and so it came to pass.

THE BAIANO REHABILITATION CAMP

The camp is half a mile outside the town adjacent to a cemetery. The entrance is flanked by two Nissen huts, one the general office, the other the Captain's office. A white-washed logo of stones spells out REINFORCEMENT REALLO-CATION AND TRAINING CENTRE. It's laid out on a tented grid system and the camp centre has a large dining tent. Across the road in a light green villa is the new 'Officers' Wing', made necessary by the increasing number of bomb-happy officers. 'It would be demoralising, phnut, for the officers to be bomb-happy in front of the phnut! ORs,' says Peters, who is bomb-happy in front of us all the time.

The setting was very tranquil, away from noise, war and volcanoes. 'You see,' said my Scots prophet, Rogers, 'we'll never be bloody heard of again.'

JUNE. A POSTING

Ah! That Italian summer in the Campania. The mornings, the cool air touching the face like an eider feather, the dawn light under the tent flap vivifying the moment, the aroma of dew on earth, the distant cockerel, the sound of the old guard standing down, the clank of the early morning tea bucket. Long before we rose the trundling of ox carts to the fields and the 'Aie!' of the calling herdsmen, all this and the lung-bursting coughing of Private Andrews.

'Who's a lucky lad then?' says Sergeant Arnolds.

I pause at my desk and answer: 'A lucky lad is the Duke of Windsor now soaking up sea and sun as the Governor of Bermuda.' No, no, the lucky boy is me. He throws me a document. From this camp of a thousand loonies I am being posted to the Officers' Club, Portici, as a wine steward. The word gets round. Milligan is leaving!!

THE OFFICERS' CLUB, PORTICI

It was a large splendid classical-style villa on the main road. I walked up a tessellated path, then right up marble steps with Venetian balustrades into a large white foyer, which had pedestalled busts of Apollo, Hermes, Aristotle and several etcs. In a large dining-room I am intercepted by a short squat thick-set Corporal of the Black Watch, complete in clan kilt. He is the image of Jerry Collona.

'I'm Gunner Milligan I –'

He pounces in. 'Ahhyes, you've come at an awkward time.'

'I could come back . . . after the war.'

No, follow him. Through an arched annexe into a sumptuous room, the beds are on a three-foot raised platform in the middle, surrounded by a Roman-style wooden railing in the St Andrew's Cross design. 'It's how the Romans used to sleep, raised up,' he explains. 'That's my bed, use the mossy-net at night and take Mepacrin.' He is Corporal Tom Ross. 'You can call me Tom, except near officers.' Right, he can call me Spike, except near railings. He is from the 51st Highland Division. Had I heard of them? Yes, we called them the 'Hydraulics' because they would lift anything. He too was bomb-happy. 'Alamein, it were tue much fer me.' I told him not to worry, it was too much for Rommel as well.

I met the staff. The cook, Franco (all Italian cooks not called Maria are Francos in Italy) two serving girls, Rosa and Maria (all Marias not called Rosa are called Marias in

Italy), girl secretary Bianca, Italian barman Carlo (all Italians not called Franco are Carlos except the Pope). The officer in charge is Lieutenant Oliver Smutts, bomb-happy, balding, with an Adam's apple which looks like a nose further down; slim, as are his chances of promotion. He interviewed me. I was to be receptionist and wine waiter.

SMUTTS: Do you know much about wine, Milligan?

MILLIGAN: Yes sir, I get pissed every night.

The club is open from midday till the wee hours. It closes when either the guests or the staff collapse. A 'Gypsy' band plays for dancing; the leader is Enrico Spoleto, who turns out to be the Town Major's batman, Eric Collins. In his black trousers, white shirt and red bandanna, he looked as much like a gypsy as Mel Brooks looked like Tarzan.

My duties are to make out the menus, check the wine stocks, and release anyone imprisoned in them. Apart from the gypsy orchestra, there's still a lot of fiddling. Tom balances the books so well we all pocket five hundred lire a week. The evil cook will do anything for fags except his wife. Rosa lays the tables and Tom lays Rosa. I sit at the door and book the officers in. It was a paid membership club, with a tendency to not remembership to pay. Like Groucho Marx said: 'Never lend people money, it gives 'em amnesia . . .'

A COLONEL INTERVENES

Yes! One evening as I sat at the reception desk varnishing walnuts and cracking them behind my knee, a man in a jeep approached. He was to be instrumental in changing my life. By instrumental I don't mean he was playing the trombone, no. The man is Colonel Startling Grope, a reddish middle-aged man, portly, used to good living, hair cuts, Horlicks, thin legs and suede desert boots. He had a body that appeared to have been inflated, and the air was escaping.

When he signed in he shot me a glance full of meaning that I knew not the meaning of.

Later that night, as he and his cronies are departing, all so pissed you could hear the cistern flushing, he enquires: 'What do you do here?' I tell him on a good day I give General Alexander his hat. Otherwise I try not to whistle the Warsaw Concerto. He is intrigued; as he should be. I am quite lovely. Seriously, I'm a wine steward and resident manic depressive. 'How would you like to come and work for me as a wine steward and resident manic depressive?' I say yes. Why? Because I have been brought up to feel inferior to everybody: priests, doctors, bank managers and officers were all Gods. To say no to them was a mortal sin

Maddaloni on a Good Day

punishable by 500 Hail Marys and an overdraft.

Within a week a jeep arrives and takes me away. The girls all cried and the men cheered.

What was happening to me? I didn't want to be a Manic Depressive Wine Waiter in Italy! I wanted to be a Manic Depressive Harry James in Catford. Why did a poofy Colonel need a wine waiter???

The jeep driver is an ex-paratrooper. Ted Noffs gives me the first warning: 'Yew wanna watch yer arsole wiv' im.' My God, a Brown Hatter! We drive in silence. Speedo says 33 mph, petrol half full, all exciting stuff. Right now my last exciting stuff, Rosa, was back at Portici. An hour's dusty drive with night approaching. A sign: MADDALONI.

'Not far now,' said Noffs. 'We korls it Mad'n'lonely, ha ha.' He was such a merry fellow, a fellow of infinite jest and a cunt. We enter a town and slow down outside a faceless three-storeyed municipal school. Turning left by its side we come to a rear back lot with a line of tents and parked vehicles. Noffs stops outside a ten-man tent. 'This is yourn.' I thank him and lug my kit into the tent which has an electric light, brighter than the three slobs lying on their beds, smoking and staring. These are khaki skivvies, the playthings of the commissioned classes. One is Corporal Rossi, London Italian Cockney. 'You the new wine steward?' Yes. He's the head barman. I'll be working under him.

I find the canteen in the main barrack block (more of it later), have a glass of red wine and a cheese sandwich. The place is full, and soon so am I. I don't know anybody and nobody wants to know me, but then I haven't been on television yet! The red wine sets me up for bed. Back under bloody canvas yet again. Like Robert Graves I thought I'd said Goodbye to All That; instead it was Hello to all This! I slept fitfully, sometimes I slept unfitfully. Variety is the spice of life, or if you live in an after-shave factory, the Life of Spice.

Raffia Party Hats. I was given orders like 'Tins to be smoothed' and 'Bar top to be desplintered'. There I was at dawn with a dopey driver driving around the streets of Caserta buying cabbages, potatoes, figs and oranges, lentils and the whole range of fresh foods for 02E Officers' Mess. Another Fine Mess I'd gotten into. Shagged out by mid-afternoon, I was then put on bar duties for the evening, serving a crowd of pissy Hooray Henrys. By the amount of drink and smoke around they must long since have died of lung cancer or cirrhosis. Disaster. The bar phone rings; they want a Major Bastard. That's how they pronounced it.

'Phone call for Major Bastard,' I yell above the din.

A man purple with rage and halitosis snatches the phone: 'Bass-*tard*, you Bastard,' he hissed. He was a real Bass-tard!

I was making a cock-up of the job. Not that I couldn't do it, I didn't want to.

'The Colonel wants to see you,' says Rossi. OK, if he looks through that window, he'll get a glimpse of me desplintering the bar.

'Look, Milligan,' says Major Startling Grope. We are in his office. 'The Sergeant says you aren't very good at your job.'

'He's a liar, sir. I'm bloody useless at my job. I could lose us the war.'

He laughed. How am I at clerking? I don't know.

'How are you at figures?'

'Terrible, you should see the women I go out with.'

'Look, Milligan, give it a try. If you don't like it, we can try something else.' Like Suicide. OK.

I work for him in 'O' Branch in the school building. A large airy office with a Sergeant Hallam, a mild-mannered poof. Then a clerk, Private Len Arrowsmith, a small lively amusing lad; then me at the bottom of the heap as filing clerk. We each have a separate desk. It's cushy. I just get files, give files and take the files back; the job has all the magic of an out-of-order phone box. It's OK to sleep in the office providing bedding is hidden during the day! So I move in and join Arrowsmith.

'You'll like it here,' says Len. 'At night you have a lovely view of the typewriter.'

ROMANCE

So far Sergeant Hallam has always carried the files to the Colonel. But I'm lovelier. So now it's me.

Announcement over the interphone. 'Send Milligan in with File X.' The Colonel is 'getting to know me'. I was going through what girls go through with in the initial chatting-up process.

'What is your – er – do sit down, Milligan, you can dispense with rank.'

'I haven't any rank to dispense with, sir.'

'You can call me Stanley.'

'Yes sir, Stanley.'

'What's your first name?'

'Spike, Stanley, sir.'

'Spike? That's not your real name.'

'No, my real name is Terence.'

At the mention of the name his eyes lit up with love.

'Terence,' he lisped. 'Yes, that's better, Terence, that's what I'll call you.' Like Private Noffs said: 'Watch yer arsole.'

I had not forgotten my trumpet. In the evening I'd practise in the office. Those notes that echoed round Maddaloni's fair streets were to lead me to fame, fortune, overdraft, VAT, Income Tax, mortgages, accountants, solicitors, house agents, nervous breakdown and divorce. It starts with a tall thin, bald, moustachioed Sergeant Phil Phillips. He leads the 02E band. Will I play for them? Yes, yes, yes, yes.

Now life took on a new meaning. Playing with the band was a bonus. We played from smoky dives to the great

Palace of Caserta which housed the Allied Forces Headquarters, though it was so far behind the lines it was
referred to as the Hind Quarters. We were given a rehearsal
room where we tried to keep up with the very advanced
band arrangements we bought from the American PX.
Playing Woody Herman's arrangement of 'Apple Honey'
nearly did for us – the top Fs gave rise to cries of 'The truss,
bring the truss.' After one appalling run-through, Stan
Britton turned to us and said, 'Gentlemen, I suggest we take
an early retirement.'

Another disaster was our first attempt at the new-fangled
samba, called 'Brazil'. After three tries, Charlie Ward put
his sax down and said, 'The defence rests.'

DANCES! DANCES!

Dances meant pretty girls and a burning sensation. At a
dance in the Caserta ballroom, I fell for – a ridiculous
phrase, 'fell for' – no, I didn't pitch forward on my face, but
when I saw her I just screamed. She was gliding past the
bandstand in another man's arms. I'd only just seen her and
she was already being unfaithful to me!! Her name was
Sheila Frances, mine was Spike Milligan. Did she come
here often, yes, and this was one of them. I try to date her
and come up with 1944. I fall for her hook, line and sinker,
and several other parts all hanging under the shirt. Blast,
she is affianced to a Sergeant. I will try again. Meantime I'll
go blind. I climb back on to the bandstand; lots of nudge
nudges wink winks.

'There's plenty more fish in the sea, Spike,' says Len
Prosser. But I don't want to go out with fish.

A DAY OUT IN A CERTAIN DIRECTION

Colonel Startling Grope to Milligan: 'Would you and Len
like to come to Ischia?'

O2E Dance Band, August–September 1944, each man a master of posing. Piano: Sgt S. Britton; Bass: L/Bdr L. Prosser; Drums: Pte 'Chick' Chitty; Guitar: Phil Phillips; 1st Trumpet: Gnr S. Milligan; 2nd Trumpet: Pte G. Wilson; 1st Alto: Sgt H. Carr; 2nd Alto: Pte J. Manning; Tenor: Pte J. Buchanan

'Yes sir, I'd love an Ischia.'

'Right, Sunday morning 0800. Bathing costume and towel.'

The day, Colonel Startling Grope, Captain Clarke, Len and myself pile on the jeep. 9.10 we arrive at the specially bombed car park on the water front at Naughty Naples. We go on board an awaiting RAF Rescue launch. 'Welcome aboard,' says a silly sea captain, all beard and binoculars. 'Cast off forrard, cast off aft,' whoosh, turbines throb and we head out into the mist-haunted sea. Our two officers are taken below for drinkypoos; we stay on deck and talk to the crew. 'Hello sailor,' I say.

The bay is calm, looking like skimmed oil. We bounce on the surface and the morning mist starts to lift. In twenty minutes looms the soaring purple head of Mount Epomeo. We draw near to the south shore, skilfully entering a little fishing mole amid red and blue fishing boats with the warding-off evil eye on the prows. We heave to as our two officers surface flushed and smiling. We jump ashore. The Colonel misses and plunges his leg up to the groin in the waters. 'Oh bother,' he says, meaning 'Oh fuck.'

With seven dry legs and one wet one, we follow the Colonel up a small path inland that leads us to a bleached white Italo-Moorish villa on the sea. A brief pull on the doorbell; the red mahogany door opens to a small, smiling, white-coated, thirty-year-old, blood group Rhesus negative inside leg forty-two, valet. He ushers us in, all the while looking suspiciously at the Colonel's one damp leg. This is the Villa San Angelo, owned by an Italian Colonello with two dry legs. He is at the moment 'away on business in Naples'. Possibly at this moment, he and two pimps are changing lire into sawdust on the Via Roma.

The Moors have left their mark here: many arches, turquoise tiled floors, latticed screens. Fazan carpets. It is a treasure house of antiques – Majolica Ceramics, Venetian Glass, Inland Moorish Muskets, Tapestried Walls. 'Homely isn't it, Terence,' says the Colonel. After a cold buffet of avocado and prawns and wine of the island, our officers retire to sleep. Len and I are directed to the private beach down a few rocky steps. The day is sunny, the sea is like champagne. We plunge into crystal clear waters that in forty years time will be floating with tourist crap and over-population. Lording over the island is Mount Epomeo, hung with a mantle of vineyards and bougainvillaea. Legend has it that the giant Typhoeus lies transfixed beneath it. A punishment for screwing one of the Naiads. I suppose one way of keeping it down is to put a mountain on it.

On this very island Michelangelo used to visit the Lady Vittoria Collona – mysterious, as he was gay.

VITTORIA: 'ows the cealin goin, Mike?
MICHEL A: I bin using the long brush but it's doin' me back in.

VITTORIA: Why don't you arst the Pope fer scaffoldin'?
MICHEL A: Oh ta, I knew these visits 'ere wouldn't be wasted.

Hours. We lie on the beach sunning and smoking, and like true smokers throw our dog ends and matches in the sea.

'Hello, down there.' The Colonel's red face is at the grilled Moorish window, his face looking equally grilled. We must come up, tea is being served. A long refectory table laden with salads and a magnificent bronze samovar. Our every whim is waited on slavishly by the little Italian. 'They're a dying breed,' says Startling Grope. (He was right. The Eyetie died the day after we left.) The officers are slopping down one Alexander after another and we all repair to the beach again; Captain Clarke in a one-piece suit that was out of date when Captain Webb swam the channel, and the Colonel in a pair of bathing drawers of 'the briefest gist'. He plunges in, comes out, and goes up to bed. Captain Clarke strikes out to sea so far that the current gradually carries him out of sight round the headland. He is not shouting 'help' but just in case we shout 'Goodbye, sir.' He disappears. Should we inform the life-guards? No, there's plenty more like him. Hours later he returned overland via the Villa Fondalillo some three miles away. When the Italian flunkey opened the door, a shagged-out Captain Clarke fell into the house, but at least he had two wet legs and a body to match.

BAND BIZ

We want to expand the band. We would like a string section. There is a fine fiddler, one Corporal Spaldo. At concerts he plays Montés Czardas. Would he like to play in our band? He shudders. No, not for him the nigger rhythm music. There is a postscript to this tale.

Many years after the war I was in a night club. The

Pte E. Edwards.
Posed with a soft filter,
facing Nor'East and
lightly oiled

cabaret is supplied by a 'Krazy Kaper' Band. I notice a violinist, wearing a larger ginger wig and beard, a football jersey, a kilt with a whitewash brush for a sporran, fishnet stockings and high heel shoes. They play 'Does chewing gum leave its flavour on the bedpost over night'. It's Spaldo! I couldn't resist it, I went over and said, 'Changed your mind, eh?'

So my lotus days in the band continued. We were paid three hundred lire a gig, my trumpet solos working out at a penny a time. Our finances were organised by Welfare Officer Major Bloore. He sometimes writes to me from the Cayman Islands.

Now I am *moved* from Filing to the Welfare Office, under the eye of Private Eddie Edwards.

I am to draw posters for the current films being shown. My first one is Rita Hayworth. No, I'm not doing it right, says Major Rodes, try again. Rita Hayworth II, no, it's not right. Rita Hayworth III, IV, V, VI, VII, VIII, no, I just can't get Rita Hayworth right for *West of Pecos*; I can't even get her right for East, North or South of Pecos.

'Sir, I didn't join the army to draw a regiment of Hayworths. I want out!'

'You fool, you little khaki fool,' losing a golden opportunity to become the great artist he could make me. The Major stamps off in a kilt-swinging rage.

'He's very temperamental,' says Eddie.

'I think he's in the change,' I reply. 'And his truss must be upside down.'

THE AQUARIUM CLUB

This is to be a new officers' drinking club. The venue is a farmhouse just outside the town.

My penance is to do murals of sea life. The Major drives me to the site. There are no men on the farm. 'Tutti nella Armata.' At the moment they were all planting cabbages in Sussex; among them Mario and Franco who were to stay on to revolutionise our eating habits with their trattorias. Only the mother and the daughter Maria were left (in Italy all daughters not called mothers are Marias). She is a rough peasant beauty, five foot seven inches, tall for an Italian, and very tall for a dwarf. She has large brown expressive legs and eyes, tousled black hair and brown satin skin. (Arrrghhh!) Her mother, pardon me, looked like a bundle of oily rags ready for sorting. She seemed ever fearful of her daughter being screwed, whereas I wasn't worried at all. They were poor and leasing out a few rooms was salvation to them. She shows us two upstairs rooms. As Maria walked up the stairs, I made a note of her shapely bottom, while the Major made a note of mine. The rooms were being painted light marine blue by defaulters. Poor devils, here they had come to face Hitler, and instead they're stripping and painting walls, just like Hitler did twenty years ago. 'No wonder he went fucking mad,' they said. On the morrow I was to apply my skills; very nice, no filing, and away from the Maddening Thomas Hardy.

THE MURALS

I'm there on the plank drawing enlarged fish, octopus, squid, dolphins and crabs; thank God I've never had them as bad. Maria drops in to see how I'm faring; there's a bit of flirting; she brings me figs, oranges, grapes. I ask her if she has a relative in Pompeii. We are repeatedly interrupted by the croaking voice of her mother – 'MARIAAAAAAAAA DOVEVI' – accompanied by sudden rushes into the room. Suspicious, yet disappointed. One arrives at the conclusion that the moment an Italian girl isn't visible to her parents she's screwing.

Their farm was a tumbledown affair, and the farm dog, Neroni, a mongrel, was a sad sight, tethered on a piece of rope that only allowed him three paces, nothing more or less than a hairy burglar alarm. The forecourt was a mess of stabling, two white longhorn oxen, a few bundles of silage, scattered farm tools and a wooden plough (in 1944!), a few chickens and goats, the latter given to the desertification of Italy. Poor Neroni, whenever I approached he would snarl and bark like crazy, but when close to, he cowered and whimpered. I got him a longer piece of rope. I stroked him, something no one had ever done before. He licked my face. I brought him some food which he wolfed down. I often think of him. Those days were among the best I'd ever have. At morning I'd breakfast and then make my way to the farm down a dusty lane. The landscape was not unlike Arles at the time of Van Gogh. I'd work through the mornings. I brought the mother some tea, sugar and tins of bully beef. She wept and kissed my hand. Never mind that, what about a screw with Maria!

By the first week in October I had completed the murals

at the Aquarium Club. I arranged to finish mid-morning so I could sneak the rest of the day off. I pack up my pots of paint, wash out the brushes. Tomorrow I will steal another day off when I come to collect them. Goodbye Maria, Momma and Neroni. I walk back by the dusty road and pass a goat flock. A large she-goat is about to deliver. The goat herder, a boy of fourteen, is stroking her and saying 'Piano, piano.' Why did a goat need a piano at this particular time? Finally the little hooves start to protrude. The boy, with consummate skill, takes the heels and pulls the kid clear, then repeats it on the twin, alley opp! The little kids, shiny and shivery, lie still as their mother licks them. In minutes they are standing on jellified legs; seconds later they are at the teat sucking vigorously. It was all miraculous in its way, as moving as a Beethoven Quartet – now that needs a piano!

OCTOBER 9

My Diary: Band gig in Rome. Whoopee!

Rome! The Eternal City! Forever young! Age makes no difference here, unless you're Henry Woods.

We travel by Welfare Charabanc. Early morning the charabanc arrives at Alexander Barracks. We eagerly pack our stuff aboard. Len Prosser is worried about the safety of his bass. In its canvas sack he appears to be smuggling a murdered body aboard. 'The man who invented this instrument never intended it to travel – it's meant for hermits or the transfixed.' Drums. Vic Shewry is coming and going. Percussion seems unending. 'When you two have finished we'd like to bloody well get on,' says Jim Manning and his alto sax. Up and away a hundred and fifty miles to go, so a cigarette and the Union Jack and I settle back. The Allies are driving the Germans back over the Po River. It must be hard on German mothers to receive telegrams.

Hitlergram No. Sieben

ZER FUHRER REGRETS TO INFORM YOU YOUR SON
HAZ BEEN DROWNED IN ZER PO.

Through ancient Capua, over the Volturno, Sparanise, Teano; all the roads I'd passed through in action. Memories of 19 Battery, the sound of the guns, the shout of fire orders, now all passing into the dreamtime. Through Cassino, and above it the ruined abbey, a monument to Allied stupidity. We rabbit, joke and laugh our way. Come evening we reach our destination. '56 Area Rest Camp Welcomes You'. It's like Belsen with food.

THE GIG

We spent the morning lazing. I cleaned my trumpet. In the afternoon band practice, listened to by crowds of soldiers. Comes evening, I couldn't believe it. Little old me from Brockley, in Rome! Back home I'd never got further than Hernia Bay. The dance is at the Crusader Club. Wow! A huge marble hotel, an officer's dream palace.

Colonel Philip Slessor greets us. 'Who's in charge?' he asks.

'You are,' we say.

Tall and saturnine, Slessor was later to become a BBC announcer. He started practising right away by announcing that we were to follow him.

The ballroom is magnificent, the stage a mass of red velvet and gold embroidery; it was an 'embarras de choix de richesses'. Slessor makes another announcement. 'There's a room for you all to change in.' We haven't anything to change into except Mr Jekyll.

'What? You're not going to play like that?' Haven't we any mess dress? No, there's another fine mess dress we haven't got into. I told him we sounded exactly the same in battle-dress as we did in mess dress.

'Huh,' he announces.

The band room is a munificence of coleslaw, the table is groaning with every sandwich possible, even a few impossible ones. Wine? Gallons. A line of bottles without labels. We tasted it, found it tasted like unlabelled wine.

Slessor is announcing again: 'We start in ten minutes, lads.' We set up behind the brocade curtains, give him the nod, and he announces: 'Ladies and Gentlemen, we have great pleasure in announcing the Band of the Officers of the Second Echelon under their conductor Sergeant Stand (yes, Stand) Britton. Take your partners for the first Waltz.' The curtains draw back as we swing into 'Song of India'. The floor is soon crammed with dancers, most of the ladies

Colonel Philip Slessor showing an officer the correct dress and stance for announcing

Italian, all desperate for food, fags and soap. It's hard to believe that the beautiful Contessa, dancing with the cross-eyed Hindu colonel, is doing it for three bars of chocolate.

I was blowing great that night. When I stood up to take a chorus it was for one of two reasons: a) Egomania or b) Piles.

The interval, and Colonel Slessor announces that he's 'Very pleased with us'. He then announces he is leaving the room.

Throughout the evening he announced every dance, the names of the tunes, the winners of the spot prize, even 'The trumpet solos were by Gunner Millington.' He really was ready for the 9 o'clock news. Finally 'The last waltz, please.' 'God Save the King', then we moved in on the scoff. It had been a great evening of dancing and announcing; we had seen lots of pretty birds but hadn't pulled any, so, as Jim Manning said, 'We'll 'ave ter pull ourselves.'

RELIGIOUS INTERLUDE

My days of sleeping on O branch office floor were over. I had found a windowless little room up a flight of stairs adjacent to the C of E chapel room at Alexander Barracks. I ask the Rev. Sergeant Beaton if I could sleep in it. Yes, but nothing else, remember! The chapel is next door and there's early services. OK, I move in, and am immediately seized upon to help. Sunday, the 'pumper' for the organ hasn't shown, can I? There, on my knees I am gainfully employed by the Lord. The handle *should* be lowered and raised with an air of delicacy, but Gunner Milligan is a jazz pumper, with a beat-me-daddy-eight-to-the-bar. There is a sickening 'CRACK', I am left with the shaft, and the only way to keep the music going is to activate the remaining four-inch stump. Panicky I pump gallantly, but just can't get enough air into the bellows. The organ fades, and wheezes back to life as the lunatic Gunner tries to keep it operating. No good, it's starting to sound like a bagpipe chanter groaning into life. The congregation are in disarray. Exhausted, I jack it in, the organ 'expires' with a long groan and 'Fissshhhhhh' as the last wind escapes.

Jesus said, ' Through suffering thou shalt come to me.' Well, I was nearly there.

After our weekly Saturday night dance, I would like to hang back and play the piano. I had the illusion that a concerto would come. I was really Cornel Wilde as Chopin. As the climax of the Finale Grandioso con Woodbines, a magnificent ATS Private in a transparent cheesecloth vest would appear and unroll a mattress: 'Come Chopin, forget your silly old Nocturnes – have something else.'

On one such evening, someone does approach. It's a Yewish sergeant who wants to say how much he has enjoyed my trumpet playing. He's just joined the unit and is also keen on show business.

Well, it was the start of a friendship. I let him move into my billet because I thought he had money.

Sgt Steve Lewis. A Yewish soldier taken in colour because he had money. (N.B. Due to the publishers' lack of money, it's black and white after all)

Help. A giant Yewish bedroll appeared, followed by a Yewish Brigade kitbag, table, chair, tea chest, camouflaged Minorah, and a secondhand copy of the Talmud. He then proceeded to erect the most complicated Heath Robinson network of strings, pulleys, hooks, weights and counter-weights. He wanted to be able to switch lights on and off, raise or lower them, drop his mosquito net, manoeuvre his mess tins and mug near or far, boil a kettle, make tea, toast bread, and open Tower Bridge, all without moving from his bed. I asked him, was he training to be a cripple? He had enough food by his bed to outlast an Atomic War and still open a shop in Golder's Green. If he had been at Masada it would never have fallen; he would have sold it to the Romans. I pointed out that his wasn't the only persecuted race. There was the Irish.

'Spike, the Irish got off light.'

'We took as much stick as you did.'

'Listen, we Jews have been persecuted since Egyptian times.'

I told him I had never read the *Egyptian Times*.

'All you suffered from was a shortage of spuds.'

'Steve, in 1680, there were eleven million Irish. Now there's only two. We lost nine million.'

'Nine million. Oh what a terrible accountant.'

'Don't joke, they were starved, killed, deported or emigrated.'

He laughed. 'You *sure* they weren't Jewish?'

We had unending arguments. 'The Irish? What did they ever have? We had Einstein, Disraeli, Pissarro, Freud. What have the Irish got? Pissed!'

'We got the Pope and Jack Doyle.'

'Jack Doyle the boxer? He's useless!'

'Yes, but we got him.'

'And there's never been an Irish Pope. How come?'

'It's the fare.'

In the shower Steve noticed I'd been circumcised. 'Why?'

I didn't know. 'To make it lighter? You know, Milligan, if Jerry took you prisoner, that could have got you into a concentration camp.' It was really something when your prick could get you sent to a concentration camp. 'Believe me, Spike,' says the Yew, 'anyone that sends someone to a concentration camp is a prick.' Amen.

This was the beginning of an ongoing Judaeo-Christian hilarity. When I heard his footsteps on the stairs, I'd call, 'Is that the Yew?' I could hear his stifled giggles.

'Listen Milligan,' he'd say. 'Believe me, the Irish are famous for *nothing*.' And so to Christmas.

Yes, Christmas, bloody Christmas. We decided to do our shopping in Naughty Naples. All up the Via Roma urchins are grabbing us and singing, 'Lae thar piss tub darn bab'. Why in the land of opera do they descend to this crap? If the reverse were to apply in London, little Cockney kids would be singing '*La Donna è Mobile*' as they begged. We make our Christmas purchases and retire to the Royal Palace, NAAFI, where, God help us, we are assailed by God bless her and keep her . . . away from us . . . Gracie Fields. She'd had a bad press at the beginning of the war about living in America, leaving poor Vera Lynn and Ann Shelton to face the bombs. Now she was making up for it. Every day she'd leave her Capri home and bear down on unsuspecting soldiers. 'Ow do lads.' Then, without warning, sing 'Red Sails in the Sunset'. After a while the lads had had enough of 'Ow do lads' and 'Sall-eeee' and the sight of her looming up the stairs would start a stampede out the back, with cries of 'Christ! Here she comes again'. Nothing personal against the dear lady, who had a big heart and an enlarged liver, but she did overdo the 'Ee ba gum, 'ave a cup o' tea lads.'

Sometimes you wouldn't know she was in, until from a distant table, you'd hear 'It's the biggest Aspidistra in the World'. To get rid of her we directed her to a table of Goumiers (Rapists by appointment to the Allies) by telling

A look-out on the Royal Palace NAAFI roof, watching for signs of Gracie Fields's boat

her they were Gurkhas. 'Sallyyyyyyy, Salleeeee,' she sang at the baffled Moroccans. They didn't even try to rape her.

CHRISTMAS EVE

Pouring, ice-cold rain. Steve and I are sitting in the festively decorated canteen. We feel seasonal but would rather feel an ATS. We are taking a little wine for our stomachs' sake, also for our liver, spleen and giblets. The strains of Sergeant Wilderspin and his 02E choir are approaching. They enter, singing 'God Rest Ye Merry, Gentlemen' and sneezing. They are collecting for ye Army Benevolent Fund and are soaked to ye skin. At eight o'clock we all file into the concert hall to see the Nativity Play. It's very good, except the dialects jarred. An Angel of the Lord: 'Thar goes t'Bethlehem, sither,' and his sidekick answers, 'Weail off tae sae him right awa.' It didn't detract from the finale around the manger, the choir singing 'Adeste, fideles'. In that moment all minds were back home by the fire, screwing on the rug. Numerous curtain calls, the Brigadier makes a speech ' . . .

a great deal of effort . . . a special debt of gratitude . . . not forgetting . . . screwing on the rug . . . also like to thank . . . A Merry Christmas to all our readers . . . has anyone seen Mademoiselle Ding?'

Christmas came and went with all the trimmings, tinned turkey, stuffing, Christmas Pud, all served to us by drunken Sergeants. Now we were all sitting round waiting for 1945. It had been a good year for me. I was alive.

JANUARY 1945

Cold and rain.

Letter from home.

Very quiet month.

Then, on 23 February 1945, this drastic message was flashed to the world from the pages of *Valjean*, the 02E house magazine.

> **Trumpeter.**
>
> Is there no stylish trumpeter in the ranks of the Echelon? At present the O2E Dance Orchestra is handicapped to a certain extent by the lack of one of these only too rare musicians. Ex-trumpeter "Spike" Milligan, who has now gone on to the production line, had to hang up his trumpet on medical grounds, so if there is a trumpeter in our midst please contact SQMS Ward of R/O.

Milligan has hung up his trumpet! A grateful nation gave thanks!

It started with pains in my chest. I knew I had piles, but they had never reached this far up before. The Medical Officer made me strip.

'How long has it been like that?' he said.

'That's as long as it's ever been,' I replied.

He ran his stethoscope over my magnificent nine-stone body. 'Yes,' he concluded, 'you've definitely got pains in your chest. I can hear them quite clearly.'

'What do you think it is, sir?'

'It could be anything.'

Anything? A broken leg? Zeppelin Fever? Cow Pox? La Grippe? Lurgi?

'You play that wretched darkie music on your bugle, don't you?'

'Yes, sir.'

'You must give it up.'

'Why?'

'I hate it.' He goes on to say, 'It's straining your heart.'

Bloody idiot. It's 1985, I'm a hundred and nine, and I'm still playing the trumpet. He's dead. At the time I stupidly believed him and packed up playing.

FURLOUGH

Yes. 'We've been furloughed,' said Steve, holding up Part Two Orders. Why had we been furloughed? In appreciation of our *Men in gitis* efforts. One whole week in the Capital again. We are away next morning, Sgt Steve Lewis, Private Eddie Edwards and Gunner S. Milligan. It looked like an old joke. 'There was this Englishman, this Irishman and this man of the Hebrew persuasion and they were all in the Army, and then one day, ha ha ha, they were all given leave to Rome, ha ha ha.' Once again it's the 56 Area Rest Camp. Steve, being senior, signs us in. 'You realise I've signed for you bastards. For God's sake please avoid the following: rape, murder, arson, little boys, gefilte fish, Mlle Ding.' We queued for a dinner of Irish stew, sponge roll and custard. Tired after a hard day's travel, we ate it, then wrote off for compensation. The Yew, Lewis, has bagged the favoured upper bunk. 'It's the English class system,' he explains. 'If a

Steve Lewis, Spike Milligan and Eddie Edwards. There was an Englishman, an Irishman and a Jew . . .

wild beast gets in it eats the lower class first, allowing the upper class to survive and re-let the bed for the next victim.' Next morning, early hot showers, singing, towel flicking on the bums etc., then breakfast of sausage, bacon, bread and jam, and we are like giants refreshed. We go on the town.

The Colosseum is to Rome what the Eiffel Tower is to Paris but less rusty. 'That's where they threw the Christians to the lions,' says Eddie. No Jews? 'No, the lions weren't kosher.' We eat gelati at a café; visit the Forum. 'Not much of it left,' says Eddie. I tell him that the Forum was destroyed by Vandals. 'I know, they did in our local phone box,' he said.

The Pantheon; two thousand years old and still intact! – the Barbara Cartland of Architecture. Within are the tombs of the Kings and Queens of Italy and there, immured in marble, is Michelangelo. Steve is very impressed. 'What did he die of?' I tell him: 'He fell off the scaffolding.' He is trying to translate the plaques.

'Pity they're in Latin.'

'Why?'

*Spike on top of
the Colosseum*

'It's a dead language.'

'Well they *are* all dead.'

I couldn't believe it! Me from Brockley standing where Agrippa stood; it was as absurd as finding Agrippa queuing for fish in Catford. Steve is telling me he has cracked it. 'Agrippa,' he says, laughing at the terrible pun. 'Agrippa is . . . Latin for hair grips.' I thought I heard a groan from the tomb of Michelangelo.

Outside we turn into the Corso Umberto and witness the great cat colony. An Italian lady is feeding them (as is the Roman custom). In answer to my query she says the cats have been here 'Lontano fa', so I tell my two chums. 'They've been here since lontano fa.' Steve says, 'That's strange – they miaow in English.'

The Fontana de Trevi and its songs in water: it cascades, gushes, ripples, drips, laughs, squirts. It is magnificent.

I toss the traditional coin in. 'What did you wish?' says Steve. I explain certain things about Candy and he is well pleased. Eddie throws his in; he won't say what, but if it was to retire and live in Southampton and go grey, it's been granted. Steve screws up his Jewish soul and throws in a low-denomination coin. What does he wish? He wishes he hadn't thrown it in. We hold back as he starts to strip.

Food. A small restaurant in the Via Flamania, a four-star place – you can see them through a hole in the roof. Here we are in the land of pasta, and I order *stew*. The photograph shows the evidence. I even had a *cup of tea* AND bread and butter. They didn't have Daddy's sauce.

APRIL 17

My Diary: My birthday. I'm 27. Had extra cup of tea.

The news tells us that the Germans in Italy are on their last legs.

FUHRER BUNKER
HITLER IS IN THE KARZI GIVING HIMSELF ONE OF DOCTOR MORRELL'S ENEMAS.
ADOLF: Allez oops! Ahhh! Dat is better.
GOEBBELS: Mein Führer, mein Führer.
ADOLF: Dere's only one of me.
GOEBBELS: In Italy our troops are running out of legs.
ADOLF: You Schwein, you haff ruined my happy enema hour.

I see Thelma Oxnevad. 'Spike, did you enjoy your leave?' Never mind that, Thelma, marry me at eight o'clock tonight. QMS Ward is asking me to come back to the band. I say, what about my impending coronary? He says that's all shit. As a qualified Quarter Master Sergeant he says I'm fit. But playing the trumpet could kill me! Yes it could, but I take the risk, so will he. OK, I'll try. There I'll be, playing a great Bunny Berrigan chorus, I hit a top G, clutch my heart and crash face downwards on a mattress. ATS Candy Withers will raise my lovely head in her arms. Have I any last request? Yes, yes, yes, if she could just take her clothes off.

Also my thespian talents are in demand! Sergeant Lionel Hamilton thinks I could play a part in *The Thread of Scarlet*. Will I be the knot? We start rehearsing, but that old Black Magic called Manic Depression attacks me and I'm put to bed with *Aspirins*. What a doctor, I suppose he's still practising. God knows, he needs to. The play goes on, and horror of horrors, it's a success!

Someone is worse off than me. Mussolini has been murdered; he and his mistresses are hanging upside down in a garage in Milan.

It was a barbaric act that puts the clock back. However, the natives seem happy. Nothing like an assassination to cheer the masses.

MAY 1

My Diary: It's over! Jerry surrenders!

I had just sat down at my morning desk still reeking of porridge when a very excited Colonel Startling Grope thundered into the office. 'Have you heard Terence? It's over! I've just spoken to Alex at AFHQ and it's OVER! General Vietinghoff von Nasty is at the Palace *now* signing the surrender.'

'Great! Do I have to sign anything, Stanley Sir? I mean, *I*

The Mussolini Massacre. They shoot horses, don't they?

haven't agreed to the surrender.' We can have the day off, he's right, it's time we had it off. The Eyeties are in the street singing 'Finito, Benito Finito' and 'Lae thar piss tub darn bab'. The bells of the churches ring out their iron victory message.

I walked back through the milling streets, lay on my bed and lit up a Capstan. I could hear the din outside and running footsteps, but I was strangely quiet. Suddenly a complete change of direction. How do you handle the end of a Campaign? I wanted to cry. Was it really over? 31,000 Allied troops had died – a city of the dead. Is a war ever really over?

A few days pass and Steve comes into the room. He is grinning: 'Have you seen? He's dead.' He shows me the headlines. ' "HITLER, SUICIDE IN BUNKER." Yes, he's dead, his tart *and* his bloody dog.' He hammered the words out like nails in a coffin.

I had better news. Back at the officers' club in Portici I had snaffled a bottle of Dom Perignon 1935. 'I've been saving this, Steve,' I said, producing the bottle from its wrapper. We toasted the end in our enamel mugs. We sat grinning in silence. It was all too much; two soldiers; just statistics; where did we fit in . . .? Mind you, they were still fighting in Berlin, but most of the orchestra had stopped playing.

V-E Night in Merry Maddaloni

The Russians are sweeping into Berlin. Their might is awesome. The Allies and the Russians meet on the Elbe. At Lüneburg Heath, Monty accepts the German surrender. It's over. Just like that. One day war, the next it's peace. It's almost absurd. The entire energy of 02E is vested in preparations for the official V-E Night celebrations. It would appear that only alcohol can generate true happiness: hundreds of bottles, barrels and fiasco are stock-piled in every available area. They are scrubbing out the fountain! Why? It's the brainchild of RSM Warburton who has ordained that it be 'filled with wine'. They had tried to get the fountains to gush, but the plumbing had long since decayed. The date is fixed. In Part Two orders.

YOU *WILL* ALL HAVE A GOOD TIME,
YOU *WILL* GET DRUNK, AND YOU WILL
ALL STAGGER AROUND . . . YOU WILL
GET SICK OVER EACH OTHER FOR YOUR
KING AND COUNTRY. THE BAND WILL
PLAY FOR DANCING UNTIL 2 A.M.

PEACE

To the victor the spoils. My spoils are a set of files. Big News!
Startling Grope is leaving us.
  'I'm being bowler-hatted,' he said. (I thought he would have been brown-hatted.) 'I leave next week, Terence, and,' he tapped his nose, it stayed on, 'I've left you a little present.'
  Me? A present? What is it, a pot of Gentlemen's Relish? A Unique Device with latent Screws? A Germolene dispenser? A leather-backed Divining Kit, a complete set of Marshmallows, a Devious Appliance with lubricating points? Any of these could be mine!
  'Who's taking your place here, Stanley Sir?'

'Nobody.'

'Well, that doesn't speak very well of you.'

'The job is being run down, Terence.'

'It was more than run down, it's down right crummy.'

So departed the Colonel, and the pretty boys of 02E breathed a sigh of relief. Bending down would never be as dangerous again.

THE GREAT NEAPOLITAN BAND CONTEST

56 Area are holding a Dance Band Contest. We'll wipe the floor with 'em. FIRST PRIZE FOR SUPERB LEAD AND SOLO TRUMPET, GUNNER MILLIGAN. We congregate in the rehearsal room. What to play?

'What's wrong with Dinah?' says Manning.

'Rheumatism,' is the answer. We choose 'Moonlight Serenade', 'Two O'clock Jump' and 'The Naughty Waltz'.

'You see! Those numbers will lose us the contest,' predicts Jim, one of the first people in 1939 to say 'The war will be over by Christmas.' We practise and practise, every

Bdr Milligan singing louder than has ever been sung before and causing the photograph to crumble

note and nuance is observed, we even play the specks of fly shit that land on the music. Nothing is wasted.

We want to wear just shirts and trousers. Major New won't hear of it: 'This is a military occasion, and you will look regimental.' OK, we can wear steel helmets, full pack, and play 'Moonlight Serenade', the other half dig slit trenches; in 'One O'clock Jump' we can all fix bayonets and charge the judges; and finally, in 'The Naughty Waltz' we'll all crawl along the stage and lob grenades at the audience.

The time is come. Backstage, musicians with extra Brylcreem in their dressing-rooms, playing scales, octaves or cards. Major New announces the draw. 'We're on first.' Groans.

'I told you we'll 'ave no luck with those fuckin' numbers,' says Manning.

'It's Kismet,' I said.

'What?'

'Kismet, that's what Nelson said to Hardy.'

'I thought it was Kiss Me Hardy.'

No, that was Stan Laurel, that's the popular version, you're very popular if you quote that version.

'U lot better get on,' says a snotty-nosed Base Depot Sergeant, one of those cringing acolytes that has always got extra fags and chocolates in their locker, a housey-housey concession, never lends money, and has never been nearer than a hundred miles to the front line.

The compère for the contest is Captain Philip Ridgeway, the announcer. He is as informed on Dance Bands as Mrs Thatcher is on Groin Clenching in the Outer Hebrides. Other judges are Lt Eddie Carrol, famed composer of 'Harlem' and Lieutenant 'Spike' Mackintosh, famous for not writing 'Harlem'.

Can you believe it – we didn't win! WE DIDN'T WIN!!! I wasn't even *mentioned*!! Why were the 56 Area Welfare Service persecuting me like this? At the contest I had heard shouts of 'Give him the Prize'. No one listened, even though

I shouted it very loud. Never mind, there would be other wars . . . !

Zounds! It's too much to believe. 'The Band are to have a week's leave in Rome,' says Major New, 'It's for the good work you've all done.'

I didn't understand. We'd never done any work. As if this is not enough, dear reader, on the 23 July my life is enriched by the legacy of Startling Grope. He's left orders that from this day henceforth I am to be promoted to Unpaid Acting Bombardier. No money, but I can put two stripes on my sleeve and I don't have to curtsy to Sergeants any more. Startling Grope has his little joke, for one day later . . . I am now PAID BOMBARDIER!

'Someone has blundered,' says Sergeant Britton, who is now only one stripe ahead! I catch lovely long Captain Thelma Oxnevad. I show her my two stripes. 'Any chance now?' I say, but before she can answer me I am laid low – not by illness, no, by treatment. Typhus inoculation. First shot.

'Roll your sleeve up,' said a Medical Orderly. 'Just a little prick.'

I said I could see he was.

'Can you feel that?' he said.

He was well pleased.

Soon I'm in bed with a high temperature.

'Have you heard the news?' says Steve, holding up a paper.

I listen. I can't hear anything. What's he mean? I *am* the news.

'They've dropped the Atom Bomb.'

Very good Steve, but *who's* dropped it on *who*? The Yanks!

Of course! They've got the money. He held up the paper. 'ATOM BOMB DROPPED IN HIROSHIMA.' I was delirious and really didn't give a bugger.

'It's their own bloody fault,' I said.

SEPTEMBER 27

Diary: Sergeants' mess dance. Raining

I was so excited at the prospect of UK leave that my swonicles were revolving at speed. Like a fool I thought I was going back to 1939. I'm still trying to get back to 1939. That was the best time. It all lay ahead of you. Now it's all behind and I don't want to look back. A letter from my mother tells me I have no home to come to. Her and dad are renting the ground floor of 40 Meadow Way, Woodhatch, Reigate at twenty-seven separate shillings to be paid at once to the landlady. Rations are short, they have eaten the couch. 'Your father has left the army and is working at the Associated Press in Fleet Street. If you come, you'll have to sleep in the box room on dad's officer's camp bed.' A camp bed! – a home fit for homosexuals. Brother is 'in Germany'. By order of the King of England he is hitting refugees who try to nick food.

OCTOBER 5

Diary: Train leaves Maddaloni at 0900 hours

A crowd of over a hundred, some even older, are waiting at the siding. Sgt Prosser is my travelling companion. It's sunny, we are all in a holiday mood.

'Here she comes,' says Prosser looking up the line.

'And there she goes,' I say, as it goes right past.

Finally a string of Wagons-Lits clank slowly into place; a scramble of khaki porridge as we fight for seats. Len and I sink down in corner seats opposite each other. It's Sergeants only, but ah! ha!, I have added a third stripe to my sleeve. A shuddering clanking as the engine is coupled, a jerking start as the engine gets up steam; gradually we gain momentum and in ten minutes rejoin the same line in Caserta. Much points changing and shouts from the railway men, and we are set fair for Rome, a hundred miles north. Thank God I had Len for company, not one of these NCOs would talk, save for an odd grunt. 'Any minute now,' I said, 'they'll go Baaa.' They brought to this sunny day the atmosphere of a Coroner's waiting-room.

All rail journeys are identical – looking out of windows, yawning, walking up corridors, smoking, the occasional exchange of conversation, sleeping, scratching, smoking, reading. We pass through war-torn Sessa Aurunca, a long tunnel through Monte de Fate, the country alternates between mountain and plain. I prefer my countryside plain, don't you? Through Minturno, the area where I had last been in action. I point out Colle Dimiano.

'That's where I was wounded,' I tell Len and the entire carriage. 'Did the Sergeant kiss it better?' says Len.

Midday, and we are on the plain approaching Cisterna, to our left the Via Appia, up into the Alban Hills dotted with white crosses from the Anzio break-out. By one o'clock we are hissing and chuffing into Rome Central Station. 'Half an hour,' shouts a voice. We debouch and stretch our legs, then taking from the vendor's trolley, stretch our teeth on sticky gooey cakes which look like noses boiled in treacle. The platforms are scurrying with Romans, all looking like unshaven Barclays Bank managers in Cricklewood. The supply of pretty Italian girls seems endless. 'They must have a factory round here,' says Len, eating what looks like a dried mango with cockroaches stuck on it. We both agree that to eat continental pastries you should be sedated or blindfolded. A sloppy, thin, violently ugly Railway Transport officer comes a-clumping and a-shouting through a bull horn: 'All Liap Pwarty number twenty-six bwack on the twain.' We had stocked up with French bread, cheese and boiled noses in treacle plus a bottle of Chianti. The guard's shrill whistle, unlike British guards', plays arias from *Madame Butterfly*: he's still blowing when we've left the station.

We are now hungry, so we start to eat the bread and cheese right away. The prognosis is we should be in Calais at exactly 'some time tomorrow'. When I wake up the train is speeding past Lake Bracciano; at the level crossing a crowd of peasants stand with open mouths. It's getting colder. So is mine. We can see snow on distant mountains. We plunge into long dark tunnels then into bright sunlight, into Umbria and through Viterbo, once in misty yesterdays an Etruscan Citadel. We are climbing, the windows are steaming up, we turn the handle from Freddo to Caldo, and soon we are nice and Caldo. Darkness descends, dingy yellow light bulbs illuminate the carriage. Heads are nodding, time for beddy-byes. I see there's room under the seat to sleep, I squirm underneath, bliss, there's a heating pipe behind me. While the dodos sleep upright, I sleep the sleep of an angel, be it fallen.

A merry Jiminy Cricket Castrati voice is calling: 'Wake up, wake up . . . we're in Milan.' 'Bollocks' is the response. It's eight o'clock on a very dull cold morning which I see through a sea of legs and boots. The smell in the carriage is like an uncleaned chicken coop on a hot day. Rasping smokers' coughs greet the morning. Milan station stands gaunt, grey and steely cold in the early gloom. The platform is almost empty save for vendors. We drink their exquisite aromatic coffee, banging our feet, expelling steam on our breath.

'How did you sleep?' I ask Len.

'Sitting up, didn't you notice?'

He hasn't slept well, because he hasn't slept at all. What did he do?

'I read the *Corriere della Sera*.' He doesn't speak Eyetie, but when you're awake all bloody night, it's amazing what you can manage.

'All Liap Pwarty number twenty-six bwack on twain.'

He's still around! With my ablution kit I spruce up in the toilet. What the hell, why not? I strip off for a stand-up bath. The train is on a dodgy bit of track. Trying to wash one leg while standing on the other, the train lurches and one leg goes down the toilet up to the groin. It's the nutcracker suite. I exit to a queue of strained faces: 'Been 'avin' a bloody barf?' says one micturated voice. Why should I tell these rough soldiers that, quite apart from crushing my nuts, I have partaken of Italian train waters and my body is now snow white and ready for leave.

What's this? A buffet car has been added? Len and I wobble along the steamed-up corridors past the odd dozy soldier. It's very nice, bright and clean with white table-cloths and friendly waiters. Our waiter is fat and looks suspiciously like Mussolini. He smiles. We order egg and chips. He stops smiling.

The scenery is now ravishing. Cobalt-tinted lakes, blue mountains with snow caps, pine forests, cascading gorges, all displayed in bright sunshine. However, in the Sergeants' carriage, it is overcast, raining, with heavy fog. An RTO Sergeant holding a clipboard is checking our documents and counting heads. God, this is exciting, this is what got Agatha Christie going on continental train murders. 'She should have travelled Southern Railways in the rush hour,' says Len. 'That's murder *all* the bloody time.' We've come to a sudden halt. I get off the floor. A look out of the window shows gangers on the line, some shouting 'twixt engine driver and gangers. Finally shouts and a whistle blowing, we chuff chuff forward. We proceed in fits and starts, starts and fits, then farts and stits.

Basle station is like Waterloo without the crap. We are greeted by another RTO Officer: 'LIAP party twenty-six? The train will be here for an hour. Refreshments have been laid on at the station buffet, no charge, just show your rail pass.' Despite 'no charge', they all charge to the buffet. What a lovely surprise to hear the pretty waitresses saying, 'We 'ave for you, ze Collation of Coldness.' Lovely – can they whistle the Warsaw Concerto to complete our happiness? But what a difference. Cold Collation here is different from Cold Collation in Catford. Here it's great slices of turkey, a whole lettuce, great dollops of thick egg-bound mayonnaise, chunky brown bread. And here was a moment of delight: one of the grim miserable sergeants bites the thick chunky bread, his teeth come out in it, and he goes on eating.

'So, the we'll-be-in-Calais-some-time-tomorrow isn't going to materialise,' says Len, not fancying another night of upright somnabulism.

'Can you hear horses galloping, Len?'

Len listens. 'No, I can't.'

'Oh, that's the second time today.'

He looks at me and shakes his head. 'It's time you had leave. Look, this is Switzerland, you could seek asylum here.'

Back in the compartment of miserable bastards, Len consults his map. 'We are about 450 miles to Calais.'

'Any advance on 450? Do I hear 460? Sold then to Sgt Prosser for 450.'

The Sergeants all steam with hate. I gain satisfaction from knowing that bloody ugly wives with faces like dogs' bums with hats on are waiting for them. Ha ha ha ha! It's getting still colder, but not as cold as Collation. Dinner? The white tablecloths are victims of sloppy eating and shunting. Would we like egg and chips? says Mussolini – if so you can scrape it off the table. Nay, we'll have some pasta. He has a heart attack. He runs screaming to the chef telling him of the breakthrough. I hear the kitchen staff singing hymns. Mussolini returns with steaming plates of ravioli. Tears come to his eyes as we eat it.

Night has encapsulated us, semaphores of light flash past the windows like speeding fireflies. We pause a while over our coffee and brandy and think of my parents possibly drinking watery Horlicks, eating the cat, and listening to the nine o'clock noise in rented accommodation. Was I really going back to that? Yes I was. I should have got off in Switzerland.

We return to our compartment. All the repulsive Sergeants are laughing and joking, but stop the moment we return. They smirk as we sit down and I wonder what's fretting at the smooth surface of their delinquent minds. I crawl under the seat to last night's sleeping niche and turn off to the sound of iron crochets of train wheels. While we slumber, the land of Jeanne D'Arc is slipping by in the D'ark.

AWAKE, MY PRETTY ONES

The sun is streaming through the carriage windows. Poplar trees are flashing past, the French countryside is a swirl of autumnal hues.

'Bonjour,' says Len, as I arise from le floor. 'It's temps pour le breakfast.'

The buffet car is crammed with bleary-eyed, travel-weary soldiers. The smell of fried breakfasts wafts along the corridors; they've started queuing, we must be getting near England. Appetite improves with waiting. Our turn. What would the messieurs like? Hot bread rolls? Oui, oui. We must be in France or luck. There's *real* unsalted Normandy butter on the table. We watch it melt on the hot rolls, heap on marmalade. 'Le Life is Très Bon,' says Len. He confers with his le map. 'Ah, we passed Chaumont in the night,' he says. Help, Doctor, Doctor, I've been passing Chaumonts in the night.

The RTO Sergeant is wobbling down the corridors: 'Calais in two hours,' he calls. I must wash and brush up. Calais, one of the Sunk Ports.

'Have you ever seen the statue of the Burghers in Calais?' says Len.

'No, I'm waiting till they make the film.'

A last coffee in the buffet car. The waiters are breathing a sigh that the culinary barbarians are leaving. But what bad cooks the English are – they even burnt Joan of Arc.

Still miles from Calais, yet the idiot Sergeants are getting their luggage down. Some are even standing at the door. In their tiny minds they think they'll get there quicker. Why don't they stand near a graveyard?

Our train is slowing. The canvas is grey, a sphaghetti of railway lines, black industrial complexes, many of them bombed skeletons. A mess of railway sidings, rolling stock, here and there a burnt-out tanker; slower and slower and then in the middle of a sea of points, we are told, 'All out!' Waiting in the grey gloom are three RTO Sergeants, all brass, blanco and bullshit. We split into two groups. 'NCOs this way please.' (PLEASE???) We two-step over a hundred yards of tracks. NO. 4 TRANSIT CAMP says the sign, and who are we to argue. 'In here, gentlemen,' (GENTLEMEN?) The sergeant shows us into a Nissen hut. Beds and an iron stove.

LAST LEG OF THE JOURNEY . . .
REVEILLE 0600
BREAKFAST 0700
PARADE 0830
EMBARK 0900–1000

It all sounds reasonable, no need to see a solicitor after all. The channel steamer SS *Appalling* (the name of the ship has been changed to protect the innocent) is waiting. A tiny almost unnoticeable sign says LIAP PARTY NO 26 ASSEMBLE HERE. We'll never do it, it's much too small to stand on. We move slowly up the gangplank like shuffling penguins. I'm humping a kitbag, big pack and trumpet case. The kitbag is vital, it contains all the hoarded underwear that my mother has promised will put me on the road to success in civvy street. And I will never be taken short. The officers in first class look down at our huddled mass from the top deck. 'There's one thing we've got over them, Len, we can see right up their noses.' A clatter of donkey engines and French steam; hawsers plummet into the waters. Cries of yo, ho, ho, and the ship slips from the quay into the muddy waters of Calais harbour, but soon we are free from the muddy French waters and out into the pure English Channel and its muddy waters. It's very choppy; ere long the first victims are starting to retch. Whereas other ranks are seasick, officers only have Mal-de-Mer, as befits the King's commission. Sleek white gulls glide alongside. In their total freedom, we must look like a bunch of caged monkeys. It's getting rougher; three green men are throwing up at the rail. Thank God for gravity.

LANDLORDS AHOY!

Frightening Folkestone on the Kardboard Kow! The golden seaport hove into view; I would rather have viewed into Hove. It's raining, and doing the gardens good. We are close to the quay.

'It looks so bloody foreboding,' Len says. 'I think I'll go back.'

I remind him that his dear little wife is at this moment panting on her bed with the heating turned up and drinking boiling Horlicks.

The customs are pretty hot. 'Read that, please,' I am handed a foolscap sheet of writing.

'Very good,' I say.

'Have you anything to declare?'

I declare that the war is over. He's not satisfied. What have I got in the case. It's a trumpet. Can he see it. He opens the case. Where did I buy this? In London. Have I got a receipt? Yes. Where is it? It's in an envelope in a drawer in my mother's dressing-table in Reigate.

He hums and haws, he's as stupid as a pissed parrot. 'Empty your kitbag.' I pour out a sea of my second-hand underwear. He turns it over and over. 'Where is it?'

'Where's what?'

'The contents.' He thinks it's the wrapping for something. Why have I got so many underpants? I tell him of my mother's forecast of the coming world shortage that will hit England soon. He is now pretty pissed off. OK. He makes a yellow chalk mark on everything. Next to me he finds a poor squaddie with a bottle of whisky. 'You'll have to pay One Pound Ten Shillingss on that,' he says with malice aforethought.

'Oh no I won't,' says the squaddie.

'Than I'll have to confiscate it.'

The squaddie opens the bottle and hands it round to us. With devilish glee we help lower the level to halfway, then the squaddie puts the bottle to his lips and drains it. The customs officer is in a frenzy, says to an MP, 'Arrest that man.'

The MP wants to know why.

'Drunkenness,' he says.

'He's not drunk,' says the MP.

'Wait,' says the customs officer.

Folkestone station and the 11.40 train to Charing Cross. London is as I left it – black, grimy, rainy but holes in the terraces where bombs have fallen. Len and I split.

'See you in four weeks' time, two stone lighter and skint,' he says.

I buy my first English newspapers for two years. The *Daily Herald*, the *Daily Mail*, the *Express*, the *Mirror*, the *News Chronicle*. I go straight for my beloved Beachcomber and find that Justice Cocklecarrot and the Red Bearded Dwarfs are still in court. He is sentencing a Mrs Grotts for repeatedly pushing the Dwarfs into people's halls.

From Charing Cross I take the tube to Archway. Soon I am knocking on the door of 31 St John's Way. A surprise for Mrs Edgington, she doesn't know I'm coming.

'Oh Spike,' she's drying her hands. 'What are you doing here?'

I tell her I'm doing leave here.

'When are you going back?'

Can I come in first? Tea, would I like some tea. Ah! at

last an *English* cup of tea and a dog biscuit (JOKE). I explain my accommodation difficulty. What is the difficulty? Accommodation. Yes, I can stay here. 'You can sleep in the basement.' Mr Edgington's not in, he's gone out to get a paper. Yes, he's well. Son Doug? He's been called up. The Army. Did I know Harry was getting married on leave? He's been caught at the customs with some material he'd bought for Peg's wedding dress and the bastards have given him detention. Mr Edgington is back. Ah Spike. 'When are you going back?' He's tall, thin, at-one-time handsome. An ex-Guards Sergeant from World War I, he was badly gassed in France. He is in receipt of a small war pension. Alas he smokes, it will do for him one day, as it would his youngest son Doug . . . I dump my gear in the basement. Would I like some lunch? Toad-in-the-hole? Lovely grub. I set myself up in the basement. There's a coal fire, but remember it's rationed! Best not light it until the evening.

Leading question. Can Mrs Edgington see to find room for Sergeant Betty Cranley for a day or so? Yes, there's Doug's bedroom going spare. I tell her, good, because I'm going spare. I phone Betty: Hello Betty, knickers and boobs, can she get up with knickers and boobs this week knickers and boobs? Yes, she can, knickers and boobs.

THE GREAT AMNESIA

I have a diary. It says: Stayed Edgingtons. Stayed Beryl. Stayed Folks. But I can't remember – so I searched for Beryl – Success – I found Beryl – she remembered, but won't charge me.

SAUCY SANDWICH

The train to Sandwich takes me through the Kent country-side. All is russet with pale gold sunshine glistening on autumn-damp trees; through the Kent orchards, the trees

My brother, mother and father, Desmond, Florence and Leo Milligan

heavy with the red green and yellow fruit. 1930s men are up splayed apple-ladders taking in the harvest. The curving line loops round Sandwich bay to the little station. There, not waiting for me, is Betty Cranley. The little cow!

I fiddle my way into town and get to the RAF depot. Like Simon Legree I burst into the kitchen and catch her. She's rolling dough for a pudding. So this is how you treat me. While I'm on the platform being lovely, you're rolling dough for puddens. She's sorry, she was put on duty owing to one of the staff being taken suddenly something or other. Would I like a cup of tea and some fruit cake? How nice.

309

Does she know 'Lae thar piss tub darn bab'? I hang around until she comes off duty. It wasn't easy in an RAF kitchen full of WAAFS, all in the prime of cooking puddens.

It was hell, folks. Betty threw me on to the bed and had her way with me. She used cold compresses, it was no good, I was getting weaker and weaker. I tell her I've got a headache. She can cure it she says, jumping up and down in a fever of sweat and pudding. In the morning she is bubbling with life, as I lie like a geriatric on my death bed, white and feeble. I must get to some Eggs and Chips soon, or a monastery. By day I lie in bed dreading the nights. She returns, strips off, and standing on the bed head, dives on me. When the woman comes to make the bed, she doesn't notice I'm in it. Twice she puts me in the laundry basket. Oh thank God, it's time to go back to Italy, dear. This is our last night, she says, we must make it last. She makes it last, I don't. I slept through the last bit.

FOLKESTONE

I report to a huge requisitioned transit hotel on the sea front, stripped of everything except the floor. I report to the Orderly Sergeant, check documents, yes the boat leaves at 0900. Bunk beds to infinity, one dull light bulb illuminates the gloom. The room gradually fills with leave-spent soldiers.

On board the steam packet, we pitch and toss on the grey spume-flecked waters, heading into a chill wind, laced with face-pecking rain. Some walk around the decks, I stay in what in better days was the saloon dining-room. Now it's just tables, chairs, tea, buns and fag ends. The eyes blink, the mind goes into neutral, the throb of the ship's engines. It's rather like taking a boat to the Styx. Alas, it's worse, soon it's Crappy Calais and the excitement of No. 4 Transit Camp with its damp beds and go-as-you-please urinal. A visit to the Hotel de Ville. Beans on toast cooked by a French chef made our journey a little more bearable.

Strange I never mentioned my travelling companion's name; and from what I remember, I'm glad. Next morning it's raining in French. It will do le garden bon. I'm glad to be on the train heading for Italy. The leave was an experience – it was like a flashback to 1940, and trying to compress it all into four weeks. We leave the dripping eaves of Calais, through its still slumbering populace. It's only seven-thirty and dark. My God, it's those Sergeants. They're all sitting opposite me again. And I don't have Len Prosser to talk to – he's on the train ahead.

RETURN TO ITALY

The morning of November the second dawns. A hurrying RTO Sergeant proceeds down the corridor. 'Maddaloni in fifteen minutes.' Familiar landscape is in view, the hills behind Caserta are light and dark in the morning sun. We wipe the steamed windows to see it. I've had breakfast: two boiled eggs, boiled bread and boiled tea. How come the Continentals can't make tea? If this is tea, bring me coffee. If this is coffee, bring me tea. The Italian waiter says they don't go much on tea. I tell him if they did it would make it stronger. The black giant locomotive groans and hisses to a clanking steaming halt, there's a long shuddering final hiss as the steam leaches out, like a giant carthorse about to die. We all climb down onto the tracks. A few thank the unshaven smoke-blackened driver. There's a clutch of lorries waiting, they are dead on time. Now the war's over the Army's getting it together. Wearily we clamber on board and arrive at Alexander barracks as the town is coming to life. Shagged-out cats are heading for home and the odd early morning dog sits on the cold pavement, freezing his bum and scratching away the night fleas.

'Wake up, Steve.' I shake the sleeping Yew. 'Wake up, God's in his heaven, all's right with the world.'

'Piss off,' he says, without opening his eyes.

'Wake up Steve my old friend, it's me, Sunny Spike Milligan, back from foreign shores with a tale to tell.'

He raises his lovely head, squints, groans, and lets his head fall back with a thud. Go away Milligan, go a long way away, take a known poison and only come back when you're dead.

I take his eating irons and bring him his breakfast. This thaws him out.

'Breakfast in bed,' he says, sitting up, pulling strings that raise the mosquito net, empty the po, release his shirt, loosen his pyjamas, bring his socks, raise his vest, lower his comb, push his boots . . . So what was England like? It's like 1939 with bomb craters and fruit cake, and there's a lot of it about. I should know, I'm just recovering. Back into the office grind. What news? During the absence of the band on leave, entertainment has come to a halt.

SHOCK HORROR ETC AND OTHER HEADLINES!

I was to get the chop! Not the leg of lamb or the kidney but the chop! While I was helping the women of England get back to normal in Sandwich, Brigadier Henry Woods has decided that either I go or he stays.

> BOMBARDIER MILLIGAN S. 954024
> With effect from November the umpteenth,
> the above will be posted to the CPA,
> Welfare Department, Naples.
> Signed H. Woods, Brigadier and midget.

So, he was the coloured gentleman in the wood pile. I swore I would never go to the pictures with him again. (He died a few years ago. I wish him well.) Why was he persecuting me like this? My only crime was my only crime. Still, like Cold Collation I could take it. I had letters to that effect from several serving women. The papers should hear of this.

A NEW LIFE AND A NEW DAWN

A truck is waiting to take me away. How many times have I done this? Yet again the kit is piled in the back, and like a sheep to market, I am driven away, all on the whim of one man who thought I played my trumpet too loud. I am puzzling over what CPA means. Captain's Personal Assistant? Cracked People's Area? Clever Privates' Annexe? None of these, says the driver. It's 'Centril Pule of Hartists (Central Pool of Artists), hits a place where orl dhan-graded squaddies who can hentertain are sent.' Was he a down-graded entertainer?

'Yer.'

'What do you do?'

'Hi sing Hopera.'

'Opera?'

'Yer, you know, *La Bhome*, *Traviahta*, and the like.'

'Were you trained?'

'Now, it cum natural like.'

'Have you ever sung in opera natural like?'

'No, I just done the horditions like. The Captain says 'ees waitin' for a suitable vehicle for me.' Like a bus, I thought.

We have driven through Naples, turned left at the bottom of Via Roma up the Corso San Antonio, which goes on for ever in an Eastern direction. Finally we arrive at a broken-down Army Barracks complex. The walls are peeling, they look as if they have mange. I report to a Captain Philip Ridgeway, a sallow saturnine fellow with a Ronald Colman moustache who looks as if he has mange as well. He sits behind the desk with his hat on. He is the son of the famous Ridgeways' Late Joys Revue that led to the Players Theatre. He looks at my papers. 'So, you play the trumpet. Do you play it well?'

'Well, er loudly.'

'Do you read music?'

'Yes, and the *Daily Herald*.'

He smiled. He would find me a place in 'one of our orchestras'. I was taken by a Corporal Gron, who looked like an unflushed lavatory, and shown to a billet on the first floor, a room with forty single beds around the walls. In them were forty single men. This being Sunday, they were of a religious order that kept them in kip until midday. I drop my kit on a vacant bed, and it collapses to the floor. 'That's why it's vacant,' laughed Corporal Gron, who laughed when babies fell under buses. Next bed is Private Graham Barlow. He helps me repair the bed with some string and money. Nice man – he played the accordion. Noël Coward said, 'No gentleman would ever play the accordion.'

I had no job as such, and as such I had no job. Breakfast was at 8.30, no parade, hang around, lunch, hang further around, tea, extended hanging around, dinner and bed. The CPA Complex had the same ground plan as the Palace of Minos at Knossos, consisting of rehearsal rooms, music stores, costume stores, scenery dock and painting area, Wardrobe Mistress, Executive offices. People went in and

The show-stopping Bill Hall Trio: J. Mulgrew on bass, Bill Hall on violin and Spike Milligan on guitar

were never seen again. The company was assembled from soldier artists who had been down-graded. They would be formed into concert parties and sent on tour to entertain those Tommies who weren't down-graded. The blind leading the blind. The facilities were primitive, the lavatories were a line of holes in the ground. When I saw eighteen soldiers squatting/balancing over black holes with straining sweating faces for the first time, they looked like the start of the hundred yards for paraplegic dwarfs.

My first step to 'fame' came when I borrowed a guitar from the stores. I was playing in the rehearsal room when a tall cadaverous gunner said, 'You play the guitar then?' This was Bill Hall. If you've ever seen a picture of Niccolò Paganini, this was his double. What's more, he played the violin and played it superbly; be it a Max Bruch Concerto or 'I've Got Rhythm', he was a virtuoso. But bloody scruffy. We teamed up just for the fun of it, and in turn we were joined by Johnny Mulgrew, a short Scots lad from the Recce Corps; as he'd left them they were even shorter of Scots. Curriculum Vitae: Pre-war he played for Ambrose and the Inland Revenue. In the 56 Recce in N. Africa. Trapped behind enemy lines at Madjez-el-Bab. Lay Doggo for forty-eight hours in freezing weather. Got pneumonia. Down-graded to B2 . . .

Together we sounded like Le Hot Club de France. When we played, other musicians would come and listen to us – a compliment – and it wasn't long before we were lined up for a show.

In the filling-in time, I used to play the trumpet in a scratch combination. It led to my meeting with someone from Mars, Gunner Secombe, H., singer and lunatic, a little myopic blubber of fat from Wales who had been pronounced a loony after a direct hit by an 88-mm gun in North Africa. He was asleep at the time and didn't know about it till he woke up. General Montgomery saw him and nearly surrendered. He spoke like a speeded up record, no one understood him, he didn't even understand himself; in fact, forty years later he was knighted for not being understood.

The Officers' Club, Naples. We were playing for dancing and cabaret, the latter being the lunatic Secombe. His 'music' consisted of some tatty bits of paper, two parts, one for the drums and one for the piano – the rest of us had to guess. We busked him on with 'I'm just wild about Harry'. He told us he had chosen it because his name was Harry, and we said how clever he was. He rushed on, chattering, screaming, farting, sweat pouring off him like a monsoon, and officers moved their chairs back. Then the thing started to shave itself, screaming, chattering and farting; he spoke at high speed; the audience thought he was an imported Polish comic, and many wished he was back in Warsaw being bombed. Shaving soap and hairs flew in all directions, then he launched into a screaming duet with himself, Nelson Eddy and Jeanette MacDonald, but you couldn't tell him apart. A few cries of 'hey hup' and a few more soapy farts, and he's gone, leaving the dance floor smothered in shaving soap. His wasn't an act, it was an interruption.

The dance continues, and officers are going arse over tip

Secombe, December 1945 – having cleared the Officers' Club, Naples, with screaming raspberries, shaving and singing – well pleased

in dozens. 'No, not him,' they'd say when Secombe's name
came up for a cabaret.

'OVER THE PAGE'

This was the show that launched the Bill Hall Trio. It was
the brainchild of Captain Hector Ross, whose play *Men in
Shadow* I had destroyed at Maddaloni. It was sheer luck:
one of the acts for *Over the Page* had withdrawn at the last
moment, a sort of theatrical Coitus Interruptus. Could the
Trio fill in? Yes. I knew that just playing jazz never was a
winner, so I persuaded the wardrobe to give us the worst
ragged costumes we could find. I worked out some patter
and introductions. I never dreamed we would be anything
more than just 'another act'.

The artistes were a mixture of Italian professionals and
soldier amateurs. Monday December 6th 1945 the show
opened at the Bellini Theatre to a packed house.

We were one incredible hit. When we came off, we were
stunned. I couldn't believe that of all that talent out there,
we had topped the lot. After the show, a Captain Reg O'List
of CPA came backstage. He had been a singer at the
Windmill in London, which was rather like being a blood
donor in a mortuary. He thinks we're great. Can he take us
to dinner? God, we were in the big time already. Off the Via
Roma is a wonderful pasta restaurant, we'll love it. Great!
Captain O'List does it in style, we go in a horse-drawn
carriage. Bill Hall plays his violin as we drift down the Via
Roma. Wow! Life is good. The restaurant is all one can
dream of: the waiters wear white aprons, the tables have red
and white check cloths, there's an oil lamp on every table, a
mandolin band playing. As soon as we enter the waiters
sweep us up in a cushion of hospitality. 'Si accomodo,
accomodo,' a bottle of wine with the manager's compliments, thank you very much with our compliments. Giddy
with success and a free dinner, we eat a mountain of

*Capt Reg O'List, Pioneer Corps, playing and singing 'When
They Begin the Beguine', Italy 1945*

spaghetti. Reg O'List can't stop telling us how good we are
and we can't stop agreeing with him. He can't believe we are
just the result of a chance meeting in a barrack room. Can
we play some jazz after dinner? Yes. 'Hey! I know! why
don't we put on a show?' etc! The customers stop eating,
they cheer and clap, encore, encore. Free wine is slopping
out of us. Enough is enough. Reg O'List is now very pissed;
he will do *his* Windmill Act; he starts to sing 'Begin the
Beguine'; he has a powerful shivery square voice.

'If he's from the Windmill,' says Gunner Hall, 'why
doesn't he take his clothes off?' The night ends with Bill
Hall splitting away from us – the last sight we had of him
was on a tram playing opera to adoring passengers. What a
night. It would lead us slowly down the road to oblivion.

BOLOGNA

Sunday. We are off to Bologna. Where the hell is Bill Hall?

Someone says Italy! We search the hotel, then his room; there's nothing in it though he's slept in both beds, left a tap running, and a pair of socks in the sink. Wait, what is this unshaven wreck with a violin case? It is he. He gets on the charabanc, ignoring the fact that we've been waiting half an hour. A desultory cheer greets him. Totally unmoved, he sits down. I watch a drip from his nose fall and extinguish his dog-end. I am seated at the back on a bench seat. I have placed my guitar case on the luggage rack and as we start, it falls off on to Hall's head. 'You have-a musica on yewer brayne,' says Mitzi. It is a good joke for a forty-three-year-old Hungarian accordion player.

Lieutenant Priest passes sandwiches down the charabanc. 'Ham and cheese,' he says. We are all stamping our feet and blowing into cupped hands. Sometimes we cupped our feet and stamped our hands: variety is the spice of life. It was an awful long cold boring darkness. It wasn't a moment too soon when we arrived in Bologna; with the Tower of Dante looming into the night sky, we pull up at the Albergo Oralogio. A fin de cycle building. All is Baroque, even the porters.

We are soon in wonderful bedrooms, faded but lovely. I have a huge marble bath with gorgon-headed taps, and a giant brass shower rose in a wooden boxed-in cabinet. The curtains are damask. It's a single room, so I'm safe from singing, farting, chattering Secombe.

Again the Bill Hall Triumph. It's getting to be a habit. With the raincoat money I bought an old Kodak camera. I filmed everything.

The streets of Bologna were swarming with Italian Partisans wearing bandoliers, their belts stuffed with German stick grenades. They sauntered the sidewalks with a braggadocio air, waving their captured weapons and shouting Viva Italia. After a while it got a bit boring and Bill Hall said to one, 'Le Guerre Finito mate.' We climbed the six hundred steps up the Tower of Dante, only to find graffiti: 'Viva La Figa.'

CHRISTMAS IN ITALY

Our last show in Bologna was on Christmas Day. It was all very strange. On Christmas Eve, after a show to a very inebriated audience, I wanted to be alone. I went to my bedroom and wished I could be back at 50 Riseldine Road with my mum and dad and brother. I wanted that little Christmas tree in the front room, the coal fire especially lit to 'air the room' for Christmas Day. The simple presents, a scarf, a pair of socks, a presentation box of 25 Player's cigarettes, my brother's box of Brittans soldiers, a drawing book with a set of pencils. Very modest fare by modern standards, but to me then, still simple and unsophisticated, it was a warming and magic day. The lunch, and *chicken*, that was something! In 1939, chicken was a luxury. And the tin of Danish ham! The huge trifle with custard and real CREAM. My father's pride in opening the Port, pretending he was a savant, smelling the cork, 'Ahhhh yes,' he would say, and pour it with the gesture of a sommelier at the Lord Mayor's banquet.

Here I was in a room in Bologna. I couldn't get it together. Outside there is roistering. Not me. I knew tomorrow there would be no stocking at the end of my bed. Father Christmas was a casualty of World War II.

FLORENCE

City of Medicis, Savonarola, and chattering raspberrying Secombe, now freezing without his leather 'love gift' jerkin. This is the city of the artist, the artisan, the connoisseur. Our Hotel Dante is just round the corner from the Piazza del Signoria. I would be able to see places that I had only read about. The hotel is one built for those rich Victorians

Spike feeding the pigeons in a piazza in Bologna. Photograph of no particular merit other than that the photographer would one day arise and find Sir in front of his name

doing the Grand Tour. Sumptuous rooms, a wonderful double bed with duck eider, like sleeping in froth. Putting my egg-stained battledress in the bevelled glass and walnut cupboard was like wearing a flat hat in the Ritz. Secombe flies past chattering and farting up the Carrara marble stairs with its flanking Venetian balustrades topped with cherubim holding bronze lanterns. He looks totally out of place, he belongs at the pit head.

I am standing on the spot, explaining that this is where Savonarola was burned. 'Oo was Savonarola?' says Gunner Hall. I tell him 'oo he is'. 'They *burnt* him?' Yes. 'Why. Were they short of coal?' I explain that he was at odds with the Medici and the state of Florence. 'Fancy,' says Hall. 'Why didn't 'e call the fire brigade?' The same indifference applies to seeing Cellini's Perseus. With the head of Medusa, Hall wants to know why statues are erected to people being burnt or having their heads chopped off. 'Why not someone normal like Tommy Handley?' Yes, of course: 'Here is Cellini's statue of Tommy Handley from ITMA.' That would look really nice in the Piazza.

321

The Pitti Palace leaves me stunned; masterpiece after masterpiece, there's no end to it. From Titian to Seguantini. You come out feeling useless and ugly. On the Ponte Vecchio Secombe and I ask Hall to take a photo of us. It comes out with the wall behind us in perfect focus, two blurred faces in the foreground. He was well pleased.

RETURN TO NAPLES

Days seem to go by like water rushing over stones. We leave Florence, having visited every possible sight. It was a city I can never forget. We are to return to Naples, with an overnight stay in Rome. There we dine again with the Eton-cropped manageress, whom we now know to be a lesbian. The discovery was made by Lt Priest who had put his hand on her leg and had it crushed in a vice-like grip, all the while smiling sweetly at him. I got a bit worried when she said to me, 'You are a very pretty boy.' After dinner she asked the trio to come to her room and play. Drinks had been laid on, including a Barolo 1930! She asked us to play 'You Go to my Head', then sang it in Italian in a deep baritone voice. If we weren't certain before, we were now. Yes, there was the shaving soap on the windowsill. The more she drank, the more masculine she became, giving us thumps on the back like demolition hammers. 'Let's get out of here,' said Hall, 'or she'll fuck the lot of us.'

Back in the old routine. Hall has been missing the days. During his absence, we transform his army bed into a magnificent four poster with a Heraldic Shield, satin drapes and a scarlet velvet bedspread. We time it to perfection. Hall comes in five minutes before the once-weekly roll-call and inspection. He walks in a moment before the Inspecting Officer. Stunned, he stands by his bed. Enter Captain O'List. He too is stunned.

O'LIST: Whose bed is this?

HALL: Mine sir.

O'LIST: How long has it been like this?

HALL: Just today, sir.

O'LIST: Why?

HALL: It's my mother's birthday, sir.

O'List couldn't contain himself. Weak-legged he walked rapidly from the room. On the stairs we could hear him choking with laughter.

BARI

Yes, we are to ancient Barium where the meal-enema was invented. We are to entertain the bored soldiery. First thing, chain Gunner Hall to the bed. Louisa Pucelli, our Italian star, has dropped out of the show, and in her place we have Signorina Delores Bagitta, an ageing bottle-blonde Neapolitan old boiler, with a voice like a Ferrari exhaust. She looked OK from a distance, about a mile I'd say. She did a Carmen Miranda act, her layers of cutaneous fat shuddering with every move. 'Amore, amore,' she'd croak. It was monumental tat.

Bari is a dusty seaport on the Adriatic. There's Bari Vecchio and Bari Nuovo. No hotel this time, but a large hostel that seemed to be under permanent siege by lady cleaners. Even as you sat on the WC a mop would suddenly slosh under the door. The streets are heavy with bored British troops, and a heavy sprinkling of Scots from the tribal areas. The old city is really a museum piece, it's a time capsule dated about 1700: the Moors were here and left their mark – many a dark skin can be seen.

Secombe appears to be inflating his head; he is even inflating his face. Somehow the wind is escaping upwards. No, the man is in real trouble. Poor Gunner, struck down in his prime! Of all things he has illness of the face. It's true, folks, he has been using cheap Italian make-up which has affected all the cuts he gave himself during his screaming farting and shaving act. It gets bad, and the swelling closes both eyes. There was little pity. We had warned him if he didn't stop it, this is what would happen. The dramatic situation of temporary blindness gives Secombe a great chance for histrionics: he becomes Gunner King Lear. 'I'm sorry lads, to have let you down like this, but remember the show must go on.' He lay in his bed, not knowing that we had left the room. He develops a high temperature which speeds him up. When the ambulance arrives to take him, he is chattering, screaming and farting at twice the speed. 'I'm sorry I'm leaving you lads, but I'll be back, the show must go on, thanks for all your help, remember me when you're on stage, tell the lads I did my best, Cardiff 3 Swansea Nil. Lloyd George knew my father, saucepanbach, Ivor Novello, when I come home again to Wales.' As they drove him away we could hear snatches of Welsh songs, rugby scores, raspberrying and screaming. When he arrived at Ben General Hospital they took him straight to the psychiatric ward where he gave three doctors a nervous breakdown.

His place in the show was taken by Delores Bagitta; dressed as a nun she sang 'Ave Maria' in a gin-soaked voice. Lt Priest pleaded with her not to, but to our horror and amazement she got an ovation! There's no telling.

Surprise, surprise, after our first show, who shows up? It's lean lovely Lance Bombardier Reg Bennett. What's he doing here? He was posted. He arrived with a letter to the Town Major who said. 'I see Bennett that you are an expert on heavy dock clearance and port maintenance.'

'No sir, I'm an insurance clerk.'

Someone had blundered. He gets the plum job of Town Major's clerk. With it goes a private flat above his office. He invited me back. We took a taxi, so he was doing all right. We arrived at the flat and opened the door to find the Town

Major screwing some Eyetie bird on the floor. 'I'm afraid the room is occupied,' he said.

We ended up at a restaurant in the Old Town; customers are up-market Italians and a few British officers. 'All black market,' says Reg.

'How can you afford all this, Reg?'

He grinned the grin of a man heavily involved in skulduggery. 'I handle the NAAFI,' he said. Ah! NAAFI, the crown jewels of military life. We spoke about an idea we had had back in Baiano. A nightclub on the Thames. It was pie in the sky. Bennett says. 'Milligan, if we're going to dream, why stop at a nightclub on the Thames, why not a hundred-storey hotel in San Francisco? We've just had four bloody years of war, why go in for more trouble? No Spike, I've thought about it, if we all clubbed together we'd just about afford two tables and six chairs.'

'We could get a bank loan.'

'OK, *eight* chairs then.'

He was right. I said so: 'You are right.' I said. 'To hell with the hundred-storey hotel and the six chairs. Waiter, another bottle of Orvieto!'

Well pissed, Bennett dropped me off at the hotel. An hour later he appears at my bedroom door. 'He's still screwing,' he said. I put him in the spare bed. 'I'm not angry, just jealous,' he said. Reg departed next morning. I was not to see him for another five years, by which time the Town Major had finished screwing.

The sound of chattering, farting and screams tells me that Secombe has been cured and released, and the hospital burnt down for safety. 'Hello hello, hey hoi hup, raspberry, scream, sing, on with the show hey hoi hup.' He revolves round the hotel at speed. What had eluded scientists for 2,000 years has been discovered by Gunner Secombe. Perpetual motion.

NEW YEAR'S EVE

AD 1946 is a few hours away as the show opens. The front row is filled with the well-scrubbed, pink and pretty Queen Alexandra Nursing Sisters, all crisp and starched in their grey, white and red uniforms. Hovering above them in the crammed gallery are hundreds of steaming Highlanders, all in the combustible atmosphere of whisky fumes. The Bill Hall Trio are a smash hit. We are going for an encore when to our horror we see, falling like gentle rain from heaven, scores of inflated rubber condoms floating down on the dear nursing sisters. Some, all merry with the festive season, start bursting them before they scream with realisation. Military police go in among the steaming Scots and a fight breaks out; to the sound of smashing bottles, thuds, screams, wallops and yells, a nun sings 'Ave Maria'. Happy New Year everyone.

After the show there's a party on stage, a table with ARGGGGHHH Cold Collation, the Bill Hall Trio play for dancing. A good time was had by all, and something else had by all was Delores Bagitta. Lt Priest drinks a toast: 'This is our last show and we will be returning to base tomorrow.'

ROMANCE 'NEATH ITALIAN SKIES

The music of 'Lae thar piss tub darn bab' floats on the air. It's spring in Napoli! Bornheim and I are sipping sweet tea as the sun streams into the golden pilasters of the Banqueting Room of the Royal Palace, Naples NAAFI, having posted a look-out on the roof for Gracie Fields. Our waitress is a Maria, and fancying me.

'Wot ewer name?'

'Spike.'

'Spak?'

'Yes, Spike.'

'Spak.'

It sounds like custard hitting a wall. My darling, can we go 'passagiere sul la Mare?' Si, si, si. When darling? Sabato. But we must be careful, we must not be seen by her parents or her familyo! Why, Maria, why? Wasn't it I, a British soldier, who has liberated Italy from the Naughty Nazis and let loose a hoard of raping, pillaging, Allied soldiers on to your streets. Does her family know I am a Holy Roman Catholic with half a hundredweight of relics of the cross to my credit, *and* a cache of secondhand underwear? No, no, no, it would be dangerous. What would happen if they caught us together? They would catch mine together and crush them. We meet then in the mysterious Vomero, she in Sunday best, me in the best I can find on Sunday. Now for a day of high romance. But no. She is in state of high anxiety, every ten seconds she clutches me with a stifled scream, she imagines one of her family appearing, knife in hand. We spend the day like two people trying to avoid the searchlights at Alcatraz, forever flattening against walls, diving into dark doorways where I give them a quick squeeze, and

Maria in a state of High Anxiety at the start of our day out

running across squares.* At the end of the day, shagged out
by a hard day's espionage and squeezing, she says goodbye
and catches a tram. Bornheim is sitting on his bed awaiting
the results.

'Did you get it?'

'No.'

Nothing? No. What did I do? About eighteen miles, I
said.

'TWAS ON THE ISLE OF CAPRI

Private Bornheim is singing the theme from the 'Pathétique'
and cutting his toe-nails with what look like garden shears.
'The good weather is coming, we should go for a trip to
Capri.' Good idea, but we must choose a day when Gracie
Fields is singing on the mainland. Ha ha ha. 'When should
we go?' As soon as he's finished cutting his toe-nails. That
could be weeks.

One fine warm spring morning, we board the ferry
Cavallo del Mare, and set fair for the Isle of Capri.
Bornheim feels fine; with toe-nails clipped he's about ten
pounds lighter. A bar on board sells cigarettes, fruit juices
and flies.

I watch as the magic isle heaves into view, blue and
purple in the morning mist, the old village in the centre, the
houses huddled together like frightened children. On the
bridge an unshaven captain in a vest, oily peaked cap and
flies, shouts to the shoreman. We approach Marina Grande,
he cuts the engines, we glide to the quay; all the while
Private Bornheim has been immersed in his Union Jack,
calling out bits of news: 'They've increased the fat allow-
ance back home.' All that and Capri!

As we disembark, Italian Dragomen and flies are waiting.
'Do you like a donkey?' No thanks, I'm a vegetarian. We

* One of the squares I ran across was Reg O'List.

The quay for the ferry to Capri – left is the Castel Uovo

board the Funicolare – up up up. At the top we walk out into the most famous square in the world, Captain Reg O'List. How are we? – he's just returning. Goodbye Reg, no – no need to sing 'Begin the Beguine', no, thank mother for the rabbit.

The main square is set up with cafés and outdoor tables, no piped music or transistors. We choose the Café Azzurra because it's nearest, and order two ice creams. What ice creams!!! Wow, a foot high, multi-coloured, and covered in cream and flies. We are the only two soldiers in the Square.

My God! the impossible! "Ello lads.' It's *her*! It's our Gracie! I wished it was *theirs*. She insists we come and have a 'nice cup of tea'. Down the lanes she takes us to her Villa Canzone del t'mare; the view is stunning but the house is rather like a very good class boarding-house in Scunthorpe. She's wonderfully warm-hearted. We sit on the balcony admiring the view; please God, don't let her sing. Is she going to say it? She does. 'Ee Bai Gom, a bit different from Blackpool.' She *must* be working from a script. We escape without any singing. 'Good luck lads, give my love t'folks back t'ome.' We'd escaped ! Not even 'Sally'!

329

I wanted to see San Michele. It's closed, says a caretaker who looked like Frankenstein's monster without the bolts. On to the site of the Villa of Tiberius, now carefully converted into cowsheds. Sloshing thru cow dung, a local shows where Tiberius threw his victims over the cliff.

'I don't see what's dangerous about that,' said Bornheim. 'It's perfectly safe until you hit the rocks.'

Lunch, midday and that warm torpor was implemented as we ate Spaghetti Marinara and drank Ruffino at a little restaurant, high over the sea.

We returned as the evening purple cascaded down on the Sorrentine peninsula.

The ferry is cloyed with chattering screaming Neapolitans and flies. At the stern a row breaks out. I can only see the pictures of a crowd of males hitting one unfortunate individual, some actually hanging over the boat railings to give better purchase for their assault. As in all mobs, anyone can join in the hitting, even though they don't know the reason for it, and even I was tempted. It's the last boat, crowded. We are the only two soldiers on board. I address a seaman: 'Hello sailor,' I say. 'Can you take our picture?' Si. The sailor smiles and points the ancient Kodak. Click! Bornheim and I are immortalised.

The cool evening air and the last warmth of the sun touched our skin. We stood at the rails watching Capri sink into the oncoming crepuscular night; in ancient times the Pharos on Capri would have been igniting its faggot fires to warn ships bearing grain from Africa of its rocky prominence. Bornheim and I were taking on glasses of grappa to light our own faggot fires, and warn those self-same ships against our own rocky prominences. Arriving back at the billets and settling back into the ways of soldiery was difficult. After lights out, we reminisced in our khaki cots. 'It didn't really happen, did it?' he said.

NICE SURPRISEY-POO

'You are very lucky fellows,' says Reg O'List, who is now not singing 'Begin the Beguine'. Why are we lucky fellows? We have been chosen to appear on the bill of the Finale of the Festival of Arts. This turns out to be nothing more nor less than a Military 'Opportunity Knocks' and, after all the contestants have done, while the summing up is going on, there is to be entertainment by the 'professionals'. Any extra money? No. Sod. OK, the Pros are Stan Bradbury, a song-plugger from the UK, the Polish Ballet, ourselves and . . . HELLLLLPPPPPP Gracie Fields and her singing! It's too late now, we've said yes and they've aired the beds.

'You'll only be there for forty-eight hours,' said Captain O'List. That would be long enough for me to carry out my solemn promise to Maria Marini that I would come back and marry her from the waist down.

'Gracie Fields,' said Bill Hall, like he's announcing the Doppelgänger.

'Don't worry,' says Reg O'List, 'I've put you on before her, so if you hurry up you can be out in the street before she starts singing. I'll try and keep the theatre doors shut so that the sound doesn't get out.'

Secombe, he's coming too, it's about time he came too. Is he going to fill the stage with soap? No. 'I'm on the spotlights,' he says, through his chattering, screaming and farting. Secombe on the spotlights?? That's like putting a man with epilepsy on a tightrope. Secombe can't keep still, he can't concentrate on anything except screaming, shaving and farting. We'll see. 'I've been specially chosen to put the spotlight on Gracie Fields in "Red Sails in the Sunset",' he says, like the Captain of the *Titanic*.

Yet again, the charabanc takes the chosen to the Holy City. This time it's just the Trio, Secombe, and a few spare wanks who will do 'odd jobs back stage'. I have no idea what odd jobs back stage are. Massaging curtains back to life? Mud-wrestling with electricians?

It's the old Albergo Universo, and our lesbian javelin-throwing manager with her fifty-six-inch chest. Can we visit her for a drink after the show? Yes. Have we any free seats? Yes, how many does she want? Seventy-three. She settles for six.

Friday March 1st. We sit in the stalls, watching the amateurs rehearsing for the finals. They are being 'produced' by Major Murray Leslie, Royal Army Service Corps, an ideal corps to produce theatricals. A short dark singer is going through 'Just a song at twilight'. We all know the joke about the short man who looks as though he's been hit by a lift: well, this is the bloke, he's been hit by one from above and another one coming up underneath. He has a good voice, but looks like a semi-straightened-out Quasimodo, and worse, he has ape-like arms. Major Leslie suggests that when the song reaches the climax he raises his arms gradually; they look like two anti-aircraft guns being raised to fire. But there you are. He finishes his song with arms raised. Major Leslie RASC waits a while and says, 'No, no, don't *keep* them up there.'

A woeful series of acts follows. The blond guardsman who recited Wordsworth's 'Daffodils'. For this Major Leslie also suggested the use of the arms, but this time they were raised alternately on 'certain words'.

I wandered lonely as a cloud (*right arm up*)
That floats on high o'er vales and hills (*left arm up*)
When all at once I saw a crowd (*right leg up?*)

and so on. Comes the night, and the hopefuls go through their paces. They get what we would call sympathetic applause, i.e. bugger all. We stand in the wings watching, and keeping an eye out for ''Ow do lads, ee bai gum.' The interval, and the judging goes on. Stan Bradbury 'entertains' at the piano. Why I don't know. A very amiable man, well-loved in the music profession, but an entertainer, no. All the while he played, the audience thought he was the warm-up pianist for a forthcoming singer who never materialised. Now, a last-minute change! The Polish Ballet are playing up and are to go on *before* us; the girls are beautiful, the boys more so; it's a stunning dance company with the full orchestra conducted by Raymond Agoult.

'And now,' it's the announcer Philip Slessor announcing an announcement, 'from the Central Pool of Artists, the Bill Hall . . .'

Before he could get the words out there was a roar from the crowd. We can do no wrong, a smash hit again. The encores keep Gracie Fields trapped in the wings. We take five curtain calls, and then the orchestra plays 'Sally'. On comes Gracie, and by the great wave of applause one realises that none of them have ever heard her Royal Palace NAAFI Naples singing sessions. But disaster lurks for poor Gracie: Gunner Secombe is now poised on the spotlight. He has been told to put the Red Jelly in for when she sings 'Red Sails in the Sunset'. Secombe is myopic: he walks into walls, over cliffs and under streamrollers and in recent years crashed into walls in horse-drawn coaches. In the dark he juggles with the jellies; Miss Fields goes rapturously into 'Red Sails' only to turn green.

'You're going mouldy, Gracie,' shouts a wag. The audience dissolves into tears. Gracie handles it well.

'Sum wun up there don't like me,' she says. Secombe realises the error and soon Miss Fields is a bright purple, yellow and then orange. Finally someone brings him down with a rugby tackle and before he can do any more damage, he's carried out screaming, shaving and farting.

ISCHIA

March 1946. Our cleaning ladies consisted of pretty young Italian things, all on the lookout for potential husbands to take them to Inghilterra. Bornheim and I are pursued by two Marias. (All cleaners in twos are called Marias in Italy.) My Maria I used for laundry, sock repairs and groping.

We decided to take the girls to Ischia as a repayment for squeezing them. When we told them, they shrieked with excitement. No, they'd never been out of Napoli, was there somewhere else? They'd certainly never been to Ischia.

On the Sunday, they turned up carrying raffia baskets full of home-cooked Neapolitan goodies. The ferry was crammed, the noise of their chattering drowning out the engines. Forty minutes and we are there; I try my luck and take us to the Colonel Startling Grope Villa of yore.

Yes, the manservant remembers me of yore – Can we use the private beach? Er – yes. The 'yes' is good, the 'er' is worrying. We disport ourselves and are soon immersed in the sparkling waters. The girls are delirious. Maria I, who is mine, I had only seen in her scruffy working clothes, but now, in her black one-piece bathing costume she is very, very dishy and ready to be squongled, and it can't be long now. The girls open the 'hamper'. In half an hour we put on a stone and sink like one. Oh, Neapolitan cooking! We must see the Grotto Azzurra, says a plying prying boatman. We argue the price and then he rows us to the enchanted hole in the cliff. We enter with our heads ducked and lo, a wondrous luminescent cavern, flickering with diaphanous sunshine on the cavern wall; by a trick of the light we appear to be floating on air. I dive over the side and give an underwater cabaret, in which I look as if I am suspended in air under the boat. It's all wondrous, the girls squeal with delight that echoes round the cavern. Out again into the white sunlight and back to the beach. On dark winter nights I recall that day – the clock should have stopped there. Our 'yes' has run out and the 'er' I was worried about is operating. Er – would we leave now as the owner is returning from Naples where he has been selling packets of sawdust.

We caught the last ferry as twilight fell across the Bay of Naples; pimples of light are starting to appear on the shore. A thousand shouts as we draw to the quay, brown hands grasp the ropes and affix them to rusting bollards. We hire an ancient Fiat taxi that looks like a grave on wheels. It chugs and rattles its way up the slopes of the Vomero. 'Qui, qui, ferma qui,' shout the girls. In the dark there's a brief kissing. We are waving the girls goodbye, when Kerash!!

Two years in the frontline – Army food!

from nowhere a drunk appears and punches through the taxi window.

'Attenzione,' shouts the driver. 'Coltello.' (Look out he's got a knife.) We leap out and set off hot foot. He is shouting something in Italian that sounds like 'My mother keeps legless goats' that can't be right. Why are *we* running away from a man whose mother keeps legless goats? Cowards all! I suddenly stop, turn, thrust my hand inside my battle-dress pocket and whip out an imaginary pistol.

'Attenzione!' I shout. 'Pistole!' He stops in his tracks and runs away. He could have sung 'Lae thar piss tub darn bab' but didn't. Very good Milligan. The day ended with a pointed finger. It wasn't the end of a perfect day, but it was an end. 'Who the fuck was he?' said Bornheim, much much further down the hill.

CIVILIAN STATUS

The Central Pool of Artists is changed to The Combined Services Entertainment. Why? I suppose it's the result of a 'meeting'. In its wake we, the Bill Hall Trio, are being offered officer status and wages if, when we are demobbed, we sign with the CSE for six months. Hedonists, we all say yes. Officer status? Cor Blimey! All the bloody months in the line and you become Lance Bombardier. Play the guitar in perfect safety, you become an officer. If I learned the banjo and the tuba I could become a Field-Marshal!

I wrote home and told my delighted parents. Mother proudly informed the neighbours that her son was a 'Banjo-playing Officer'.

A DAY OUT

Seven of us hired a taxi and went swimming at Bagnoli. The beach was in the ancient Campi Flegrei, one-time watering place of the Roman rich. A pumice-coloured beach, a few run-down bathing huts, the doors swung on rusty hinges, the cabins now used by beach whores for 'quickies'; a dying Italian hires out worn umbrellas. Several fishing craft bob in the morning calm sea. A rip-roaring day with skylarking in and out of the sea. We hire a row boat and soon we are going in all directions; we round the headland of the Isle of Nisidia and turn into a horseshoe bay. We discover caves! Wow, it's an omni-directional day; totally mindless, we strip off and dive off the jagged lava rocks.

Bang, bang! Bullets are flying over our heads.

'It's World War Three and they've started without us,' I shouted, ducking for cover. From down the craggy hillside come armed carabinieri. They are shouting. We take to the oars and row like mad in all directions; we would have moved faster if we had just drifted. I am shouting 'Ferma! Sono Inglese.'

A good-looking Italian captain, speaking like George Sanders with garlic, asks what we are doing. What a sight we make, three of us naked save shirts, two totally naked, one naked with socks on, me in a pair of groin-crippling underpants pretending I am Tarzan in my brown boiled boots.

'We are swimming,' I say, forgetting I am standing on land.

'This is a prohibited area,' he says.

I tell him *we* are prohibited people, but he doesn't understand.

'This is a top security island,' he says, 'where war criminals are being held.' I ask him what part are they being held by, but he still doesn't understand and waves his Beretta pistol. I wave back, he is getting angry, we must leave.

In total disarray we clamber into our craft. Have you read *Three Men in a Boat*? – well, multiply that by seven. Everyone rowed furiously in a different direction, the boat was coming apart. As the Italians were threatening and shooing us away, the Captain said something to his men and they all burst out laughing. As they were laughing in Italian we couldn't understand it. I looked at my motley crew and realised how lucky Captain Bligh had been.

My God! A squall blows up! Soon we are bailing for our *lives*! A boatman from the shore takes us in tow, we are very grateful until he asks for two hundred lire. We argue, he explains that we would never have made it back on our own. 'Fuck off,' says Barlow to a man who has just saved our lives. What a day!

'Dear Mother, Today we went swimming and were nearly shot at by Italians and drowned, wish you were here.'

We jump aboard one of the shuttle passion waggons throbbing on the beach, filled with spent soldiers. Why are we waiting? 'My mate's having a shag in that hut.' He points to a fragile beach hut shaking backwards and forwards under the assault from within, then there's a pause. ''Ees 'avin a rest,' says the soldier, the hut starts to vibrate again, the door opens and out comes a weed of a soldier who gets a desultory cheer from his mates, a portly tart hoisting up her bathing costume frames in the doorway, waving him goodbye with the money.

'Orl finished shaggin'?' cries the driver, cries of yes, and we lollop forward over the sand onto the road and away. As we sped down the coast road I was stricken with the divine

view and had a shot at taking a photograph. It doesn't exactly do justice to the scene, but it's evidence to say that I'm not making this all up.

June 17th 1946. Barbary Coast opened at the Bellini Theatre: a packed house, with soldiers queuing all day. Again the Bill Hall Trio, with a lot more gags in the act, steal the show; a corps de ballet from Rome did next best – all top-class dancers and only in this show because Rome Opera House is temporarily closed.

Great write-ups the next day! Then the icing on the cake: we are to tour, but this time we are to include Venice and Vienna! Someone should have told us, 'Man, these are the best days of your life, eat them slowly.'

Sunday morning, all bustle and packing kit onto the charabanc, Gunner Hall as usual is missing.

'She must be late paying him,' says Bornheim. All set, we pile onto the CSE charabanc with Umberto the fat Eyetie driver pinning Holy Pictures on the dashboard to ward off the devil, accidents, Protestants and the husband of the woman he is knocking off.

It's a sparkling day, the sun streaming through the holes in Bornheim's underwear. 'What's this Venice like?' he says. I tell him when you step out the front door you go splash! People don't take dogs for a walk, they take fish. Wasn't the city resting on piles? Yes, it was agony for the people underneath.

Lieutenant Priest boards the charabanc. 'Answer your names,' he says. 'Bornheim G.' 'Sah,' we all shout. 'Mulgrew J?' 'Sah' we all answer. He tears up the list in mock defeat; the charabanc and its precious cargo of piss artists proceeds forth. We inch thru the unforgettable fish market off the Piazza Capuana, displaying everything from waterfleas to tuna on the barrows. The mongers douse their catches with water. 'Fools,' says Bornheim. 'They'll never revive them.' The church bells are anointing the air, each peal sending flocks of pigeons airborne on nervous wings.

Through the machicolated crowds we edge, finally arriving at the peeling front of the Albergo Rabacino, which roughly translated means Rabies. Ronnie Priest flies into its front portals. He's annoyed – the Italian ballerinas from our cast are not ready. 'They had to go to holy bloody mass,' he says. We all get out and stretch our legs and are immediately beset with vendors. I am casting my eye on a tray of watches that gleam gold like the riches of Montezuma. They are in fact cheapo watches dipped in gold-plating. I knock the price down from ten million lire to ten thousand. OK, I buy the watch. Of course it doesn't give the date, phases of the moon, high tide in Hawaii, it doesn't light up in the dark, doesn't give electronic peals every half hour, and it doesn't ring like an alarm in the morning. All it does is tell the silly old time.

I paid the vendor and told him the time, I said hello to Mulgrew and told him the time, I called Bornheim over and told him the time and I wrote a letter to my mother telling her the time. Looking at the watch I realise it's time to close this fifth volume of my War Time Trilogy. It was the year I had left the front line and found various Base Depot jobs. I had much to be thankful for and now I knew the time. In Volume Six I will tell the time and the story of my love affair with Maria Antoinetta Fontana the Italian ballerina who in a way changed my life and made me abandon my store of second-hand Army underwear. The time is 11.20 a.m.

VOLUME SIX

GOODBYE SOLDIER

ROME

JUNE 1946. The charabanc, with its precious cargo of bisexual soldier artistes, seesaws through the narrow Neapolitan streets. It is a day of high summer. We pull up at our destination, the Albergo Rabacino. The sunlight plays on its golden Baroque chiselled façade. Lt Ronnie Priest hurries into its mahogany portals, only to return downcast of visage. 'The bloody girls will be a while; they've just got back from Mass.' He lights up a cigarette. 'Bloody females,' he adds. We all debouch to stretch our legs and other parts. Immediately, we are set on by street vendors. I was taken up with a tray of chrome and gilt watches – I needed a watch badly, a good heavy one that would stop me being blown away. As we barter, the Italian Corps de Ballet usher forth with their luggage. Our balding driver, Luigi, is rupturing himself stowing the bulging cases into the rear locker – all this while I have just clinched a deal for a watch that looks like a burnished gold Aztec altar, a huge lump of a thing. On me, it made my wrist look like an Oxfam appeal for food. I had bargained the price down from ten million lire to seven thousand and the vendor was running away at full speed while counting the money. I was winding it when a female voice diverted me: ''Ow much you payer for that?' I turned to see a petite, mousey haired, blue-eyed, doll-like girl.

The first clash of eyes was enough. It was, no, not *love* at first sight – that came later – but it most certainly was *something* at first sight. (Darling, I feel in something at first sight.)

'I paid seven thousand lire.'

She 'tsu-tsu-tsued' and shook her head. 'You know all watch stolen.' No, I didn't know that. 'Let me see,' she

Maria Antoinetta Fontana

said, in a semi-commanding voice. She examined the watch.
'Maybe, yes,' she said, returning it.

I said it was a very good watch, it told the time in Italian
as well as English. What was her name?

'My namer is Maria Antoinetta Fontana, but everyone
call me Toni.'

'I'm Spike, sometimes known as stop thief or hey you!'

344

'Yeser, I know.' She had found my name on the programme and had obviously set her sights on me. I would make good target practice. Maria Antoinetta Fontana was understudy for the Première Ballerina at the Royal Opera House in Rome. From now on, it was goodbye Bing Crosby, lead soldiers and Mars bars. She was so petite! Five feet four inches! We are 'all aboarding' the Charabong, I notice that Toni has lovely legs and the right amount, two. I tried to sit next to her, but in the mêlée I ended up in the seat behind her as Ricky Trowler, our crooner, had fancied her and beat me to it. If he looked at her, I would kill. Do you hear me? KILL! Didn't he know with me around he hadn't a chance! Me, the Brockley Adonis? Poor blind little fool. Me, the Harry James of St Cyprian's Hall, SE26! 'Hold very tight and fares please,' says Lt Priest in mock cockney bus conductor tones as we set off for the Holy City.

The journey passes with Toni turning to cast me eye-crippling glances. She dangles her hand in the lee of her seat for me to hold. Arghhhhhhhhh! It's small, sensuous, soft and perfumed. It's giddy-making. Oh, but how lovely!!! I'm falling, falling, falling! and no safety net!

Mulgrew's keen Scottish eye has noticed my new watch. He assesses it and says, 'That's the sort of present a mean millionaire would buy for a blind son.' He asks how much. I tell him. He bursts out laughing. Laugh he may, in a year's time that selfsame watch would save him and the Bill Hall Trio from ruin. Of that, more in my next book! Bill Hall is killing the boredom by playing his fiddle. I join in on the guitar. We play some jazz and a few Neapolitan melodies, 'Cuore Napolitano', 'Non Me Scorde', 'Ah Zaz Zaz Za'.

Ceprano is a halfway halt. We are taken to a large NAAFI where we are given lunch. Ahhhhhhhgghhhh, Cold Collation!!! The most dreaded meal in the English Culinary calendar: the dead chicken, the dead lettuce, the watery mayonnaise, the lone tomato ring! It's the sort of meal you leave in your will to your mother-in-law.

'You no lak,' says Toni who is sitting opposite.

'No, I no lak,' I said.

'Can I have you chicken?' she says, her head inclined to one side. I watch as the dead fowl disappears through her delectable lips. I sip the red tannic-acid-ridden tea that must have been put on to boil the day after we all landed at Salerno.

Toni and I saunter out to the Charabong, the journey continues. The swine Trowler assumes his seat next to *my* Toni, the blind fool. Hasn't he noticed her adoring glances?? My matchless profile from Brockley SE26?

Late evening and the dusty chugging Charabong enters Rome through the Porta Maggiore. It's a Sunday evening and the sunlight is turning to rose-petal pink. The streets

The Bill Hall Trio in a now derelict prisoner-of-war cage, trying desperately to be funny en route to Rome, where the Pope lives

are full of the populace taking their evening strolls – elegant Romans are *really* elegant, they wear clothes well. But! None of them are wearing sensible brown English shoes like me. More of them later. The Charabong comes to rest outside the Albergo Universo. *I'll* help Toni with her luggage to her bedroom. Her mother wants her to go home, but because she wants to be near me – lies – and tells momma the company rules insist she stays at the hotel. Ha! Ha! Love finds a way.

BARBARY COAST

Barbary Coast opened at the Argentina Theatre on Monday 24th June. It was an immediate success and the Bill Hall Trio again the hit of the show. Wait till England heard about us, rich, rich, rich!!!

ROMANCE AND TEA

27th June 1946. On the day she visited her mother, Toni arranged to meet me in the gardens of the Villa Borghese. There, we would have tea. I was walking on air! Our budding romance was the talk of the company.

'We will meeta under theee statue of Goethe,' she had said smilingly.

Of course, Frederick Von Goethe the well-known German singer and dancer! I wore my dark blue trousers, white silk shirt, satin blue tie, navy blue velvet jacket and my sensible strong brown outsized convulsed English shoes. I took one of Rome's dying Fiat taxis. He had never heard of the statue of Frederick Von Goethe, singer and dancer, but we kept driving till we found it.

I arrived early as I wished to choose a suitable pose to strike for when Toni arrived. I chose a Spanish oak against which I leaned like Gary Cooper and smoked a cigarette like Humphrey Bogart. By the time she arrived, I'd run out.

Toni drew up in a taxi, I posed heavily as Robert Taylor. As she approached, all the juices in my metabolism started to revolve. I think I was actually vibrating: as she drew near I would appear to her as a blue blur. She was dressed in a blue polka dot dress, her clean brown limbs glowed in the Roman sun and I was speechless in the face of her smile.

'Bon Giorno Toni,' I said going light-headed, only the weight of my sensible English shoes keeping me earthbound.

'Hello Terr-ee,' she said and held out her hand.

I took it and she led me away.

'Come,' she said.

Through leafy glades she led me to a teahouse. We sat at a table, all the others were deserted, perfect! A crisp white-coated waiter still smelling of shaving soap attended us. Would I like tea, asks Toni. Yes, I say. What kind, she says. What's she mean what kind? Tea, there's only one kind. Toni orders in Italian and the waiter speeds to her bidding.

'Isn't it a lovely day?'

Yes, Toni, and I love you.

'The trees are at their best this time of the year.'

Yes, Toni, and I love you.

My first photograph of Maria Antoinetta Fontana – the Villa Borghese gardens, Rome, where the Pope lives

The tea arrives – ah! and Italian pastries. Good old Char. Toni watches as I mix mine with half milk, five spoons of sugar and stir it into a treacly goo. What's that she's drinking in a tall glass enclosed in a silver holder? There's a lemon floating in it. Careless waiter! Shall I get it out for her? What? It's meant to be there? Russian Tea? Oh, I'm sorry I can't speak Russian, so how should I know?

'I show you nice things,' says Toni arising. 'Having you ever seen Temple of Aesculapius?'

No I have never seen his temple; the only Temple I've seen is Shirley. We walk through boulevards of roses, many a small fountain laughing in the sun. We talked, I know we talked but it was all coming to me through a long tube. I was spellbound by this girl by my side. We saw the temple and I took an amateur snapshot to enshrine the moment.

So we walk, walk, walk, talk, talk, talk. The walking involves my sensible brown English brogues. Let me describe them. At first glance they look like semi-deflated rugby balls. I have a small foot, size seven, but the shoe is size ten. The leather is convulsed, the soles are an inch thick with a rubber heel. I had bought them off a stall in Deptford. Basically, they made me look like a cripple. I wondered why people stood up for me in buses. Now Toni, elegant Toni, has noticed them. I suppose to her Italian mind they would appear to look like two giant stale salamis with shoelaces inserted. She tries to be tactful.

'Terr-ee, why you wear you Army boots with nice clothes?'

Army boots???? What was wrong with the girl? I told her these were my best shoes and the height of fashion in England in the 7s. 6d. range. I was the talk of Deptford! She stifled a laugh with her handkerchief. She is wearing delightful feather-light Ferragamo shoes.

'You only 'ave one pair of shoes?'

Of course, that's all one needs – one sensible pair weighing ten pounds each.

'You must buy one more best pair,' she said and we left it at that. That magic afternoon wandered on and still does . . . We stop at a stall and have a lemonade each. We sit sipping them through straws.

We have arrived at the Spanish Steps. The flower sellers fade into drabness among the urgently growing flowers. Red roses! of course! I buy Toni a small bouquet – I had never bought flowers for a girl before. I passed them to her, they glowed red in the afternoon sun. She took them, looking intently at me as she did. Still looking at me, she withdrew one lone rose and gave it to me. It's a moment in time frozen in my memory. I take the rose and try to put it into my buttonhole. But there isn't one, is there, so I stick it in my pocket. Toni giggles, it sounds like water splashing in a pond.

'My love is like a red, red rose that blooms in early spring.'

She smiled with her eyes, 'You write that?'

'Yes,' I said.

If you're going to tell a lie, tell a big one.

FAREWELL OLD SHOES

28th June 1946. Toni and I meet at the Café Minosko on the Via Veneto. Toni wants to get me to a shoe shop to buy a pair of decent shoes. I arrive first and order.

'Tea,' I say. 'Tea à la Russe con Lemone.'

I am quick to learn. Suddenly, as I'm sipping the new-found concoction, she draws up beside me. She, too, has Russian Tea. Tea over, she holds out her hand; I take it and follow. We walk and talk. We could have run and talked, I suppose; or, rather, Toni could have run and talked while I stood and listened. God, she had lovely legs. Those lovely legs stop outside a shoe shop. In she hikes me. A totally bald fat Italian salesman with a fixed grin attends us. Toni rattles off something in Italian, during which the salesman glances off something in Italian, during which the salesman glances in horror at my sensible English shoes. He is gone and returns with a pair of black moccasins.

'Terr-ee,' she smiles. 'You try theseeeee.'

I sit while the salesman unlaces my shoes. He braces himself like a man about to neutralise an unexploded bomb. With a low moan, he eases them off and drops them to the floor with a loud Thud!

My shoes lie on their sides looking like an accident. He slips on one moccasin, then the other. I feel light-headed. I feel naked, I look in the mirror – gone are the two Frankenstein lumps at the bottom of my legs. Now, all is trim and elegant. Toni has made her first move in civilising me.

The salesman wants to know if I want the old shoes. Yes, I say, I want to take them to Lourdes to see if there's a cure. The change in shoes is unbelievable. I'm a stone lighter, I can cross my legs without having to lift my leg manually, dogs have stopped barking at or trying to mate with them. A small step for Spike Milligan, a giant step for mankind.

Toni wants me to meet her family. Why not? I've already met mine and it took to me. We sit in a café on the Via Veneto with Rome passing by. She tells me her father died at the beginning of the war, that he had owned various enterprises in Abyssinia but they had all collapsed and been impounded by the British who he hated. The main one was a soap factory; when they closed that, he had a heart attack and died. I had been out with a girl whose father was a mechanic in Norwood, one who was a bookmaker in Crofton Park and one who was a thief in Brockley, but never a soap factory owner. Still, everything comes to he who waits. But before I meet her family, she must break the news to her 'boyfriend' Arturo who is an officer in the Alpine Brigade. She has already written to him saying it was *finito*.

'I only know him a leetle,' she said.

Sunday, 30th June, 1946. All packed up and on to the Charabong. This time, I sit next to Toni. Our destination, the ancient town of Padua. We are travelling on a Sunday morning and families are coming or going to church. The sound of church bells hangs on the morning air; we pass several religious processions.

'One fing about Caflicks,' says Gunner Hall. 'They always play ter full 'ouses.'

Bornheim agrees. 'It's all that communion wine they swig free, that gets 'em in' – he who hasn't been inside a church since his christening day.

I, too, had lost touch with my religion. I had stopped going to church the moment I joined the Regiment. No more could my mother nag me into God's presence. However, Toni was a practising Catholic. Why are they always practising? When do they become good enough not to?

When I put that to Toni, she said, 'I don't understand you, what are you talking about.'

I said about twenty words a minute.

She didn't understand, but laughed and said, 'I love you beautiful eyes.'

How strange! All those years in the Army and my Sergeant never said I had beautiful eyes. 'Beautifulll eyeeesss front!' No, it doesn't sound right.

We are driving across Italy from west to east. We can't make Padua in a day; it's some six hundred kilometres away. We stay that night in a hotel on the sea at Riccione. It's a large rambling hotel built in the thirties, a square building built by squares for squares. The rooms are comfortable – strange I've *never* found an uncomfortable Italian bed.

From the windows in the passage off our bedrooms, we can see the outdoor cinema which is showing Nelson Eddy and Jeanette MacDonald in something like 'give me some men who are stout-hearted men' etc. etc. etc. Toni and I stand at the window for the freebie. I have my arm round her waist; it's like an electric shock. We watch as Jeanette and Nelson shriek at each other, face to face. 'I am thineeeeeeee, for everrrrrrr.' It ends with them kissing on a balcony. So to bed. I kiss Toni goodnight only to be caught by Johnny Bornheim.

'Here, here, here,' he cautions. 'No kissing ballerinas between six and midnight.' He pretends to produce a notebook and pencil. 'Now then, how many kisses and what time?'

Toni giggles and disappears into her bedroom. 'Goodnight Terr-ee.'

Bornheim tells me he has found a grand piano in a room. Would I like to hear it? I troop down with him and he plays Puccini, Ellington and more Ellington. By then it is midnight. I hie me to my bed, my head full of flowers and Toni. Oh, those kisses, there must be a word somewhere that explains the feeling. Spazonkled! That's it, it was like being Spazonkled, Spazonklified!! I lay in bed smoking a cigarette and steaming with love. Where will it all end?

PADUA

Let's see, what do I know about Padua? There was St Anthony's, and 'Fred' Giotto had some murals in the Palazzo della Regione. So I didn't know much about Padua. If only the coach stopped in Catford. I knew a lot about Catford. There was the Fifty Shilling Tailors, where I had ordered a dreadful suit that made me look deformed. It was like something you get on prescription from a doctor.

It's evening when the dusty Charabong with its passengers singing 'Hey, Girra, Girra, Girrica' shudders to a steaming halt outside the Leone Bianco Hotel.

'Ah, Leone Bianco,' says Bornheim, 'The Blancoed Lion'.

'Che stufa,' says Toni.

It's her twentieth 'Che sufa' of the journey. We sort out

our luggage. Mulgrew says, 'Oh fuck,' the handle of his suitcase has come off.

'Ah, now you can join the knotted string brigade,' I say.

We lollop into the hotel which is soon echoing to the sound of lollops. Blast! I am sharing a room with Mulgrew and his second-hand clothes store. Toni's bedroom is the next floor up, blast again.

'It'll never stretch that far,' says Mulgrew.

'Will you stop making suggestive remarks about me and Toni,' I said. 'Our love is pure,' I said with hand over heart and the other raised heavenwards.

A tap on the door and enter a pretty girl with tea trolley.

'*Signori* tak tea, yes?'

Yes, please! We sipped our tea and smoked.

'Sooo,' says Mulgrew. 'This is New York.'

I unpack.

'You know, Johnny, you look taller in bed.'

'What are you suggesting? I only meet people lying down?'

'Well, yes. You can get up for shaking hands and then lie down again.'

There was a silence and Mulgrew blew smoke ceiling-wards.

'I wonder where that silly bugger Hall is.'

It was a worry. Hall had this horror film visage – he was lucky no one had tried to drive a stake through his heart. We were to open in Venice tomorrow. Would Hall make it?

'I mean, the streets are made of water. No good trying to run,' says Mulgrew, scratching his groins.

'Is it the old trouble?' I say.

'That was a wee smasher who brought in the tea,' he said.

More groin scratching. Aloud, he starts to read the notice on the door – anything to save buying a book.

'Dinner between eight and ten-thirty, unless a late meal is requested.'

There it is at the bottom . . . Arghhhhhhh Cold Collation!

Barbary Coast Co. – on the Grand Canal Bornheim reading the
Union Jack

It's followed me, there are special Cold Collation units that
are following me.

'Sir, he's heading for Padua.'

'Quick, send a despatch rider with several Cold Colla-
tions, and hurry.'

I run a bath; I undress in front of the mirror. The more
clothes I remove, the more I look like a Belsen victim. I
immerse what is called a body in the bath. I sing merrily,
adjusting the taps with my toes.

I spruce up and take the lift down to see Toni, who is
walking down the stairs to meet me. I go down to meet her,
she comes up to meet me, and so on until we make it. A
lovers' stroll through the town: being a university town,
there are numerous book shops and the cafés are full of
students talking excitedly. Toni stops at a sweet shop and
buys coloured sugared almonds.

'Thee blues ones are for your eyes.'

Gad, I must have been lovely then. One thing for sure, she must never see me naked. I had a body that invited burial, that and my ragged underwear.

We walked and talked. Sometimes, we stood still and talked – that's like walking with your legs together (eh?). Back to the Blancoed Lion and dinner. *Gnocchi*? What's a Gnocki? Who's that Gnocking at my door? It was the first time I'd had it.

'Eeet is a Roman speciality,' says Toni.

She asks me if I've ever been to Venice. I say no, but I've seen it in a book. 'All the city built on – how you say?'

'Piles,' I said.

Yes, the whole of Venice suffered from damp piles. She doesn't understand.

Lieutenant Priest approaches, 'Is everything all right?'

Yes, *molto buono*.

He tells us that Chalky White has gone forward with the scenery, which will be transported to the theatre by barge. Priest laughs at the thought.

'My God, he had difficulty unloading on dry land.'

We repair to the lounge bar where most of the cast are drinking.

'What will you have?' says Bornheim.

'I will have a Cognac and Toni will have a lemonade.'

'Well, I'm sure the barman will serve you,' he laughed – the swine! 'Sorry, Spike, I'm broke. You'll have to lash out.'

'You sure Bornheim isn't a Jewish name?' I said. 'So, what'll *you* have?'

Of course, it's double whisky, isn't it. Wait, what's this? Through the door, covered in dust, unshaven, his fiddle case under his arm, is the late Gunner Bill Hall.

''Ere, they didn't bleedin' wait for me,' he says. 'I bin cadging lifts all day. My bloody thumb's nearly coming off.'

He wants to know if dinner is still on. I gaze at my Aztec gold watch and holding it in a position for the whole room to see, I tell him he is just on the right side of ten-thirty. He departs, him and his reeking battle-dress – the jacket is open from top to waist, over a crumpled shirt (off-white shirt). Because of his thin legs he wears two pairs of trousers – they billow out like elephants' legs. God, what a strange man, but a genius of a musician. When he died a few years ago, I realised that a genius could die unsung.

So, as the surgeon said, we're opening tonight. All excitement – we're on our way to the Theatre Fenice in Venice. Toni gave my arm a squeeze but nothing came out.

'Now,' she says. 'Theese is for you.'

It's a small tissue-wrapped package.

'Oh, how lovely! It's what I've always wanted, a tissue-wrapped package!'

I remove the tissue. It's a silver cigarette case. I look for the price tag.

'Now you throw away dirty tin, eh?'

'No, no I can't throw it away. That tin has been under mortar and shell fire with me, danced with girls with me, even had an attack of piles with me!' From now on, I'll have to keep it out of sight.

VENICE

The Charabong is taking us through medieval Mestre and on to the causeway. The sun bounces off the yellow waters of the Lagoon. On the right, the blue-grey of the Adriatic, neither of which looked clean. We de-bus in the Piazza Roma where a CSE barge is waiting – oh, the fun!

'Hello Sailor,' I say to a deckhand.

I lift my guitar case carefully on board, then turn to help Toni – Blast! A deckhand is helping her. I'll kill him, he *touched* her, my Brockley SE26 blood boiled. He's lucky to be alive.

We glide down the Grand Canal: on our right, the magnificent Palace Vendramin Calergi, its mottled stone

Our pier – at 86 Area HQ Venice

catching the sun, pigeons roosting along its perimeters. We slide under the Ponte Rialto and look up people's noses – the sheer *leisure* of water travel. Toni and I are in the back of the barge by the rudder; I look into the brown waters to see romantic discharge from a sewer. Slowly, we come to the landing stage for the theatre.

Our dressing-rooms are wonderful: red plush with gilt mirrors, buttoned furniture.

'Och, now! Och, this is more like it,' says Mulgrew.

What it is och more like, he doesn't say. That bugger Bill Hall is missing again! Will he turn up? Mulgrew shrugs his shoulders. Suddenly, he notices my new cigarette case.

'It's from Toni,' I tell him.

An evil grin on his face, Mulgrew says, 'Is that for services rendered.'

How dare he!

Next day is bright and sunny. We are awakened by a nubile waitress with the tea trolley. What a luxury! She has nice legs and a wobbly bottom with the consistency of a Chivers jelly. Mulgrew lights his first cigarette of the day, has a fit of coughing that sounds like a plumber unblocking a sink. With a contused face and eyes watering, he says, 'Oh, lovely! Best fag of the day.' Then falls back exhausted on the pillow.

Toni has gone on the roof to sunbathe. 'I want brown all over,' she says. 'If you come up, make a noise.' I promise I will yodel like Tarzan. Ah! Some more mail has caught up with me and a parcel! My mother's letter is full of warnings about show business: 'It can ruin your health, and knock yourself up'. How does one knock oneself up?

> INSTRUCTOR: Take up the normal standing position, clench fist, then start to rotate the arm, getting faster and faster. When going at good speed, thud fist under chin and travel upwards.

Terry Pellici is leaving today to be demobbed. He asks us all to have a farewell drink; so, I say farewell to my drink and swallow it. I ask Terry was it awkward, being Italian by descent, having to serve in the Allied army and fight his own people? 'That's the way the cookie crumbles. I'm an Eyetie Cockney. In a war you got to be on somebody's side, so I was on somebody's side.'

'You got relatives living here?'

'Yer, in Cattolica. I went to visit them. It was funny – most of 'em were in the Eyetie army. I thought,' here he started to laugh, 'one of them might say, you shoota my uncle.' Terry had been in the 74 Mediums, a sister regiment to the 56 Heavy. 'They used me as an interpreter. I did well with Eyetie POWs: I tell them first thing they had to give up was their watches. I made a bomb on them in Tunis.' He brandishes an expensive chronometer: 'Eyetie colonel.'

He asks me for my home address and promises to contact me when I return. He never did. In 1976 I phoned him. 'Is that Pellici's Café?'

'Yer, oo is it?'

'You wouldn't know me. I was killed in the war.'

'Oo *is* that?'

'Gunner Milligan.'

'Spike! I bin meaning to write you.' Thirty years he's been meaning to write!

We finish the booze up and Terry gets on his Naples-bound lorry. First, I take a posed picture of him sorrowing at his departure.

Toni! She should be nude by now. I tiptoe up the stairs with Bornheim, my camera ready to click. She must have heard because by the time we got there she had her petticoat on. I got Bornheim to hold her while I took this memorable shot.

Terry Pellici's farewell pose

Toni resisting being snapped in her petticoat

TRIESTE

It's another bright sunny day as we board our, by now, dodgy Charabong. Lieutenant Priest has a quick roll-call, and has a heart attack when Bill Hall answers his name.

Trieste is a combustible city on the Adriatic, the Allies have a large force there to deter combustible Marshal Tito who is claiming that Trieste is Yugoslavian. It's a hundred miles to go as we settle down for the trip. Our route runs across the Gulf of Venice – all agricultural land, very green, very lush. The cattle are fatter up here than their scrawny cousins in the Campagna.

Behind me, on the bench seat, Bornheim says, 'Who said "What the fuck was that?"' We don't know. 'The Lord Mayor of Hiroshima.'

'They should never have dropped it.'

'What else can you do with a bomb but drop it? Can't keep it in the fridge.'

'They asked for it.'

'Wot you mean *asked* for it? You think they phoned up Roosevelt and said please drop honourable bomb?'

'OK, what would you have done to end the war?'

'Well, something else.'

'I think we should have dropped Cold Collation on them,' I said. 'That, or watery custard. Can't you see the head-lines?

Cold Collation destroys Hiroshima. Thousands flee Custard.

'If they'd have got it, you can be bloody sure they'd drop it on us.'

'It still wouldn't be right. What about us and Cassino?'

'What about us and Cassino?'

'We bombed it, didn't we?'

'There were Germans in it.'

'No, there wasn't.'

So the argument raged. From atom bombs to wages is a big jump, but that was what they were on about next. In a *sotto voce* Hall is telling Mulgrew and me that he thinks we should be on more money.

'Aren't you satisfied with ten pounds a week?'

'No, we are the hit of the show.'

'It's ten pounds a week all found,' I said.

'I've never found anything,' says Mulgrew.

'We should be on twenty-five pounds a week,' says Hall.

'If you're going on what it *should* be, why not fifty pounds?' says Mulgrew.

'Why stop at *should* be fifty?' I said. 'How about *should be* a hundred?'

And that was the end of the should bes. Bill Hall produces his violin and launches into an insane version of a very bad musician playing jazz. He crosses his eyes, puts on a fixed maniacal grin with his head shaking like a speeded-up metronome and plays 'Honeysuckle Rose'. Every note is exquisitely sharp or flat. To musicians, it's hysterically funny. He plays and sings Irving Berlin's tune.

> Wot'll I do, when you
> Are far away and I am blue
> Wot'll I do
> Kiss my bottle and glass.*

Bornheim starts to conjure up tunes that have just missed being winners – like, 'That's Why the Lady is a Trampolinist', or 'Honeysuckle Nose' again, 'Saint Louis Browns', 'Tea for One', 'We'll Meet Occasionally', 'On the Good Ship Lollibang' and so on. He reverts to his *Union Jack* newspaper. It has a report on Dachau. 'How can there be places like this and there be a God?' I told him that my mother used to answer that question by saying God works in mysterious ways.

'Seven million Jews dead. That's not mysterious, that's bloody cruel,' says Bornheim.

Seven million Jews killed, I couldn't get it in perspective.

'Perhaps it *is* God's will,' says Hall.

'I never knew he left a will,' I said.

Toni has fallen asleep on my shoulder and my arm now has pins and needles. I try clenching and unclenching the fist, but she wakes up with a start. 'Where are we, Terr-ee?' I told her Italy. We now have the sea on our right – a cobalt blue, looks very inviting. We pass the ill-fated Castello Miramar, where some aristocrat shot himself – his ghost is seen on the battlements. As we enter the precincts of Trieste, lots of signs '*Abbasso con* Tito,' '*Trieste è Italiano*'.

* Bottle and glass (cockney slang)=arse.

There are shrines to partisans murdered by Germans, faded bouquets hang on bullet-ridden walls, the partisans still strut the streets with great bandoliers of bullets and machine pistols.

There is a general cast call at eleven o'clock, so into the Charabong. En route Italians keep banging angrily on the side. By looking out the window I see that some silly bugger has chalked VIVA TITO on the side of the bus. It was Mulgrew and his Scottish Highland sense of humour. I told him, 'We could all have been bloody killed.' He says that was the general idea.

As we de-bus at the stage door of the Theatre Fred, there's a loud explosion – a bomb has gone off. Civil and Military Police start whizzing by in jeeps, all armed to the teeth – some were only armed to the throat, some to the knee. The theatre was built for opera, it has an excess of Italian kitsch. We are assembled on the stage and Jimmy Molloy says that parts of the show are slack so we are to run through those bits.

John Angove is not feeling well. He is taken to the Medical Officer who diagnoses that he has measles. Measles at twenty-five! He is put into a quarantine ward and is out of the show. I wonder if they are always caught in the plural?

PATIENT: What is it doc?
DOC: You've caught *a* measle.
PATIENT: Just one?

I mean, bronchitis is in the singular.

PATIENT: What is it doc?
DOC: You've caught bronchitises.

We try out a new gag for the show. I announce that I will fire the slowest bullet in the world. Mulgrew stands one side holding a water biscuit; I, from the other side, aim and fire.

There's a count of five and then Mulgrew crumples the biscuit manually with a cry of Hoi Up La.

In our dressing-room, there are signs of occupation scrawled on the wall: 'Harry Secombe was here', 'Norman Vaughan was here', 'Ken Platt was almost here'. We dutifully add our names. The manager, a voluble fat Italian tells us many famous people have been here, including Elenora Duse. He tells us the story of how after she had had a leg amputated, she returned to the stage and people wondered how she would manage with an artificial wooden leg. On the first night, the theatre was crowded with the cognoscenti. It is French theatre custom to bang a mummer's pole thrice behind the curtain. When the audience heard 'boom boom boom', one said, 'My God, here she comes now!'

GRADO

Next day, we are all in the Charabong looking forward to the day at Grado. We are singing, 'Why Are We Waiting'. In this instance, it's Bill Hall. He finally appears blinking in the unaccustomed sunlight. Luigi lets the clutch in and we are on our way.

Grado is a spit of land accessible by a causeway. It's apparently a fisherman's paradise. It's not much of a paradise for us. The beach is brown and so is the water. It's all due to a muddy bottom, of which I'd seen a few. However, it's a clear blue sky and hot. Toni and I hire a boatman who rows us to where the sea turns blue. We dive over the side. It's like swimming in champagne, you can see the bottom. We sun ourselves and take a few snaps.

We sit in silence, holding hands, watching the wake of the boat. The boatman smiles, he knows we're in love. '*Buona*, eh?' he smiles. Plimping (yes, *plimping*) on the sea are fishing boats, small two-men affairs – and, let's face it, in those days two-men affairs were not that frequent. It was all very stimulating – the salt water drying on your body, the tranquillity and being in love.

Our time is up; the boatman heads for the shore.

Mulgrew greets us. 'Ahoy, there. Welcome to Grado.'

'You're welcome to it, too,' I said.

Mulgrew has buried Bill Hall in the sand and shaped it like a woman's body, with huge boobs. Alas, I lost that photo. 'How much was the boat ride?' he says. I tell him a hundred lire for half an hour. 'A *hundred* lire,' he said, his Scots face wincing with pain. 'Why you can get three bottles of wine for that!' I agreed but said they wouldn't float as good as a boat.

There's a sort of beach café with a straw-matted roof. Toni and I sit on high stools sipping fresh orange juice. Mulgrew has lemon juice.

'It's got more vitamins in.'

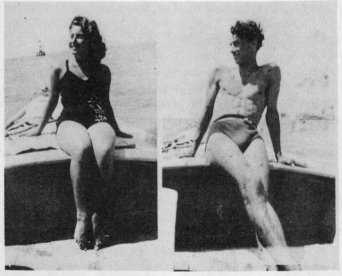

Toni taken by me in Grado   *Me taken by Toni, Grado*

'What is vitamin?' says Toni.

'You know, vitamins A, B, C, D.'

'That's a funny way to spell vitamins,' I said.

Marisa is coming out of the water saying, '*Aiuto! Aiuto!*' She's been stung on her bum by a jellyfish, who seemed to know what he was doing. From then on no one would venture into the water. Toni and I walked along the beach about a mile, stopping at any rock pools and looking for fish trapped by the tide. Sometimes, we'd splash our feet in the shallows. It was like being a child again.

The sun is setting the sea on fire as it lowers itself into the Adriatic. Dancing waves catch the deflected light and semaphore in silver gold flashes. It's been a wonderful day. The beach café wants to know do we want dinner. If so, they can make us sardines and rice. We ask the all-in price and Lieutenant Priest thinks it reasonable – so, OK. We sit eating it as a new moon like a lemon slice appears in the eastern night sky and, blow me, there's the sound of Bill Hall's violin. Soon the Italians are singing.

Vicino Mare
Vicino Amore

In the half-light, I lean over and kiss Toni on the shoulder. As I do so, she places a kiss in my hair – that hair that had lived with washing with Sunlight soap, Lifebuoy, Pears, Carbolic (never had a shampoo) and Brylcreem and Anzora hair goo. Yes, she kissed all that. We quaff white wine. Some of the boys collect driftwood and make a fire. We sit in a circle watching our dreams burn into embers. The tide rises and washes away our footprints in the sand. Sand from a shore that neither of us would see again. Already that sand was running out.

It was eleven when we drove back to the hotel, all pleasantly tired. Tomorrow? Who cared about tomorrow?

> A FORCED LABOUR CAMP IN SIBERIA. HITLER IS
> SHOVELLING SHIT AND SALT.
> HITLER: I care about tomorrow. You see, Von Rund-
> stedt and the Tenth Panzer Army will break through and
> rescue me.

I kiss Toni goodnight, *buona notte a domani*.

So passed the week in Trieste. This morning, we all embark for Austria. Austria, land of Strauss and the naughty waltz – men and women dancing face to face! Land of Franz Josef, the Hussars, the woods and the liver sausage! I massage my clothes into my suitcase, I sit on it and finally lock it. It looks pregnant. I've got half an hour to get breakfast. I dash down to the dining-room. Toni and the girls are at a table laughing and giggling. 'Oh, Terr-ee, you late. You must hurry.' I wolf down marmalade and toast and a cup of lemon tea.

KRUMPENDORF

'Oh Terr-ee,' says Toni. 'You choke yourself.' What a headline:

Man Strangled by Marmalade

Lieutenant Priest is rounding up the latecomers. 'Come on, we haven't got all day,' he fusses.

Aboard the Charabong, everyone is excited at the thought of Austria, especially Greta Weingarten. 'Now I vill be able to speak mein own language,' she says with an air of superiority.

Toni is in her drab khaki clothes, her hair in a bandana. She looks shapeless, but ah ha! I know what lies under-neath, heh, heh, heh! She asks, 'In Vienna, we see Russian soldiers?'

'Yes, my dear.' But what's this Lieutenant Priest is

saying? 'Before Vienna, we have to play Krumpendorf.'
Krumpendorf? Isn't that a disease of the groin? He goes on,
'Then we play Graz and *then* Vienna.'

'You been in Austria before Terr-ee?' No, I had travelled
extensively in Catford, Lewisham and Brockley SE26, but
somehow never Austria. The trams didn't go that far.

Oh, no! The coach engine is faltering. We pull over and
Luigi raises the bonnet. He is joined by Ricky Trowler who
is a whizz kid at engines. He tells Lieutenant Priest, 'It's the
distributor.'

'Wait until I see the bastard,' says Priest.

Trowler does some minor adjustments and we are on our
way again. It's another sunny day with a few mare's-tails in
the sky, where do they get such a name for clouds? Like
mackerel – what was that poem?

> Mackerel sky, mackerel sky,
> Not long wet, not long dry.

To pass the time, we play noughts and crosses. I show Toni
how to play noughts and crosses for idiots.

We are heading north and gradually climbing. On looking,
we can see Trieste spread out below us with the Yugoslav
coast disappearing in the morning haze. On one side, we
have a sheer drop; on the other, vine terraces looking like
giant steps. It reminds me of Daumier's drawings from
Dante's *Paradise Lost*. But then anything made me think of
Paradise Lost. I remember in Lewisham where I was paying

some money into my Post Office savings account, I was served by an old dear of sixty with huge ill-fitting false teeth and I thought, '*Paradise Lost!*' Another time I saw a mongrel sniffing a lamppost and I thought of *Paradise Lost*. What a good headline:

PARADISE LOST! POLICE AND ARMY IN SEARCH

We cross the border at Thorl. There is no customs barrier, we just motor straight through. 'Ladies and Gentlemen,' says Priest in mock German tones. 'Ve are now in Austria,' and gives the Nazi salute. We all give a cheer and Bill Hall, as though on cue, launches into 'The Blue Danube' and a selection of cloying German tunes ending with 'Grinzing' – that's another name I am baffled by. What or why is Grinzing?

MOTHER: Where have you been at this time of night?
ME: I've been out Grinzing, mother dear.

Mulgrew clips on a prop Hitler moustache, gives the *Sieg Heil* salute and says, 'Ve are now in zer Fatherland. From now, all Jews will haff their circumstances confiscated!'

Outside Thorl, the Charabong stops for lunch. We are surrounded by fir-tree covered hills. I climb up a hillock and get a wonderful view. I call to Toni to come up, then do a few yodels à la the Von Trapp family. Toni starts to clamber up and I take yet another photo.

Mulgrew has heard me yodel, so he yodels back. Others join in and soon the hills are alive with the sound of yodels.

We are looking down on a valley with a torrent running through it. Anything done in this stream today will arrive in Italy tomorrow. It was very pretty, Toni and I stood enjoying the view. Helpppp! They are breaking out the lunch rations. If we don't get down, the bloody lot will be

Toni climbing a hill to join me and the view, Austria

gone. They see us running down the hill; they are eating as fast as they can. But we manage to intercept some cheese and pickle sandwiches.

Lunch over, Lieutenant Priest herds us on to the Charabong – all bleating and mooing. The Charabong lurches off with a promise of further distributor trouble, but it doesn't materialise and the engine settles down as Luigi crosses himself with relief. Now we are seeing Austrians: some diehards are wearing Lederhosen (leather shorts). Greta Weingarten points them out, saying, 'Is *gut, ja?*'

'I bet they're all bloody ex-Nazis,' says Bill Hall rolling a cigarette.

'Zey are not all bloody Nazis,' assures Greta. 'Many people not like ser Nazis.'

Priest is standing at the front peering out the window. 'Ah, this is it, folks,' he says as the Charabong pulls right off the road in front of a large guest house surrounded by chalets.

We troop into reception where a fierce German lady by the name of Frau Hitz welcomes us with penetrating blue eyes and a big nose. 'Velcom to zer Krumpendorf Guest House,' she says. 'Your rooms are all ready for you.'

'I wonder where the gas chamber is,' said Mulgrew, his shoulders heaving with silent mirth. 'She's a dead ringer for Bill Hall,' he said.

We all check in. Hall, Mulgrew and myself have a chalet to ourselves. We dash to it to get the best bed. Fleet-of-foot Milligan gets in first and bags the bed near the window which overlooks a rose garden. It's very simple furnishing, but very comfortable. No show tonight, so we relax. Toni has a room in the main guest house (BLAST, there go my knee tremblers again). From now on it's goodbye Italian cuisine and hello German. No more pasta, but meat and veg, dumplings and stodgy puddings. For dinner that night we had Wiener Schnitzel mit zer Sauerkraut, and it was delicious.

BLOODY AWFUL

Next day, after breakfast, it's a real hot day. I tell Toni we must try and get a swim in the Wörther See. We take our costumes and make for the lake. But everywhere it's reeds, reeds, reeds and where there is access, it's mud, mud, mud. So, we settle for a sunbathe. Oh, the heat. Toni so close, covered in oil – it's almost frying her. 'Terr-ee, some more oil on my back, please.' So Terree obliges, taking his time to rub the oil on her satin skin. Ohhhh, the heat. Ohhhh, the oil. God, we all need a button on us that says SEX ON-OFF. Right now, I'm fumbling for the off switch. Through the lazy afternoon we talk with our eyes closed, sweet nothings that would bore any but us. Being in love, everything seems important. Small things. God, why did I have a small thing?

'What's going on here?' I open one eye to see Bornheim and Mulgrew; the latter, who hasn't learned his lesson, is holding a fishing rod. 'You know there's no mixed bathing allowed in the long grass,' he says.

'Go away, Mulgrew. Weren't you ever young?'

'Yes,' he says. 'It was on a Thursday.'

It is tea-time, so we give in and the four of us head back to the guest house. I need a shower to get the oil off and a cold one to reduce the swelling. Toni came down to tea in an all-white dress to show off her suntan, and lovely she looked.

The show that night was pretty hysterical. A lone drunk in the middle of the hall started to shout out, 'It's bloody awful, bloody awful.' It took a time to evict him. Then, in the second half he obviously somehow got back in because he shouted from the gallery, 'It's still bloody awful, bloody awful,' again he was thrown out, only to reappear through a front row Fire Exit direct from the street. 'It's bloody awful from here, as well,' he shouted, before doing a bunk. It caused great laughter in the audience and the cast.

The next morning broke sunny and warm. Across the road from us was a little Austrian beerhouse, so at lunch-time Bornheim and I toddled over and sat outside. We ordered a bottle of white wine and some cheese, then another bottle of white wine. Two Austrians in Lederhosen with over-muscled legs and blue staring eyes asked us to join them for a 'drink of zer Schnapps' and my God we got pie-eyed. We wobbled back to our chalets. I was sick and crashed out groaning on the bed. Toni was horrified, I've never been drunk before. She sees the drunken wretch and says, 'Terr-ee, you, you, bludy awful,' bursts into tears and runs out. I stumbled after her and crashed to the floor where I was sick yet again. I now looked like a walking Irish stew on legs. By evening I was coming to and drank a lot of black coffee, brought in by faithful Mulgrew who knew drunkenness. That night on stage I *was* bloody awful. I muffed the announcements, got the wrong intros and generally buggered up the act. But we still went down well.

'Just bloody luck,' said Bill Hall.

'What did you get pissed for?' said Lt Priest. 'About thirty Schillings,' I said. 'We were very economical.'

Lt Priest seeks me out. Tomorrow Bill Hall and I are to report to Villach Demob Camp to be issued with civilian clothes, how exciting! Next morning a 15 cwt truck takes us to the depot. Giant sheds loaded with military gear. We hand in our papers and discharge sheets, then we are given the choice of three suits – a grey double-breasted pinstripe suit, a dark blue ditto or a sports jacket and flannels. This photograph shows us with our chosen clobber.

Milligan and Hall, their first meal as civilians

I had chosen clothes three times too large for me and Hall had chosen some three sizes too small. The distributing sergeant was pretty baffled. We duly signed our names and walked out. England's heroes were now free men. No more 'yes, sir, no, sir', no more parades. Back at the guest house, we have our first meal as civilians. As I remember it was spaghetti.

We had one more demob appointment. That was with the Army MO. This turns out to be a watery eyed, red-nosed lout who was to medicine what Giotto was to fruit bottling.

'It's got you down here as B1,' he says.

'That's right, I was downgraded at a medical board.'

'It says "battle fatigue".'

'Yes. "Battle fatigue, anxiety state, chronic".'

'Yes, but you're over it now, aren't you?'

'No, I still feel tired.'

'So, I'll put you down as A1.'

'Not unless I'm upgraded by a medical board.'

'Oh, all right. B1.'

He then asks me if my eyesight is all right.

'As far as I know.'

'You can see me, can't you?'

'Yes.'

'Then it's all right.'

It ended with him signing a couple of sheets of paper and showing me the door. Why didn't he show me the window? It was a nice view. To give you an idea of the creep, here is his signature.

D. **Fitness for further service.**

Is the member fit for further service? *Yes*
If so, in what medical category? *B1*
(If considered permanently unfit for further service he should be brought before a medical board with a view to invaliding.)

E. Is the member a known or suspected carrier of infectious disease? *No*

Date of Examination *20 - 8 . 46.* Signed *G.P.*   ← Who?

Place *25. MM I. Room* Personal No. and Rank *276921 CPt.*
Klagenfurt   *RAMC*

FSS A 4652 500M 6-45

That was it. I was a civilian and B1.

Ah, Sunday, day of rest and something. On Monday we

will travel to Graz and do the show. In the morning I lie abed smoking.

'What's it feel like to be a civvy?' says Mulgrew.

'Well, I've felt myself and it feels fine.'

'Lucky bugger. I've still got two months to go,' he said, coughing his lungs up.

'You sound as if you're going now.'

Bill Hall stirs. 'Wot's the time?'

I tell him, 'It's time you bought a bloody watch.'

Lying in bed, Hall looks like an activated bundle of rags. Poor Bill – he, too, had been to the creep MO, who had passed him out as A1. He didn't know it at the time but he had tuberculosis, which would one day kill him. So much for bloody Army doctors.

I take a shower and sing through the cascading waters. 'Boo boo da de dum, can it be the trees that fill the breeze with rare and magic perfume?' I sing. What a waste, singing in the shower. I should be with Tommy Dorsey or Harry James.

Mid-morning, Hall, Mulgrew and I agree to give a concert in the lounge. It is much enjoyed by the hotel staff. All blue-eyed, blonde, yodelling Austrians, who have been starved of jazz during the Hitler régime. They have a request. Can we play 'Lay That Pistol Down Babe'? Oh, Christ, liberation had reached Austria. To appease them we play it. Hall plays it deliberately out of tune. 'I'll teach the bastards,' he says, *sotto voce con espressione*. They applaud wildly and ask for it again!! Hall can't believe it. 'They must have cloth ears,' he says and launches into 'Deutschland Uber Alles' as a foxtrot. 'Take your partners for the National Anthem,' he says. Hitler must have turned in his grave.

HITLER: No, I'm not. I'm still shovelling shit and salt in Siberia.

No sign of Toni so far, then Greta tells me she's in bed with tummy trouble. I go up to her room. She's asleep, but awakes as I come in. 'What's the matter Toni?'

She is perspiring and looks very flushed. 'I think I eat something wrong,' she says. 'All night I be sick.' Oh dear, can I get her anything on a tray like the head of John the Baptist? 'No, I just want sleep,' she says in a tiny voice. So, I leave her.

That afternoon, Lt Priest has arranged a picture show just for us. We all go to the Garrison Cinema in Klagenfurt to see the film *Laura*, with George Sanders and Clifton Webb. It has that wonderful theme song 'Laura', after which I would one day name my daughter. We are admitted free under the banner of CSE.* The cinema is empty, so we do a lot of barracking.

'Watch it, darling, 'ees going ter muder yer' etc.

''Ee wants to have it away with you darlin'.'

'Look out, mister, watch yer ring! He's a poof!'

Having destroyed the film, we return home like well-pleased vandals.

Tea is waiting and Toni is up and dressed, she feels a lot better. No, she won't eat anything except a cup of coffee, so I get her a cup of coffee to eat. I light up my after-dinner fag and pollute the air. Toni flaps her hands. 'Oh, Terr-ee, why you smoke?' Doesn't she know that Humphrey Bogart never appears in a film without smoking? We spend the evening playing ludo with small bets on the side. Suddenly, *I* feel sick. It's the same as Toni. Soon, I have both ends going. I take to my bed and only drink water. That night, I have a temperature. What a drag! I fall into a feverish sleep.

GRAZ

Next morning, I'm still discharging both ends. Wrapped in a blanket, doused with Aspros, I board the Charabong.

* Combined Services Entertainment.

'How you feel Terree?' says Toni.

'Terrible.'

I semi-doze all the way to Graz, showing no interest in food or drink. When we arrive in Graz, I hurriedly book in and make for my room. It's a lovely hotel with double glazing and double doors to the room, so it's very quiet except for the noise of me going both ends. I take a hot bath and take to my sick bed. I get visits from everyone. Do I need a doctor? I say, no, a mortician. Will I be doing the show tomorrow? Not bloody likely. Bornheim will have to take my place on the squeeze box; I am delirious. Toni visits me and tells me she loves me. That's no bloody good. I love her too, but I've still got the shits. Can she hurry and leave the room as something explosive is coming on. I fall into a deep sleep. I awake in the wee hours to do a wee. I'm dripping with sweat. What's the time? 3 a.m. I take a swig at my half-bottle of whisky. When I awake in the morning, I seem to have broken the back of it – it feels as if I've also broken its legs and arms. Twenty-four hours had passed away but I hadn't. In two days I'm back to my normal, healthy, skinny, self. How did the act go with Bornheim deputising for me? It was great! Curses. So I rejoin the fold.

The show is at the Theatre Hapsburg, a wonderful, small intimate theatre – one mass of gilded carvings of cherubim. This night the trio get rapturous applause from a mixed audience of Austrians and soldiers. Hall is stunned.

'Bloody hell,' he said. 'We weren't *that* good.'

'Rubbish,' says Mulgrew. '*They* weren't good enough!'

Dinner that night was a treat – first food for forty-eight hours. It's Austrian Irish stew. Bill Hall tells the waitress that his meat is very tough. She calls the chef, a large Kraut. He asks what's wrong.

'This meat is tough.'

'Oh,' says the Kraut. 'You are zer only von complaining.'

'That's 'cause I got all the 'ard bits, mate.'

'It's zer luck of the draw,' says the Kraut, who takes it away.

The waitress returns with a second portion.

'Yes, this is better,' says Hall. The excitement is unbearable.

It was one unforgettable night in Graz that Toni and I consummated our love. When it was over, we lay quite still in the dark. Neither of us spoke. I could hear her breathing, then she started to cry.

'What's the matter, Toni?'

'I am different now. I am not girl anymore.'

'Are you sorry?'

'No.'

With one act, everything was changed. We had made an invisible bond. Only time would test its strength. I lay watching her dress in the half-light – every move was etched in my mind. I can still see it quite clearly.

Next morning, when we met at breakfast, everything seemed different. Yet, it was only us. We seemed speechless, but our hearts beat faster. It was as though we were caught in an invisible net, each a prisoner of the other. Primitive emotions held us in their timeless grasp.

That afternoon, the Trio met in Hall's room for a practice of some new numbers.

'You're bloody quiet these days,' he says.

'I'm in love, Bill. That's why.'

'Love, me arse. All you want is a good shag and you'll be right as rain.'

'I'll bear that in mind.'

'Are you thinking of marryin' this bird?'

'It crossed my mind and body, yes.'

'You'll see, she'll be fat as a pig at forty.'

'Don't listen to him,' says Mulgrew. 'He should talk, with all those old boilers he goes out with.'

'They're not old boilers,' says Hall. 'They are mature,

experienced women, who know all the tricks of love.'

'Tricks,' guffaws Mulgrew, 'like cracking walnuts in the cheeks of their arse.'

The session over, I rose to leave the room. 'You'll see,' says Hall, who is now playing the Trout Quintet. 'At forty, you'll be able to roll her home.'

I am writing home asking my folks for more razor blades and pile ointment – at the same time, telling them that I'm considering marrying Toni. My mother's reply is full of advice. I mustn't marry till I have a decent job and have 'settled down', whatever that means. Two *can't* live as cheaply as one; she knows, she's tried it. Even one can't live as cheaply as one. My ninety pounds savings won't go far. I don't know, though; it's got as far as the Post Office in Lewisham. My mother should talk! In the days of the British Raj, her father was dead set against her marrying my father. He chased my father through the Poona Cantonments on a bicycle, my father escaping in a *tonga*.

VIENNA

Ah yes, Vienna. *Tales of Vienna Woods*, were they true or was it gossip? The Blue Danube, now called the Brown, the Emperor Franz Josef, Freud.

The journey passes uneventfully. Hall and I occasionally break the monotony by playing some jazz and lead a few sing-songs. Towards late evening, we reach the outskirts of Vienna.

It's rush hour in Vienna; the streets are crammed with commuters all hurrying home. The city is unfolding itself. It is a bounty of grand and stately buildings, palaces and fountains. We pass in the shadow of St Stephen's. I tell Toni this is where Bach played the organ. She doesn't like Bach too much. 'He, too, how you say, mathmetica.' She likes *dolce* music like Puccini. 'You like Bach?' she said. I don't know, I've never met him.

Street lights are coming on. It's fun to see trams again. There's evidence of the quadrilateral occupation. American jeeps and the green-grey of Russian lorries with po-faced Russian soldiers. We pass the giant Ferris wheel that has survived the war – there had been a move to dismantle it as it was a focal point for bombers.

On we trundle through busy streets. We get lost several times, but no one notices the difference. We stop and Lieutenant Priest flags down a British Military Police patrol, which turns out to be lost itself. We are looking for the Franz Josef Hotel in Gustav Strasse.

'We're bloody lost,' moans Hall.

'No, we're not,' says Priest. 'I know exactly where we are.'

'Where?' says Hall.

'Here,' says Priest with a chuckle.

More by luck than judgement, we finally arrive, at which there is a dull cheer. But wait! Uniformed porters are coming out to *carry* our luggage. There's Bill Hall's bulging cardboard suitcase tied with knotted string. We trail behind them and are shown into a wood-panelled reception hall, all very, very chic. The receptionists are super-polite. There's lots of heel-clicking and '*jawohl*'s. They are all wearing gold trimmed uniforms. 'I bet they're all ex-Nazis,' says Hall. It's a culture shock to see the smart porter carrying Hall's grotty luggage, followed by an even grottier Hall.

Toni is excited by the magnificence of the place. 'How beautiful, Terr-ee. *Che eleganza*.' My room looks like Madame du Barry's. It has a four-poster bed with velvet swags, a gold-plated chandelier, a burgundy carpet with fleur-de-lis motif. There must be some mistake. My phone is buzzing. It's Toni. She is in raptures over her room. She also says she loves me 'and you beautiful eyes'.

The State Opera House is a two-thousand seater. When I think of all those bums making contact. The dressing-rooms? Well, you could have lived in them. 'This is better than the house my folks live in,' said an amazed Hall; but reflected that *anything* was better than the house his folks lived in. In London, Hall lived in a room with a gas ring that served as a) stove b) heater c) decoration.

Our first night had a very mixed audience: Americans, Russians, British, Austrians. The Russians are in a box and we are chuffed when they laugh uproariously at the Trio.

'If nothing else,' says Mulgrew, 'they've got a sense of humour.'

'Sense of humour?' said Hall. 'Have you read what they did to the women when they captured Berlin? Very funny.'

'They weren't the only ones,' said Mulgrew. 'I've seen some of our squaddies and GIs behaving pretty abominable.'

'You sayin' we're as bad as the Russians?'

'Given the opportunity, yes.'

'Listen, they raped everything from schoolgirls to grandmothers.'

'Listen, mate. Some of the grandmothers were very grateful,' said Mulgrew with a sadistic chuckle,

These Hall vs. Mulgrew arguments never got anywhere; both were implacable. Their arguments ranged from who should turn out the light when neither bed was more than three paces from the switch, to why the Conservatives had lost the post-war election.

'Churchill was going gaga, that's why,' insisted Hall.

'Rubbish,' retorts Mulgrew. 'He's in his prime. Attlee has the personality of an overlaundered vest.'

Next day, Toni and I set out to see the sights. Toni has a small booklet in Italian telling what to see. Under her guidance, we visit Kartnerstrasse. Helpppppppp!!! It's the most expensive shopping centre in Austria, and me down to my last few Schillings! Helpppppp!!

She stops at a window with a magnificent tulle white

wedding dress. 'Oh, Terr-ee – look, how beautiful!'

'I couldn't wear it,' I said. 'It's the wrong colour.'

It was another one of my jokes that didn't register. If there was a graveyard for failed jokes, it would be overflowing with mine.

A JOKE MORTICIAN'S SHOP.
ME: I've come to bury a joke.
MORTICIAN: I'm sorry sir, the graveyard is full. It's been a good year.
ME: What do you suggest?
MORTICIAN: Cremation, sir. You can have the ashes of your favourite joke in an urn. In moments of depression, you can take the lid off and have a good laugh.

That night, the most embarrassing night of my life, the act ends with my trousers falling down. OK, I hear you say, what's embarrassing about that? This night we arrive at the end of the act, I pull the string that drops my trousers – down they go. Then came the moment of truth: I had forgotten my underpants! My shirt *just* covered my willy, but people standing in the wings can see the lot. Two of the ballet girls, Luciana and Marisa call out, 'Bravo, Terr-ee, che bellino' (Well done, what a beauty) and who was I to disagree with experts? However, it was a near-run thing. That night Toni, Mulgrew, Bornheim and I dine together. It's Bornheim's birthday. He splashes out on a bottle of champagne. It's Austrian – called Schlocknut, which sounds like part of a diesel engine and almost tastes like it.

'Don't you like it?' he enquires.

'Not much, it's too dry for me.' Ugh, it has almost sucked my cheeks together.

How old is he now? Can we guess? He gets a selection: twenty-nine? twenty-six? twenty-seven? No, no, no, all wrong. One more guess – sixty? Silly bugger, Milligan, no.

*Private J. Bornheim –
soldier friend and twit*

'I am this day twenty-five.' We wish him *bon voyage* on his journey through life as a furrier in Leeds. What more can a man want of life?

We eat our dinner to the accompaniment of the quintet who are playing, as usual, waltzes. Bornheim orders another bottle of the diesel oil, then another, and I notice that Toni is getting squiffy. She is giggling into her food and missing her mouth. Enough is enough, I beg Bornheim not to give her any more.

'Just because you're falling behind, there's no need to persecute this poor girl.'

'Don't you listen to him, Toni,' says Mulgrew, who is himself starting to slur his words.

The evening ended with me helping her to her room, a giggling female who was very unsteady on her feet. I retire to my room, where I'm suddenly awakened from a deep sleep by Mulgrew and Bornheim. Both are smashed out of their minds.

'Schpike, SCHPIKE! Cwan on hev a drink he he he he,' says Mulgrew trying to make me drink from his glass.

'Schjust hev hay liddle schippy poos,' says Bornheim standing or rather swaying behind him. I have to get up and gradually push the unintelligible lunatics out into the corridor, where I hear them stumbling along talking gibberish. What made it amazing was that they semed to understand each other!! How I envied them in that blissful state.

We come to our last day in Vienna sausage. It starts with a disaster for Johnny Bornheim: he left his shoes outside his room for the Boots to clean and someone has pinched them. 'The thieving bastards,' he rages. He reports the theft to the manager, a short, fat, bald, puffing Austrian with pebble-glass spectacles.

'Hi am zo zorry, *mein Herr*.'

He is full of profuse apologies and halitosis. He, in turn, phones the police and duly, an Austrian plain-clothes policeman arrives and takes details. What colour were the shoes? Brown. How old were they? About seven years. The detective tries to stifle a laugh. Bornheim knows he hasn't a hope in hell of getting them back and, until he buys a new pair, has the embarrassment of wearing white plimsolls. He looked a real Charlie as he came down to breakfast.

'Anyone for tennis?' ribbed Mulgrew.

'They were my best pair,' moaned Bornheim. He could have fooled me.

The last night, full house again – show goes extremely well. There is an after-the-show drink on stage with Lieutenant Priest. Chalky White and his helpers are starting to dismantle the set and load it onto lorries. Back to the hotel. It's half-past ten, I borrow Priest's little radio and take it to my room. Bornheim and Mulgrew join me. We sit and smoke as the programme is announced. 'A Date with the Duke,' says the announcer to the strains of 'The "A" Train.' I can't remember now the tunes he played after that, but it went on till eleven-thirty when the station closed down. I have missed dinner; I go down and enquire if there's anything to eat. Ahgggggggggggg, Cold Collation!

PADUA YET AGAIN

The long journey back starts. We all board the Charabong at nine o'clock. Our destination is Rome, nearly nine hundred miles away. We will be staging tonight at Padua. It's going to be a long haul; none of us are looking forward to it. When we arrive in Rome, we are to do another week of the show at the Argentina Theatre. Toni says if I like, I can stay part of the time at her home in the Via Appennini.

At eight of the clock, our Charabong lurches to a halt outside the Leone Bianco and we wearily de-bus. All I want is a bath, some dinner and bed – preferably, with Toni. We are all allocated to our rooms. By coincidence, I have the same one as previously. The hotel is pretty empty so we all have a room on our own. Ahhhh! I exclaim, as I dip myself into a hot bath. I had taken many baths in my time and this was one of them. Ahhhh! The bath has a shower attachment. The shower rose is in the shape of a blossom. People say a shower is cleaner than a bath – wrong! I turn this one on. The shower rose falls off and hits me square on the head. A lump appears on my head. I had had many lumps in my time and this was one of them. Dressing at speed, I hasten down to the dining-room, where everyone is tucking in. I order a double portion of Spaghetti Neapolitan. In no time I had caught up with the rest of them, passed them and gone into the lead.

Bornheim is ogling a waitress. 'Cor look at that,' he says, as a nubile waitress, all boobs and bum, passes the table, sending out coded sexual vibrations in all directions. I had seen many coded sexual vibrations in my time and these were some of them.

Everyone is travel-weary; most go up to their rooms.

Toni and I finish off a coffee. 'Oh good,' she says, 'tomorrow Roma! *Grazie a Dio*.' Yes, I can, if I wish, stay with her at her mother's flat. But I realise that Toni won't be as available under mother's eagle eye, so I give her a loose yes. When we get desperate, we can retire to the hotel as a second line of defence. So it's to bed. Ah, bed! It was not long before I was in the arms of the angel of sleep. Please don't drop me, dear.

ROME AGAIN

We have only travelled a kilometre outside Padua when there is a hold-up. Ahead, there has been an accident: two lorries have collided – one is a lorry containing chickens and now lies on its side, blocking the road. The two drivers are shouting at each other and gesticulating. Add to this a hundred chickens clucking. Some of their cages have broken open and chickens are running around, pecking by the road side or perching on the side of the lorry. A black mongrel dog has joined in and is chasing the chickens into the middle distance. It was chaos as a police patrol arrived and joined in the shouting.

Luigi backs up, turns round and finds another route.

So we rumble on. By eight that night, we enter the northern suburbs of Rome down the Via Flamania. We all give a groan of relief, the Italians bravely strike up a song and Luigi pulls up outside the Albergo Universo. It's not over yet. There's the unloading of the baggage by two little porters and we all register at reception. And there is the lesbian manageress. 'Ahh, Terr-ee,' she says and seemed genuinely pleased to see me.

'Before we all break up,' announces Priest, 'the show is tomorrow at 7.30 p.m. Coach leaves here at 6.00 p.m. prompt – Bill Hall, please note.'

Morning comes bright and sunny. Mulgrew and I lie in bed smoking.

'What you doing today?' he says. I tell him I think I'm having lunch with Toni and her mother. 'Getting your feet under the table, eh?'

'It's not like that. I have been genuinely accepted into the family, I am a *persona grata*.'

At this, he guffaws. There's no winning with him.

I must look my best for the lunch. I put aside my khaki travelling clothes and lay out my blue ensemble. I borrow a fresh razor blade from Mulgrew. It's strange, in those days people lent freely – soap, cigarettes, money. What happened, then? I shave very carefully, avoiding any nicks or cuts, have a shower, first testing the shower rose. I dress as far as shirt, trousers and tie, then Brylcreem my hair, all the while watched by the bemused Mulgrew. 'You're looking loverly, darling,' he says. And, though I say it, I was looking lovely. God, I've only got fifteen minutes to have breakfast. I dash downstairs to the dining-room. No Toni. I order toast and jam and tea. Still no Toni. I ask John Angove where she is. She had breakfast earlier; also, Lieutenant Priest has some mail for me. Lovely! I find Lieutenant Priest in the foyer. He is phoning Naples HQ. Still engaged on the phone he hands me two letters and a small parcel. I can tell by the over-cautious wrapping and endless knotted string that it is from my mother. As to the contents, it's marked socks. In the bedroom, I eagerly unwrap it. It contains chocolate, cigarettes and pile suppositories. Ah, how sweet, something for each orifice. The letters are from my mother and ex-girlfriend, Lily Dunford of 45 Revelon Road, Brockley SE26. Mother harps on about not forgetting to go to church. She thanks me for the photo of Toni that I sent her, but feels she would rather have had a medical report. Don't forget to put paper on the toilet seat. If I can't, do it standing up, etc. Lily Dunford's letter is really just a progress report on her life. The man she had ditched me for had left her. But for Toni, I might have made it back with her again. Too late, 'the bird has flown and has but a little way to fly' (Omar Khayyam).

I break open the chocolate bar, giving some to Mulgrew. 'Fruit and Nut,' he mutters, 'my favourite.' But then, if it was free, *anything* was favourite with him. What is he going to do today? If he can get an advance of wages he'll go to the vino bar and then the Alexander Club. Then? Then back to the vino bar.

I buzz Toni on the interphone. 'Good morning, Toni, bon giorno,' what time are we going to mother's? *Mezzogiorno.* Good, that gives me time for a job long overdue – the cleaning of my trumpet and guitar. I dismantle the trumpet and run hot water through it. I dry and polish the valves, re-oil them and put them back in the cylinders. A general overall polish and that's that. The guitar, I give a thorough polishing and a set of new strings. What a busy little bee I am. Midday and Toni, all shining and new, is waiting in the foyer. We stroll out and flag down an ancient Fiat taxi. Toni gives him the address and we sit back and watch Rome flash by. It's a city of unending interest. We pass the great piazzas with their vibrant gushing fountains, the Colosseum, the National Monument, then into the suburbs.

Via Appennini is on a slight slope. The taxi stops at 53 but starts to roll back as his brakes are dodgy, so we have to leap out at the run. Mrs Fontana is at the window looking out for us. Gioia, the maid, opens the door, is all blushes and embarrassment.

Toni's mother greets us. 'Ah, Terr-ee, *come sta?*' I am sta beni and running out of Italian.

We are seated in the lounge where we are joined by her sister Lily. 'Ah, Terr-ee, *come sta?*' I am still sta beni.

Soon I am lost to view as Toni and her mother exchange all their news. I can understand bits of the conversation with words like, *si, no, buona.* Now and then Toni translates bits concerning me. Rather like discussing the dog with an occasional 'Good boy' and a pat on the head. Lily speaks

The Bill Hall Trio on stage in Rome, where the Pope lives

broken English. She wants to come to the show. Neither she nor her mother have seen it. I promise two tickets. Toni's mother works in an Italian tourist agency called CIT which, when pronounced, sounds like shit. Lily works as a secretary and between the three of them they earn enough to live modestly well.

It's a splendid lunch: spaghetti then chicken liver risotto with white wine. Mrs Fontana asks about my family. I explain my brother is still in the Army and *almost* an officer. My father is in Fleet Street and *was* an officer. Only my mother has never been an officer. I plug the fact that my mother is a very good Catholic. This is well-received as Mrs Fontana is herself a good Catholic. As yet, I haven't told her I am a bloody awful Catholic. When do I want to come and stay? Is tomorrow all right, *domani*? Si si buona allora domani.

Toni and I taxi back to the hotel. I want to write some letters, so retire to my room. I dash one off to mother and another for Lily Dunford. I tell my mother that not only am I putting paper on the seat but, just in case, I do it standing up. Dear Lily Dunford, I commiserate with her over the

loss of her husband (HA HA HA). After carrying the torch
for her for nearly nine years, like an evil swine I felt some
measure of revenge. I didn't tell her I was in love again, but
said perhaps we could meet when I came back to London
and see what happened. Good luck (HA HA HA). Yes,
revenge is sweet but not fattening.

First night at the Teatro Argentina: very good show and a
great first-night audience. Feel very good, feel lively, feel
Toni. I'm healthy with lire, so I ask her if she'd like to go
out to dinner. Yes, she knows a place I would like. Great.
We grab a taxi with a driver who sings all the way,
badly. The restaurant is the Trattoria San Carlo. It is small,
bustling with waiters and pretty full. Nevertheless, we get a
table in a corner near the resident accordion player. He
plays, very *sostenuto*, Italian favourites.

'*Che desidera signore?*' says an *allegro* waiter.

I'm desperate for a drink to bring me down from my
post-show 'high'. 'Una bottiglia Orvieto abboccato, per
favore,' I say in ill-pronounced Italian.

It's to be a lovey-dovey evening. It's difficult for us two to
be alone like this; now we are, and it's beautiful.

'You lak it here, Terr-ee?'

Yes, *si, si,* it's lovely and you are lovelier.

We spend a lot of time looking at each other. I won't try
to describe the feeling in detail, but it caused vibration of
the Swonnicles. *Allegro* waiter pours the wine. Toni and I
touch glasses. All is sweetness and light. As I spill some
down my shirt, in a flash the *allegro* waiter is at my side with
a napkin. Toni giggles as he helps me mop up. We sit
drinking, enjoying the music and the ambience. At this time
of night Rome comes alive and takes you with it.

Time to order: I'm a sucker for it, spaghetti Neapolitan
please! Chicken à la Roman for Toni. This latter is baked in
clay, the mould broken open at your table. 'You try,' she
says, passing a piece on her fork. Mmmmm, delicious, but

it can't seduce me from my spaghetti. Paradise would be to be buried under a mound of spaghetti, having to eat my way out. Toni complains, 'You eat much food but you never get like fat.' Who do I take after, my mother or father? For piles, I take after my father; for thinness, it's my mother. My mother has legs thinner than Gandhi. If my mother stands with her legs together, it looks like one normal leg.

I've had four glasses of wine and am feeling good. God, I fancy Toni like mad. Oh, for a room at the Grand Brighton! I tell Toni, 'I want you very much.'

She gives a small understanding smile, which doesn't give any relief. 'Not possible, Terr-ee.'

There is the last resort, a secret knee-trembler – but no, I couldn't introduce her to that. That was for taller women. Of course, there was always the orange box. No! These were all sexual fantasies. I don't want the evening to end, but end it does and we take a taxi back to Albergo Universo. It's one o'clock. 'Good morning,' I say, as I kiss her goodnight.

Mulgrew is still awake. 'Did you get it?'

'Oh, Mulgrew, must you?'

'Yes, I must keep a check on the state of play.'

I undress, still with a warm glow from the evening with Toni.

'You know, I'm a better size for Toni,' says Mulgrew.

'What do you mean, better size?'

'I'm the right height.'

'Height? You haven't got any, you're doomed to be a short-arse.'

'Listen, Napoleon was short.'

'Napoleon never went short. There was Josephine for a start.'

'Well, he had to start somewhere.' Mulgrew giggles reflectively. 'He must have looked funny with his clothes off.'

It was a thought. Mind you, most of us look funny without clothes.

'Could he have conducted his battles nude?' said Mulgrew.

'Not unless he wore his sideways hat.' I pull the covers over me and turn off the light. 'Goodnight, Johnny.'

Another day in my life had ended. It was all going by so quick, but it was in the main very enjoyable. I didn't know it but these were to be among the most memorable days.

Another good attendance. For a two-thousand seater, we are getting the sort of audiences that London impresarios would like. 'Mind you,' says Bill Hall, 'compared with the office takings, we get peanuts. Someone's getting a good rake-off.' To this day, I often wonder if somebody was. It was so easy to fiddle during the war. Fortunes were made by soldiers who had sterling posted to them which they exchanged, at inflated rates, on the black market, then changed back into sterling at a profit. But *I* didn't have to do that; *I* was on ten pounds a week!

During tonight's show, I take time to watch Toni in her 'Dance of the Hours'. She had been the start of my love affair with ballet. I love the grace, the posturing, the elegance, I see her spinning like a top around the stage, my ballerina. Aw, shucks.

Priest comes backstage to tell us that our favourite, Gracie Fields, is in tonight.

'She's in a box,' he says.

'Well, screw the fucking lid on,' says Hall, who can't stand her singing.

'She wants to come backstage after the show,' says Priest.

'Oh, Christ,' says Hall, 'she's not going to sing, is she?'

Priest laughs: No, she wants to say hello to the cast.

During our act, I can see Gracie who laughs and applauds with enthusiasm. She's not a bad old stick, if only she didn't sing. After the show we dutifully await her visit. Finally it comes to us.

''Ow do, lads,' she says. ''Aven't seen you since the CMF Arts Festival.'

She then introduces us to an old dear, a Mrs Biddick of

ENSA Welfare, who is 'frightfully pleased to meet us'. She is *very* interested in Bill Hall. 'I say, you play your fiddle frightfully well.' Hall mumbles something like 'Ta'. A few more boring pleasantries and Miss Fields and Mrs Biddick leave our sphere of influence.

Our chorus girls like her. 'She speak little Italian,' said Toni, who herself is a little Italian. 'She says if we go Capri, she like to see us.'

With that threat hanging over us, we board the returning Charabong. Luigi, our driver, is very happy. He has heard from his wife who has, this day, given birth to his seventh child. '*Una ragazza.*' At dinner, we open a bottle of Asti Spumante and wet the baby's head. Mulgrew goes on to wet the arms, the body and the legs.

'Christ,' says Hall, 'they don't 'arf have big families.'

'It's very simple,' says Mulgrew. 'They do it more often.'

Hall shakes his head, but no noise comes from it. Toni is telling her friend Luciana about our proposed Capri holiday. Of *course*, she won't tell anyone else – except the entire company.

The javelin-throwing champion, lesbian manageress of the hotel asks Mulgrew and me to have a goodbye drink in her flat. She doesn't invite Hall as she freely admits she thinks he's got leprosy. I can vouchsafe that his underwear has. We take the lift to the top floor and press the buzzer. A very tall, willowy blonde answers the door. She's the sister, Claudia. She leads us down the hall into the lounge, beautifully furnished with modern furniture – very Mussolini-modern.

'*Si accomodino,*' says lesbian manageress. We settle for wine. Yes, she had enjoyed our show and loved our 'jizz'. She gives us little nibbly snacks. Her radio is tuned into the American Forces Network with unending big bands playing. Right now, it's Ray Ventura. It was all so accessible those days. Nowadays, I have to journey to Ronnie Scott's to hear any.

We don't stay long. She won't be here on Sunday morning when we leave, so she'll say goodbye now. So we all say 'Goodbye now.'

As we go down in the lift, Mulgrew makes a certain sign. 'Oh, her sister, 'ow!'

'Ah, more's the pity, Johnny,' I said. 'I know you could have given her four inches. The trouble is she could give you six.'

On that note, we ended the evening.

Time for the last show. We gather chattering in the foyer, then board the Charabong through the Roman cacophony of motor horns. Toni has recovered her demeanour and I have put my Y-fronts back on the right way, and the Swonnicles are revolving normally. Tonight our strong man, Maxie, will try and break his own weightlifting record of umpteen pounds. We all watch from the wings as the dwarflike strong man strains to get the weights above his head. The silence is broken by his grunts and strains, the veins stand out on his head. Finally, with a gasp, he gets them above his head. He takes the applause.

'What a way to make a bloody living,' says Hall. 'I bet one day 'e'll get a double rupture.'

There's a sense of sadness in the air. This company has been together every day for three months; it has become as familiar as a family. As the trio are taking an encore, I think well that's it; the next time we play will be in England. Then what? I can still hear that applause on the last night . . .

A SUNDAY

Yet another glorious, sunny Roman day. I draw the curtains; the light falls on the slumbering Mulgrew, who stirs with a few mouthy sounds like 'Abregibera'. I have a quick shower, singing 'Love thy neighbour, wake up and say how be yer boo boo da de dum.'

Oh, what a waste! Mulgrew is awake; he calls out, 'While you're there, have one for me.'

The packing, and I'm baffled as to why each time I do it, there seems to be more stuff than last time. 'The suitcase is shrinking,' says Mulgrew, having the same trouble. We lug the cases down to the care of the porter.

Toni is in the dining-room; she's not eating. 'No I wait for you my love,' she says with a morning-bright smile. I mouth the words 'I love you'. She smiles again, her head inclined to one side. Was her neck giving way? No, it's just a posture of hers, ha ha. Lovely hot toast, melting butter and conserve – there *is* a God.

We are all wearing our rather shapeless travelling clothes. Toni's are too big for her, while I'm too thin for mine. People keep knocking on my shirt to see if I'm in. Lieutenant Priest looms large. 'Are you all packed?' he says. 'We board in ten minutes. All hurry along.' Dutifully, we mounted our motorised steed for the haul to naughty Naples. This journey will be interesting to me as we will be passing over ground that my regiment has fought over.

We leave Rome by the Via Appia Nuova, flanked on the left side by the Roman aqueduct that once fed Rome its water. Despite the ravages of time, lots of it is intact, rather like Bill Hall's body. We pass tall cypress trees and the occasional Roman tomb, where occasional Romans were buried. 'I suppose the bombin' did all that,' said Hall, referring to the ruins. That's right, Bill; these are specially bombed Roman ruins. Somewhere along this road would one day live Sophia Loren, who once squeezed my hand at a dinner table. But more of that in the future.

We are passing through the great frascati vineyards where the grapes are being harvested. Peasants with coloured clothes are speckled in the fields. We are on Route Six which will take us through Cassino. It's a quieter coachload than normal; there's a sense of anticlimax (why anybody should be anticlimax, I don't know). Nobody talks much. Toni breaks he silence, 'I so excited to go Capri,' she said and squeezed my hand extra hard.

The warmth, the rumbling along, the scenery flashing past; I nod off to sleep, waking up with a start when my head starts to fall off. 'You tired, Terr-ee?' No, just sleepy. 'Tell me, Terr-ee, you lak opera, Italian Opera?' Yes, I love it. Good, if and when we go back to Rome, she will take me to one. 'Which one you lak?' I lak *Madame Butterfly*, *Aida*, any romantic ones. 'You lak *La Bohème*?' Yes, *mi piace molto*. Good we will go and see all of them; after, we'll have dinner and I can sleep at her mother's place. Good, now I can go back to sleep again.

I nod on and off until in the early afternoon we pull over under the shadow of the now ruined monastery at Cassino. I carry the sandwich box onto the grass verge while John Angove brings up the vacuum tea container. We arrange ourselves on the grass and help ourselves to the sandwiches. Toni and I sit in the shade of a tree. I lean against the trunk and look up at the sad spectacle of the ruined monastery. Bornheim sees me and reflects, 'Bloody madness, eh?' Yes, bloody madness.

'You fight here, Terr-ee?' says Toni, with a full mouth.

'No, I was over that side.' I point behind me. Was it as bad as Cassino? Bad enough.

Luigi is walking round the Charabong, looking at the tyres. They are like Bill Hall, starting to go bald and will just about last the journey. I wonder if I will.

After an uneventful lunch, we are back on board. We turn left round a bend and there ahead is the skeleton of the town of Cassino, looking like a First World War setting. A road has been bulldozed through the rubble, but that is all. There are people in the ruins, but where they live, God only knows. Here and there are a few street stalls selling vegetables and fruit – how resilient is the human race.

Bornheim is reading his *Union Jack*. 'You're Irish, aren't you, Milligan?' he says.

'I couldn't afford anything else,' I said. 'Why?'

'Well, it says here, in the human race today, the Irish came last.'

Bloody cheek. It must have been the first of the Irish jokes.

'Remember this, mate: General Montgomery and Alexander were both Irish. Till they took charge, the English were having the shit knocked out of 'em, ha!'

In the early evening we are entering the northern outskirts of Napoli. '*Grazie a Dio*,' says Toni, yawning and stretching but not getting any longer. On to the Via Roma with its bustling life and traffic, Luigi weaves in and out, shouting and blowing his horn. He's happy. Soon he'll be setting up his wife for *bambino* no. 8; he has already loosened his trousers. Finally we pull up at the Albergo Rabacino, where all the Italian artistes disembark. I kiss Toni goodbye; I'll see her tomorrow morning. We wave goodbye as we turn off in the direction of the CSE barracks. It's only ten minutes later when we draw up to the grotty façade of the barracks. I go to the Q stores and pick up my belongings, and back on the bus. Hall and I are to go to the Army Welfare Hotel in the Vumero.

'Fancy you two lucky buggers staying at a hotel,' says Mulgrew.

I remind him that Mr Hall and I are now officer status and that they are still soldiers in service of the Crown and are thus khaki minions serving their time, and good luck with the food.

This fragrant moment in time over, Hall and I re-bus and are taken to our hotel. It's a middle-class affair, called Albergo Corsica in the Vomero. It's run by the WVS with Italian staff. A Mrs Laws is the manageress, a portly matron in the tweed uniform of the WVS. She hopes we'll be comfortable; so do we. A terribly weak little Italian porter with a trolley takes our luggage to the lift, or tries to. It takes his entire energy. In the lift, sweating, he leans against the wall, giving a sickly grin that only normally comes on deathbeds.

I am shown to a room on the second floor. It is at the back and therefore, though the room is high up and the hotel overlooks the bay, I overlook the rear streets. Bill Hall is next door, not for long – what's my room like? It's as the matron said, comfortable, just about – a bed, a table, a cupboard, a dressing table, the standard quartet of furnishings. Bill Hall sits on my bed. What's he going to do?

'I think I'll hang around a couple of weeks, sort of holiday.'

Holiday?

'We've been on one long holiday,' I said.

'There's some friends here I want to visit.'

We both go down for dinner. The dining-hall is crowded with ENSA and AWS bods, all no doubt having a bloody good time at the expense of the taxpayer. My God, they were good days for skiving. As the apparition of Hall enters, the buzz of conversation stops, rather like when a gunman enters a saloon bar. I order minestrone and pasta. 'I'll 'ave the same,' says Hall, mainly because he can't pronounce the Italian names himself.

We discuss things we have to do and both agree to visit the British Consulate on the morrow to collect our passports. It's too late and I'm too tired for any activity save bed. When I return to my room, the maid is turning down my bed and I hadn't even offered it to her. '*Mi scusi,*' she smiles, showing those magnificent white teeth, and that's all she was going to show me. '*Buona notte, dormi bene,*' she says and leaves. I survey my ex-Army kit: there's a big pack, small pack and my big stencilled kitbag. I'll attend to that on the morrow. I fall asleep to the distant sounds of the streets.

I awake at nine of the clock. I have much to do; I do some in the WC and some in the bathroom. My toilet complete, I knock on Hall's door to be greeted by a stunning silence. I push the door open. The curtains are closed and so are Hall's eyes. I awake him as gently as an 'OI WAKE UP!' will allow. He gradually comes to; I count him down to consciousness,

Passport photo of the bearer

7, 6, 5, 4, 3, 2, 1! Wide awake now, Hall; hands off cocks, on socks! He'll see me in the foyer in half an hour. Yes, but will I see him? I take breakfast in my stride.

Hall is *not* in the foyer. I phone up to his room. Yes, yes, he's coming. Together we get a taxi, I tell the driver Via Roma. We are looking for a passport photographer. Hall looks out the left side and I look out the right. Hall has the eye of an eagle and legs to match. He spots one.

'There, over there,' he says, rapping on the driver's window.

'*Fermare!*' I shout.

'Ah, *si capito*,' says our photographer, a tall Italian with slick black hair parted in the middle, a little pencilled-over moustache and a grey tight chalk-striped suit. He looked the ideal co-respondent in a divorce case. Yes, si, si, he can have the photographs ready in '*un'ora*'. So, after presenting our visages we have an hour to kill.

'Let's kill a policeman,' I say.

We pass the time window-shopping and having a cup of

coffee at the big NAAFI in the Via Roma. We duly collect our photos, which aren't as bad as some.

It looks as if I've been on drugs. Hall looks as if he's been dead a month. Thus supplied, we take a taxi to His Majesty's Britannic Consul in the Piazza Bagnoli. At a desk with a 'Ring Bell for Service', we attract a middle-aged, slightly balding, thin, pale-faced Englishman wearing pebbled glasses that makes his eyes stand out like organ stops. Ah, yes, he has received our applications. Have we the photographs? We present them. He looks at them at arm's length, drawing them towards him then away again. Finally, he says 'Which is which?' I point out me; he writes my name on the back. If we come back in a week, they will be ready. Bring five thousand lire each.

Now Hall and I split, me to the cashier at CSE barracks to sort my finances out. Another taxi. The cashier is a corporal in the Queen's. Have I the CSE contract? I produce it from other papers. Yes, I'm in CSE for another six weeks; yes, I can have it all in advance. God, I'll be so rich! It's almost 72,000 lire! I must be careful; Naples is full of thieves, commonly known as the British Army.

I taxi to Toni's hotel. It's lunch-time and I find her in the dining-room, which abounds with the smell of garlic. Toni greets me; it's all coming from her – yes, she just had scampi with garlic sauce. What a sauce! She's anxious to know what day and garlic are we going to Capri? I tell her possibly the day after tomorrow. Only, she will only be allowed to stay at this hotel and garlic for another five days. Don't worry, I will save her and garlic long before then. That evening would she like to go to the Bellini Theatre where they are showing *Night Must Fall*? Oh, she and her garlic would love to. OK, I will pick her up at seven and put her down again at one minute past. What am I talking about? Only time will tell. So saying, I catch taxi number three and take me and my 72,000 lire back to my hotel.

I enquire from the hotel porter about the ferry to Capri.

Oh, yes, there are four a day: two in the morning and two in the afternoon. He shows me a printed brochure with times and prices, so I am set fair for the romantic isle where dwells the Goddess Gracie Fields. In my bedroom, I lock the door then do an hour's gloating over my 72,000 lire. I lay it on the bed next to me to have a rest. I shut my eyes. When I open them, the money is still there; the room appears to be safe. Aloud, I say seventy-two thousand lire. It sounds good. I carefully fold the money and place it in my jacket pocket to see if it makes a bulge. No, it doesn't look like 72,000 lire. I take it out again and it does. I hold it up to the mirror, where it now looks like 144,000 lire! So, I spend a pleasant afternoon's gloating.

Comes evening and I pick Toni up in a taxi and we drive up the Via Roma to the Theatre Bellini. Good heavens, Captain O'List is the manager for the show. 'How nice to see you again, Spike,' he gushes. 'I hear that the tour went very well.' Pay for seats? No, no, no, we can have complimentaries. Obviously this man doesn't know that I'm carrying 72,000 lire. What posh! Captain O'List gives us a box for two. 'See you in the interval for a drink in my office,' are his parting words.

Night Must Fall. Toni cannot follow the dialogue, I am constantly having to translate in a hushed whisper. True to his word, Captain O'List is waiting for us during the interval and we have 'drinky-poos'. Are we going steady? Yes, Toni and I are going steady.

'We're going for a week on Capri,' I tell him.

'Oh,' he says, and lets it hang in the air like the Sword of Damocles. 'Oh, Capri, eh? Ha, Ha,' he says, the whole shot through with innuendo. Why, oh, why doesn't he ask me how much money I'm carrying? 'I'm due for demob in four weeks,' he says.

'Are you going back to the Windmill?'

'Yes, Vyvyan van Damn has kept the job open.'

'Do all those wankers who come to the Windmill to see

naked birds listen to you singing?'

'Not many, but it's a living.'

The second half puzzles Toni even further, especially the head in the hatbox.

'What he got in the box?'

'A head.'

'Head?'

'Yes, *una testa*.'

'Ah, *testa*.'

I enjoyed the play in which Miss Fontana took a leading part.

At the exit, Captain O'List wishes us goodbye and 'Have a nice time on Capri!' Taxi? No, it's a warm night so we walk down the Via Roma hand in hand and I unravel the play for Toni. By the time we get to the bottom of the Via I have done all the play again and, though I say it, played all the parts better than the actors managed. I flag down one of Napoli's fleet of decaying taxis.

'Where we go?' says Toni.

'Ah ha,' I say, 'somewhere nice – Zia Theresa.'

The driver nods.

In the taxi, I give Toni a long, lingering, burning kiss causing steam in my trousers. We arrive at the restaurant on the water-front at Santa Lucia and walk down the side facing onto the bay. Zia Theresa is over a hundred years old; the roof is made of raffia-like straw with rough wooden poles as support. In the centre of the restaurant is the cooking area with a metal cowling over the top. I give the Maître d' a thousand lire note. 'Una tavelo vicina mare, per favore,' I say, and we get a table directly on to the sea. As we sit down, night fishermen are hoving to, selling fresh fish to the chef. At the back of the restaurant are a guitar and a violin player plus a singer. '*O, mare lucido*' he sings.

'Theese is lovelee, Terr-ee,' says Toni, beaming with happiness.

We have an entire fish meal: fresh mussels and scampi.

The wine was one of my favourites: Est Est Est. All this and tomorrow, Capri; walking on clouds wasn't in it. What a view! At the end of a pier, on the right, the ancient Castello del Ovo, where I believe Cicero once had a villa; then, the broad sweep of the bay circling to our left, its winking lights following the curve to distant Sorrento; out in the crepuscular night, a ghostly image of Capri; above us all, the giant shape of Vesuvius, now black and silent but always threatening.

'How you find theese place?' she says. Well, before *Barbary Coast* one night we asked a taxi driver for a good restaurant and he brought us here. 'How lucky,' she said. '*Che romantico.*'

Yes, how romantic, and the wine fortifies that feeling.

Midnight: the singer and the duo are visiting the tables. He reaches us; I ask him for 'Vicino Mare'. We sit back sipping wine as the silvery voice floats on the balmy night air. After this, I call for the bill. When it arrives I flourish the 72,000 lire, peeling off the notes in time to the music. A very impressive performance enjoyed by the waiter. I give him a handsome tip and turn a normal human being into a subservient, grovelling hulk.

On the way home, I tell Toni about the arrangements for the morrow. I'll pick her up at ten and we'll catch the eleven o'clock ferry. 'I don't think I sleep tonight,' she said as she kissed me goodnight, causing more trouser steam. It's one o'clock by the time I turn my light out. I close my eyes, undress Toni and fall asleep.

CAPRI

Lovely! It's a sunny day, nice and warm with a cool breeze. I pack my suitcase, only taking the bare essentials – like me. I'm too excited to eat breakfast, so I have a cup of tea. I buzz the porter and ask him to get me a taxi. When it arrives, he buzzes me: '*Taxi pronto, signore!*' Toni is waiting in the foyer of her hotel: she is all beaming and giggles. She lights up when she sees me; she must know that I'm carrying what *was* 72,000 lire. Our taxi turns into numerous buzzing backstreets on the way to the Porto Grande. There, waiting for us, is our dream boat – Spirito del Mare.

At the quayside ticket office, I buy our two returns and we board. We go into the airy saloon bar: we are early, the saloon is empty save for the barman. Can we have two coffees? '*Si accomodino.*' We sit at a window overlooking the deck; we hear the engines start up. There are only a few passengers carrying bundles. All of them appear to be peasants who have come to Naples to shop or collect something. They are all much more sunburnt than the mainland Italians.

We hear the bell on the ship's telegraph; there are shouts as the hawsers are slipped and the donkey engine takes them in. Expertly we move away from the quay; Toni and I finish the coffee and go to the ship's rail. We turn slowly; clear of the harbour wall, we increase speed and the ship vibrates to the engines. There is that gorgeous sound of a ship slicing through warm waters. We leave the brown waters behind and soon are into the clear blue waters of the Bay of Naples. The city starts to recede, is gradually obscured by the heat haze. Capri lies about twenty-five kilometres ahead.

A few vest-clad crewmen are moving about the ship, all looking rough and unshaved. They shout their conversations even when face to face. I always thought it made you go blind; apparently, it makes you go deaf.

'What did you say Toni?'

'I feel sick.'

Oh, my God, she's allergic to sea travel. She runs to the ladies and is in and out of there for the whole trip. What bloody luck. I breathe a sigh of relief as we pull up to the Marina Grande. We disembark, with me carrying Toni's case and mine and Toni holding a handkerchief over her mouth. I ask a tourist guide for the nearest hotel; he points to one five minutes away.

'Albergo Grotta Azzurra, *signore*.'

'*Grazie, grazie*.'

We walk uphill to the hotel. Up a few steps in reception, a smiling old Italian greeted us. Are there any vacancies? *O, si, si, molto*. Would we like 'una camera matrimonia?' No no no, I say; we would like separate rooms with adjoining doors. '*Ah, si, si*.' We register in our own names, killing any breath of scandal. They are modest, old-fashioned, unpretentious rooms with a view of the sea. We didn't know it, were totally ignorant, that this was the 'poor' part of the island. Further up on the far side, was where it was all happening, which we would in time find out – only, too late.

Toni is still feeling queasy, so she'll have a lie-down. OK. I repair to my room, unpack my few belongings and read Mrs Gaskell's *Life of Charlotte Brontë*. Will I never finish? I'm taking longer to read it than she lived. From my window I can see down to the Marina Grande, which is primarily a fisherman's port. Little boats are beached on a laticlave of sand; painted on each prow is an eye to ward off evil. They all appear to be looking at me. At about four o'clock Toni comes into my room; she's feeling a lot better. What would she like to do? Why not a swim? OK, we change into our costumes and walk down to a small beach this side of the Marina. No one else is in the water. We have a good hour's swimming.

Then a little sunbathe. It's so peaceful; in the distance, we can hear the chatter of the fishermen's wives and their children. We decide that we will have dinner at our hotel and really start exploring the island tomorrow. Toni says she is feeling much better now; *I* am feeling much better now. We *both* feel so much better that we get back into bed, which is even better than better. We watch the twilight approach.

'I think I'll have a bath, Toni – wash all the salt water off.'

She laughs a little. What is it?

Milligan the human skeleton escaping from jellyfish, Capri

Maria Antoinetta Fontana swimming from the knees down

She says, 'I think you wash you self away.'
She's referring, I think, to my thinness.

I return to my room and turn the light on. It is a very low voltage bulb that just about illuminates the room. The same bulb in the bathroom. I have a lovely long hot bath in braille. I get out before I pull out the plug, just in case. All together, now:

> SING: Your baby has gone down the plug 'ole
> Your baby has gone down the plug
> The poor little mite
> Was so thin and so slight
> He should have been washed in a jug.

Toni and I are the only couple in the dining-room. The waiter says the season is '*passato*'. It's a fixed menu, under celluloid: potato soup, vermicelli, then fish and the wine of the island, Vino Capri Scala, Grotta Azzurra – a light white, very fruity. We eat in silence with three unemployed waiters and a waitress standing in attendance. 'Food very nice,' says Toni. When we've finished, we are bowed out of the room.

We decide to take the funicular up to the piazza. We wait as the little box car descends and climb in. It's a slow ascent to the top. The view is a night setting: in the distance, we can see the lights of Naples and the bay winking in the dark. It's a clear night, cool with a starry sky; the air is like velvet. We reach the top and usher out into the piazza. All is brightness with the shops around still open. We sit ourselves at a table outside the Caffè al Vermouth di Torino. A few American officers and their wives/birds are in evidence. It's two coffees and two Sambuccas, that daring drink that they set on fire. Our waiter speaks English.

'You here on holiday?' he said.

'Yes.'

'Ah, good time – not many people on the island.'

In the square, a few landaus with sorry-looking horses wait for customers. Around us, at other cafés, people are partaking of the night. Among them are the élite of Capri, well-dressed, haughty, never looking left or right as though the rest of the world doesn't exist, and on Capri, it doesn't. The waiter puts a match to our Sambuccas, a blue flame appears. We watch it whisper on the surface as they burn the coffee beans. It's the first time Toni has had one. We blow out the flames, wait for the glasses to cool; we clink them together.

'To us, Toni.'

'Yes,' she says and clinks again. 'To us', which she pronounces 'to hus.' (I'd better explain that Toni spoke with a pronounced accent, which I have straightened out for the benefit of the reader.)

She sips it rather like a food taster at the court of the Borgias.

'Ummm!' she says, closing her eyes. 'Very good. What they make it with?'

I tell her it's Strega, a drink that can revive dead horses

and cause Brongles to rise earlier than normal. 'I no understand.'

'What a pity. I was hoping you'd tell me.'

She knows I'm out of my mind and it's showing.

We don't want to go to bed; the air is so invigorating. Let's have another two Sambuccas. Yes, why not? The night is young even if I'm not. Again the two flames burn in the night; shall *we* blow them out or call the fire brigade? Toni says, 'You mad, Terr-ee!' As an inspired guess that was pretty accurate. After the second Sambucca, Toni says she feels really fine and I say that I am really fine. So we go back to the hotel, get into bed and have a fine time, bearing in mind that my mother would say 'You are ruining your health.'

NAPLES AGAIN

Seven days later, I awake to the sound of various church bells, wassatime? Nine o'clock. We have to catch the eleven o'clock ferry. I leap from my bed and hastily pack my suitcase, then collect Toni for breakfast. Is she packed? No, but her clothes are, ha ha ha. Mario knows we are leaving today – most important to him is how much. I settle the bill with Mr Brinati.

'I hope you enjoy Capri,' he says.

'Apart from the shit-strewn sea, we have.'

It's cost us ten thousand lire.

As we leave the hotel, Mr Brinati stands at the door and waves us goodbye.

Lugging Toni's suitcase and mine, I lead down the little path to the Marina Grande. We can see that the ferry has docked. From where we are the ship looks like a toy. As we get nearer, it gets bigger. Not many people boarding. At the top of the gangplank, I present our return tickets to a scruffy-looking sailor with all the animation of a wooden leg. He is to sea travel what Charles Manson was to vegetarianism.

We go into the saloon and sit on the bench seat like lost children. At the bar, the barman is polishing glasses. 'I hope I no sick this time,' says Toni. It would certainly be a messy end to the holiday. She sits in anticipation, I give her hand a squeeze, she smiles back. A few more passengers are hurrying up the gangplank – an Italian family with two young children. They enter the saloon, the woman whoops out one of her boobs and starts to feed the baby. You don't get that on the 74a tram going to Forest Hill.

The engines throb into life and there are shouts from the bridge as the tie-off hawsers are freed from the bollards. Slowly, the ferry appears to turn on its axis and the vessel heads out to sea. Thank God, it's totally calm and by the time we are halfway across, Toni is still all right. We have made our way to the deck above and stand at the rails in the ship's slipstream. It's a hot day but the sea air is delightfully cool, like real cool man. Behind us Capri is getting smaller; we stay the same size.

We must have got off just in time. Napoli and its giant Mount Vesuvius are appearing through a morning haze. Naples is getting bigger – by the time we arrive, it's the right size to accommodate us. I realise that all through the trip, neither of us had said a word. As we are docking, Toni looks at me: 'All finish,' she says with a note of sadness. 'Never mind,' says Merry Milligan, tomorrow we journey to the Eternal City and stay with 'Momma' where our sex life will come to a grinding halt. Still, there are other things – ice cream, spaghetti, rug-weaving and light groping.

After Capri, Naples is like a madhouse – the noise! And a variety of smells, from stale fish to guardsmen's socks.

'*Che massa,*' says Toni, as we thread our way through the dockside crowds.

'*Scusi, scusi,*' I repeat *ad nauseam*.

The taxi we catch is a scream: at the back, it's down on its springs; the front points up so the driver has to permanently elongate his neck to see the road. We at the back are in the semi-prone position. All my life I'd been prone to semis (Eh?). Toni and I discuss tomorrow's arrangements. We have to catch the 10.30 train to Rome in the morning; I'll call for her at etc., etc., etc. I drop her at the Albergo Rabacino; a goodbye kiss, and I'm off to mine.

When I arrive I go straight to Bill Hall's bedroom – my God, he's still in bed! Has he been up since I left him? ''Ow you get on with your bird in Capri?' he says, searching for his fags. 'Shagged out, are you?' What has he been doing? 'I done some local gigs with Bornheim and Mulgrew. We got one tomorrer night at the Officers' Club. You want to sit on guitar?'

'No, Bill, I'm off to Rome with Toni. Any news about the boat passage?'

'No, it's being arranged through Major Philip Ridgeway at CSE. 'Ee thinks it will be on the *Dominion Monarch*. 'Ee said 'ee thinks it will be sailing on 15 September.'

'He *thinks*? Doesn't he know?'

'Don't ask me, mate. That's wot 'ee told me.'

15 September – that would give me a good clear week of rug-making and light groping in Roma, and a few days to spare in Naples.

Evening. Hall wants to know if I want to come down to a club on the Via Roma.

'It's a nightclub. Lot of 'mericans down there, plenty of Eyetie birds – got a good Eyetie band. They let me sit in.'

I'm at a loose end and it's frayed, so OK. Yes, Bill, let's go in there and beat up a storm – yeah, wow, beat me, daddy, eight to the bar. I'll bring my guitar along.

We duly enter the door of a place called The Den. We descend stairs to a basement, where a band is trying to be heard above the noise of the customers. It's a postage-stamp-sized room, the smoke so thick the band on the far side are hardly visible. Everyone is on the floor jiving.

Around the perimeter are chairs and tables; we manage to get a couple in the corner by the band. The leader, one Franco Pattoni, plays tenor sax. He sees Bill and waxes lyrical.

'Ah, Beel, *vieni, vieni,*' and beckons him to come up.

'We drink first,' says Bill, miming the action.

''Ello, big boy,' I look up at an overmade-up but very pretty Italian girl of statuesque proportions, smiling down at me. 'You buy drink, I dance weese you,' she says.

I'm looking up at her directly under her prominent boobs that give a promise of pneumatic bliss. No, I won't dance but she can sit and have a drink. She pulls up a chair and crosses her legs, a good safety move.

'You American?' she asks.

'No, I'm not.'

Straightaway, I lose marks. Can she have a cigarette? Yes. Can she have a light? Yes, anything else? Is there any laundry she wants doing? Yes, she'd like a brandy and coke. She also wants to know if I'm married. No, I'm single and have to depend on Swedish massage. Her name is Bianca Bianci, mine is Spike Milligan.

Bill Hall leans over with a gleam in his eye. 'If you play your cards right, you could catch it off her,' he says.

After a drink, we both get on the stand and join in the jazz. It's a very good combo, playing music of a professional standard. Bianca sits and watches – I hope she also listens. She recrosses her legs; it must be hell in there. She is whisked away by a drunken GI and waves me goodbye over his shoulder. Another woman in my life gone! How they pile up.

By midnight no one has asked us to play 'Lay That Pistol Down, Babe' – it must be some kind of record. I've had enough. As I put my guitar away, I'm confronted by both of Bianca Bianci's.

'You want good time?' she says.

No, thank you, I've just had one but don't let me stop

you having one. She really likes me, lays a hand on my lapel.

'Oh, why you say no,' she says, pouting.

'Pouting is such sweet sorrow,' I say.

I leave – it had been a near thing for Toni. By taxi, back to the hotel where I ask the night porter could he get me some food. 'No, *signore.*' I hold up a hundred lire note and 'Yes, *signore.*' He raids the kitchen and comes into my room with – Arghhhhhhhhhhhh, no, it's Cold Collation! It's better than nothing, but only just! I eat it by closing my eyes and thinking of England. I next indulge in a hard night's sleeping in the kneeling load position (What am I talking about. Helppppp.)

ROME YET AGAIN

Monday morning finds me packing my best clothes for the Rome trip. I pack my Bing Crosbys, my Robert Taylors and my Leslie Howards. At breakfast Bill Hall, who in the morning looks like a mummy with the bandages off, wants to know do I want a gig tonight. No, I'm going to Rome with Toni. "Aven't you had enough rumpo?' he says. How can he be so crude about my love affair? It's not rumpo I'll be after in Rome, it will be ice cream, spaghetti, rug-weaving and light groping in between mother-in-laws. Will he still be in Naples when I get back?

'I suppose so. 'Oo wants to go back to bloody England in the winter?'

'Oh, don't you want to see the old folks at home?'

'No.'

'Why not?'

'Because they don't want to bloody well see me. They only written to me once – that was to tell me they'd let my room.'

Toni is waiting at the front door of the hotel. I collect her and her two suitcases and we are on our way to the Central

Station. The crowds there are frightening. I book two first class tickets, '*Piattaforma numero due*,' says the ticket office man. Through a nightmare of people with a high garlic content, we struggle to the platform where the train is now standing. We find two seats in a *non-fumare* carriage. Thank God, we're early. Soon the train fills up with what appear to be peasant families and their furniture fleeing the wrath of Saracen invaders. Fathers shout, mothers scream, children howl. Obvious third class passengers crowd into our carriage and the corridors. I look at Toni, who seems quite cool and undisturbed.

'Is it always like this?'

'No,' she says, 'this is a good day.'

I'd never seen congealed people before.

It is with a gasp of relief that we steam into Rome Central and fall out of the carriage. We throw ourselves in a taxi and thank God it's all over. On on on to Via Appennini! Signora Fontana is waiting at the door with sister Lily and maid Gioia. There's endless embracing and kisses on each cheek. '*Benvenuto,* Terr-ee,' they all say as the kissing roundelay continues.

'Come, Terr-ee, I show you your room.'

Toni leads me to a neat, small bedroom at the back of the apartment. I dump my bags.

Mangiare mezzogiorno has been laid on. Fussing like a mother hen, Signora Fontana shows us our seat placings. 'Terr-ee, *qui*,' she gestures.

'How did the show go in Naples?' asks sister Lily, who will have to be killed.

'Oh, the show in Naples? Very well. Oh, yes, my word, the show in Naples, ha ha, it was splendid.'

Signora Fontana tells us there has been a one-day strike of tram drivers. Oh, really? How interesting. Does Signora Fontana know that the price of butter has gone up in Poland, and there are no dry-cleaners in Peru, and a Negro vicar has crossed Scotland on one leg, medicine is now free in England and so is illness? Soon I'm left out of the conversation as they all talk in Italian at a speed too fast for me by far. I just sit and when they all laugh I join in like an idiot. When the meal ends, Toni remembers me again. 'My mother have bought ticket for opera tomorrow night. You like see?' Yes, I'd like see. The meal ends with zabaglione. 'Gioia make for you, she know you like,' says Toni. Delicious! Now it's announced that all the ladies are going to afternoon Mass. Do I want to come, too? No, I've got this bad leg.

I spent a relaxing afternoon listening to the Allied Forces Network which played unending programmes of big band music. This afternoon, I remember, it was Artie Shaw. I didn't know at the time that the days of the big band were numbered (I think this was number six). Swing music was the 'in' thing and I was part of the scene, man. When the ladies returned from Mass, they found me stretched out on the sofa, asleep, with the radio on. It had been a boring service with an old priest who couldn't enunciate well and dribbled. Now some tea: Gioia disappears into the kitchen. The Signora wants to give me a present, a book, *Italia Paese dell' Arte* – was this Artie Shaw?

We sit round drinking tea and drumming up conversation. What will I be doing when I get back to England? As I step off the boat, I will immediately become famous – that's what. The Bill Hall Trio will be up there in lights, London will be at our feet, shins and groins! Toni tells her mother how successful we are. Oh, yes, her mother knows, had she not seen us triumph at the Argentine Theatre, even if she herself was a bit baffled by the act? I remember her mother had no idea of jazz and couldn't understand why we all wore rags, and *why* were people laughing at us? It wasn't fair. How is my mother? My mother is very well. And my father? He's well, too. What about my brother? Would you believe he's well as well. The phone goes, Lily rushes to it. It's her beau. Immediately her body turns to jelly and she speaks *sotto voce*, blushing and giggling, running her finger up and down the wall. Toni smiles, 'This new boyfriend.' Lily is now rocking backwards and forwards and her finger is going up and down the wall faster. What *is* he saying to her?

Toni unwraps the presents she bought on Capri. They are all delighted. Gioia is delighted with her pincushion and hugs it to her; Signora Fontana tries on her headscarf. Lily is weaving from side to side and trying to drill a hole in the table with her index finger. She is nodding her head – how can he hear that on the phone? She seems to be going into a trance. Who is she speaking to, Svengali? I have another cup of tea. They want to know have I any plans for the evening? Yes, but I left them in my other jacket pocket – I remember, though. I thought Toni and I might go to the pictures. 'Oh, yes,' says Toni enthusiastically. Splendid, her mother is expecting an old schoolfriend and will no doubt spend the evening going over the old school exams. 'Do you remember $2 \times 2 = 4$?' 'As if it were yesterday.'

A new dawn, a new day, the same old me. I awake to catch Toni emerging from the bath, wrapped in a towel. Temptation at this time of the morning: she looks glowing. I grab her and kiss her – holding her up so her feet leave the ground, only to drop her at the approach of Gioia who will *have* to be killed.

Toni has arranged for us to have our photo taken by 'Very good photograph man, best in Rome.' Go on, say it, and the most expensive!! I remember the great days when my roll of money was 72,000 lire – now it's down to 30,000, just a ghost of itself! The photographer's trade name is Luxardo; his real name is Il Conto Julio Di Sacco. He is of noble blood and six foot tall – so good-looking, it hurts. He speaks flawless English, has been to Caius College, Cambridge, wears a dazzling white shirt and trousers and a black silk neckerchief and is as queer as a coot.

'Good morning,' he says. 'Let's see, it's,' he looks up his leather appointments book, 'Mr and Mrs Fontana.' Wrong. Mr Milligan and Miss Fontana. 'Oh, I'm so sorry.'

From his posh front office, we enter his studio: very large, a mass of equipment and lights and a young boy. 'This is Francesco, my assistant.' And queer as a coot. Would we like to sit on this couch? He stands behind a large wooden box camera, talks rapidly in Italian to the lad who is putting a plate in. The Count comes forward and arranges us with our heads together. He's different, he *doesn't* want us to say cheese, he doesn't take pictures of those unending grinning idiots that plague the world of photography. 'I want you both to look serious.' He pauses for a look through the lens. 'Are you both in love?' Yes, I'm both in love. 'Good, then you think that when I say ready.' He takes a

giant stride twix us and the camera, very much like Jacques Tati. Finally, he settles. 'Ready? In love, hold it.' Hold what? A light flashes. 'Very good,' he says to himself. 'Now I'm going to take you individually. Miss Fontana, then.' He giantstrides towards her and places her hand under her chin. 'Like that, very good.' He giantstrides back, lights a cigarette, tosses his head back to eject the smoke and aims through the lens.

'Think nice things,' he says. The flash of a light, then it's my turn. Please, God, can he make me look like Robert Taylor. 'No, don't look at the camera, Mr Milligan, just to the right. Think nice things.' I think of my nice things – a flash and it's all over. 'They'll be ready day after tomorrow.' With great courtesy, he bows us out.

So, dear reader, we come to two blank days. However, on 23 September my diary continues. 'Lazy day, went to Parco Botanico. Lunch in park. Carriage drive back home. *Madame Butterfly* in evening, awful singing. Toni tells me organised by black marketeers, claque in evidence.'

Yes, *Madame Butterfly* was at the Rome Royal Opera House. Toni has two free tickets that her mother had given to her by a customer at the CIT travel agency. What a treat to look forward to! But it was a night of suppressed hysterical laughter. The whole opera was financed and cast by black marketeers. I couldn't believe it. When first I saw Madam Butterfly, she was *huge*, with a heaving bosom. I thought, out of this frame will come a most powerful voice. When she opened her mouth to sing, you could hardly hear anything. To accentuate the short-coming, she overacted, throwing her arms in the air, clasping her hands together, falling on her knees with a groan, running across the stage with loud, thudding feet – all to thunderous applause from an obvious claque. Then we wait for Lieutenant Pinkerton: my God, he's half her size! He can't be more than five foot five inches and so thin that when he stood behind her, he vanished. He has a piercing tenor voice, high up in the nose, with a tremendous wobbly *vibrato* that fluctuates above and below the real note. He is obviously wearing lifts in his shoes that make him bend forward from the ankles as though walking in the teeth of a gale. If that isn't all bad enough, he is wearing what must be the worst toupee I've seen. It appears to be nailed down, the front coming too far forward on the forehead with a slight curl all round where it joins his hair.

Trying to laugh silently, I'm almost doubled up in pain. All around me are Mafia-like creatures – one wrong move and I'll be knifed. So be it, no comedy could exceed this. We notice that when Pinkerton tries for a high note, he shoots up on his toes, putting him at an even more alarming angle. When he and she embrace, she envelops him completely, his little red face appearing above her massive arms as though he's been decapitated. I'm carried on the tide of enthusiasm. When the claque jump up applauding, so do I. '*Bravo, encore,*' I shout. It was a night I can never forget.

At the little restaurant after the show, I keep breaking into fits of laughter as I recall it all. Toni is split down the middle, both halves being equal to the whole. She's ashamed that something so bad should go on at the Royal Opera House. '*Disgrazia,*' she says, but continues to laugh through it.

I remember that, as we sat outside eating, for no reason it started to rain. We retreat inside while a waiter rescues our food. The waiter is amusing; he apologises for the rain and says even though some has settled on the food, there'll be no extra charge.

Seated inside, Toni suddenly says to me, 'You know, in two day you leave me.'

My mood changed, was it that soon? I was so impervious to days that each one came as a shock. Why wasn't time timeless?

'Toni,' I said, 'I'll come back as soon as I can and I'll write as much as I can.'

That's followed by us just looking at each other in silence.

'I miss you very much, Terr-ee.'

She looks so small and helpless; I *feel* so small and helpless.

'I tell you what, we have some champagne, yes?'

She pauses reflectively. 'OK,' she says.

The restaurant hasn't any champagne. '*Tedeschi hanno bevuto tutto*,' says the waiter. Would we like Asti Spumante? Yes, when in Rome.

When midnight strikes in some campanile, we toast each other. We'd done it so often before, but this time it's a little more meaningful – our sand is running out. In the taxi back, I sit with my arm around her, her head on my shoulder (sounds like a transplant). I hum her favourite tune, 'La Valzer di Candele' . . . We tiptoe into the apartment and I instinctively wait for my mother's voice, 'Where have you been at this time of night.' No, it's Signora Fontana asking is that Toni. Yes, so goodnight.

Comes the morning of my final departure. I put on my CSE uniform for the journey, then comes amnesia, folks. I remember that I made the return journey by military lorry, a three-tonner returning empty to a depot in Salerno – but as to why and how I managed to get a lift on it, I can't remember. I've racked my brains, I've even racked my body and legs, but to no avail. Anyhow. There I was, saying goodbye to the Fontanas: they all cry, even Gioia, the maid. So with one suitcase and a much-reduced bankroll, I depart.

I depart to amnesia because where I picked up the lorry is lost for ever. However, I remember the journey back. The driver was a northcountryman, he hardly said a bloody word all through the journey. I sat there in silence with Rome falling farther and farther behind. It was a hot, dusty day and I dozed frequently in the cab. When we reach the

Garigliano plain, I can see Colle Dimiano where I was wounded. It all seemed so unreal now, but I think I left part of myself up there forever; after the incident, I was never the same.

Suddenly, as we near Naples, the creep driver seems to speak. 'Do you know what time is?'

'Yes,' I say. Period. I'd make the bugger suffer.

He pauses and repeats, 'Do you know what time is?'

'Yes.'

'Oh, what is it then?'

Finally, I tell him. He nods his head in acknowledgement, his vocabulary expended. He drops me at the bottom of the Via Roma. I delighted in saying goodbye. 'Tatar, you little bundle of fun,' I said.

I'm in the welter of the Neapolitan rush hour and garlic. I manage to get a taxi back to the hotel. The old fragile porter grabs my bag; he'll take it to my room. He strains and staggers to the lift. I have to wait for him, I have to help him into the lift where he stands gasping for breath. He must be training for a coronary. On my floor, he staggers behind me. I offer to carry it. '*No, no signore, tutto a posto*', he'll just have a little rest in the corridor. I go ahead and wait in my room – poor old bugger, he's doing it in anticipation of a tip or death, whichever comes first. I give him two hundred lire – it's a good tip. '*Mille grats, signor,*' he says in Neapolitan dialect and shuffles out the room. I put through a phone call to Toni. After a delay it comes through.

'Hello Toni.'

'Terr-ee,' she gasps, 'my Terr-ee, you go all right Napoli?'

'Yes, I go all right in Napoli.'

''Ow lovlee 'ear your voice, mio tesoro. I miss you much already. Why you go away?'

'What are you doing?'

'Just now we have dinner. Tell me you love me.'

'I love you.'

A little more of that type of chat and we finish. Yes, I promise I'll phone tomorrow. No, I won't go out getting drunk with Mulgrew. No, I won't go near other girls. Now, where is that man Hall. I buzz his room.

''Oos that?'

'Me, Spike. Are there any gigs going? I'm at a loose end till the boat sails.'

No, no gigs tonight. There's one tomorrow. Do I mind playing in a sergeants' mess? Well as long as it isn't too big a mess.

'Wot you doing tonight?'

'I'm not doing anything tonight.'

'Well, good luck with it,' he says.

I meet him in the dining-hall for dinner. Has he seen Mulgrew or Bornheim lately? Yes, he's done a couple of gigs with them. What about the *Dominion Monarch* and the sailing date? That's all fixed, I have to collect my ticket from Major Ridgeway. So the end is in sight: it's goodbye Italy and hello Deptford.

The remaining days were very very boring. So I won't bore the reader. I do a couple of band gigs on guitar with Hall, Bornheim and Mulgrew at military establishments. I collect my boat ticket and passport and I buy a few trinkets for my mother and father. Most days I spend in my room reading books from the hotel library. The very last one was the story of San Michele by Axel Munthe, a most moving story about Capri.

The night before I sail, Jimmy Molloy checks into the hotel. He's booked on the same ship as me. He wants to have a night out; he knows a good officers' nightclub on the seafront. OK, I'll come with him and wear the suit. It's the Club Marina, 'Officers Only'. We show our CSE passes. Down a corridor to a large room with a central dance floor, where a good Italian band are playing the music of our time. There are hostesses at the bar: no, Jimmy, I'm not interested. Well, he is. He goes over and chats to one and brings her back to our table. Ah, good, wait till she sees my suit. She is pretty stunning, small, petite, saturnine-dark with a pair of giant olive eyes.

'This is Francesca,' says Molloy.

'Piacera,' I say.

She throws me a dazzling white-toothed smile. More than that, as the evening progresses I realise that she fancies me and my suit. 'I fink I've picked a loser here,' chuckled Molloy. Do I want to take her over? No no no, Jimmy, I am promised to another. He gives me a disbelieving look. 'Come on, a bit on the side won't hurt.' I told him I had no bits on my side, all my bits were at the front, so I'd be the wrong fit for her. However it's nice flirting with her.

The lights go down: a spotlight on the stage illuminates an Italian MC in a white jacket. 'Laddies and Gintilmin, nower oura starer of thee cabereter, Gina Escoldi.' He points left, the band strikes up and a ballerina on points pirouettes onto the floor and sings 'a hubba hubba hubba' with red-hot accompaniment. She has a coarse croaky voice,

On board SS Dominion Monarch *from Naples to the UK*

loaded with sex – all the while standing on points. It was a head-on collision between jazz and ballet, but very successful. She goes down big with what is in the majority, an American officer audience.

At the end of the evening Molloy says, 'You takin this bird or not.' I decline, cursing the fact that I have a conscience. 'One day,' he laughs, 'you'll regret this decision!' What did he mean 'one day', I was regretting it *now*. While he offs with her, I off to the hotel and bed. While I lay there, my mind was going through the long years away from home. Had I really been in action in North Africa? Had I really taken part in the Tunis Victory Parade? Did I land at Salerno? It all seemed unreal, like a distant dream ending up in the most distant dream of all – Toni and me on Capri. Would the sun ever shine like that again?

On departure morning I awake and, first thing, put in a call to Toni. We say our final goodbyes – tears on the phone from Rome. At breakfast, I meet Jimmy Molloy. 'That bird last night, what a con. When we get to 'er place, she just kisses me goodnight then pisses off. I think it was all your bloody fault, Milligan.' Smugly, I say, yes, it undoubtedly was.

Our ship sails at midday. We have to start boarding at 10.30. We take a taxi to the quay where the *Dominion Monarch* awaits. We both have first-class passages – I'm nominated a cabin on the port side. A young English steward carries my bag and calls me sir. It's a fine, single-berth cabin with a porthole for looking out – or, if you hang on the outside, for looking in. 'If there's anything you want, sir, just ring the service button.' I locate the Purser's Office where a grim-faced staff change my lire into sterling, which looks much less. Up on the promenade deck I find Molloy and I get him to take my photo.

The ship is alive with bustle, with sailors shouting yo ho ho and pouring hot tar down the hatches. At midday the gangplank is removed, the ship gives a long mournful blast on the hooter and a tug starts to manoeuvre us out to sea. Molloy and I stand at the rail. Slowly, the great ship puts on speed, the Italian mainland recedes into the distance, finally lost in a haze. It's over: it's goodbye Italy, goodbye Toni and goodbye soldier.